Communications
in Computer and Information Science 935

Commenced Publication in 2007
Founding and Former Series Editors:
Phoebe Chen, Alfredo Cuzzocrea, Xiaoyong Du, Orhun Kara, Ting Liu,
Dominik Ślęzak, and Xiaokang Yang

Editorial Board

More information about this series at http://www.springer.com/series/7899

Tadeusz Czachórski · Erol Gelenbe
Krzysztof Grochla · Ricardo Lent (Eds.)

Computer and Information Sciences

32nd International Symposium, ISCIS 2018
Held at the 24th IFIP World Computer Congress, WCC 2018
Poznan, Poland, September 20–21, 2018
Proceedings

 Springer

Editors
Tadeusz Czachórski (iD)
Institute of Theoretical and Applied
  Informatics
Polish Academy of Sciences
Gliwice
Poland

Erol Gelenbe (iD)
Department of Electrical and Electronic
  Engineering
Imperial College London
London
UK

Krzysztof Grochla (iD)
Institute of Theoretical and Applied
  Informatics
Polish Academy of Sciences
Gliwice
Poland

Ricardo Lent
University of Houston
Houston, TX
USA

and

Institute of Theoretical and Applied
  Informatics
Polish Academy of Sciences
Gliwice
Poland

ISSN 1865-0929   ISSN 1865-0937 (electronic)
Communications in Computer and Information Science
ISBN 978-3-030-00839-0   ISBN 978-3-030-00840-6 (eBook)
https://doi.org/10.1007/978-3-030-00840-6

Library of Congress Control Number: 2018954765

This Springer imprint is published by the registered company Springer Nature Switzerland AG
The registered company address is: Gewerbestrasse 11, 6330 Cham, Switzerland

Preface

The ISCIS series of conferences were launched in Ankara, Turkey, in 1986 at Bilkent University, and the 31st such event took place in Krakow, Poland, in 2016. Recent ISCIS symposia have centered broadly on computer science and engineering. Their proceedings have been published by Springer and attracted hundreds of thousands of paper downloads over the years [1–7].

Thus, these are the proceedings of the 32nd International Symposium on Computer and Information Sciences (ISCIS). This year's symposium was co-organized in Poznan, Poland, by the Institute of Theoretical and Applied Computer Science of the Polish Academy of Sciences, in conjunction with the 2018 World Computer Conference of the International Federation of Information Processing Societies (IFIP). We are grateful to Springer for publishing these proceedings.

We were unable to accept most of the papers that were submitted to ISCIS 2018 because of the need to remain selective and to have a single track of oral presentations within a two-day program.

In 2018, in addition to the present 32nd ISCIS 2018 conference, we were fortunate to organize the very successful First International ISCIS Security Workshop 2018, named Euro-CYBERSEC 2018, which took place in London, UK, during February 26–27, 2018. Its proceedings contain papers from several European Cybersecurity projects including FP7 NEMESYS [10], the H2020 Projects KONFIDO [11], GHOST [12], and the new H2020 Project SerIoT coordinated by the Institute of Theoretical and Applied Informatics of the Polish Academy of Sciences [13]. The complete proceedings of Euro-Cybersec 2018 can be found in [9].

I am particularly grateful to all the authors who kindly submitted papers to this 32nd ISCIS 2018 event. I am also very grateful to the co-chairs of this symposium and co-editors of these ISCIS 2018 proceedings, Tadeusz Czachórski, Krzysztof Grochla, and Ricardo Lent, for their major contributions to this event and to these proceedings. Their active participation in refereeing, selecting, and improving the papers was essential.

August 2018   Erol Gelenbe

References

1. Gelenbe, E., Lent, R., Sakellari, G., Sacan, A., Toroslu, I. H., Yazici, A. (eds.): Computer and Information Sciences - Proceedings of the 25th International Symposium on Computer and Information Sciences, London, UK, September 22–24, 2010, Lecture Notes in Electrical Engineering, vol. 62. Springer (2010), https://doi.org/10.1007/978-90-481-9794-1
2. Gelenbe, E., Lent, R., Sakellari, G. (eds.): Computer and Information Sciences II - 26th International Symposium on Computer and Information Sciences, London, UK, 26–28 September 2011. Springer (2011), https://doi.org/10.1007/978-1-4471-2155-8
3. Gelenbe, E., Lent, R. (eds.): Computer and Information Sciences III - 27th International Symposium on Computer and Information Sciences, Paris, France, October 3–4, 2012. Springer (2013), https://doi.org/10.1007/978-1-4471-4594-3
4. Gelenbe, E., Lent, R. (eds.): Information Sciences and Systems 2013 - Proceedings of the 28th International Symposium on Computer and Information Sciences, ISCIS 2013, Paris, France, October 28–29, 2013, Lecture Notes in Electrical Engineering, vol. 264. Springer (2013), https://doi.org/10.1007/978-3-319-01604-7
5. Czachórski, T., Gelenbe, E., Lent, R. (eds.): Information Sciences and Systems 2014 - Proceedings of the 29th International Symposium on Computer and Information Sciences, ISCIS 2014, Krakow, Poland, October 27–28, 2014. Springer (2014), https://doi.org/10.1007/978-3-319-09465-6
6. Abdelrahman, O. H., Gelenbe, E., Görbil, G., Lent, R. (eds.): Information Sciences and Systems 2015 - 30th International Symposium on Computer and Information Sciences, ISCIS 2015, London, UK, 21–24 September 2015, Lecture Notes in Electrical Engineering, vol. 363. Springer (2016), https://doi.org/10.1007/978-3-319-22635-4
7. Czachórski, T., Gelenbe, E., Grochla, K., Lent, R. (eds.): Computer and Information Sciences - 31st International Symposium, ISCIS 2016, Kraków, Poland, October 27–28, 2016, Proceedings, Communications in Computer and Information Science, vol. 659 (2016), https://doi.org/10.1007/978-3-319-47217-1
8. Czachórski, T., Gelenbe, E., Groschla, K., Lent, R.: The 32nd International Symposium on Computer and Information Sciences, ISCIS 2018, Poznan, Poland, to appear, Springer Verlag, (2018)
9. Gelenbe, E., Campegiani, P., Czachorski, T., Katsikas, S., Komnios, I., Romano, L., Tzovaras, D. (eds.): First International ISCIS Security Workshop 2018, Euro-CYBERSEC 2018, London, UK, February 26–27, 2018, vol. 821. Lecture Notes CCIS, Springer Verlag (2018)
10. Gelenbe, E., Gorbil, G., Tzovaras, D., Liebergeld, S., Garcia, D., Baltatu, M., Lyberopoulos, G.: Security for smart mobile networks: The NEMESYS approach. In: Privacy and Security in Mobile Systems (PRISMS), 2013 International Conference on. pp. 1–8. IEEE (2013)
11. Staffa, M., Coppolino, L., Sgaglione, L., Gelenbe, E., Komnios, I., Grivas, E., Stan, O., Castaldo, L.: KONFIDO: An OpenNCP-based secure ehealth data exchange system. In: Gelenbe, E., Campegiani, P., Czachorski, T., Katsikas, S., Komnios, I.,

Romano, L., Tzovaras, D. (eds.) Recent Cybersecurity Research in Europe: Proceedings of the 2018 ISCIS Security Workshop, Imperial College London. Lecture Notes CCIS No. 821, Springer Verlag (2018)

12. Collen, A., Nijdam, N.A., Augusto-Gonzalez, J., Katsikas, S.K., Giannoutakis, K. M., Spathoulas, G., Gelenbe, E., Votis, K., Tzovaras, D., Ghavami, N., Volkamer, M., Haller, P., Sanchez, A., Dimas, M.: GHOST - safe-guarding home IoT environments with personalised real-time risk control. In: Gelenbe, E., Campegiani, P., Czachorski, T., Katsikas, S., Komnios, I., Romano, L., Tzovaras, D. (eds.) Recent Cybersecurity Research in Europe: Proceedings of the 2018 ISCIS Security Workshop, Imperial College London. Lecture Notes CCIS No. 821, Springer Verlag (2018)

13. Domanska, J., Gelenbe, E., Czachorski, T., Drosou, A., Tzovaras, D.: Research and innovation action for the security of the internet of things: The SerIoTproject. In: Gelenbe, E., Campegiani, P., Czachorski, T., Katsikas, S., Komnios, I., Romano, L., Tzovaras, D. (eds.) Recent Cybersecurity Research in Europe: Proceedings of the 2018 ISCIS Security Workshop, Imperial College London. Lecture Notes CCIS No. 821, Springer Verlag (2018)

Organization

The 32nd International Symposium on Computer and Information Sciences was held in Poznan, Poland, in conjunction with the 2018 IFIP World Computer Conference.

Symposium Chairs and Organizers

E. Gelenbe
T. Czachorski
K. Grochla
R. Lent

Program Committee

Manfred Broy	TUM, Germany
Fazli Can	Bilkent University, Turkey
Sophie Chabridon	Institut Telecom, Telecom Sud Paris, France
Tadeusz Czachorski	ITAI PAS, Poland
Gökhan Dalkılıç	Dokuz Eylul University, Turkey
Mariangiola Dezani	Università di Torino, Italy
Nadia Erdogan	Istanbul Technical University, Turkey
Taner Eskil	Isik University, Turkey
Stephen Gilmore	University of Edinburgh, UK
Ugur Güdükbay	Bilkent University, Turkey
Attila Gursoy	Koç University, Turkey
Yorgo Istefanopulos	Isik University, Istanbul, Turkey
Alain Jean-Marie	LIRMM University of Montpellier, France
Sylwester Kaczmarek	Gdansk University of Technology, Poland
Jacek Kitowski	AGH University of Science and Technology, Poland
İbrahim Körpeoglu	Bilkent University, Turkey
Stefanos Kollias	NTUA Athens, Greece
Jerzy Konorski	Gdansk University of Technology, Poland
Ricardo Lent	University of Houston, USA
Albert Levi	Sabanci University, Turkey
Peixiang Liu	Nova Southeastern University, USA
Jozef Lubacz	Warsaw University of Technology, Poland
Chris Mitchell	Royal Holloway, University of London, UK
Marek Natkaniec	AGH University of Science and Technology, Poland
Sema Oktug	Istanbul Technical University, Turkey
Ender Özcan	University of Nottingham, UK
Oznur Ozkasap	Koc University, Turkey
Ferhan Pekergin	Université Paris 13 Nord, France

Contents

Data Analysis and Algorithms

Security in Cyber and Physical Systems

Machine Learning and Applications

Applications to Linguistics, Biology and Computer Vision

Systems and Networks

Tandem Networks with Intermittent Energy

Yasin Murat Kadioglu(✉)

Intelligent Systems and Networks Group,
Electrical and Electronic Engineering Department,
Imperial College, London SW7 2BT, UK
y.kadioglu14@imperial.ac.uk

Abstract. Energy harvesting may be needed to operate digital devices in locations where connecting them to the power grid and changing batteries is difficult. However, energy harvesting is often intermittent resulting in a random flow of energy into the device. It is then necessary to analyse systems where both the workload, and the energy supply, must be represented by random processes. Thus, in this paper, we consider a multi-hop tandem network where each hop receives energy locally in a random process, and packets arrive at each of the nodes and then flow through the multi-hop connection to the sink. We present a product-form solution for this N-hop tandem network when both energy is represented by discrete entities, and data is in the form of discrete packets.

Keywords: Tandem networks · Energy packet network
Renewable energy

1 Introduction

Energy is one of the primary concerns for digital devices capable of processing and transmitting information such as computers, Internet of Things (IoT) and network nodes (e.g. sensors), as the total electrical energy use by ICT has been approaching 10% of total electricity consumption worldwide [1]. Therefore, many studies investigate the use of energy harvesting to reduce the dependency of such devices on non-renewable energy sources [2]. Harvested energy is also very useful for devices in remote locations such as stand-alone sensors, and in systems which are difficult to reach to change batteries. However, harvested energy is generally intermittent and limited, so that the Quality of Service (QoS) depends on the interaction between energy availability and the workload that the device must process. Since queueing models are useful for the analysis of communication and computing systems, the use of intermittent energy in queueing models was introduced in the "Energy Packet Network" (EPN) paradigm [3] where an energy queue is a battery, while a data or work queue is a usual queue of jobs or packets.

In this paper we present new results using a somewhat different modeling approach introduced in [4] where it is assumed that the sensing process that

© Springer Nature Switzerland AG 2018
T. Czachórski et al. (Eds.): ISCIS 2018, CCIS 935, pp. 3–9, 2018.
https://doi.org/10.1007/978-3-030-00840-6_1

generates packets and the energy harvesting process that collects energy are both much slower than the forwarding (or service times) for the data packets (DP), with further work in [5]. A model with transmission errors, so that several energy packets (EP)s may be needed for a successful DP transmission, is discussed in [6,7]. A two-hop feed-forward network was analysed in [8]. Since tandem systems are of interest in several areas such as production lines, supply chains and optical transmission lines [9,10], in this work, we consider an N-hop tandem network model and present its product-form solution [11,12] for the joint probability distribution of backlog of DPs and EPs. Similar model without external data arrival at each node will also appear in extended form elsewhere [13].

2   N-Hops Tandem Network

The tandem network model shown in Fig. 1 is studied. Each node is assumed to sense traffic as discrete data packets (DP)s, and harvest energy as discrete energy packets (EP)s. The arrival of both DPs and EPs at Node-i are assumed to be independent Poisson processes with rate λ_i and Λ_i, respectively. It is also assumed each node has unlimited energy storage (e.g. battery or capacitor) and data buffer. Energy leakage occurs due to natural discharge characteristic of batteries, and DP loss occurs due to impatience or errors. The leakage rate at node i is μ_i (γ_i) when there are more than one EPs (DPs) at node i, and is μ_i^0 (γ_i^0) when there is just one EP (DP) at the same node.

With current electronic technology, the DP transmission time will be in the nanoseconds, while the constitution of a full DP through sensing of external events, the harvesting of a significant amount of energy, the leakage of an EP and the loss of a DP due to impatience or errors will take much longer time. Thus, we can assume that the DP forwarding times are negligibly small compared to these other time durations.

The state of node $i \in \{1, \ldots, N\}$ at time t can be represented by the pair (x_i^t, y_i^t) where the first variable represents the backlog of DPs at the node, while the second variable is the amount of energy (in EPs) available at the same node. As with the single node model we must have $x_i^t \cdot y_i^t = 0$ since if there is both an EP and a DP at a node, the transmission occurs until either all DPs or all EPs are depleted at node i. Thus the state of a node may be represented by a single variable $n_i^t = x_i^t - y_i^t$. If:

- $n_i^t > 0$, then node i has $n_i^t = x_i^t$ DPs waiting to be forwarded, but it does not have the EPs at that node to start the transmission from that node,
- $n_i^t < 0$, then node i has a reserve of $-y_i^t$ EPs, but does not have any DPs to transmit,
- $n_i^t = 0$, then node i does not have any DP and EP in their respective buffers.

The tandem network is then represented by the vector of positive, negative or zero integers: $\bar{n}^t = (n_1^t, \ldots, n_N^t)$, $t \geq 0$, and $\bar{n}$ denotes a particular value of the vector, so that we study the probability $p(\bar{n}, t) = Prob[\bar{n}^t = \bar{n}]$.

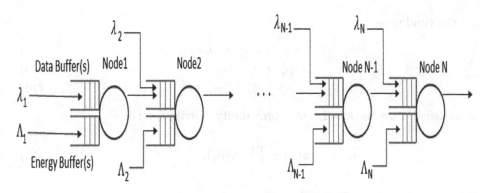

Fig. 1. Tandem network comprised of several store-and-forward layers that forward data packets (DPs) to the devices that collect the data and monitor the sources of the data.

Let $\bar{e}_i \triangleq (0, 0, \cdots, 1, \cdots, 0)$ be a vector whose i^{th} element is 1 and other $N - 1$ elements are 0. The equilibrium equations for the steady-state probability distribution $\pi(\bar{n})$ for this system are:

$$\pi(\bar{n}) \sum_{i=1}^{N} [\lambda_i + \Lambda_i + \gamma_i \delta_{n_i > 1} + \gamma_i^0 \delta_{n_i = 1} + \mu_i \delta_{n_i < -1} + \mu_i^0 \delta_{n_i = -1}] \tag{1}$$

$$= \sum_{i=1}^{N} [\pi(\bar{n} + e_i)(\gamma_i \delta_{n_i > 0} + \gamma_i^0 \delta_{n_i = 0} + \Lambda_i \delta_{n_i < 0} \delta_{i \neq N} + \Lambda_N \delta_{i = N})] \tag{2}$$

$$+ \sum_{i=1}^{N} [\pi(\bar{n} - e_i)(\mu_i \delta_{n_i < 0} + \mu_i^0 \delta_{n_i = 0} + \lambda_i \delta_{n_i > 0} \delta_{i \neq N} + \lambda_N \delta_{i = N})] \tag{3}$$

$$+ \sum_{j=1}^{N-1} \sum_{i=j}^{N-1} [\pi(\bar{n} - \sum_{k=j}^{i+1} e_k)\lambda_j \prod_{k=j}^{i} \delta_{n_k \leq 0}(\delta_{1+i=N} + \delta_{n_{i+1} \geq 1} \delta_{1+i \neq N})] \tag{4}$$

$$+ \sum_{j=1}^{N-1} \sum_{i=1}^{j} [\pi(\bar{n} + e_i - \sum_{k=1}^{N-j} e_{i+k})\Lambda_i \delta_{n_i \geq 0}(\delta_{N-j \leq 1} \cdot \tag{5}$$

$$\cdot + \delta_{N-j \geq 2} \prod_{k=1}^{N-j-1} \delta_{n_{i+k} \leq 0})(\delta_{i=j} + \delta_{n_{N+i-j} \geq 1} \delta_{i \neq j})]$$

Theorem 1. Let:

$$v_1 = \lambda_1, \tag{6}$$

$$v_{i+1} = \lambda_{i+1} + \sum_{j=1}^{i} \lambda_j \prod_{k=j}^{i} \frac{\Lambda_k}{\Lambda_k + \gamma_k}. \tag{7}$$

and the conditions

$$v_i - \gamma_i = \Lambda_i - \mu_i, \tag{8}$$
$$\mu_i^0 = v_i + 2\mu_i, \tag{9}$$
$$\gamma_i^0 = \Lambda_i + 2\gamma_i. \tag{10}$$

are satisfied, then the steady state probability distribution:

$$\pi(\bar{n}) = \prod_{i=1}^{N} \pi_i(n_i), \tag{11}$$

where $\bar{n} = (n_1, n_2, \cdots, n_N)$ and

$$\pi_i(n_i) = \begin{cases} P_i, & \text{if } n_i = 0 \\ \frac{1}{2} P_i (\frac{v_i}{\Lambda_i + \gamma_i})^{n_i}, & \text{if } n_i \geq 1 \\ \frac{1}{2} P_i (\frac{\Lambda_i}{v_i + \mu_i})^{-n_i}, & \text{if } n_i \leq -1 \end{cases}$$

where the normalising constant P_i is:

$$P_i = (1 + \frac{v_i}{2\mu_i} + \frac{\Lambda_i}{2\gamma_i})^{-1}. \tag{12}$$

Equation 8 indicates that the net inflow of DPs, after removal of those that time-out, should be the same as the total inflow of EPs minus the loss of EPs due to leakage. The product-form solution of the joint probability distribution enables the rigorous computation of all the performance metrics (throughput, average backlog of DPs, energy efficiency, average response time) for such systems operating with intermittent energy.

Proposition 1. The steady-state arrival rate of DPs to Node 1 is obviously $\alpha_1 = \lambda_1$, and for Node i, $i > 1$:

$$\alpha_i = v_i. \tag{13}$$

Proposition 2. The DP throughput of Node-i in steady-state is:

$$o_i = \sum_{n_i > 0} \pi(n_i)\Lambda_i + \sum_{n_i < 0} \pi(n_i)v_i \tag{14}$$

$$= \frac{v_i \Lambda_i}{\Lambda_i + \gamma_i}. \tag{15}$$

Proposition 3. The average backlog of DPs waiting at Node-i in steady-state is:

$$<n_i> = \sum_{n_i > 0} n_i \pi(n_i) \tag{16}$$

$$= \frac{v_i}{\mu_i} \frac{\gamma_i}{\gamma_i + \mu_i}. \tag{17}$$

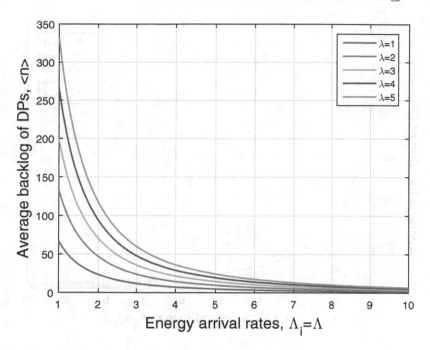

Fig. 2. The total average backlog of DPs at all of the $N = 5$ units, versus the arrival rate of EPs. We see that the values of N, Λ and λ impact the DP backlog time significantly. Note that the total energy arrival rate to the system is $N\Lambda$.

Proposition 4. The energy efficiency of Node-i can be defined as:

$$\eta_i = 1 - \frac{\mu_i}{\gamma_i + \Lambda_i}. \tag{18}$$

Proposition 5. The effective average response time (T_i) of Node-i in steady-state can be calculated as:

$$\frac{<n_i>}{v_i} = T_i(1 - l_i) + \frac{l_i}{\gamma_i} \tag{19}$$

$$T_i = \frac{\frac{<n_i>}{v_i} - \frac{l_i}{\gamma_i}}{1 - l_i} \tag{20}$$

$$T_i = \frac{1}{\Lambda_i}[\frac{\gamma_i}{\mu_i}\frac{(\Lambda_i + \gamma_i)}{(\mu_i + \gamma_i)} - 1] \tag{21}$$

where $l_i = \frac{(v_i - o_i)}{v_i}$.

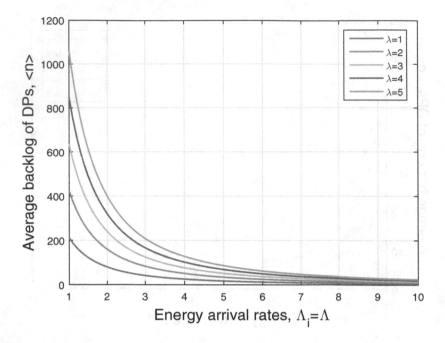

Fig. 3. The total average backlog of DPs at all of the $N = 10$ units, versus the arrival rate of EPs. We see that the values of N, Λ and λ impact the DP backlog time significantly. Note that the total energy arrival rate to the system is $N\Lambda$.

3   Conclusions

This paper introduces a mathematical model of a tandem network of very fast digital devices (i.e. having negligible service time) with limited and intermittent energy sources. The system times are determined by the speed at which energy is harvested and the speed at which data enters into the network. The nodes also suffer from EP losses due to battery leakage and some DP losses due to time-outs or due to the lack of energy in the system. We have explicited the conditions under which this model has product form solution, and presented the product form, jointly for both the EP "queues" (i.e. batteries) and the DP buffers at each of the nodes. Numerical results illustrate the usage of the model. In Figs. 2 and 3 we show the average backlog of DPs for different energy and data arrival rates, and different numbers of nodes N. We set identical values at all units $\Lambda_i = \Lambda$, $\lambda_i = \lambda$. Other parameters are $\gamma_i = 0.1\lambda_i$, $N = 5$ (Fig. 2) and $N = 10$ (Fig. 3), respectively. As one would expect, when the EP arrival rate increases, the average DP backlog decreases significantly since DPs are more rapidly transmitted. More nodes in tandem networks will result in higher overall packet backlogs since the net inflow of DPs will be higher.

In future work, the model can be generalized to time-varying data and energy arrival rates at each node, and dependent inter-arrival times.

References

1. Gelenbe, E., Caseau, Y.: The impact of information technology on energy consumption and carbon emissions. Ubiquity **2015**(June), 1 (2015)
2. Rodoplu, V., Meng, T.H.: Bits-per-joule capacity of energy-limited wireless networks. IEEE Trans. Wireless Commun. **6**(3) (2007)
3. Gelenbe, E.: Energy packet networks: ICT based energy allocation and storage. In: Rodrigues, J.J.P.C., Zhou, L., Chen, M., Kailas, A. (eds.) GreeNets 2011. LNICST, vol. 51, pp. 186–195. Springer, Heidelberg (2012). https://doi.org/10.1007/978-3-642-33368-2_16
4. Gelenbe, E.: Synchronising energy harvesting and data packets in a wireless sensor. Energies **8**(1), 356–369 (2015)
5. Kadioglu, Y.M.: Finite capacity energy packet networks. Probab. Eng. Inf. Sci. **31**(4), 477–504 (2017)
6. Kadioglu, Y.M., Gelenbe, E.: Packet transmission with k energy packets in an energy harvesting sensor. In: Proceedings of the 2nd International Workshop on Energy-Aware Simulation, p. 1. ACM (2016)
7. Kadioglu,Y.M., Gelenbe, E.: Wireless sensor with data and energy packets. In: 2017 IEEE International Conference on Communications Workshops (ICC Workshops), pp. 564–569. IEEE (2017)
8. Gelenbe, E., Marin, A.: Interconnected wireless sensors with energy harvesting. In: Gribaudo, M., Manini, D., Remke, A. (eds.) ASMTA 2015. LNCS, vol. 9081, pp. 87–99. Springer, Cham (2015). https://doi.org/10.1007/978-3-319-18579-8_7
9. Dallery, Y., Gershwin, S.B.: Manufacturing flow line systems: a review of models and analytical results. Queueing Syst. **12**(1–2), 3–94 (1992)
10. Ramaswami, S.: Optical Networks: A practical Perspective, 2nd edn. Academic Press (2002)
11. Balsamo, S., Harrison, P.G., Marin, A.: Methodological construction of product-form stochastic petri nets for performance evaluation. J. Syst. Softw. **85**(7), 1520–1539 (2012)
12. Marin, A., Balsamo, S., Harrison, P.G.: Analysis of stochastic petri nets with signals. Perform. Eval. **69**(11), 551–572 (2012)
13. Kadioglu, Y.M., Gelenbe, E.: Product form solution for cascade networks with intermittent energy. IEEE Syst. J. (2018). Accepted for publication

Adaptive Allocation of Multi-class Tasks in the Cloud

Lan Wang[✉]

Imperial College London, London, UK
lan.wang12@imperial.ac.uk

Abstract. Cloud computing enables the accommodation of an increasing number of applications in shared infrastructures. The routing for the incoming jobs in the cloud has become a real challenge due to the heterogeneity in both workload and machine hardware and the changes of load conditions over time. The present paper design and investigate the adaptive dynamic allocation algorithms that take decisions based on on-line and up-to-date measurements, and make fast online decisions to achieve both desirable QoS levels and high resource utilization. The Task allocation platform (TAP) is implemented as a practical system to accommodate the allocation algorithms and perform online measurement. The paper studies the potential of our proposed algorithms to deal with multi-class tasks in heterogeneous cloud environments and the experimental evaluations are also presented.

Keywords: Random Neural Network · Reinforcement learning
Sensible algorithm · Task allocation · Cloud computing
Task dispatching

1 Introduction

Cloud computing enables the inhabitation of an increasing number of applications from the general public or enterprise users which generate diverse sets of workloads in terms of resource demands and performance requirements [2]. For example, Web requests usually demand fast response and produce loads that may vary significantly over time [18]; Scientific applications are commonly computation intensive and might undergo several phases with varied workload profiles [10]; MapReduce jobs consist of different tasks of various sizes and resource requirements [18]. The consolidation of highly heterogeneous workloads in shared IT infrastructure causing inevitable interference between co-located workloads [20] can also degrade performance. Furthermore, the heterogeneity in the hardware configuration of physical servers or virtual machines in terms of the specific speeds and capacities of the processor, memory, storage, and networking subsystems further complicates the matching of applications to available

© Springer Nature Switzerland AG 2018
T. Czachórski et al. (Eds.): ISCIS 2018, CCIS 935, pp. 10–18, 2018.
https://doi.org/10.1007/978-3-030-00840-6_2

machines. Therefore, it is really challenging for cloud service providers to dispatch incoming tasks to servers with the assurance of the quality and reliability of the job execution required by end users while improving resource usage efficiency.

Much research have been carried out on task allocation approaches for QoS improvement in the cloud, such as DAC-based modeling [11,14], genetic algorithms [9], colony optimization (ACO) [1], Particle Swarm Optimization [13], Random Neural Networks [7], and auction-based mechanisms [17]. The authors in [2,12] focus on modeling the diversity among applications on heterogeneous servers. The trade-off between energy consumption and QoS was addressed in [5,6,15,19]. Workload distribution across multiple clouds has been discussed in [16].

In this paper we evaluate the two adaptive task allocation algorithms, the sensible algorithm [4] and the Random Neural Network-based Reinforcement Learning algorithm [3], that make measurement based fast online decisions to address quality of service (QoS) with low computational overhead. With no priori knowledge of workload characteristics and the state of servers in terms of resource utilization and load conditions, our approach exploits on-line measurement related to the user required QoS and make judicious allocation decisions based on the knowledge learned from the observations, adapting to changes in workload and on-going performance of the cloud environment. It is designed for the cloud service providers that use the SaaS model where the service provider sets up the VMs with the installed software components which provide the services requested by the customers.

In order to conduct experimental evaluations, we also use the Task Allocation Platform (TAP) [8], which is a Linux based portable software module and can be easily installed on a machine with Linux OS, to accommodate the distinct static or dynamic allocation algorithms and perform online measurement. In TAP, users are allowed to declare QoS goals such as fastest job execution or optimising cloud provider's profit while maintaining service level agreements (SLAs). TAP accepts these directions and carries out constant monitoring and measurement in order to keep awareness of the state of cloud environment and service performance related to the QoS goals. On receiving the jobs, TAP employs the accommodated allocation algorithm and dispatches the jobs to the selected machines.

Experiments are conducted on a multiple host test-bed which is heterogeneous regarding processing speed and I/O capacity, running with low to high loads that are achieved by varying arrival rates of tasks. We study the potential of our proposed algorithms when there is greater diversity both in the types of jobs, the class of QoS criteria and the SLA they request. Multi-class tasks in terms of resource requirements, such as the capacities of CPU and I/O, or agreed SLAs are injected into TAP simultaneously. We also complicate the QoS goal from minimising job execution time to economic cost of executing tasks: this cost includes the *penalty* that the cloud provider would have to pay to the end user when a SLA (service level agreement) is violated, as well as the intrinsic economic cost of using faster or slower hosts.

2   Multi-class Task Allocation

It is quite common in cloud environments that the services requested by customers generate multiple workloads which are characterised differently in terms of their resource and performance requirements. For example, for an online financial management and accounting software providing SaaS services, the web browsing requests which retrieve files from web servers generate I/O bound workload, while the profit and loss accounting services which need a large amount of computation requiring high CPU capacity. Thus, the response time of the above two different web requests provided by a server relies on its capacities of the I/O and CPU respectively. TAP is designed to support multi-class tasks by assigning a distinct QoS class to a class of tasks.

2.1   Multiple QoS Classes

To illustrate the multi-class task allocation, we emulate two different classes of tasks in our experiments. We first introduce a web browsing workload generated using HTTPerf which is a web server performance tool. It originates HTTP requests which retrieve files from web server, such as Apache 2 HTTP server, thereby generating I/O bound workload on the web server without much CPU consumption. The load on the I/O subsystem relies on the size of the retrieved files. In our TAP test-bed, the Apache server is deployed on each host in the cluster. The HTTPerf generates HTTP requests at a configurable rate and TAP receives the requests and dispatches them to the web servers. The second class corresponds to the web services which require a large amount of computation, mainly stress CPU and thus can be emulated by the CPU intensive job which is a "prime number generator with an upper bound on the prime number being generated". We compare the RNN based algorithms with the Sensible Algorithm, both using the goal of minimising the response time. Round-Robin scheduling is also applied as a baseline.

We conduct our experiments on a hardware test-bed as shown in Fig. 1. The three hosts (with 2.8 GHz, 2.4 GHz, and 3.0 GHz, respectively, dual-core CPU respectively) are used for task execution, while a dedicated host (2.8 GHz dual-core CPU) accommodates the allocation algorithms.

The test-bed is in the small scale as we can easily vary the load of the system and evaluate the algorithms under low, medium and high (including saturation) load conditions. The job requests arrive at TAP following a Poisson process with different average rates of $1, 2, 3, 4$ tasks/sec. To built the heterogeneous server environments, we introduce a background load which stresses I/O distinctly on each host, namely Hosts $1, 2, 3$, resulting in relative processing speeds of $6 : 2 : 1$ with respect to I/O bound services, while a background load which stresses CPU differently, resulting in the relative processing speed of $2 : 3 : 6$ for the CPU bound services.

The results in Fig. 2 show that our proposed algorithm, the RNN based algorithm and the sensible algorithm, outperform Round-Robin as they are aware of the distinct and updated performance level offered by the hosts by effective

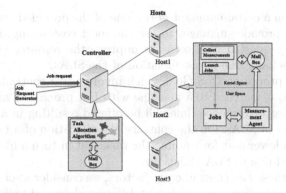

Fig. 1. The test-bed for the task allocation platform with a central controller on a test-bed

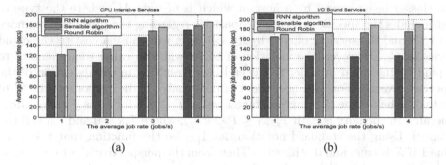

Fig. 2. Average response time experienced by CPU intensive services and I/O bound services in a heterogeneous cluster. We compare Round-Robin with RNN based Reinforcement Learning and the Sensible Algorithm.

learning from the historical job experience. The RNN based algorithm performs particularly better due to its potential to make more accurate decisions (compared with Sensible) which direct I/O bound tasks to the hosts which provide better I/O capacity and transfer CPU intensive tasks to the hosts with higher processing speed. In the experiments, we also reduced the background load in terms of both CPU and I/O stress on the *Host* 2 to the lowest level as compared with the *Hosts* 1, 3. The RNN based algorithm was found to be able to detect the load changes and dispatch the majority of subsequent tasks of both classes to *Host* 2, which also shows the host which is heavily loaded in terms of CPU can still offer good performance to I/O bound tasks and thereby improving the resource utilization.

2.2   Contradictory QoS Requirements

In previous sections, we focus primarily on the simple QoS goal of minimising job execution/response time which is of interest of end users. From the perspective of cloud service providers, the economic cost of job execution is of greater importance. Given a certain amount of revenue of the provided services with the agreed SLA, the provider manages to use the most cost-saving machines while maintaining the requested QoS so as to improve the resource efficiency while minimising the penalty due to the violation of the SLAs.

Thus we can propose a QoS Goal which involves two contradictory requirements: if a task is dispatched to a machine with fast processors and thus higher running cost, a better response time will be offered resulting in a lower penalty due to the respect of SLAs. On the contrary the allocation of a task to a slower machine causes a lower cost for running the task, but in turn a higher possibility of being penalised due to SLA violations.

To formalise these two contradictory factors, we consider a set of host servers having distinct processing capacities, and different classes of tasks with distinct SLA agreed objects. We use I_j to represent the revenue generated by serving the tasks of a class j with the agreed SLAs. Next, we assume that the task of a class j being served by a host m which is of type M_i, where the type of host includes the specific processing capacities regarding the processor, memory and I/O, and the services offered by its software, will cause a cost to the cloud service of C_{ij}. However, the violation of SLAs will also cause some penalty to be paid by the cloud provider to the end user, resulting in the reduction of the expected revenue. For instance, there is no penalty if the response time T of the task is below the SLA agreed target value $T_{j,1} > 0$ for class j tasks. More generally, the penalty is c_{jl} if $T_{j,l-1} \leq T < kT_{j,l}$, where $T_{j0} = 0$ and $c_{j0} = 0$ (no penalty). Using the standard notation, let $1_{[X]}$ be the function that takes the value 1 if X is true, and 0 otherwise. Then from the perspective of a task of type j which is served by the cloud service, the *net income* obtained after deducting the host operating cost and the eventual penalty due to SLA violations, can be written as:

$$I_j^* = I_j - C_{ij}1_{[m=M_i]} -$$

$$\sum_{l=0}^{n}\{c_{jl}1_{[T_{j,l}\leq T<T_{j,l+1}]}\} + c_{j,n+1}1_{[T\geq kT_{j,n+1}]}.$$

Obviously, the cloud providers is willing to *maximise* I_j^*, while I_j is pre-defined in the service agreement.

Thus in this section we apply the task allocation algorithm with the goal of minimising the *net cost* function:

$$C_j = C_{ij}1_{[m=M_i]} + \sum_{l=0}^{n}\{c_{jl}1_{[T_{j,l}\leq T<T_{j,l+1}]}\} \tag{1}$$
$$+c_{j,n+1}1_{[T\geq kT_{j,n+1}]}.$$

We consider the above online financial management and accounting service as an example in the real world, the bookkeeping service requires fast response as they are frequently-used operations, while users are tolerant of the long response time for bank reconciliation service which is the time-consuming operation.

It gives us an example of the tasks of two classes with the distinct SLA agreed response time and thus the distinct penalty functions.

To illustrate the preceding discussion with experiments, we use CPU intensive jobs which either are "short" with an execution time of 56 ms, or "long" with an execution time of 190 ms as measured on the fastest host. With regard to the first term in (1), we have $M_1 : C_{1j} = 1000$, $M_2 : C_{2j} = 2000$ and $M_3 : C_{3j} = 4000$ coinciding with our assumption that the faster machines cost more. The penalty function, which is the second term in (1), for the two distinct classes of tasks is shown in Fig. 3 where the job class 2 is tolerant of longer execution time. We emulate a heterogeneous host environment where there is a fast host, a slow host and a medium speed host by stressing the CPU of each host differently, resulting in the relative processing speeds of $1 : 2 : 4$ for Host $1, 2, 3$. Tasks of both classes were generated following a Poisson process with varied task arrival rates of $1, 2, 3, 4$ tasks/sec. The RNN based algorithm is compared with the Sensible Algorithm.

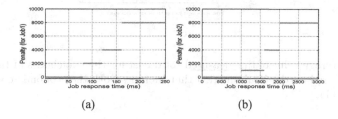

(a)   (b)

Fig. 3. The penalty function for tasks belonging to Class 1 (left) and Class 2 (right), versus the task response time on the x axis.

We can see that the RNN-based algorithm does better in reducing the overall cost plus SLA violation penalty (indicated as the Total Penalty in the y-axis) as shown in Fig. 4(c). Because the RNN is able to accurately dispatch the jobs which require fast response to the faster machines resulting in fewer SLA violations and direct the jobs which have the tolerance of long response to slower machines which can maintain the agreed SLA and thereby avoiding the interference with each other which further improves the performance.

3   Conclusions

The present paper presents the design and the evaluation through experiments, of some adaptive dynamic allocation algorithms that take decisions for task allocation to servers, based on on-line and up-to-date measurements, and make fast online decisions to achieve desirable QoS level. To this effect, a Task allocation platform (TAP) is implemented as a practical system to accommodate the allocation algorithms, perform online measurement and carry out performance evaluations. Our experiments have shown the potential for enhanced performance

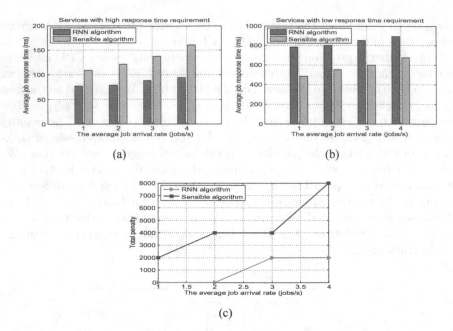

(a)

(b)

(c)

Fig. 4. The average value of the <u>measured</u> total cost for the two classes of tasks, when allocation is based on the Goal function that includes both the economic cost and the penalty as in (1).

offered by our proposed algorithms, namely the RNN-based algorithm and the Sensible algorithm, to deal with multi-class tasks. These algorithms outperform the Round-Robin scheme due to their ability to be aware of the heterogeneity in both the workload and the machine hardware, and regarding changes in load conditions in the Cloud over time. The performance of RNN based algorithm with Reinforcement-Learning stands out among the others as it offers fine-grained QoS-aware and accurate task allocation decisions.

References

1. Chen, W., Zhang, J.: An ant colony optimization approach to a grid workflow scheduling problem with various qos requirements. IEEE Trans. Syst. Man Cybern. Part C Appl. Rev. **39**(1), 29–43 (2009). https://doi.org/10.1109/TSMCC.2008. 2001722
2. Delimitrou, C., Kozyrakis, C.: QoS-aware scheduling in heterogeneous datacenters with paragon. ACM Trans. Comput. Syst. **31**(4), 12:1–12:34 (2013). https://doi. org/10.1145/2556583
3. Gelenbe, E., Fourneau, J.: Random neural networks with multiple classes of signals. Neural Comput. **11**(4), 953–963 (1999)

4. Gelenbe, E.: Sensible decisions based on QoS. Comput. Manag. Sci. **1**(1), 1–14 (2003)
5. Gelenbe, E., Lent, R.: Trade-offs between energy and quality of service. In: Sustainable Internet and ICT for Sustainability (SustainIT), pp. 1–5. IEEE (2012)
6. Gelenbe, E., Lent, R.: Optimising server energy consumption and response time. Theor. Appl. Inform. **4**, 257–270 (2013). https://doi.org/10.2478/v10179-012-0016-1
7. Gelenbe, E., Timotheou, S., Nicholson, D.: Fast distributed near-optimum assignment of assets to tasks. Comput. J. **53**(9), 1360–1369 (2010). https://doi.org/10.1093/comjnl/bxq010
8. Gelenbe, E., Wang, L.: Tap: A task allocation platform for the EU FP7 PANACEA project. In: The proceedings of the EU projects track, September 2015
9. Hou, E., Ansari, N., Ren, H.: A genetic algorithm for multiprocessor scheduling. IEEE Trans. Parallel Distrib. Syst. **5**(2), 113–120 (1994). https://doi.org/10.1109/71.265940
10. Iosup, A., Ostermann, S., Yigitbasi, M., Prodan, R., Fahringer, T., Epema, D.H.J.: Performance analysis of cloud computing services for many-tasks scientific computing. IEEE Trans. Parallel Distrib. Syst. **22**(6), 931–945 (2011). https://doi.org/10.1109/TPDS.2011.66
11. Kwok, Y.K., Ahmad, I.: Dynamic critical-path scheduling: an effective technique for allocating task graphs to multiprocessors. IEEE Trans. Parallel Distrib. Syst. **7**(5), 506–521 (1996). https://doi.org/10.1109/71.503776
12. Moreno, I.S., Garraghan, P., Townend, P., Xu, J.: Analysis, modeling and simulation of workload patterns in a large-scale utility cloud. IEEE Trans. Cloud Comput. **PP**(99), 1–1 (2014). https://doi.org/10.1109/TCC.2014.2314661
13. Pandey, S., Linlin, W., Guru, S., Buyya, R.: A particle swarm optimization-based heuristic for scheduling workflow applications in cloud computing environments. In: 2010 24th IEEE International Conference on Advanced Information Networking and Applications (AINA), pp. 400–407, April 2010. https://doi.org/10.1109/AINA.2010.31
14. Topcuouglu, H.: Hariri, S., you Wu, M.: Performance-effective and low-complexity task scheduling for heterogeneous computing. IEEE Trans. Parallel Distrib. Syst. **13**(3), 260–274 (2002). https://doi.org/10.1109/71.993206
15. Wang, L.: Online work distribution to clouds. In: 2016 IEEE 24th International Symposium on Modeling, Analysis and Simulation of Computer and Telecommunication Systems (MASCOTS), pp. 295–300, September 2016. https://doi.org/10.1109/MASCOTS.2016.64
16. Wang, L., Brun, O., Gelenbe, E.: Adaptive workload distribution for local and remote clouds. In: 2016 IEEE International Conference on Systems, Man, and Cybernetics (SMC), pp. 003984–003988, October 2016. https://doi.org/10.1109/SMC.2016.7844856
17. Zaman, S., Grosu, D.: A combinatorial auction-based dynamic vm provisioning and allocation in clouds. In: 2011 IEEE Third International Conference on Cloud Computing Technology and Science (CloudCom), pp. 107–114, November 2011. https://doi.org/10.1109/CloudCom.2011.24
18. Zhan, J., Wang, L., Li, X., Shi, W., Weng, C., Zhang, W., Zang, X.: Cost-aware cooperative resource provisioning for heterogeneous workloads in data centers. IEEE Trans. Comput. **62**(11), 2155–2168 (2013). https://doi.org/10.1109/TC.2012.103

19. Zhang, Q., Zhani, M., Boutaba, R., Hellerstein, J.: Dynamic heterogeneity-aware resource provisioning in the cloud. IEEE Trans. Cloud Comput. **2**(1), 14–28 (2014). https://doi.org/10.1109/TCC.2014.2306427
20. Zhuravlev, S., Blagodurov, S., Fedorova, A.: Addressing shared resource contention in multicore processors via scheduling. SIGPLAN Not. **45**(3), 129–142 (2010). https://doi.org/10.1145/1735971.1736036

The Mapping Between TFD and IEEE 802.11 User Priorities and Access Categories

Robert R. Chodorek[1]($\boxtimes$) and Agnieszka Chodorek[2]

[1] Department of Telecommunications, AGH University of Science and Technology,
Al. Mickiewicza 30, 30-059 Krakow, Poland
chodorek@agh.edu.pl
[2] Faculty of Electrical Engineering, Automatic Control and Computer Science,
Kielce University of Technology, Al. Tysiaclecia P.P. 7, 25-314 Kielce, Poland
a.chodorek@tu.kielce.pl

Abstract. The modern approach to the quality of service (QoS) claims
that problems of assurance of the required QoS parameters may occur
not only in core networks (as the classic approach assumes), but also
in access networks (including local networks, or LANs), especially if the
access network is of broadcast type, such as the IEEE 802.11 wireless
LAN. In the case of broadcast LANs, QoS assurance in the network
layer should be associated with the QoS assurance in the data link layer.
The aim of this paper is to propose such an association between the
802.11 QoS assurance and the QoS assurance based on the Traffic Flow
Description (TFD) option of the IP protocol. The TFD was specified by
the Authors in the IETF's working document (Internet Draft), and was
intended to describe Internet traffic for the purpose of dynamic resource
reservations. The TFD-based QoS assurance offers dynamic reservations
for micro-flows (single data real-time streams or non-real-time flows).
The proposed method associates TFD and 802.11 QoS architectures in a
way similar to the association of the DiffServ architecture and the 802.11
QoS, i.e. by the mapping of corresponding signalling. This mapping was
designed and then implemented by the Authors in a Linux kernel. Results
of laboratory experiments carried out in a test network show that the
proposed mappings sufficiently promote traffic described by the TFD
option in 802.11 WLAN and protect it against degradation. The proposed
method includes the mapping of static signalling. Mapping of dynamic
information conveyed in the TFD option is also possible and will be
a subject of further research. The mapping between TFD and IEEE
802.11 user priorities and access categories will allow a 802.11 network
to preserve TFD-based QoS in wireless links.

1 Introduction

From the information dissemination point of view, communication networks can
be divided into three classes. Point-to-point networks, where one sender physically sends information to one and only one receiver. Broadcast networks, where

© Springer Nature Switzerland AG 2018
T. Czachórski et al. (Eds.): ISCIS 2018, CCIS 935, pp. 19–27, 2018.
https://doi.org/10.1007/978-3-030-00840-6_3

one sender is able to physically send information to one or more receivers. Broadcast networks offer natural (on a level of a physical link) broadcast and multicast services, which is often associated with random access to a link shared by two or more stations. The third class is non-broadcast networks, which also offer one-to-N transmissions, where N is equal to or larger than 1, but their broadcast and multicast services are emulated in non-broadcast links. Core networks, typically built with the use of fiber optics or radiolinks (including satellite radiolinks), usually belong to point-to-point or non-broadcast classes. Access networks, including local area networks (LANs), often belong to the broadcast class.

The point-to-point and non-broadcast networks allow the network layer of the Open Systems Interconnection (OSI) model to assure quality of service (QoS) by the use of suitable buffering. Thus, the main efforts of the creators of the classic approach to quality of service (QoS) were focused on two fundamental QoS architectures, based on two alternative methods of signalling. They are the Integrated Services (IntServ), based on the Resource Reservation Protocol (RSVP) and the Differentiated Services (DiffServ), based on the differentiated services code point (DSCP). The broadcast environments are not able to assure end-to-end QoS in the same way because of the random access of sending stations to shared medium.

The classic approach to QoS works around the problem of BMA networks by the assumption that the performance of access networks, including local area networks (LANs), is both much larger than the performance of the core network and large enough to assure required QoS parameters. As a result, the problems with QoS should occur only in core networks. Nowadays this assumption is not always met, so the modern approach to QoS states that in broadcast networks QoS assurance in the network layer should be associated with the QoS assurance in the data link layer. An example that can be used is the popular wireless LAN technology, IEEE 802.11 (WiFi), which allows the user to associate DiffServ and 802.11 QoS assurance (formerly 802.11e, now included in 802.11). Mapping between the DiffServ's DSCPs and IEEE 802.11 access categories and traffic classes are widely described in the literature ([3–5], just to list a few), although it still remains an open issue [6].

The Traffic Flow Description (TFD) is an experimental option of the Internet Protocol (IP), proposed in the IETF's working document [1], intended for the description of traffic in real-time streams and non-real-time flows for Quality of Service (QoS) purposes. The option is devoted to conveying detailed knowledge about forthcoming traffic (valid in a short time horizon) from a sender, through intermediate nodes, to a receiver. This knowledge was successfully used for the individual (made for each flow or stream) dynamic resource allocation of multiple video streams [2]. However, to utilize TFD descriptions, TFD-capable intermediate nodes (routers) are needed and the connection of TFD-capable and TFD-incapable networks may result (and, usually, results) in the degradation of QoS.

In this paper, an unequivocal mapping between a subset of the TFD flags and IEEE 802.11 user priorities and access categories is proposed. The proposed method maps the static part of the TFD option into user priorities and access categories of IEEE 802.11 Wireless LAN. As a result, QoS-protected traffic avoids medium contention and receives QoS guarantees from a 802.11 network.

The rest of the paper is organized as follows. The next section describes the TFD option. The third section proposes the mapping between the TFD and IEEE 802.11 QoS signalling, while the fourth section describes implementation of proposed mapping in the Linux kernel. The fifth section presents experimental results. The sixth section summarizes our experiences.

2   Traffic Flow Description Option

The TFD option of the IP protocol is intended to be used as optional fields of the header of the IP version 4 (IPv4) datagram or as an optional header of the IP version 6 (IPv6) datagram.

The option conveys both dynamic knowledge about forthcoming traffic and static information about the described real-time stream or non-real-time flow. The dynamic part assures signalling that allows for the building of the dynamic resource allocation systems. The static part can be used as a code point, which enables the coding of QoS requirements.

The option consists of five fields (Fig. 1). The first two bytes are occupied by two option control fields. The next, Flags field occupies the next two bytes of the option. This field conveys, among other things, static information about data transmitted stream or flow. Each of the last two fields, Next Data and Next Time, occupy four bytes. They are designed for the transmission of dynamic knowledge about forthcoming traffic. The Next Data field includes the amount of data (in bytes) that will be transmitted during the time (in ms) given in the Next Time field.

The Flags field consists of seven 1-bit flags and one 9-bit field Res, reserved for future flags (Fig. 2). The first two flags describe features of the Next Data field (number format and indication of maximum value). The next two flags describe how data transmitted in the Next Data Field were acquired (buffer analysis or prediction). The last three fields describe properties of the transmitted traffic. The S and E fields indicate the type of traffic - streaming (inelastic) or elastic, respectively. The L field indicates that large amounts of data will be transmitted.

3   LSE-to-UP and LSE-to-AC Mappings

Apart from dynamic knowledge about forthcoming traffic, conveyed mainly in NextData and NextTime fields, the TFD option carries static general information (some bits of the Flags field) about the transmitted stream or flow. This information is too general to be able to serve as a basis of per-stream or per-flow reservations, but describes streams or flows well enough to serve as code points that indicate traffic classes. In this case the L, S and E bits of the Flags field are the most important.

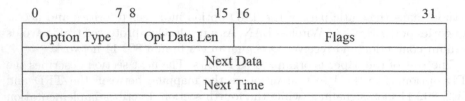

Fig. 1. IPv6 traffic flow description option

The L, S and E bits indicate QoS requirements of given traffic. The values of the so-defined code point (hereafter referred to as 'LSE') can be mapped to corresponding values of IEEE 802.11 user priorities (UP) and access categories (AC). The mapping table of LSE QoS information to IEEE 802.11 UP and AC is presented in Table 1.

Table 1. LSE to UP/AC mapping

L	S	E	UP	IEEE 802.1D designation	AC
0	0	0	0	BE	AC_BE
1	0	0	0 or 1	BE or BK	AC_BE or AC_BK
0	1	0	6	VO	AC_VO
1	1	0	5	VI	AC_VI
0	0	1	3	EE	AC_VO
1	0	1	4	CL	AC_VI
0 or 1	1	1	–	–	–

S and E bits equal to zero denote that TFD-based assurance is not in use and the transmission should be carried out using typical best effort service. This LSE code point is mapped to UP equal to zero (IEEE 802.1D Best Effort or BE). However, if the L bit is set and the nature of traffic allows, user priority can be set to 1 (IEEE 802.1D Background or BK). The S bit set indicates streaming traffic (voice or video transmission). The distinction between voice and video is based on the size of streaming information, indicated by the L flag. If the L bit is set, UP will be set to 5 (IEEE 802.1D Video or VI). If the L is clear, UP will be set to 6 (IEEE 802.1D Voice or VO). In the case of the above LSEs, mapping between UP and AC is in accordance with the IEEE 802.11 standard [7].

Elastic traffic (E bit set) is usually not covered by the QoS guarantees. However, such guarantees may be desirable for certain applications, such as the Internet of Things (IoT) or e-health. The Authors then propose to use UP equal to 3 (IEEE 802.1D Excellent Effort or EE) in the case of a small amount of transmitted data (L = 0) and UP equal to 4 (IEEE 802.1D Controlled Load or CL) otherwise (L = 1). AC set to AC_VI (video), in the case of UP set to

4, is compliant with IEEE 802.11 specification [7]. In the case of UP set to 3, the Authors propose to use the AC_VO (voice) access category rather than the AC_BE (best effort), specified in [7].

The situation where the S bit is set to 1 and the E bit is set to 1 is forbidden in the document [1].

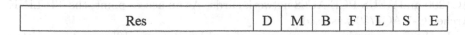

Res	D	M	B	F	L	S	E

Fig. 2. Flags field of the TFD option

4 Implementation

The above mapping was implemented in the Linux kernel. The Linux kernel IEEE 802.11 framework consists of two main components: mac80211 and cfg80211. The mac80211 is a framework used for writing drivers for SoftMAC wireless devices. The cfg80211 is the configuration API for IEEE 802.11 devices in Linux. It bridges userspace and drivers and offers some utility functionality.

The implementation of mapping includes both LSE-to-UP mapping and the improvement of UP-to-AC mapping. In so far as LSE-to-UP mapping only needs changes in the kernel, the UP-to-AC mapping also needs changes in the driver of the network card, introduced as firmware extensions. Firmware extensions and some default parameters of 802.11 devices are sent from the Linux kernel drivers to 802.11 network adapters during startup of the operating system.

As a result, changes were made both to the mac80211 module (net/mac80211 - "Linux softmac layer") and to the util.c module of the wireless section (net/wireless - "Wireless utility functions"). The implementation defines the QoS map structure (according to Table 1) and adds the TFD mapping to the cfg80211_classify8021d function, which determines the 802.1p/1d tag assignment. The QoS map is defined using the Linux kernel nl80211_set_qos_map function. Because, during transmission, TFD option fields are analyzed and user priorities and access categories are set and the ieee80211_select_queue function, which indicates the queue used for transmission, was also modified.

5 Experiments and Preliminary Results

Experiments were carried out in a local 802.11n network, working at 2.4 GHz, 144 Mbps. As foreground traffic, media streams from a VLC media server [8] or elastic flows transmitted by the Transmission Control Protocol (TCP) were used. As background traffic TCP flows were used. Foreground traffic was QoS protected with the use of the TFD option and background traffic was transmitted without QoS guarantees (the best effort service). End systems worked under the control of the Linux operating system. To enable TFD signalling, implementation

[9] of the TFD option in the Linux kernel was used. Video streams were High Definition Television (HDTV) sequences [10], owned by NTIA/ITS, an agency of the U.S. Federal Government and created in 2008 under Project Number 3141012-300, Video Quality Research. TCP flows were generated by the iPerf tool [11]. Video streams and TCP flows were transmitted from senders, through the access point, to receivers. End systems were equipped with Archer T4U AC1200 and ASUS PCE-AC68 network cards. As an access point, the TP-LINK Archer C-7 AC1750 was used.

In the first experiment, a sequence of 8 video streams [10] were transmitted together with N TCP flows ($N = 0, 1, ..., 10$). The topology of the test network is depicted in Fig. 3. Each test sequence lasted about 760 s and was build by repeating the transmission of 8 clips five times (each clip lasts for 19 s and the target bit rate set to 20 Mbps), with clips starting from randomly chosen moments. Figure 4 shows the comparison of averaged (over 10 times) packet error rates (PER) of the video transmission with and without the TFD signalling. The LSE code point was set to 110 (L and S bits set, E bit clear), which gives UP equal to 5 and AC set to AC_VI (Tab. 1). As is depicted in the figure, LSE-to-UP mapping allowed for the achievement of nearly errorless transmission (only in the case of 9 and 10 competing TCP streams was PER larger than zero, i.e. 0.3% and 0.5%, respectively), while without QoS protection one competing TCP flow was enough to achieve average PER of 17.4% (and 36% for $N = 10$).

In the second experiment, a single TCP transmission (bulk data transfer) competed for bandwidth with N TCP flows ($N = 0, 1, ..., 10$). Topology of the test network is depicted in Fig. 5. The LSE code point was set to 001 (L and S bits clear, E bit set), which gives UP equal to 3 and AC set to AC_VO (Tab. 1). Each transmission lasted for 500 s and results were averaged over the 10 transmissions. Figure 6 presents average throughput achieved for transmissions with and without QoS protection based on the TFD option. As is shown in the figure, LSE-to-UP mapping allows one to obtain larger throughput if more than one TCP stream competes with QoS protected elastic traffic. In the case of $N = 6$ protected traffic achieved about two times larger throughput than non-protected (7.08 Mbps vs. 3.7 Mbps), and if $N = 10$, more than three times larger (7.01 Mbps vs. 2.3 Mbps).

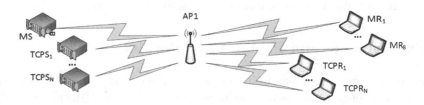

Fig. 3. Topology of the test network used in the first experiment. Legend: MS - media (video) server, $MR_i - i$th media (video) receiver, $i = 1, ..., 8$, $TCPS_j - j$th TCP sender, $TCPR_j - j$th TCP receiver, $j = 1, ..., N$

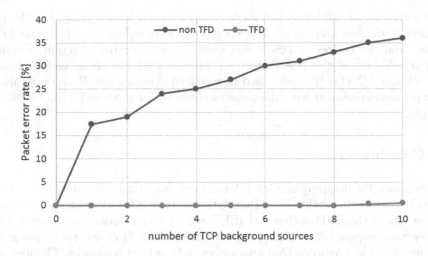

Fig. 4. Error rate of video transmission vs TCP background sources

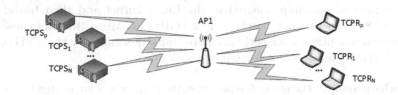

Fig. 5. Topology of the test network used in the second experiment. Legend: $TCPS_p$ - TCP sender (QoS-protected traffic), $TCPR_p$ - TCP receiver (QoS-protected traffic), $TCPS_j - j$th TCP sender, $TCP_j - j$th TCP receiver, $j = 1, ..., N$

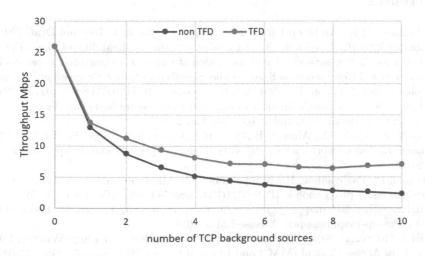

Fig. 6. Throughput of TCP transmission with multiple TCP background traffic connections

For the sake of validation and verification of the implementation described in the Sect. 4, the first and the second experiments were repeated without the TFD option, and the DiffServ's DSCP was used as the indicator of required traffic category. Values of the DSCP were so selected that the same traffic classes (AC_VI and AC_VO) [12] were used in repeated experiments. Results obtained for repeated experiment were the same as obtained for proposed TFD-to-802.11 mapping.

6   Conclusion

In this paper, the mapping of static information about transmitted flow or stream (described using the Traffic Flow Description option of the IP protocol) between chosen bits of the TFD option and IEEE 802.11 user priorities and access categories was proposed. Such mappings are created for QoS assurance purposes and are aimed at providing QoS guarantees in broadcast networks. The method of mapping is similar to classic DSCP-to-UP and DSCP-to-AC mappings that enable the preservation of DiffServ's QoS guarantees in 802.11 networks. The proposed method was implemented in the Linux kernel and then tested in a laboratory 802.11n network, working at 2.4 GHz, 144 Mbps. Results show that the proposed mappings sufficiently promote traffic described by the TFD option in 802.11 WLAN and protect it against degradation.

Acknowledgement. The research reported in the chapter was supported by the contract 11.11.230.018.

References

1. Chodorek, R.R.: An IP option for describing the traffic flow. Internet Draft (2017)
2. Chodorek, R.R., Chodorek, A.: An analysis of the applicability of the TFD IP option for QoS assurance of multiple video streams in a congested network. In: International Conference on Systems and Signals and Image Processings, Poznan, Poland, May 2017, pp. 1–5 (2017). https://doi.org/10.1109/IWSSIP.2017.796559
3. http://www.cisco.com/c/en/us/support/docs/wireless-mobility/wireless-lan-wlan/81831-qos-wlc-lap.html/. Accessed May 2018
4. Malik, A., Qadir, J., Ahmad, B., Yau, K.L.A., Ullah, U.: QoS in IEEE 802.11-based wireless networks: a contemporary review. J. Netw. Comput. Appl. **55**, 24–46 (2015)
5. Yegani, P., Pazhyannur, R., Kaippallimalil, J.: Mapping quality of service (QoS) procedures of proxy mobile IPv6 (PMIPv6) and WLAN. RFC 7561 (2015)
6. Hiertz, G.R.: UP mapping. https://mentor.ieee.org/802.11/dcn/17/11-17-1445-00-000m-up-mapping.pptx. Accessed May 2018
7. IEEE Std 802.11-2016, IEEE Standard for Information technology-Wireless LAN Medium Access Control (MAC) and Physical Layer (PHY) specifications (2016)
8. http://www.videolan.org/vlc/. Accessed May 2018

9. Chodorek, R.R., Chodorek, A.: A Linux kernel implementation of the traffic flow description option. In: Zgrzywa, A., Choroś, K., Siemiński, A. (eds.) Multimedia and Network Information Systems. AISC, vol. 506, pp. 161–170. Springer, Cham (2017). https://doi.org/10.1007/978-3-319-43982-2_14
10. ftp://vqeg.its.bldrdoc.gov/HDTV/NTIA_source/. Accessed May 2018
11. https://iperf.fr/. Accessed May 2018
12. Szigeti, T., Baker, F. Henry, J.: Mapping Diffserv to IEEE 802.11. RFC 8325 (2018)

Design of a Multidomain IMS/NGN Service Stratum

Sylwester Kaczmarek[iD] and Maciej Sac[(⊠)][iD]

Faculty of Electronics, Telecommunications and Informatics,
Gdańsk University of Technology, 11/12 Narutowicza Street,
80-233 Gdańsk, Poland
{kasyl,msac}@eti.pg.edu.pl

Abstract. The paper continues our research concerning the Next Generation Network (NGN), which is standardized for delivering multimedia services with strict quality and includes elements of the IP Multimedia Subsystem (IMS). A design algorithm for a multidomain IMS/NGN service stratum is proposed, which calculates the necessary CSCF servers CPU message processing times and link bandwidths with respect to the given maximum values of mean call set-up delays $E(CSD)$ and mean call disengagement delays $E(CDD)$ for all types of successful call scenarios. These delays are standardized call processing performance parameters, which are very important for satisfaction of users and overall success of the IMS/NGN concept. In the paper a block diagram of the algorithm and details regarding its operation are described. Using the implemented algorithm several multidomain IMS/NGN service stratum designs are performed for different data sets and their results are discussed.

Keywords: IMS · Network design · NGN · Service stratum
Teletraffic engineering

1 Introduction

The Next Generation Network (NGN) [1] is a standardized network architecture including elements of the IP Multimedia Subsystem (IMS) [2] (thus the names "IMS-based NGN" and "IMS/NGN" are frequently used) and dedicated to satisfy current and future needs of information society for delivering high quality multimedia services. For a commercial success IMS/NGN should be properly designed [3], to guarantee values of quality parameters, which are satisfactory for users. It particularly concerns standardized call processing performance parameters [4, 5], which include mean call set-up delay $E(CSD)$ and mean call disengagement delay $E(CDD)$.

The paper proposes a design algorithm for resources of a multidomain IMS/NGN service stratum. The algorithm takes into account maximum values of $E(CSD)$ and $E(CDD)$ defined separately for all types of successful call scenarios (intra- and inter-operator) generated in particular domains. Calculations utilize the analytical traffic model of a multidomain IMS/NGN, which was a subject of our previous research [6–8]. Basic information about this model is provided in Sect. 2. Section 3 is dedicated to the proposed algorithm and contains the description of its block diagram and

© Springer Nature Switzerland AG 2018
T. Czachórski et al. (Eds.): ISCIS 2018, CCIS 935, pp. 28–37, 2018.
https://doi.org/10.1007/978-3-030-00840-6_4

performed operations. In Sect. 4 results of several multidomain IMS/NGN service stratum designs are presented and discussed. The paper is summarized in Sect. 5.

2 Model of a Multidomain IMS/NGN

In the paper a multidomain IMS/NGN is considered with two domains administered by two operators [6–8]. Each domain consists of the following elements [2, 9]: User Equipments (UEs), Call Session Control Function servers (P-CSCF – Proxy-CSCF, S-CSCF – Serving-CSCF, I-CSCF – Interrogating-CSCF), SUP-FE/SAA-FE (Service User Profile Functional Entity/Service Authentication and Authorization Functional Entity), RACF (Resource and Admission Control Functions). To distinguish between the elements of different domains, numbers 1 and 2 are added to the above mentioned names (e.g. P-CSCF 1, I-CSCF 2). As both operators have their own core and access networks, letters "A" and "C" are additionally used for RACF units (e.g. RACF A1 controls the resources of access network of operator 1).

In the assumed network 16 different service scenarios are performed (registration as well as intra- and inter-operator calls, which can be successful or unsuccessful due to lack of transport resources) [6–8]. In terms of this paper the most important are successful scenarios, for which $E(CSD)$ and $E(CDD)$ are calculated by our analytical traffic model of a multidomain IMS/NGN [6–8]: b1 (intra-operator call, domain 1, the same access area, success), b2 (intra-operator call, domain 2, the same access area, success), d1 (intra-operator call, domain 1, different access areas, success), d2 (intra-operator call, domain 2, different access areas, success), f1 (inter-operator call, originated in domain 1, success), f2 (inter-operator call, originated in domain 2, success). To obtain $E(CSD)$ and $E(CDD)$, mean values of theoretical delays introduced by network elements are calculated and properly summed. These component delays include:

- mean message waiting times in communication queues (buffering messages when links are busy); for calculation of these times mathematical models of queuing systems are used;
- message transmission times (message lengths divided by links bandwidths);
- propagation times (equal to 5 µs/km – optical links are assumed);
- mean message waiting times in CSCF servers CPU queues, which store incoming messages when CSCF servers CPUs are busy (for calculation of these times mathematical models of queuing systems are used);
- mean message processing times by CSCF servers CPUs as well as RACF and SUP-FE/SAA-FE elements; they are given by the input parameters [6–8].

The described analytical traffic model was implemented in the MATLAB environment and thoroughly tested with different queuing system models for communication queues and CSCF servers CPU queues (M/M/1, M/G/1, G/G/1 approximations, PH/PH/1 based on moments and whole experimental histograms) [6–8, 10, 11]. It was also successfully verified with a simulation model [8] implementing the operation of real network elements and standardized call scenarios (the simulated elements process SIP and Diameter messages according to standards), and thus reflecting the phenomena taking place in real IMS/NGN network.

As a result of the above mentioned research, we decided to move from the problem of network analysis to network design. In the next section, based on the described analytical traffic model of a multidomain IMS/NGN, a design algorithm is proposed, which allows calculations of service stratum resources: CSCF servers CPU processing power (message processing times) and link bandwidths.

3 Design Algorithm

The algorithm described in this section calculates the resources of service stratum of a multidomain IMS/NGN with respect to the defined maximum values of $E(CSD)$ and $E(CDD)$ for all types of successful call scenarios (Sect. 2). The proposed method does not assume particular contribution of network domains in $E(CSD)$ and $E(CDD)$ for multidomain calls. It optimizes parameters of all domains to possibly the best fulfill the designer requirements. As the structure of a multidomain IMS/NGN is complicated and the numbers of service scenarios as well as network parameters are large, an iterative approach is used.

The block diagram of the proposed design algorithm is described in Fig. 1. The general idea is to start from the maximum available IMS/NGN service stratum resources (low CSCF servers CPU processing times, high link bandwidths) and in each iteration modify parameters of the least loaded network element (CSCF server CPU or link) to increase its load. If such a modification leads to unacceptable $E(CSD)$ or $E(CDD)$ values, it is cancelled and the selected network element is excluded from further calculations. Computations stop when there are no elements, which parameters can be changed. More details about the performed operations are provided later.

The proposed algorithm was implemented in the MATLAB environment as the design_IMS_NGN() function, which returns the following output parameters:

- TINV: vector with SIP INVITE message processing times [s] by P-CSCF 1, S-CSCF 1, I-CSCF 1, P-CSCF 2, S-CSCF 2, I-CSCF 2; times of processing other messages by the CSCF servers CPUs are proportional with the a_k factors [6–8];
- b: vector with link bandwidths [bit/s]; due to space requirements, its full contents (38 elements) will not be presented;
- ECSD: vector with guaranteed mean call set-up delays [s] – for the b1, b2, d1, d2, f1, f2 call scenarios (Sect. 2);
- ECDD: vector with guaranteed mean call disengagement delays [s] – for the b1, b2, d1, d2, f1, f2 call scenarios (Sect. 2);
- load_CPU: vector with loads offered to CSCF servers CPUs [Erl] (order the same as in TINV vector);
- load_link: vector with loads offered to links [Erl] (order the same as in b vector).

It can be noticed that two first output parameters (TINV, b) describe required resources of IMS/NGN service stratum. During iterations of the algorithm these parameters are modified to assure proper values of $E(CSD)$ and $E(CDD)$. Additionally, the information about offered loads in the network is returned (load_CPU, load_link vectors). For the operation of the algorithm the following input parameters are used:

- ECSD_max, ECDD_max: vectors with maximum values of $E(CSD)$ [s] and $E(CDD)$ [s] (order the same as in ECSD, ECDD vectors);
- TINV_min, TINV_max: minimum and maximum values [s] for all elements of TINV vector;
- b_min, b_max: minimum and maximum values [bit/s] for all elements of b vector;
- TINV_step, b_step: the changes in elements of TINV vector [s] and b vector [bit/s] possible in a single algorithm iteration;
- num_iter_max: maximum number of iterations;
- lambdaR: vector with registration request (SIP REGISTER) intensities [1/s] in domain 1 and 2;
- lambda1d: vector with intra-operator call set-up request (SIP INVITE) intensities [1/s] (domain 1 and 2);
- lambda2d: vector with inter-operator call set-up request (SIP INVITE) intensities [1/s] (requests originated in domain 1 and 2);
- rC: vector with ratios of calls involving multiple access areas to all intra-operator calls (domain 1 and 2);
- pb: vector with probabilities of transport resource unavailability in access 1, core 1, access 2 and core 2;
- EX: vector with mean message processing times [s] by RACF A1, RACF C1, RACF A2, RACF C2;
- EY: vector with mean message processing times [s] by SUP-FE 1/SAA-FE 1, SUP-FE 2/SAA-FE 2;
- d: vector with link lengths [m] (order the same as in b vector);
- queueing: the type of queuing system models used in calculations (Sect. 2); M/M/1 and M/G/1 models are available;
- S: vector with message lengths [bit]; due to space requirements, its full contents (31 elements) will not be presented.

The mentioned input parameters of the algorithm can be divided into four categories: requirements on $E(CSD)$ and $E(CDD)$ (ECSD_max, ECDD_max), constraints on the designed resources (TINV_min, TINV_max, b_min, b_max), parameters of algorithm iterations (TINV_step, b_step, num_iter_max), input parameters of the analytical traffic model of a multidomain IMS/NGN (lambdaR, lambda1d, ..., S; [6–8]).

As already mentioned, at the beginning of the algorithm maximum available IMS/NGN service stratum resources are assumed (Fig. 1): all elements of the TINV vector are set to TINV_min and all elements of the b vector are set to b_max. For such a network configuration the values of the ECSD, ECDD, load_CPU, load_link vectors are calculated using the analytical model of IMS/NGN (Sect. 2; the same model is later used to update the above mentioned values). If any element of the obtained ECSD, ECDD vectors exceeds the given maximum values (ECSD_max, ECDD_max vectors), the design process stops with a proper warning message.

Otherwise, the algorithm starts the first iteration (i = 1) of its main "for" loop. The number of iterations can be limited using the iter_max input parameter. When i > iter_max the values of the ECSD, ECDD, load_CPU, load_link vectors are updated and the algorithm returns its output parameters. The same situation occurs when

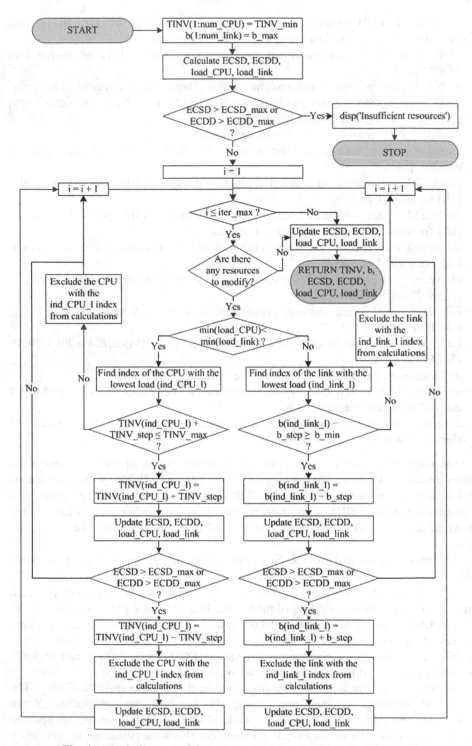

Fig. 1. Block diagram of the proposed design algorithm for IMS/NGN.

parameters of all CSCF servers CPUs and links are fixed and there are no resources to modify (all CPUs and links are excluded from calculations – more details later).

The next operation in each iteration is to determine the type of the least loaded network element (CSCF server CPU or link). It is performed by comparing minima of the load_CPU and load_link vectors. Subsequently, the index of the least loaded element is found (ind_CPU_l for CSCF servers CPUs or ind_link_l for links). To increase the load offered to this element, its resources are modified (SIP INVITE message processing time of the CSCF server CPU is increased by TINV_step, bandwidth of the link is decreased by b_step). Before performing this operation the constraints on TINV and b are checked (TINV_max, b_min input parameters). When they are violated, no resource modifications are performed, the selected network element is excluded from further calculations and the next algorithm iteration starts.

After modifying resources of the least loaded network element, the values of the ECSD, ECDD, load_CPU, load_link vectors are updated. If no element of the updated ECSD, ECDD vectors exceeds the given maximum values (ECSD_max, ECDD_max vectors), the algorithm continues its operation in new iteration. Otherwise, the performed resource modification is cancelled (SIP INVITE message processing time of the CSCF server CPU is decreased by TINV_step, bandwidth of the link is increased by b_step), the selected network element is excluded from further calculations, the values of the ECSD, ECDD, load_CPU, load_link vectors are updated and then the next algorithm iteration starts.

4 Results

We present several multidomain IMS/NGN service stratum designs using the proposed algorithm. In experiments the following input parameters of the algorithm were used: TINV_min = 0.05 ms, TINV_max = 10 ms, b_min = 1 bit/s, b_max = 50 Mbit/s, num_iter_max = 100000, lambdaR = [50, 50] 1/s, lambda1d = [50, 50] 1/s, lambda2d = [50, 50] 1/s, rC = [0.5, 0.5], pb = [0, 0, 0, 0], EX = [10, 10, 10, 10] ms, EY = [10, 10] ms, d = [200, 200, ..., 200] km, M/M/1 queuing system models.

The results of the performed investigations are presented in Fig. 2 (data set 1) and Fig. 3 (data set 2). Each of them includes six subfigures with mean call set-up delays for particular call scenarios (b1, b2, d1, d2, f1, f2 – Sect. 2; e.g. $E(CSD)_{b1}$ concerns the b1 scenario). Due to space limitations analogical subfigures for mean call disengagement delays are not demonstrated in the paper. All subfigures of Figs. 2, and 3 include three charts: maximum values of $E(CSD)$ given at the input of the design algorithm (elements of the ECSD_max vector) – blue circles, values obtained for the network designed using the algorithm with TINV_step = 0.5 ms, b_step = 0.5 Mbit/s (red "x" signs) as well as TINV_step = 0.1 ms, b_step = 0.1 Mbit/s (green squares).

In experiments with data set 1 the elements of the ECSD_max and ECDD_max vectors (blue circles in Fig. 2) increase linearly (ECSD_max = k*[45, 45, 45, 45, 90, 90] ms; ECSD_max = k*[25, 25, 25, 25, 40, 40] ms; k = 1, 2, ..., 10). It can be noticed that for different TINV_step, b_step values (0.5 ms, 0.5 Mbit/s – red "x" signs; 0.1 ms, 0.1 Mbit/s – green squares) the designed networks fulfill the condition of ECSD ≤ ECSD_max. For small k values (1–3) the obtained $E(CSD)$ are very close to the maxima given at the input of the design algorithm – for all call scenarios. However, when k > 3 a similar situation occurs only for the f1 and f2 scenarios and for the other scenarios there are visible differences between the assumed maximum and the obtained call set-up delays. These differences are smaller when smaller TINV_step, b_step values are used, which makes network design process more time consuming.

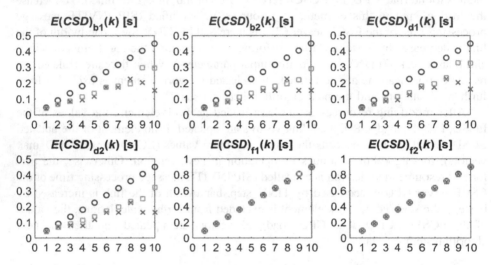

Fig. 2. Mean call set-up delays for the b1, b2, d1, d2, f1, f2 call scenarios (data set 1).

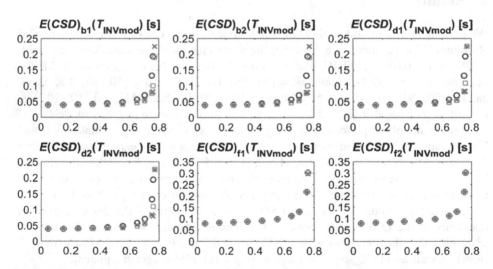

Fig. 3. Mean call set-up delays for the b1, b2, d1, d2, f1, f2 call scenarios (data set 2). The values of TINVmod are given in miliseconds.

The reason for the above mentioned differences is the complexity of a multidomain IMS/NGN. This results in the fact that there are certain relations between call set-up and disengagement delays for particular call scenarios, which additionally change with network load. The relations assumed in data set 1 (Fig. 2) are fixed (all maximum $E(CSD)$ values grow linearly) and only for $k < 3$ the algorithm can find network parameters, which give satisfactory mean call set-up delays for all call scenarios.

To further investigate this matter, the experiments with data set 2 were performed (Fig. 3), where the ECSD_max and ECDD_max vectors were taken from the analytical model of a multidomain IMS/NGN (Sect. 2) with bmod = 50 Mbit/s and TINVmod = 0.05…0.8 ms. bmod represents link bandwidth, which was constant and the same for all links. TINVmod is SIP INVITE message processing time by CSCF servers CPUs – it was changed during consecutive analytical model runs but always the same values were applied for all CPUs.

Using the approach presented in Fig. 3 proper relations between call set-up and disengagement delays for particular call scenarios are preserved. This way IMS/NGN service stratum designs using the proposed algorithm lead to $E(CSD)$ and $E(CDD)$ results very close to the assumed maxima. Despite such a good conformity, the designed networks have different resources than the parameters used to calculate the ECSD_max and ECDD_max vectors with the analytical model (Table 1). For example for TINVmod = 0.25 ms, TINV_step = 0.1 ms, b_step 0.1 Mbit/s the algorithm returns TINV = [0.05, 0.15, 0.25, 0.05, 0.15, 0.25] ms and b = [26.3, 50, 12.3, 26.3, 50, 32.8, …] Mbit/s, while during calculation of ECSD_max and ECDD_max the values of TINVmod = 0.25 ms were used for all CSCF servers CPUs and the values of bmod = 50 Mbit/s were used for all links. This demonstrates that there are different sets of IMS/NGN parameters, which give very similar $E(CSD)$ and $E(CDD)$ results. It is also very helpful for the designer to know the operation of the network and the relations between call set-up and disengagement delays for particular call scenarios.

Table 1. Selected IMS/NGN service stratum design results for data sets 1–2 (Figs. 2 and 3).

data set	TINV_step [ms]	b_step [Mbit/s]	TINV [ms]	b [Mbit/s], first 6 elements
1, k = 2	0.5	0.5	[0.55, 0.55, 1.55, 0.55, 0.55, 1.55]	[4, 11.5, 2, 4, 8.5, 5, …]
1, k = 2	0.1	0.1	[0.45, 0.55, 1.25, 0.45, 0.55, 1.25]	[3.7, 11.9, 1.7, 3.7, 8.8, 4.6, …]
1, k = 3	0.5	0.5	[0.55, 0.55, 1.55, 0.55, 0.55, 1.55]	[2.5, 10, 1.5, 2.5, 7.5, 3, …]
1, k = 3	0.1	0.1	[0.55, 0.75, 1.65, 0.55, 0.75, 1.65]	[2.9, 9.3, 1.3, 2.8, 6.9, 3.5, …]
2, TINVmod = 0.15 ms	0.5	0.5	[0.05, 0.05, 0.05, 0.05, 0.05, 0.05]	[30.5, 50, 14, 30.5, 50, 38, …]
2, TINVmod = 0.15 ms	0.1	0.1	[0.05, 0.05, 0.15, 0.05, 0.05, 0.15]	[33.5, 50, 15.7, 33.6, 50, 42, …]
2, TINVmod = 0.25 ms	0.5	0.5	[0.05, 0.05, 0.55, 0.05, 0.05, 0.55]	[31, 50, 14.5, 31, 50, 38.5, …]
2, TINVmod = 0.25 ms	0.1	0.1	[0.05, 0.15, 0.25, 0.05, 0.15, 0.25]	[26.3, 50, 12.3, 26.3, 50, 32.8, …]

5 Conclusions

The paper continues our research concerning call processing performance parameters (mean call set-up delay $E(CSD)$ and mean call disengagement delay $E(CDD)$) in a multidomain IMS/NGN, which are very important for satisfaction of users and overall success of this concept. We move from the problem of network analysis, investigated earlier, to the aspect of network design. Based on our analytical traffic model, a design algorithm for a multidomain IMS/NGN service stratum is proposed, which returns CSCF servers CPU message processing times and link bandwidths for given maximum values of $E(CSD)$ and $E(CDD)$ for all types of successful call scenarios.

A block diagram and details regarding the operation of the algorithm are described. It is also implemented and tested for several data sets. The performed research demonstrate that the algorithm works properly – the designed networks are close to the assumed maxima of $E(CSD)$ and $E(CDD)$, but do not exceed them. However, for some sets of input parameters it may be not possible to get very near to these maxima for all call scenarios, as for particular scenarios there are certain relations between call set-up and disengagement delays, which additionally change with network load. Therefore, it is advisable for a designer to know some details about the network operation and learn the above mentioned relations.

References

1. General overview of NGN, ITU-T Recommendation Y. 2001, Dec 2004
2. IP Multimedia Subsystem (IMS); Stage 2 (Release 14), 3GPP TS 23.228 v14.3.0, Mar 2017
3. Hadžialić, M., et al.: Problem of IMS modeling – solving approaches. In: CTRQ 2012 : The Fifth International Conference on Communication Theory, Reliability, and Quality of Service. Chamonix/Mont Blanc, France (2012)
4. Call processing performance for voice service in hybrid IP networks, ITU-T Recommendation Y. 1530, Nov 2007
5. SIP-based call processing performance, ITU-T Recommendation Y. 1531, Nov 2007
6. Kaczmarek, S., Sac, M.: Traffic model of a multidomain IMS/NGN. Telecommun. Rev. Telecommun. News (8–9), 1030–1038 (2014)
7. Kaczmarek, S., Sac, M.: Call processing performance in a multidomain IMS/NGN with asymmetric traffic. In: Grzech, A., et al. (eds.) Information Systems Architecture and Technology: Selected Aspects of Communication and Computational Systems, pp. 11–28. Oficyna Wydawnicza Politechniki Wrocławskiej, Wrocław (2014)
8. Kaczmarek, S., Sac, M.: Verification of the analytical traffic model of a multidomain IMS/NGN using the simulation model. In: Grzech, A., Borzemski, L., Świątek, J., Wilimowska, Z. (eds.) Information Systems Architecture and Technology: Proceedings of 36th International Conference on Information Systems Architecture and Technology – ISAT 2015 – Part II. AISC, vol. 430, pp. 109–130. Springer, Cham (2016). https://doi.org/10.1007/978-3-319-28561-0_9
9. Functional requirements and architecture of next generation networks, ITU-T Recommendation Y.2012, Apr 2010

10. Kaczmarek, S., Sac, M.: Analysis of IMS/NGN call processing performance using G/G/1 queuing systems approximations. Telecommun. Rev. Telecommun. News (8–9), 702–710 (2012)
11. Kaczmarek, S., Sac, M.: Analysis of IMS/NGN call processing performance using phase-type distributions based on experimental histograms. In: Świątek, J., Borzemski, L., Wilimowska, Z. (eds.) Information Systems Architecture and Technology: Proceedings of 36th International Conference on Information Systems Architecture and Technology – ISAT 2017. AISC, vol. 656, pp. 138–155. Springer, Cham (2018). https://doi.org/10.1007/978-3-319-67229-8_13

Performance Evaluation

Dynamic Capping of Physical Register Files in Simultaneous Multi-threading Processors for Performance

Hasancan Güngörer$^{(\boxtimes)}$ and Gürhan Küçük

Department of Computer Engineering, Yeditepe University, Istanbul, Turkey
hasancangungorer@gmail.com, gkucuk@cse.yeditepe.edu.tr

Abstract. Today, Simultaneous Multi-Threading (SMT) processors allow sharing of many datapath elements among applications. This type of resource sharing helps keeping the area requirement of a SMT processor at a very modest size. However, a major performance problem arises due to resource conflicts when multiple threads race for the same shared resource. In an earlier study, the authors propose capping of a shared resource, Physical Register File (PRF), for improving processor performance by giving less PRF entries, and, hence, spending less power, as well. For the sake of simplicity, the authors propose a fix PRF-capping amount, which they claim to be sufficient for all workload combinations. However, we show that a fix PRF-capping strategy may not always give the optimum performance, since any thread's behavior may change at any time during execution. In this study, we extend that earlier work with an adaptive PRF-capping mechanism, which tracks down the behavior of all running threads and move the cap value to a near-optimal position by the help of a hill-climbing algorithm. As a result, we show that we can achieve up to 21% performance improvement over the fix capping method, giving 7.2% better performance, on the average, in a 4-threaded system.

Keywords: Processor performance · Shared resource management · Simultaneous Multi-Threading

1 Introduction

Simultaneous Multi-Threading (SMT) processors are merely superscalar processors, which allow simultaneous execution of instructions coming from multiple threads. Compared to single-thread superscalar processors, they promise better throughput by allowing more efficient utilization of available datapath resources. To keep the design cost at its lowest level, many of the resources are shared among running threads. For instance, Physical Register Files (PRFs) are not replicated but are enlarged to compensate renaming requests coming from multiple threads. Here, one faulty assumption is that threads show similar behavior and do not harm each other. However, shared resources give SMT processors a major disadvantage over their superscalar counterparts: resource conflicts. These resources can be claimed by any of the running threads at any given time, and, unfortunately, the assumption about the behavior of different threads being similar is almost always wrong. Some of the threads are resource hungry

© Springer Nature Switzerland AG 2018
T. Czachórski et al. (Eds.): ISCIS 2018, CCIS 935, pp. 41–48, 2018.
https://doi.org/10.1007/978-3-030-00840-6_5

but do not commit too many instructions. We can classify such threads as harmful, since they can easily clog one or many shared datapath resources up, and, as a result, they can reduce the overall system throughput, almost instantly. In contrast, some of the threads may request just enough resources to keep their throughput at a reasonable pace. Such threads can be classified as genuine threads, since they become the reason for achieving high overall system throughput. These threads do not ask for any unnecessary amount of resources. Finally, there is also a third class of threads, which hardly asks for any type of resources. We can classify them as harmless threads, since they have low instruction level parallelism resulting in no claim for any resources.

There is considerable amount of work involved in this research area. On reducing the pressure on PRF, Lo et al. apply compiler and operating system extensions to release PRF entries as soon as they are detected to be useless [1]. For instance, all PRF entries allocated for an idle thread might be immediately released. The authors also propose techniques to release PRF entries immediately after their last use. In another study, Monreal et al. propose virtual physical registers that do not require any storage bindings [2]. With the help of virtual physical registers PRF allocation time can be delayed, again reducing the pressure on the PRF. Here, in our proposed method, we also reduce pressure on the PRF by dynamically capping it according to runtime behavior of threads.

There is also a variety of resource partitioning techniques that target better resource utilization [3]. Choi et al. propose a hill-climbing based method, which runs in periods of time called epochs. At each epoch, one of the threads is given more resources than its actual share, and the overall performance is recorded. After testing each thread's performance with extra resources, a greedy-type decision algorithm selects the thread with the best performance and increases its allocated resource size. In another study, Wang et al. focus on a metric, which they call Committed Instructions Per Resource Entry (CIPRE) [4]. Again, the execution time is divided into epochs, and the CIPRE value of all running threads are calculated at the end of each epoch. The thread with the highest CIPRE value is selected to receive a resource increase, since it proves that it can give the best throughput per allocated resource entry. Finally, Cazorla et al. propose the DCRA mechanism, which is an acronym for Dynamically Controlled Resource Allocation [5]. Here, threads are classified as slow/fast and active/inactive, and slow threads receive more resources than fast threads can have. Active and slow threads receive the largest share of the resources. All these techniques require a complex hardware for collecting hardware statistics and partitioning multiple datapath resources.

In an earlier study, the authors propose a PRF-capping mechanism that allocates a small amount of PRF entries for each thread [6]. They claim that, with this simple mechanism, they can regulate the Issue Queue (IQ), the Re-Order Buffer (ROB) and the Load/Store Queue (LSQ). They also show that a fixed cap size is enough to satisfy any type of workloads, and they report up to more than 44% IPC improvements for a 4-threaded SMT system.

In this study, we show that a fixed cap size does not really gives optimal performance in all workload combinations as stated in the earlier work. As shown in Fig. 1, there are a variety of cap sizes that give near-optimal IPC values for different workloads. Here, benchmarks from the SPEC CPU 2006 suite are combined to create a set of 4-threaded workloads mixtures (see Table 2). When we examine the figure, we see that PRF cap size of 8 is the best for Mix 1, whereas the same cap size gives the worst performance for Mix 2 and Mix 5. We also see that Mix 10 is almost insensitive to cap size. In this study, our main motivation is to dynamically pinpoint a near-optimal cap size and use it. Our results show that our proposed method tracks down the optimal cap size for each of these workloads and achieves up to 21% better performance compared to a fixed cap size approach as proposed in [6].

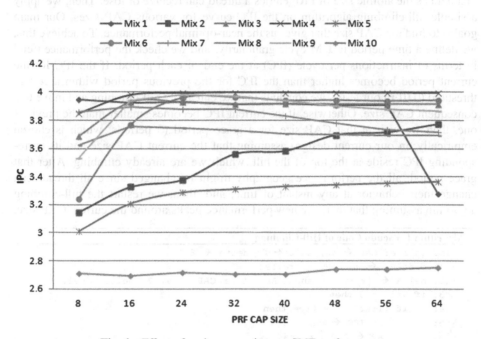

Fig. 1. Effect of various cap sizes on SMT performance

2 The Proposed Method

Physical Register Files (PRFs) are one of the most critical resources to achieve high throughput in SMT processors. At the instruction dispatch stage, each decoded instruction with a destination register is given a PRF entry to eliminate false data dependencies among instructions. This is known as the register renaming process. When the PRF becomes full, the frontend of the pipeline is stalled until some instructions in the backend commits and releases precious PRF entries. In a single-thread superscalar processor, PRF should be kept large enough to support multiple names for each architectural register, and the size of the PRF might be the sole design problem that we can face. In a SMT processor, though, there are other problems originating from the nature of the processor. Instructions from multiple threads race on the same datapath and allocate PRF entries. A harmful thread, which holds too many resources but executes too few instructions, may easily render the whole system into a thrashing state.

In an earlier study, the authors propose the fixed capping of the PRF after a detailed analysis. But, a fixed cap size becomes a problem when a genuine thread looks for extra resources for improving its throughput or when a harmless thread does not make use of any allocated resource to itself. We believe that such inefficiencies can be easily avoided with a mechanism that can move the CAP size to an appropriate position when it is needed. In our proposed design, we set the lower and the upper bound for the CAP size to 8 and 64, respectively. In our experiments, we also selected a delta value of 8 that defines the atomic size of PRF entries a thread can receive or lose. Then, we apply a simple hill-climbing algorithm on the IPC curve for various CAP sizes. Our main goal is to find the CAP size that gives us the near-optimal performance. To achieve this, we define a time period in 1 M-cycle granularity, and we check the performance trend in terms of instructions per cycle (IPC) at the end of each period. If the IPC for the current period becomes higher than the IPC for the previous period within a certain threshold (0.01 in our tests), we conclude that we can apply hill-climbing and move to a consequent CAP size. Otherwise, if the current IPC becomes smaller than the previous one, than we wait at that CAP size for a grace period (5 periods, which is chosen empirically, in our current design) assuming that the current CAP size and its corresponding IPC reside at the top of the hill, which we are already climbing. After that grace period, all the performance geography might be changed since all threads can change their behavior at any instant of time, and, then, we restart the hill-climbing algorithm assuming that there are new performance peaks around the current CAP size.

Algorithm 1. Pseudo Code of Hill-Climbing

```
Initialize: CAP ← 40, wait ← 0, delta ← 8
 1: diffIPC ← currIPC - prevIPC
 2: delta ← (wait = 0 and (CAP = 8 or CAP = 64) ? -delta : delta)
 3: if wait = 0 then
 4:    if firstTime = true then
 5:        prevIPC ← currIPC
 6:        CAP ← CAP + delta
 7:        firstTime ← false
 8:    elseif diffIPC > 0.01 then
 9:        prevIPC ← currIPC
10:        CAP ← CAP + delta
11:    else
12:        wait ← 5
13:    end if
14: else
15:    wait ← wait - 1
16: end if
```

Algorithm 1 given above shows the details of our hill-climber. The most important feature of the algorithm is its bouncing delta value. It is initially, set to +8, which enables us to search cap sizes in one direction starting from 8 up to 64. But, when the algorithm reaches the CAP size of 64, the delta value becomes -8 to enable a hill-climb process in the reverse direction.

3   Experimental Methodology

In this paper, we use M-sim simulator to run SPEC CPU2006 benchmarks [7]. Configuration details of the simulated processor are given in Table 1. Our hill-climbing algorithm is run every one million cycles. We also tested other periods but one million cycle period gives the best results. We fast-forwarded each benchmark for 100 million cycles and run cycle-accurate simulations for 200 million cycles. The workload mixtures that we use in our simulations are given in Table 2.

Table 1. Configuration of the simulated processor

Parameter	Configuration
Machine width	4-wide fetch/dispatch/issue/commit
L/S Queue size	48 Load/Store queue
ROB & IQ size	128 entry ROB, 32-entry IQ
L1 I-cache	64 KB, 2-way set-associative 64-byte line
L1 D-cache	64 KB, 4-way set-associative 64-byte line, write-back, 1-cycle access latency
L2 Cache unified	512 KB, 16-way set-associative 64-byte line, write-back, 10-cycle access latency
BTB	512 entry, 4-way set-associative
Branch predictor	Bimod: 2 K entry
Memory	32-bit wide, 300 cycles access latency

Table 2. 4-threaded workloads

Workloads	Benchmarks
Mix 1	libquantum, dealII, gromacs, namd
Mix 2	hmmer, sjeng, gobmk, gcc
Mix 3	libquantum, dealII, gobmk, gcc
Mix 4	gromacs, dealII, lbm, cactusADM
Mix 5	hmmer, sjeng, lbm, bzip2
Mix 6	libquantum, sjeng, lbm, gcc
Mix 7	namd, dealII, hmmer, milc
Mix 8	namd, gcc, lbm, milc
Mix 9	gobmk, gromacs, cactusADM, bzip2
Mix 10	sjeng, namd, cactusADM, hmmer

4   Tests and Results

In our tests, we test the adaptive nature of our algorithm, first. Figure 2 shows the percentage of time each cap size is visited across all workload mixtures in an elevation-map form. From the figure, we learn that cap size of 32 and above are quite popular among workloads. We also see that there is a variety of cap sizes utilized in each workload proving the dynamic tracking ability of the algorithm.

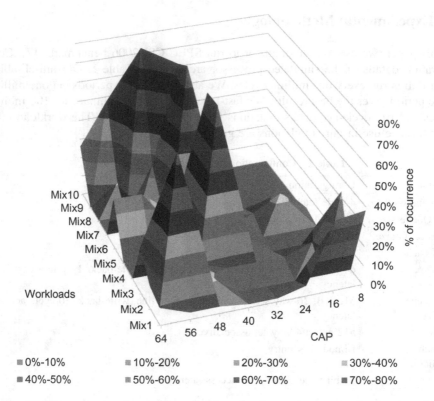

Fig. 2. 3D Histogram showing number of visits of each cap size across simulated workload mixtures

We also studied how well the algorithm tracks the actual peak performance of the workloads given in Fig. 1. Figure 3 shows the percentage of time our algorithm dynamically selects the cap sizes corresponding to within 1%, 2%, 3% and 5% tolerance range of the peak performance value. For instance, from the figure we see that our hill-climber successfully locates 55% of the cap sizes within 1% tolerance range of the peak performance, on the average. But, when the tolerance range is within 2%, the algorithm sweeps more than 90% of the near-optimal cap sizes, and we believe that this is a great success for pinpointing peak performance points of workloads at runtime. Tolerance ranges of 3% and 5% have 94.2% and 95.5% coverage of performance at peak cap sizes, respectively. From the figure, we also see that our algorithm is not perfect for all type of workloads. For instance, when we observe Mix 3 from Fig. 1, we see that it shows a very low performance for cap size of 8. However, our adaptive algorithm spends its 33% of time at this cap size, and, therefore, its coverage is constant at 67% for all tolerance ranges that we study.

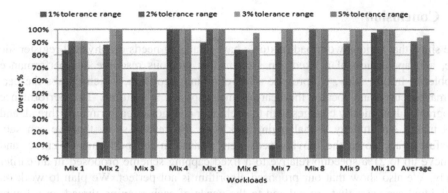

Fig. 3. Coverage percentage of cap sizes with peak performance points for various tolerance ranges

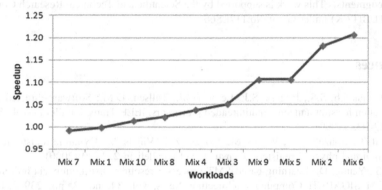

Fig. 4. Speedup of our proposed algorithm compared to the original algorithm proposed in [6].

In Fig. 4, we report the speedup of our hill-climber compared to the fix cap size algorithm suggested in [6]. Here, we see that Mix 7 shows a worse performance compared to the original algorithm. When we observe Fig. 1, we see that Mix 7 has a low sensitivity to PRF cap size. But, it still shows slightly better performance values for cap sizes less than 32. Unfortunately, as we examine Fig. 2, we find that our algorithm spends most of its time on the opposite range (i.e. cap sizes 32 to and up) assuming that it is already close to the peak of the performance curve. Therefore, its coverage percentage becomes quite high (90%) even with a tolerance range of 2%. However, the coverage result (10%) with the tolerance range of 1% tells us the real story. Mix 7 fools our algorithm and its performance becomes worse than the original fixed cap size approach. But, the good news is we successfully track the actual peak performance points in the rest of the workloads, and achieve 7.2% better performance, on the average. Our best results are observed with Mix 2 (18%) and Mix 6 (21%), which are two genuine class workloads always hungry for resources.

5   Conclusion

We show that various workload mixtures have changing needs on physical register file use, and application of a fixed cap size on this precious resource has performance problems. In this study, we propose a hill-climbing algorithm, which climbs the performance curve and locates the near-optimal cap size at runtime. The performance geography dynamically changes with the behavior changes of each running thread, and this makes our strategy a challenging task. Our test results show that we can successfully track down the moving peak performance in the performance curve, and achieve up to 21% speedup relative to a fixed capping scheme proposed in an earlier study. We also show that our proposed algorithm is not perfect. We plan to work on individual cap sizes that are tailored to the needs of each running thread, in a future study. We believe that this new strategy may solve the problems that we encountered and left unsolved in this study.

Acknowledgments. This work is supported by the Scientific and Technical Research Council of Turkey (TUBITAK) under Grant No:117E866.

References

1. Lo, J.L., Parekh, S.S., Eggers, S.J., Levy, H.M., Tullsen, D.M.: Software-directed register deallocation for simultaneous multithreaded processors. IEEE Trans. Parallel Distrib. Syst. **10** (9), 922–933 (1999)
2. Monreal, T., González, A., Valero, M., González, J., Viñals, V.: Dynamic register renaming through virtual-physical registers. J. Instr. Level Parallelism **2**, 1–20 (2000)
3. Choi, S., Yeung, D.: Learning-based SMT processor resource distribution via hill-climbing. In: ACM SIGARCH Computer Architecture News, vol. 34, no. 2, pp. 239–251. IEEE Computer Society (2006)
4. Wang, H., Koren, I., Krishna, C.M.: An adaptive resource partitioning algorithm for SMT processors. In: Proceedings of the 17th International Conference on Parallel Architectures and Compilation Techniques, pp. 230–239. ACM, Oct 2008
5. Cazorla, F.J., Ramirez, A., Valero, M., Fernandez, E.: Dynamically controlled resource allocation in SMT processors. In: Proceedings of the 37th Annual IEEE/ACM International Symposium on Microarchitecture, pp. 171–182. IEEE Computer Society (2004)
6. Zhang, Y., Lin, W.M.: Efficient resource sharing algorithm for physical register file in simultaneous multi-threading processors. Microprocess. Microsyst. **45**, 270–282 (2016)
7. Sharkey, J., Ponomarev, D., Ghose, K.: M-Sim: a flexible, multithreaded architectural simulation environment. Technical Report CS-TR-05-DP01, Department of CS, SUNY-Binghamton (2005)

Minimizing Latency in Wireless Sensor Networks with Multiple Mobile Base Stations

Mehdi Achour[1](✉) and Jamel Belhadj Taher[2]

[1] High Institute of Computer Sciences and Communication Technologies,
Street GP1, 4011 Hammam Sousse, Tunisia
achour.mhd@gmail.com

[2] National School of Engineers, BP 264 Erriadh City, 4023 Sousse, Tunisia
belhadjtahar.jamel@gmail.com

Abstract. Among the main issues in wireless sensor networks is the minimization of response time for the delay sensitive applications. Such applications require a fast response time because of their emergency nature; we can site for example battlefield surveillance and health monitoring applications. Despite the importance of latency minimization, we can't forget energy conservation which is almost always present in many works on wireless sensor networks. In this paper we study the impact of the utilization of multiple mobile base stations on the latency minimization and network lifetime elongation which make a twin gain. Simulation results show the efficiency of the used technique in comparison with the utilization of one base station or multiple fixed base stations.

Keywords: Wireless sensor networks · Delay sensitive applications
Latency · Network lifetime · Multiple mobile base stations

1 Introduction

Wireless sensor networks (WSN) are very widespread today. This because of their capacity to detect useful information in the environment where they are deployed and send the detected information to a one or more base stations to be treated and serve the final user. Wireless sensor networks are deployed in different types of applications and contain usually a predefined number of base stations and a high number of inexpensive and small sensors [1].

Delay sensitive applications emerge nowadays because of the changes that appear in the lifestyle in which speed is the most important factor. For example, in a health monitoring application which could measure blood pressure, heart rate and breathe rate, a delay in the arrival of these measurements can threaten the patient's life. So wireless sensor networks that are deployed in such applications must be adapted to be as fast, in data collection and delivery, as the application requirement. This type of wireless sensor networks is called real time wireless sensor networks for its capacity to provide bounded delay guarantees [2].

© Springer Nature Switzerland AG 2018
T. Czachórski et al. (Eds.): ISCIS 2018, CCIS 935, pp. 49–56, 2018.
https://doi.org/10.1007/978-3-030-00840-6_6

In wireless sensor networks, when an event occurs, sensors communicate information to the base station in multi-hops manner. This leads to a high response time because data have to cross long paths. A simple idea consists at using multiple base stations to segment the network and make the paths shorter. We thus obtain a fast response time. The mobility is massively used to minimize the energy consumption [3, 4]. When the base station moves around the network, the sensors close to it and which relay a large amount of traffic will no longer be the same. So we exploit the mobility of the base station in a multiple mobile base station technique to jointly conserve energy and minimize latency.

In [3], authors proposed a linear programming model that produce a mobile sink movement patterns and sojourn times. This model improve the network lifetime up to five time compared with a static sink model.

A previous work that treated the problem of minimizing Latency in WSN [8] consists at optimizing data gathering in order to minimize the latency of data delivery and making a tradeoff with energy consumption. An accurate network model was proposed to capture that tradeoff.

In another work [7], authors use dynamic sinks synchronized by distributed algorithm to receive data from all sensor nodes with reduced latency time and energy consumption.

In this paper, we first present a linear programming framework aiming to minimize the energy consumption and thus maximizing the network lifetime. We exploit the base station mobility to make that. Then present the network architecture of the multiple mobile base stations approach and the optimization problem. We conclude by the simulation results and the comparisons.

2   Network Model and Optimization Problem

Let N be the set of sensor nodes and L be the set of stop positions of the base station.

We assume that the order of visits to different positions does not affect the network's lifetime. The residence time of the sink at position l belonging to L is denoted by zl. The sum of all sojourn times in all stop positions is in fact the network lifetime denoted by T.

Let $y_{ij}^{(l)}$ be the total data quantity sent from sensor i to j when the sink is in the position l. Let $C_{ij}^{(l)}$ be the required energy to send one unit of data from sensor i to j when the sink is in the position l. Finally each node i has an initial energy E_i and generate date at a constant rate d_i. Table 1 summarizes all notations.

Table 1. Notations.

Symbol	Description
N	Set of sensor nodes
L	Set of stop positions
l	A stop position belonging to L
z_l	The residence time of the sink at position l
T	The network lifetime
$y_{ij}^{(l)}$	Data quantity sent from sensor i to j when the sink is in the position l
d_i	Data rate of node i
E_i	Initial energy of node i
$C_{ij}^{(l)}$	Required energy to send one unit of data from sensor i to j when the sink is in the position l
γ	Required energy to receive one unit of data

We adopted the well-known mobile base station model. The problem of maximizing the network lifetime is the following [5]:

$$Max\, T = z_1 + z_2 + \ldots + z_{|L|}$$

Subject to:

$$\sum_{j \in N(i)} y_{ij}^{(l)} - \sum_{k:i \in N(k)} y_{ki}^{(l)} = z_l . d_i \tag{1}$$

$$\sum_{l=1}^{|L|} \left(\sum_{j \in N(i)} C_{ij}^{(l)} . y_{ij}^{(l)} + \sum_{k:i \in N(k)} \gamma . y_{ki}^{(l)} \right) \leq E_i \tag{2}$$

$$x_{ij}^{(l)} \geq 0$$
$$z_l \geq 0$$
$$i,k \in N, j \in \hat{N}, l \in L$$

Where $\hat{N} = N \cup L$ and $N(i)$ is the set of neighboring nodes of node i and γ is a constant.

The first constraint represents the flow conservation for all nodes when the sink is in position l. Constraint (2) is the energy conservation constraint, it means that the energy consumed by node i in all stop positions cannot exceed the initial energy of the node.

3 Multiple Mobile Base Stations Approach

3.1 Network Architecture

Our approach consists at dividing the network geographically into many contiguous zones. The number of zones depends on the number of mobile base stations. Each mobile sink moves in its own area and cannot pass it to another zone. The network contains two types of sensor nodes: static ordinary sensor nodes sensing the data and mobile sinks collecting the data from the ordinary sensor nodes.

Our proposed approach reduce energy consumption because it adopts the mobility and at the same time reduces the delay because since the use of many base stations increases the rate of data collection. Another benefit of this approach is fault tolerance. Since there are several base stations in the network, when one fails the zones are concatenated and the network continues to operate. For this reason, the base stations must be in communication to act rapidly to a possible breakdown (Fig. 1).

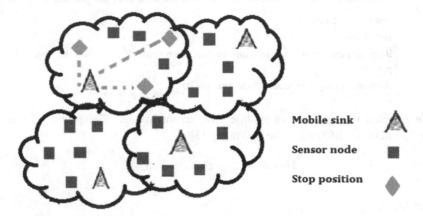

Fig. 1. Network architecture with multiple mobile sinks.

3.2   Optimization Problem

Since the network is made up of several mobile base stations, the network lifetime becomes the sum of the sojourn times of all base stations in all stop positions. The residence time of the base station number i in position p is denoted by $z_{n,l}$. Let S denotes the set of the mobile base stations. The optimization problem then becomes:

$$Max\ T = \sum_{n=1}^{|S|} \sum_{l=1}^{|L|} z_{n,l}$$

Subject to:

$$\sum_{j \in N(i)} y_{ij}^{(l)} - \sum_{k: i \in N(k)} y_{ki}^{(l)} = z_{n,l}.d_i \qquad (3)$$

$$i, k \in N, j \in \hat{N}, l \in L, n \in S$$

$$\sum_{l=1}^{|L|} \left(\sum_{j \in N(i)} C_{ij}^{(l)}.y_{ij}^{(l)} + \sum_{k: i \in N(k)} \gamma.y_{ki}^{(l)} \right) \le E_i \qquad (4)$$

$$i, k \in N, j \in \hat{N}, l \in L$$
$$y_{ij}^{(l)} \ge 0$$
$$z_{n,l} \ge 0$$

4 Performance Evaluation

The above optimization problem was solved by the linear programming solver LPsolve [6]. All sensors have the same initial energy amount, a different data generation rate and they are randomly deployed in a bi-dimensional area. We have used up to seven mobile sinks in our experiences. We have studied the impact of sink multiplicity on latency and the impact of mobility on network lifetime.

In the rest, unless otherwise specified, we assume the initial energy $E_i = 2000$ joules and the required energy to send one unit of data from sensor i to j when the sink is in the position l, $C_{ij}^{(l)} = 2$ joules/time unit. For simplification we assume the required energy to receive one unit of data $\gamma = 1$.

In Table 1, many computational experiments show the advantage of using mobile sinks against the use of fixed sinks. We have fixed a varied number of sinks in some positions and we calculated the network lifetime. Then we mobilize these sinks and we recalculated the network lifetime. It is clear from the table that network lifetime increases significantly in general. For example in the third experience we have three sinks fixed near to sensors number 1, 4 and 7, we obtained a network lifetime equal to 13.4 time units. This experience is compared with the seventh one using also three sinks but mobile in positions 1, 2 and 7 then in 1,4 and 3. We obtained a better network lifetime equal to 17.4 time units. For a better comparison we mobilized the sinks in a set of positions including those of the fixed sinks (Table 2).

Table 2. Comparison between mobile and fixed sinks for a 20 sensors network.

Experience number	Number of sensors	Number of sinks	Sinks description	Network lifetime (time units)
1	20	1	Fixed in sensor number 1	6.13
2	20	2	Fixed in 1 and 7	12.8
3	20	3	Fixed in 1, 4 and 7	13.4
4	20	1	Mobile in 4 and 7	9.46
5	20	1	Mobile in 1, 4 and 7	11.8
6	20	2	Mobile in 1 and 7 then in 1 and 4	12.1
7	20	3	Mobile in 1, 2, 7 then in 1, 4, 3	17.4

We have done many other experiences with other network models. All show the efficiency of the mobility technique. Figure 2 illustrates the values of the lifetime for a 16 sensors network.

In the following, we present some experiments to evaluate the performance of the approach of multiple mobile base stations.

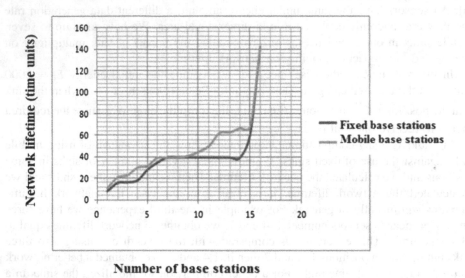

Fig. 2. Values of network lifetime for mobile base stations and fixed base stations.

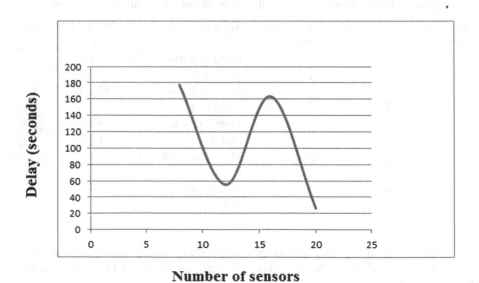

Fig. 3. Delay values versus number of sensors.

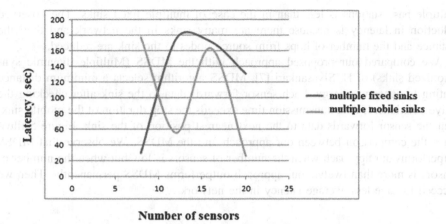

Fig. 4. Values of latency according to the number of sensors.

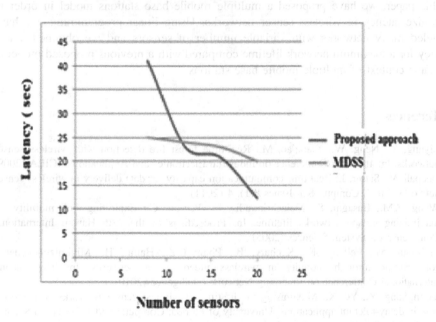

Fig. 5. Comparison between the proposed approach and the MDSS.

Figure 3 illustrates the delay values according to the number of sensors. The delay is the time required for a packet to be transmitted from a source node to the nearest mobile base station.

In the next experiment, we compare the use of mobile base stations against the use of fixed base stations in terms of response time (latency). In this experiment we have used three mobile base stations covering the whole network and each of these stations has two stop positions ($|L| = 2, |S| = 3$). In Fig. 4, the latency in the case of using multiple base stations is less than in the case of multiple fixed sinks. The observed reduction in latency is because there are many sinks in the network and then the distance and the number of hops from source nodes to the sink are reduced.

We compared our proposed approach with the MDSS (Multiple dynamic synchronized sinks) of H. Sivasankari [7]. MDSS algorithm selects a minimum distance routing to conserve energy. Each sensor forwards data to the sink after checking the active positions. If data transmission time exceeds the stop duration of the mobile sink, then the sensor forwards data to the next nearest position of the sink. Figure 5 illustrates the comparison between our approach and the MDSS. We observe that MDSS outperforms our approach when the number of sensors is low but when the number of sensors is more than twelve, our approach outperforms MDSS permanently. Then we succeed to have less average latency in the network.

5 Conclusion

In this paper, we have proposed a multiple mobile base stations model in order to minimize latency in wireless sensor networks. Using linear programming, we have modeled many networks with variable number of sensors and we obtained a less latency for a maximum network lifetime compared with a previous proposed model in the same context of multiple mobile base stations.

References

1. Liyang, Y., Neng, W., Xiaoqiao, M.: Real-time forest fire detection with wireless sensor networks. In: 4th IEEE Conference on Industrial Electronics and Applications, ICIEA (2009)
2. Deepali, V., Satbir, J.: Real time communication capacity for data delivery in wireless sensor networks. Int. J. Comput. Sci. Issues **8**(1), 4 (2011)
3. Wang, Z.M., Basagni, S., Melachrinoudis, E., Petrioli, C.: Exploiting sink mobility for maximizing sensor networks lifetime. In: Proceedings of the 38th Hawaii International Conference on System Sciences (2005)
4. Maimour, M., Fellahy, K., Kechary, B., Pham C.Z., Haffaf, H.: Minimizing energy consumption through mobility in wireless video sensor networks. In: The Second International Conference on Emerging Network Intelligence (2010)
5. YoungSang, Y., Ye, X.: Maximising the lifetime of wireless sensor networks with mobile sink in delay-tolerant applications. University of Florida, Computer and Information Science and Engineering Department
6. Lp_solve Reference Guide. http://lpsolve.sourceforge.net/5.5/
7. Sivasankari, H., Shaila, K., Venugopal, K.R., Patnaik, L.M.: Multiple dynamic sinks to maximize the lifetime and conservation of energy in wireless sensor networks. Int. J. Comput. Theor. Eng. **4**(1) (2012)
8. Borghini, M., Cuomo, F., Ricciato, F.: Optimal data delivery in wireless sensor networks in the energy and latency domains. In: First International Conference on Wireless Internet, Budapest (2005)

Solving Large Markov Models Described with Standard Programming Language

P. Pecka[✉], M. P. Nowak, A. Rataj, and S. Nowak

Institute of Theoretical and Applied Informatics, ul. Bałtycka 5, 44-100 Gliwice, Poland
mateusz@iitis.pl

Abstract. Continuous time Markov chains (CTMC) are one of the formalisms for building models. This paper discusses OLYMP2 - a system for solving big CTMC models (exceeding 10^9 states), described with a standard programming language - Java. OLYMP2 is primarily aimed at modelling of computer networks, so its formalism comes from networking concepts, like queueing systems. Using Java as a model description allows for greater flexibility in comparison to model-checker specific languages that often do not employ complete features of an object-oriented programming. Using Java also makes the parsing of models relatively fast, due to optimised Java run-time environment. Introducing dedicated compression of transition matrices allows for keeping memory usage at reasonable level even for large models.

Keywords: Markov chains · Model checker · Performance evaluation

1 Introduction

Probabilistic model checking [1] is a recognised method of system verification. It often employs Continuous time Markov chains (CTMC) formalism for models. Along with model checkers or other software that analyses continuous–time Markov chain models [11] there is a host of languages for representing these models. These languages, usually being at the fringe of the effort focused on analysis of the models themselves, typically lack expressiveness and employ outdated programming paradigms.

One of the best recognised model checkers, Prism, employs state-of-the-art algorithms for solving the models, but at the same time supports only a simple model description language. SPIN model checker [7] is able to embed a standard language like C into their model description, still the Promela language into which the C code is embedded represents a simple procedural approach to programming. XBorne 2016 [5] which evolved to a general purpose framework, uses C language for description of the models. It is focused however on Discrete time Markov chains (DTMC), and as a consequence of choosing C as a model description language, lacks the advantages of object-oriented approach.

© Springer Nature Switzerland AG 2018
T. Czachórski et al. (Eds.): ISCIS 2018, CCIS 935, pp. 57–67, 2018.
https://doi.org/10.1007/978-3-030-00840-6_7

This paper proposes using another standard language for description of Markov Chains model. In OLYMP2 we use Java for model description and our domain are CTMC models. It is object-oriented, and able to to handle complex data types. Java is well-known among software developers, so user of OLYMP2 probably needs not to learn specialised model description language, and can use its favourite compiler, debugger and IDE.

We developed OLYMP2 not only due to the will to use our favourite programming language for formal modelling of systems. We did it also because the Prism language was hard to use for clean and optimised description of the models we examined. We also lacked the tools specialised for modelling queueing models. There is a wide class of models, including computer networks and systems, communication protocols, traffic engineering, and also the design of factories, shops, offices and hospitals, which can be described using queueing theory. The existing model checkers (Prism, Uppaal [2]) miss the tools for queueing models formalism support, and specialised software for modelling queueing systems, like PEPSY-QNS [8] or MACOM [9], is no longer maintained.

At the internal representation and model solving side we decided to follow traditional way of sparse matrices. However, thanks to the use of jit-compiled code and dedicated compression we aimed at keeping the computation speed and memory complexity at an acceptable level. OLYMP2 consists of a front-end library on top of Java, aimed at representing models in that language and translate these models into transition matrices, and back-end numerical libraries (in an efficient C implementation), that employ known numerical methods for solving big systems of equations typical for complex CTMC models. As the front-end part presents the new approach, the paper in its bigger part is devoted to it. Due to the potentially very large sizes of a model's transition matrix, its generation using OLYMP2 is parallelised, and the matrix can be compressed on-the-fly using a dedicated compression based on finite-state automata [13].

2   Similar Work

We are not aware of any CTMC library for a C–like language (we mean C++, Java, C#, Objective-C, D etc.), that offers a functionality of describing model with standard, object-oriented programming language, beside OLYMP [12], from which stems OLYMP2. There are, though, some projects that treat a Java application as a process with a *discrete* time, like JavaPathFinder [17] or Java2TADD [14,15,18]. The former is a kind of the Java Virtual Machine, that is able to test complex production applications, but it does not translate these applications into transition matrices. The latter is, in contrast, limited to a small subset of Java grammar and requires the analysed application to be instrumented, but translates it to a form, that can be easily transformed to a transition matrix, which in turn can be reused by a lot of model checking software.

3   Basic Concepts

The basic assumption is to use the style and concepts found in the Java language and in the formalism of queueing systems, that describe computer networks or similar systems. The former stems obviously from choosing Java as the model representation, the latter from the fact, that models which can be described according to queueing theory, like models of computer networks, are commonly modelled and checked using CTMC.

To realise the assumption, we aimed at making the model representation similar to an implementation of a computer network in Java.

3.1   Nodes and Connections

Let a *node* be an entity, that, on basis of the current state vector, decides on a fragment or a whole of the new state vector, and on its contribution to the respective transition rate to that new state vector.

A node is thus a generalisation of a queueing theory's server, in the sense that there can be an arbitrary number of elements of the input state vector and in the output state vector, that are respectively read or written to by a node.

The essence of the system description using the queueing theory is the possibility of transferring some elements between the nodes. Following the original paper of Erlang [4] the elements are usually referenced as customers. In a computer network, an event is typically a transfer of a packet from one node to another. In other application areas the customers may be also in fact tasks to do, or even physical entities like people or vehicles. In OLYMP2 system and in further part of a paper we prefer to use the term token.

Let a *connection* in OLYMP2 be a way, though which a *token* can be sent. Per a connection, there is a single sender node, and a number of receiver nodes. A token, to be successfully transferred, must be sent by the sender and accepted by the receivers. Sending a token is the only possible way of an event to occur in OLYMP2. Thus, there is a negotiation needed between a number of nodes for every event to occur. In a degenerated case, a single node sends a token to itself to change its own internal state, what also is a case of a negotiation.

3.2   A Node is a Class

A node in OLYMP2 is a Java class, that directly of indirectly extends AbstractNode. A node can contain a number of *state fields*. All state fields in all instantiated nodes create together the state vector.

3.3   Negotiation Details

AbstractNode needs two of its methods to be defined by subclasses – transit and receive. The former method is called by OLYMP2 as a way of querying a node, if, for a given input state vector and a given connection c, the node can asynchronously initiate an event. A node, within `transit`'s code, reads the input state and then, on basis of the values read, may try to send a token through c, by calling via `OLYMP2` the `receive` methods of the receiver nodes assigned to the other, receiving end of c.

A `receive` method defines token acceptance and, if the token is accepted, a contribution to the rate and the output vector of a respective transition. The token sender, again within `transit`, on basis of these return values of the called `receive` methods, determines the resulting transition rate and returns it through `transit`'s return value to `OLYMP2`. If the token has been accepted, the return rate is non–zero, otherwise, it is zero. If the rate is non–zero, `OLYMP2` reads the output state from node's state fields and completes the transition matrix.

3.4   A Library

`OLYMP2` comes with a library of standard components. The library extensively uses the objective programming paradigm. For example, an abstract class of a server `AbstractBufferedServer` is extended by a subclass `ErlangBufferedServer`.

3.5   Further Implementation Details

In this section, some further implementation details are discussed.

Explicit State Variables As discussed, a node can contain various fields, but it explicitly lists to `OLYMP2` the subset of these fields, that are a part of the state vector. It does that using a field annotation. The annotation supports two parameters `min` and `max`, that define the range of values, into which fits the state variable. If not defined, these limits default to $\langle -32768, 32767 \rangle$.

Example of a state variable:

```
@State{min = 0, max = MAX_BUFFER_SIZE}
int packetsNum = 0;
```

A node's initial state is determined while its construction. In the example, an initial value of 0 is assigned to the part `packetsNum` of the state vector.

Refreshing the State Variables `OLYMP2` must set the state variables to the input state before calling `transit`. Some non–public state variables might be not set, as discussed in the next section. Anyway, `OLYMP2` might refresh these variables before each receiver's `receive` is called, but to reduce the computational complexity, there is a instead rule, that the sender is not allowed to modify the state variables within `transit` before trying to send a token. If there is more than a single receiver in a connection, though, the state variables are refreshed between two successive calls to `receive`, along with saving of the modifications to the vector state made by the methods, of course. This is substantiated by the peer nature of the receivers – there is no asymmetry like the sender/receiver asymmetry, so all receivers equally receive the input vector in the state variables. The sender should not rely on the state variables after a token is accepted, as their values are undefined. After the acceptance, the sender may only write to the state variables, to specify the output state.

Sending a Token There is a method `accept` that serves as OLYMP2's layer between the sender and the receivers. The method calls the `receive` methods in turn – a sender should never directly call `receive`.

A node can send a token to itself. It can do so using a looped connection, but it can also do so using a so called internal token transfer.

To support th case of a looped connection, the `receive` methods have an additional parameter `me`, that represents, if the token to accept was send by the same node. This way, a node knows, that it may yet modify the output vector in `transit`, after `receive` returns. That knowledge is sometimes crucial, what is illustrated by the example described in Sect. 6.1.

An internal token transfer can be used, when using a looped connection would be unnatural. For example, a server having the service time given by the Erlang distribution, whose example is given in Sect. 6.1, changes its phase before the serviced task is released. Due to OLYMP2 rules, such a change must involve a token transfer, just as any other event. But, in queueing terminology, servers with Erlang service time do not possess a looped connection just for changing the phase. An internal token transfer could thus be used instead. That type of transfer is realised by by a variant of the method `accept`.

The method `accept` also computes the value r_r. The return value of that method is specifically $r_r r_a$, where r_a is the method's argument decided by the sender. This eases computing r_s, as it is typical that the sender multiplies the 'acceptance factor' r_r by a given factor to create r_s. An example of it is shown in Sect. 6.1, where r_a is the rate of reaching a new phase by a server.

Caveats of Parallel Execution OLYMP2 is able to work concurrently. As the model is not reentrant, it is copied into a number of clones, accessed concurrently. If the model happens to have references to the other nodes in a model, then these references must obviously be changed in the clone models.

To update the references, OLYMP2 scans all fields in the nodes for types being `AbstractNode` or its subclass, and replaces these fields with references to cloned nodes. If such references are hidden outside the node fields, OLYMP2 is not able to reach and replace them. Such hidden references should thus not be used.

Adding a Receiver to a Source All sources in the library implement an interface `SourceInterface`, which has a method for adding new receivers. The method adds the receivers to a single connection, instead of adding a separate connection for each receiver.

The effect is, that a token generated by the source goes to all receivers at once. If this is not the desired behaviour, a number of separate sources should be declared, what will effect in independent tokens being sent to each receiver.

3.6   Receiving the Results

The raw results of work of OLYMP2 is probability vector, containing probability of particular CTMC states. To allow the user to conveniently receive modelling results, simple interpreter of PCTL language [6] is introduced. The user can ask question abut results using P, S or M operators, respectively for probability in not-steady state, steady state and mean value.

4   Solving the Matrix

Numerical solving of CTMCs means solving the sets of equations defined by transition matrix $\boldsymbol{Q}$, such that it fulfils [16]:

1. Linear equations
$$\boldsymbol{Q}^T \pi = 0 \tag{1}$$

2. Differential equations
$$\frac{d\pi(t)}{dt} = \boldsymbol{Q}^T \pi(t) \tag{2}$$

where π is a solution vector of probability of every state in Markov process. Linear equations are used for determining the probability of particular states in steady-state, after infinite time of system activity. Differential equation must be used when modelling the state of system after particular amount of time – in transient state. Detailed description of methods used exceeds the limits of the paper. Methods used for solving the equations were initially introduced in [12].

5   Compression of the Sparse Matrix

Because the nodes are currently a black-box to OLYMP2, the transition matrix is not stored in a symbolic form. This might make it very large. The transition matrices in OLYMP are sparse and there are only a few (usually less than 10) non-zero elements per row. A natural representation of such matrices is to store for each row only a number of non-zero elements and pairs (column index, value) for each such element. In a typical case, this leads to memory requirements (expressed in bytes) two orders of magnitude larger than matrix dimension. For matrices of dimension 10^8 it means about 10GB, which is usually too much or almost too much for typical workstations. The memory constraint limited OLYMP applications to models of up to 10^8 states.

To reduce memory requirements, MetaRLE – a dedicated compression of the matrix using finite state automatons is used. The algorithm uses semi-dynamic finite state automata (FSA), More details about the method along with detailed performance results can be found in [13]. MetaRLE compression ratio highly depends on the structure of the matrix but experiments show that it often exceeds 10^3.

6   Examples

Following sections contain two examples of CTMC model, simple and complex one.

6.1   Simple Example – A Buffered Server

Let us analyse an example – a simple buffered server with a service time given by the Erlang distribution. In OLYMP2, there is a class ErlangBufferedServer, that defines the service time only, as the buffer is defined in a superclass AbstractBufferedServer. Let us look into the superclass first. The buffer only receives packets, it never sends them over thenetwork – the latter is done by the server itself. The packet reception is modelled straightforwardly by a token reception – AbstractBufferedServer defines the method receive for that end:

```
@Override
public double
receive(boolean me, AbstractToken token, int num) {
  if(queueSize <maxQueueSize + (me ? 1 : 0)) {
    ++queueSize; return 1.0;
  }
  else
    return 0.0;
}
```

The subclass ExpBufferedServer defines service time. It simply means, that it declares sending a single packet from its buffer elsewhere with some rate μ. As sending a packet is represented by the server's token being accepted by a node that agrees to receive that packet, the subclass needs only to declare an appropriate transit method:

```
@Override
public double
transit(Connection t, int num) {
  double rate;
  if(queueSize > 0) {
    if(phase < phasesNum - 1) {
      rate = model.accept(this, phaseMu, null);
      ++phase;
    }
    else {
      rate =  model.accept(t, phaseMu, getToken());
      if((rate != 0) {
        --queueSize;
        phase = 0;
      }
```

```
    }
  }
  else
    rate = 0.0;
  return rate;
}
```

As can be seen, the class changes the phase of processing the packet several times using internal token transfers, until finally the packet is sent to the network. Transitions that represent the change to the next phase have a rate $phaseMu$, and the transition that represents sending the already processed token out of the server has that rate as well.

6.2   Complex Example – Database System

The presented example describes a large database system at an assurance company. The system includes a server with a database and a local area network with a number of terminals where the company employees run applications that introduce documents or retrieve them from a database.

We present a model of clients activities. Measurements were collected inside the working system: the phases at each users application were identified and their duration was measured. The collected data are used to construct a synthetic model of applications activities which is then applied to predict the system behaviour in case of the growth ofthe number of users.

Some features of the system:

- built on the Microsoft Windows software called the ComplexIT System (CITS),
- the system performs about 100 million of accountancy operations monthly (in Poland),
- 40 billion calculations in numerous specially created data centres (monthly),
- under the pension insurance currently serves 1.6 million active accounts of the payers and 14.4 million of insured accounts,
- system affects more than 260 million billing documents annually.

We are investigating only a single branch office of this system. The branch office consists of 30 Cisco switches linked with a multimode fibre, and 10 servers. The architecture of the system is shown at Fig. 1.

There are five applications working in the system, $A_1, ..., A_5$. Every application loads payers, and for every payer a number of documents is downloaded subsequently, according to rough scheme shown at Fig. 2.

For every application a number of real time distributions were measured – time to download a payer, time to download a document, distribution of the number of documents downloaded for one payer, time-gap before demanding a new document, time-gap before demanding a new payer. Details of the model are included in [3], but short description follows. The measurements indicate that data server is the bottleneck of the system, LAN may be omitted, hence queueing model of the system is extended machine-repairman model with 5 customers classes and 6 parallel servers. Besides, customers dynamically change their character, as each customer class has two forms - an application alternatively represents either a payer or a document. Modeling results are shown and discussed in original paper (Table 1).

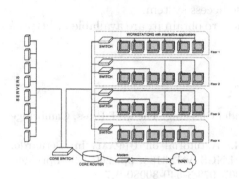

Fig. 1. LAN at database location   **Fig. 2.** Scheme of application work

Table 1. Number of states in Markov chain

No. of clients	No. of states
50	31500
100	133000
150	304500
200	546000
400	2212000
800	8904000
3200	143136000

Dynamic character of the model caused problems for modeling software. We were increasing the number of customers in the system, what resulted in increasing number of states.

OLYMP2 was able to solve the model for as high as 3200 customers in the system, what gave the transition number ca. 1.4×10^8. With Prism maximal size of the model turned out to be 100 customers (133 000 states). Though, the matrix compression ratio was as low as 10%. For less sophisticated models, however, e.g. ring model presented in [10], efficiency of OLYMP2 appeared comparable Prism.

7   Conclusion and Future Work

Thanks to use of sparse matrix compression performance of OLYMP2, exploiting traditional sparse matrices scheme, is in some cases competitive to well recognised Prism, that uses symbolic representation of the model. Our further plans provide work on further speed-up of building the model (matrix Q generation) by caching of node behaviour. We also plan on improving compression scheme by finding factors within a rate values, what might substantially improve compression of models like described database access system.

Current information on OLYMP2, and how to obtain it, are available at http:// modeling.iitis.pl/software/olymp-2.

References

1. Baier, C., Katoen, J.-P.: Principles of Model Checking. The MIT Press, Cambridge (2008). ISBN-13:978-0-262-02649-9
2. Behrmann, G., David, A., Larsen, K.G.: A tutorial on UPPAAL. In: Bernardo, M., Corradini, F. (eds.) SFM-RT 2004. LNCS, vol. 3185, pp. 200–236. Springer, Heidelberg (2004). https://doi.org/10.1007/978-3-540-30080-9_7
3. Czachórski, T., Grochla, K., Józefiok, A., Nycz, T.: Simulation, markov chain and diffusion approximation models–a case study. In: Computer Science & Information Technologies (CSIT2011) (2011)
4. Erlang, A.: Solution of some problems in the theory of probabilities of significance in automatic telephone exchanges, post office. Electr. Eng. J. **10**, 189–197 (1918)
5. Fourneau, J.M., Mahjoub, Y.A.E., Quessette, F., Vekris, D.: XBorne 2016: a brief introduction. In: Czachórski, T., Gelenbe, E., Grochla, K., Lent, R. (eds.) ISCIS 2016. CCIS, vol. 659, pp. 134–141. Springer, Cham (2016). https://doi.org/10. 1007/978-3-319-47217-1_15
6. Hansson, H., Jonsson, B.: A logic for reasoning about time and reliability. Form. Asp. Comput. **6**(5), 512–535 (1994)
7. Holzmann, G.J.: The Spin Model Checker: Primer and Reference Manual, 4th edn. Addison-Wesley, Boston (2008). OCLC:254420839
8. Kirschnick, M.: The performance evaluation and prediction system for queueing networks-PEPSY-QNS. Technical Report TR-I4-18-94, Department of Computer Science 4, Universität Erlangen-Nürnberg, Germany (1994)
9. Krieger, U.R., Muller-Clostermann, B., Sczittnick, M.: Modeling and analysis of communication systems based on computational methods for markov chains. IEEE J. Sel. Areas Commun. **8**(9), 1630–1648 (1990)
10. Nowak, M., Pecka, P.: Reducing the number of states for markovian model of optical slotted ring network. In: Balandin, S., Dunaytsev, R., Koucheryavy, Y. (eds.) NEW2AN/ruSMART -2010. LNCS, vol. 6294, pp. 231–241. Springer, Heidelberg (2010). https://doi.org/10.1007/978-3-642-14891-0_21
11. Parzen, E.: Stochastic Processes. Classics in applied mathematics. Society for Industrial and Applied Mathematics (1999)
12. Pecka, P.: Obiektowo zorientowany wielowątkowy system do modelowania stanów nieustalonych w sieciach komputerowych za pomocą łańcuchów Markowa (in Polish). PhD thesis, IITiS PAN, Gliwice (2002)

13. Pecka, P., Deorowicz, S., Nowak, M.: Efficient representation of transition matrix in the markov process modeling of computer networks. In: Kacprzyk, J., Czachórski, T., Kozielski, S., Stańczyk, U. (eds.) Man-Machine Interactions 2, vol. 103, pp. 457–464. Springer, Berlin (2011)
14. Rataj, A.: More flexible models using a new version of the translator of Java sources to timed automatons J2tadd. Theor. Appl. Inform. **21**(2), 107–114 (2009)
15. Rataj, A., Woźna, B., Zbrzezny, A.: A translator of java programs to TADDs. Fundam. Inf. **93**(1–3), 305–324 (2009)
16. Stewart, W.J.: Introduction to the Numerical Solution of Markov Chains. Princeton University Press, Princeton (1994)
17. Visser, W., Pasareanu, C.S., Khurshid, S.: Test input generation with java PathFinder. ACM SIGSOFT Softw. Eng. Notes **29**(4), 97 (2004)
18. Zbrzezny, A., Woźna, B.: Towards verification of Java programs in VerICS. Fundam. Inform. **85**(1–4), 533–548 (2008)

Performance of a Buffer Between Electronic and All-Optical Networks, Diffusion Approximation Model

Godlove Suila Kuaban[1,2], Edelqueen Anyam[2], Tadeusz Czachórski[1(✉)], and Artur Rataj[1]

[1] Polish Academy of Sciences, Institute of Theoretical and Applied Informatics, Baltycka 5, 44–100 Gliwice, Poland
{gskuaban,tadek,artur}@iitis.pl, gkuaban@polsl.pl
[2] Institute of Informatics, Silesian Technical University, Akademicka 16, 44–100 Gliwice, Poland
edelqueen2014@gmail.com

Abstract. We present a model of the edge router between electronic and all optical networks. Arriving electronic packets of variable sizes are stored at a buffer the volume of which is equal to the fixed size of optical packet. When the buffer is filled, its content becomes an optical buffer and dispatched to optical network. To avoid excessive delays, the optical packet is sent also after a specified deadline. The model is based on diffusion approximation and validated by discrete event simulation. Its goal is to determine the probability distribution of the effective optical packet sizes an distribution of their interdeparture times as a function of the interarrival time distribution, distribution of the electronic packet sizes, the value of deadline and the size of buffer. We use real traffic data from the CAIDA (Center for Applied Internet Data Analysis) repositories.

1 Introduction

In all-optical networks which are still a technology under development, switching is performed by optical nodes and the optical signal is not converted to electronic form along the whole way through the network. This may improve substantially the network performance. However, it is not easy to organize. Electronic nodes are able to queue and prioritize packets, to decide the further routing, while the optical ones may only, if needed, delay the signal in special fibre loops. That is why the ingress router should do as much work as possible: incoming electronic packets are here sorted by destination and by class of service (e.g. CoS1, CoS2, Best Effort). We consider the performance of a single buffer where packets of the same destination and class are stored.

The high demand for more bandwidth and high speed networks have motivated a lot of research in the design, optimization and performance evaluation of IP over all-optical networks [6]. There is a great need to improve the efficiency of the packetization process since the delay in IP over all optical network is the

© Springer Nature Switzerland AG 2018
T. Czachórski et al. (Eds.): ISCIS 2018, CCIS 935, pp. 68–75, 2018.
https://doi.org/10.1007/978-3-030-00840-6_8

sum of the delays in the packetization process, the delays in the buffer where the packets are scheduled into the all optical network, the propagation delays in the optical transmission links and the delays in the optical nodes.

Here, we use diffusion approximation which is an analytical tool developed to evaluate the performance of queueing systems with general arrival and general service time distributions, [12,13]. The diffusion process represents here the process of assembling and framing electronic IP packets into optical packets. Our study is based on the packetization model proposed in [7] which we formerly studied in [6] using Markovian model solved numerically with a Probabilistic Model Checker (Prism).

The diffusion models are validated by a discrete event simulation model developed using the JAVA programming language. We use a synthetic traffic in form of Poisson process and real traffic traces from the CAIDA repositories. The performance measures we consider are the distribution of optical packet inter-departure times (delays introduced by packetization and regularity of traffic at optical side) and the distribution of the size of content in optical packets which are of constant size but may be only partially filled (throughput).

2 Packetiztion in IP over All-Optical Networks

Packetization in IP over all optical networks is the process of grooming smaller electronic IP packets into larger optical packets. It is carried out in the edge node where the incoming IP packets are classified based on their QoS classes, destination and other relevant parameters, queued in a buffer until the buffer is full or until the filling deadline expires. This has given rise to two types of packetization algorithms adopted in IP over all optical networks. These are the maximum time (Max Time) and the maximum time maximum size (Max Time Max Size) algorithms described in detail in [8]. In the Max Time algorithm, after a predefined deadline T, the content of the buffer is emptied while in the Max Time Max Size, the buffer is emptied after the predefined deadline has expired or after the maximum size of the buffer N is reached, even if the deadline has not yet expired.

The authors in [4,6,7] adopted the Max Time Max Size algorithm but with the modification that if the mean size of the arriving IP packet say m, is larger than the free available space in the buffer, the buffer is considered to be full, its content is dispatched as an optical packet and the rejected IP packet is rescheduled in the next filling cycle. The authors in [9] proposed two adaptive packetization (assembly) algorithms which are packet-based dynamic-threshold algorithm for burst assembly (dyn-threshold-packet) and the byte-based dynamic threshold algorithm for burst assembly. They used synthetic traffic (Poisson traffic and Markov Modulated Poisson Process traffic) and the real traffic traces from a traffic data repository maintained by the measurement and analysis on the WIDE Internet (MAWI) working group of the WIDE Project to demonstrate that the dynamic threshold-based assembly algorithms perform substantially better than the usual timer-based schemes. The authors in [14] are proposing a packetization scheme with adaptive expiration times, determined in response to local and/or global queue sizes.

In this paper, we considered the first two criteria above and then solve diffusion equations without considering the influence of the deadline (MTMS-S) and in another case without considering the influence of the buffer size (MTMS-T), that is considering the influence of the deadline. However, we still considered the packetization mechanism that we used in [6], alongside the first two criteria.

3   Simulation Model

A discrete event simulation model written in Java was prepared. In simulation we used traffic traces from CAIDA (Center for Applied Internet Data Analysis) [1] repositories. CAIDA routinely collects traces on several backbone links, in the examples that follow we used measurements of the size of IP v4 packets and their interarrival times from Equinix Chicago link collected during one hour on 18 February 2016, having 22 644 654 packets belonging to 1 174 515 IPv4 flows, [2].

In the model we compare the performance of the buffer in presence of the resulting intensity of CAIDA traffic flow (in bytes per time unit) with Poisson traffic of the same intensity. The dispersion of the real traffic intensity is clearly larger and limited only by the maximum throughput of the link. The time unit is 0.01 sec, in this scale the burstiness of traffic is seen the best. The same time unit was then applied in diffusion model.

The assumed size of the buffer was $N = 10000$ bytes, corresponding to the size of about 15 (14.32) average packets or 6.66 maximum packets size. The simulation results concerning the distribution of interdeparture times of optical packets and their filling without and with deadline $T = 0.02$ s are in next sections compared with diffusion approximation results.

4   Diffusion Approximation Model Without Deadline

In this section we develop diffusion approximation model for the interdeparture times of optical packets with no deadline. Since the incoming IP packets are queued up in the buffer until the buffer is full we can treat this system as a queueing system with mean interarrival rate λ and mean service rate $\mu = 0$.

The principle of the diffusion approximation is to replace the number of customers in a queueing system by the value of diffusion process $X(t)$, [12,13]. The solution of the diffusion equation

$$\frac{\partial f(x,t;x_0)}{\partial t} = \frac{\alpha}{2}\frac{\partial^2 f(x,t;x_0)}{\partial x^2} - \beta\frac{\partial f(x,t;x_0)}{\partial x} \tag{1}$$

where βdt and αdt represent the mean and variance of the changes of the diffusion process at dt, defines the conditional probability density function (pdf) of the diffusion process $f(x,t;x_0) = P[x \leq X(t) < x + dx \mid X(0) = x_0]$ of $X(t)$.

The density of the unrestricted diffusion process starting from x_0 is, e.g. [3]

$$\phi(x,t;x_0) = \frac{1}{\sqrt{2\Pi\alpha t}} \exp\left[-\frac{(x - x_0 - \beta t)^2}{2\alpha t}\right] \tag{2}$$

and in case of starting the process at $x_0 = 0$ and having the absorbing barrier at $x = N$ (i.e. the process is ended when it comes to the barrier, $f(N,t) = 0$ for $t > 0$), is

$$\phi(x,t) = \frac{1}{\sqrt{2\Pi\alpha t}}\left\{\exp\left[-\frac{(x - \beta t)^2}{2\alpha t}\right] - \exp\left[\frac{2\beta N}{\alpha} - \frac{(x - 2N - \beta t)^2}{2\alpha t}\right]\right\}. \tag{3}$$

The first passage time from $x = 0$ to the barrier has density $\gamma_{0,N}(t)$

$$\gamma_{0,N}(t) = -\frac{d}{dt}\int_{-\infty}^{N}\phi(x,t)dx = \frac{N}{\sqrt{2\Pi\alpha t^3}}\exp\left[-\frac{(N - \beta t)^2}{2\alpha t}\right]. \tag{4}$$

This first passage time approximates the time of filling the buffer and also the interdeparture time between optical packets. The filling of the buffer starts at $x = 0$ when $t = 0$, and ends at the barrier at $x = N$ where N corresponds to the size of the buffer. The value x of the diffusion process at time t represents the current filling of the buffer.

The number of bytes arrived at a unit of time is a product of two independent random variables: X – the number of packets and Y – the size of packets. The mean of a product variable XY is $E(XY) = E(X)E(Y)$ and the variance is

$$Var(XY) = E(X^2Y^2) - (E(XY))^2 =$$
$$Var(X)Var(Y) + Var(X)(E(Y))^2 + Var(Y)(E(X))^2,$$

the mean number of arrived at a time unit packets is $E(X) = \lambda$ and the variance is $Var(X) = \lambda^3\sigma_A^3$, therefore the mean of arrived at time unit bytes is $\beta = \lambda m$ and the variance of number of arrived at a time unit bytes that define α is

$$\alpha = \lambda^3\sigma_A^2\sigma_m^2 + \lambda^3\sigma_A^2 m^2 + \sigma_m^2\lambda^2$$

We may refine this model having in mind that the interdeparure time includes time the buffer stays empty, that means completion time of the interarrival time (below, for simplicity we take the interarrival time distribution $f_A(x)$ of packets after which the diffusion is started not at zero but at a point corresponding to the size of the first arriving packet, i.e. at $x_0 = \xi$ given by the distribution $f_H(\xi)$ of the packet size:

$$\gamma(t) = f_A(t) * \int_0^H \gamma_{\xi,N}(t)f_H(\xi)d\xi$$

where $*$ is the convolution operation.

5 Diffusion Approximation Model with Deadline

If we do not consider the deadline, the optical packets leaving the buffer are always full. In case of deadline T, the expression (4) of the first passage time evaluates the density of probability $\gamma_{0,x}(x)$

$$\gamma_{0,x}(x) = -\frac{x}{\sqrt{2\Pi\alpha T^3}} \exp\left[-\frac{(x-\beta T)^2}{2\alpha T}\right] \tag{5}$$

that the filling of the buffer ends at position x (provided that the process was not ended on its way to x) because of the deadline T. Dispatched this way the optical packet contains x bytes, the remaining $N - x$ of its volume being empty: The probability density that the diffusion process will end exactly when the deadline T is reached is given by:

$$\gamma_{0,N}(T) = \int_T^\infty \gamma_{0,N}(t)dt = N\left[2 - \operatorname{erfc}\left(\frac{N-T\beta}{\sqrt{2T\alpha}}\right) + e^{\frac{2N\beta}{\alpha}}\operatorname{erfc}\left(\frac{N-T\beta}{\sqrt{2T\alpha}}\right)\right] \tag{6}$$

where

$$\operatorname{erfc}(t) = 1 - \operatorname{erf}(t), \qquad \operatorname{erf}(t) = \frac{2}{\sqrt{\Pi}}\int_0^t e^{-\xi^2}d\xi.$$

Figure 1 compares the interdeparture times obtained by simulation and diffusion approximation in case of deadline and Poisson input. The influence of deadline is hardly seen as the passage time in case of Poisson traffic are usually shorter than T. In case of more dispersed real traffic the passage time may be larger and probability that the filling ends with deadline, expressed by Eq. 6 is distinct. The solutions for the model without deadline are quite similar to those in the figures except spikes resulting from deadline.

When the deadline is reached, the buffer should be cleared and the diffusion equation should be provided with jumps performed from the point x to $x = 0$ with the density $\gamma_{0,x}(x)$. Some similar models of diffusion with jumps back were discussed in [10]. Here, the diffusion equation

$$\frac{\partial f(x,t,x_0)}{\partial t} = \frac{\alpha}{2}\frac{\partial^2 f(x,t,x_0)}{\partial x^2} + \beta\frac{\partial f(x,t,x_0)}{\partial x} - \gamma f(x,t,x_0) \tag{7}$$

in steady state becomes a second order homogeneous linear differential equation with solution

$$f(x) = C_1 e^{z_1 x} + C_2 e^{z_2 x}$$

where z_1, z_2

$$z_1 = \frac{\beta}{\alpha} + W, \quad z_2 = \frac{\beta}{\alpha} - W, \quad W = \sqrt{\frac{\beta^2}{\alpha^2} + \frac{2\gamma}{\alpha}}$$

are the roots of the characteristic polynomial

$$\frac{\alpha}{2}z^2 - \beta z - \gamma = 0$$

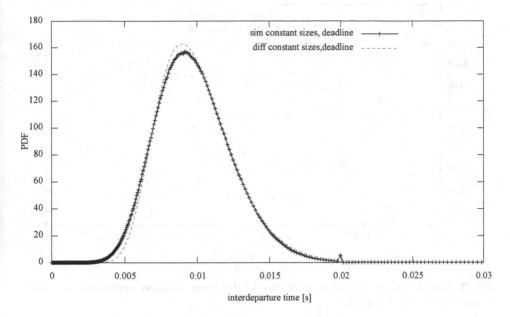

Fig. 1. Interdeparture times, simulation and diffusion approximation with deadline (Poisson input).

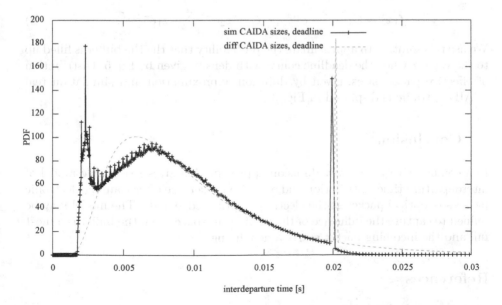

Fig. 2. Interdeparture times, simulation and diffusion approximation with deadline (CAIDA input).

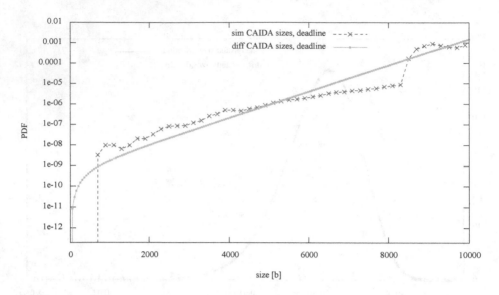

Fig. 3. Distribution of packet sizes in case of deadline, diffusion approximation and simulation, (CAIDA input).

Using the border condition $\lim_{x \to 0} f(x) = 0$ ($C_1 = -C_2$) and the normalization $\int_0^N f(x)dx = 1$, we have

$$f(x) = C(e^{z_2 x} - e^{z_1 x}), \quad C = z_2 e^{-z_2 N} - z_1 e^{-z_1 N}. \tag{8}$$

We use this solution to approximate the probability that the the buffer is filled up to the value x when the deadline comes with density given by Eq. 5. Distribution of effective packet sizes, given by diffusion approximation and simulation real (CAIDA) traffic is displayed in Fig. 3.

6   Conclusions

In a comparatively easy way diffusion approximation gives reasonable model of interdeparture time distribution and of useful packet size after framing electronic packets to optical packet at the electronic-optical edge node. The model may be refined to capture the influence of the insufficient space when the buffer is almost full and the incoming packet starts a new filling cycle.

References

1. http://www.caida.org/home/
2. https://data.caida.org/datasets/passive-2016/equinix-chicago/20160218-130000. UTC/

3. Cox, R.P., Miller, H.D.: The Theory of Stochastic Processes. Chapman and Hall, London (1965)
4. Domańska, J., Kotuliak, I., Atmaca, T., Czachórski, T.: Optical packet filling, In: 10th Polish Teletraffic Symposium PSRT2003 (2003)
5. Kuaban, G.S.: Markovian queuing model for performance evaluation of the edge node in IP over all-optical networks, Masters thesis, Silesian University of Technology (2017)
6. Suila, K.G., Czachórski, T., Rataj, A.: A queueing model of the edge node in ip over all-optical networks. In: Gaj, P., Sawicki, M., Suchacka, G., Kwiecień, A. (eds.) CN 2018. CCIS, vol. 860, pp. 258–271. Springer, Cham (2018). https://doi.org/10.1007/978-3-319-92459-5_21
7. Kotuliak, I.: Feasibility study of optical packet switching: performance evaluation. Ph.D. thesis, University of Versailles-St-Quentin-en-Yveline (2003)
8. Li, H., Thng, I.: Edge node buffer usage in optical burst switching networks, Photonic Netw. Commun. 13(1), 31–51. Springer Science+Business Media, LLC (2006)
9. Toksöz, M.A., Akar, N.: Dynamic threshold-based assembly algorithms for optical burst switching networks subject to burst rate constraints. Photonic Netw. Commun. 20(2), 120–130. Springer Science+Business Media, LLC (2010)
10. Czachórski, T.: A diffusion process with instantaneous jumps back and its application, Archiwum informatyki Teoretycznej i Stsowanej, t.2 (z.1-2) 27–46 (1990)
11. Czachórski, T., Domański, A., Domańska, J., Rataj, A.: A study of IP router queues with the use of markov models. In: Gaj, P., Kwiecień, A., Stera, P. (eds.) CN 2016. CCIS, vol. 608, pp. 294–305. Springer, Cham (2016). https://doi.org/10.1007/978-3-319-39207-3_26
12. Gelenbe, E.: On approximate computer systems models. J. ACM 22(2), 261–269 (1975)
13. Gelenbe, E.: Diffusion approximations: waiting times and batch arrival. Acta Inf. 12, 285–303 (1979)
14. Atmaca, T., Kamli, A., Rataj, A.: Adaptation of the NGREEN architecture for a bursty traffic. In: Proceedings of CN 2018. Institut Mines-Telecom, Gliwice, France

The Influence of the Traffic Self-similarity on the Choice of the Non-integer Order PI^α Controller Parameters

Adam Domański[1], Joanna Domańska[2], Tadeusz Czachórski[2($\boxtimes$)],
Jerzy Klamka[2], Dariusz Marek[1], and Jakub Szyguła[1]

[1] Institute of Informatics, Silesian University of Technology, Address Akademicka 16,
44-100 Gliwice, Poland
[2] Institute of Theoretical and Applied Informatics, Polish Academy of Sciences,
Address ul. Bałtycka 5, 44-100 Gliwice, Poland
tadek@iitis.pl

Abstract. The article discusses the problem of choosing the best parameters of the non-integer order PI^α controller used in IP routers Active Queue Management for TCP/IP traffic flow control. The impact of the self-similarity of the traffic on the controller parameters is investigated with the use of discrete event simulation. We analyze the influence of these parameters on the length of the queue, the number of rejected packets and waiting times. The results indicate that the controller parameters strongly depend on the value of the Hurst parameter.

Keywords: Active queue management · Network congestion control
Parameters of the non-integer order PI^α controller

1 Introduction

The first Active Queue Management (AQM) mechanism was proposed in 1993 by Floyd and Jacobson [11]. Still in use, it is called *Random Early Detection* or *Random Early Discard* (RED) algorithm and is based on a drop function giving probability that a packet is rejected. This probability is defined on the basis of the walking average queue length. The walking average is computed as the weighted sum of the current queue length and the previous walking average and serves as a low-pass filter which eliminates fast queue changes and detects long term trends. A loss of packets at a congested IP router is a signal to the TCP protocol that the sender should lower the intensity of connection traffic to avoid congestion. The authors have discussed the RED algorithm and its several modifications in [3,5–7,9,10]. One of the observations is that a more detailed account of history of the flow values than in case of the moving average may improve the control, see [4]. This may be done by e.g. fractional order integration and differentiation. A proportional-integral-derivative controller (PID controller) is a traditional mechanism used in feedback control systems. Its fractional-order

© Springer Nature Switzerland AG 2018
T. Czachórski et al. (Eds.): ISCIS 2018, CCIS 935, pp. 76–83, 2018.
https://doi.org/10.1007/978-3-030-00840-6_9

version $PI^\alpha D^\beta$ has more flexibility and therefore is currently extensively studied, e.g. [15]. It may be also applied in TCP/IP traffic control, which is in fact a closed loop control, and may replace RED mechanism and its role will be the same: determination of the packet loss probability on the basis of the current and past traffic but in a way more complex than in case of the moving average.

The latter part of the paper is organized in the following way: Sect. 2 discusses $PI^\alpha D^\beta$ controllers, Sect. 3 briefly reminds definitions of self-similar traffic. Section 4 presents our experiments and their results. The conclusions are presented in Sect. 5.

2   AQM Mechanism Based on PI^α Controller

Our papers [7–9] describe how to use the response from PI^α controler with non-integer α to define packet loss probability. It is given by a formula:

$$p_i = max\{0, -(K_P e_k + K_I \Delta^\alpha e_k)\} \tag{1}$$

where K_P, K_I are tuning parameters, e_k is the error in current slot $e_k = Q_k - Q$, i.e. the difference between current queue Q_k and desired queue Q.

The Fractional Order Derivatives and Integrals (FOD/FOI) definitions unify the notions of derivative and integral to one differintegral definition. The most popular formulas to calculate differintegral numerically are Grunwald-Letnikov (GrLET) formula and Riemann-Liouville formulas (RL) [1,18,19].

Differintegral is a combined differentiation/integration operator. The q-differintegral of function f, denoted by $\Delta^q f$ is the fractional derivative (for $q > 0$) or fractional integral (if $q < 0$). If $q = 0$, then the q-th differintegral of a function is the function itself.

In the case of discrete systems (in the active queue management, packet drop probabilities are determined at discrete moments of packet arrivals) there is only one definition of differ-integrals of non-integer order. This definition is a generalization of the traditional definition of the difference of integer order to the non-integer order and it is analogous to a generalization used in Grunwald-Letnikov (GrLET) formula.

For a given sequence $f_0, f_1, ..., f_j, ..., f_k$

$$\Delta^q f_k = \sum_{j=0}^{k} (-1)^j \binom{q}{j} f_{k-j} \tag{2}$$

where $q \in R$ is generally a non-integer fractional order, f_k is a differentiated discrete function and $\binom{q}{j}$ is generalized Newton symbol defined as follows:

$$\binom{q}{j} = \begin{cases} 1 & \text{for } j = 0 \\ \dfrac{q(q-1)(q-2)..(q-j+1)}{j!} & \text{for } j = 1, 2, ... \end{cases} \tag{3}$$

e.g.

$$\Delta^{0.5} f_k = 1 f_k - 0.5 f_{k-1} - 0.125 f_{k-2} - 0.0625 f_{k-3} \dots$$
$$\Delta^{-0.5} f_k = 1 f_k + 0.5 f_{k-1} + 0.375 f_{k-2} + 0.3125 f_{k-3} \dots$$

Articles [7–9], show that using the non-integer order $PI^\alpha D^\beta$ controller as AQM mechanism has advantages over the standard RED mechanism and improves the router performance. These articles present results for arbitrary sets of controller parameters. Here, we try to find an optimal set of the parameters.

3   The Self-similar Network Traffic

In the article we consider the PI^α AQM mechanism in presence of self-similar network traffic with different Hurst parameters. In simulations presented in the next section the traffic intensity was represented by fractional Gaussian noise (fGn). This stochastic process was proposed in [17] for description of the long-range dependence in a variety of hydrological and geophysical time series. At the moment the fGn model is one of the most commonly applied self-similar processes in network performance evaluation [16].

Let $B_h(t)$ be a fractional Brownian motion process. Then the sequence of increments:

$$X(t) = B_h(t) - B_h(t-1)$$

is an exactly self-similar stationary Gaussian process with zero mean, referred to as fGn process. The autocorrelation function of fGn process is given by [13]:

$$\rho^{(m)}(k) = \rho(k) = \frac{1}{2}[(k+1)^{2H} - 2k^{2H} + (k-1)^{2H}],$$

which is the sufficient condition for second-order self-similarity. The fGn process is the only stationary Gaussian process that is exactly self-similar [20]. For $0.5 < H < 1$ the auto-correlation decays hyperbolically [2]:

$$\rho(k) \sim H(2H-1)k^{2H-2}$$

so the process exhibits long-range dependence.

The spectral density of fGn process is given by [16]:

$$f(\lambda) = c|e^{J\lambda} - 1|^2 \sum_{i=-\infty}^{\infty} |2\pi i + \lambda|^{2H-1},$$

where $\lambda \in [-\pi, \pi]$, $0.5 < H < 1$ and c is a normalization constant such that $\int_{-\pi}^{\pi} f(\lambda)d\lambda = Var(X)$.

4   Selection of Optimal PI^α Controller Parameters

Our goal is to find experimentally the optimal, in the sense of a chosen objective function, parameters of PI^α controller. It was done with the use of a series of simulations. Two objective functions were defined: f_1 is the mean packet waiting time:

$$f_1 = E[W]$$

and f_2 is a weighted sum of the mean waiting time $E[W]$, the number of rejected packets N_{loss}, the longest series of successive losses $N_{loss-in-raw}$, and average queue length $E[N]$:

$$f_2 = a_1 E[W] + a_2 N_{loss} + a_3 N_{loss-in-raw} + a_4 E[N].$$

We looked for the minimum of the objective functions in the 3-dimensional space of the parameters K_P, K_I, α. It was done with the use of Hooke and Jeeves direct search method [12,14].

At each iteration Hooke and Jeeves algorithm compares the value of the objective function for current set of parameters K_P, K_I, α (base point) with values of the objective function (with their arguments given by simulations) at six neighboring points

$$K_{P\,new} = K_P \pm \delta \qquad K_{I\,new} = K_I \pm \delta \quad \alpha_{new} = \alpha \pm \delta$$

with the same $\delta = 0.0001$ for all parameters. The smallest value of the function indicates the next base point. To make the process more efficient, six separate computer threads were used. If the result is not better at any of these six points, the step δ is doubled. This way the risk of ending the algorithm at a local minimum is reduced. One experiment to determine minimal value of objective function takes about 5–6 h.

The model of the router queue assumed that the desired queue length Q is 100 packets and the maximum queue length Q_{max} is 300 packets. The Hurst parameter was increased from 0.5 by 0.1 to 0.9. The input traffic intensity was always the same $\lambda = 0.5$, the service intensity μ was equal 0.5. In each simulation run 500 000 packets went through the router with PI^α controller. The simulator was written in Simpy.

Table 1 and Fig. 1 show the searching process for $H = 0.5$ and the second objective function. The algorithm found the best set of parameters in 25 iterations ($K_P = 0.00089$, $K_I = 0.01$, $\alpha = 0.$).

Table 2 and Fig. 2 show the results for $H = 0.9$ i.e. strongly self-similar traffic.

Table 1. Searching process for $H = 0.5$ and second objective function.

	K_P	K_I	α	Mean waiting time	Rejected packets
0	0.00050	0.0011	−0.35	7.912	125
1	0.00050	0.0010	−0.35	7.885	101
2	0.00050	0.0045	−0.35	7.687	154
3	0.00051	0.0045	−0.35	8.890	200
...					
8	0.00052	0.0075	−0.25	8.679	222
9	0.00052	0.0075	−0.20	8.038	16
10	0.00052	0.0075	−0.10	7.253	171
11	0.00052	0.0075	0	10.352	84
12	0.00051	0.0075	0	8.631	57
13	0.00051	0.0086	0	7.869	114
14	0.00053	0.0086	0	10.556	51
...					
24	0.00039	0.0100	0	7.784	12
25	0.00089	0.0100	0	7.429	3

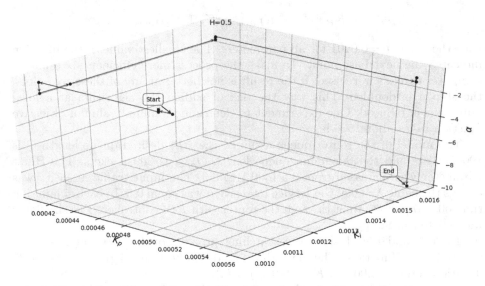

Fig. 1. Searching process for $H = 0.5$ and second objective function.

5   Summary

The Internet Engineering Task Force (IETF) recommends that IP routers should use the active queue management mechanism (AQM). The basic algorithm for AQM is the RED algorithm. There are many its modifications and improve-

Table 2. Searching process for $H = 0.9$ and second objective function.

	K_P	K_I	α	Mean waiting time	Rejected packets
0	0.00050	0.0011	−0.30	15.446	9527
1	0.00050	0.0014	−0.30	14.853	9614
...					
...					
31	0.00054	0.0023	−0.35	13.143	9747
32	0.00055	0.0023	−0.35	12.914	9651
...					
35	0.00309	0.0034	−0.35	12.708	9887
36	0.00305	0.0034	−0.35	12.715	9702
37	0.00322	0.0034	−0.35	12.564	9826

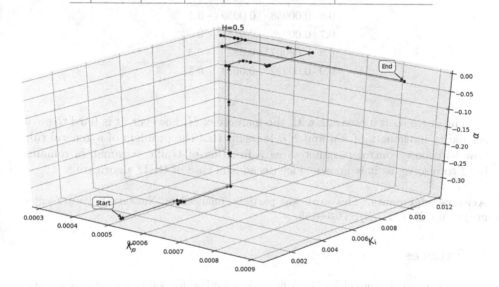

Fig. 2. Searching process for $H = 0.9$ and second objective function.

ments. One of them is the introduction of PI^α controller. Our previous work has shown the advantage of this solution. However, the proper selection of the controller parameters is important in adaptation to various types of traffic (degree of self-similarity or various intensity).

The article considers the problem of choosing the optimal PI^α – in the sense of two objective functions – controller parameters. One is focused on delay introduced by the router, the other takes also losses into account.

We remark that the traffic self-similarity the great influence on AQM process and controller parameters, see Tables 3 and 4.

Table 3. Hurst parametr and obtained controller parameters, first objective function

H	K_P	K_I	α
0.5	0.00056	0.0016	−0.7
0.6	0.000001	0.01381	−0.95
0.7	0.000001	0.011	−0.9
0.8	0.00048	0.0361	−1.0
0.9	0.000841	0.0117	−1.0

Table 4. Hurst parameter and obtained controller parameters, second objective function

H	K_P	K_I	α
0.5	0.00089	0.01	0
0.6	0.00058	0.0059	−0.1
0.7	0.00225	0.0181	0
0.8	0.000071	0.032	−0.4
0.9	0.00322	0.0034	−0.35

The degree α is increasing with the increase of H, however, it is hard to see a regularity in changes of K_P and K_I. It seems that the problem of a general rule how to choose control parameters as a function of traffic parameters remains hard to resolve, as it is known since decades in case of RED algorithm.

Acknowledgements. This work was partially financed by National Science Center project no. 2017/27/ B/ST6/00145.

References

1. Leszczyński, J., Ciesielski, M.: A numerical method for solution of ordinary differential equations of fractional order. In: Wyrzykowski, R., Dongarra, J., Paprzycki, M., Waśniewski, J. (eds.) PPAM 2001. LNCS, vol. 2328, pp. 695–702. Springer, Heidelberg (2002). https://doi.org/10.1007/3-540-48086-2_77
2. Cox, D.: Long-range dependance: a review. In: Statistics: An Appraisal, pp. 55–74. Iowa State University Press (1984)
3. Domańska, J., Augustyn, D., Domański, A.: The choice of optimal 3-rd order polynomial packet dropping function for NLRED in the presence of self-similar traffic. Bull. Pol. Acad. Sci Tech. Sci. **60**, 779–786 (2012)
4. Domańska, J., Domański, A., Augustyn, D., Klamka, J.: A RED modified weighted moving average for soft real-time application. Int. J. Appl. Math. Comput. Sci. **24**(3), 697–707 (2014)
5. Domańska, J., Domański, A., Czachórski, T.: Fluid flow analysis of RED Algorithm with modified weighted moving average. In: Dudin, A., Klimenok, V., Tsarenkov, G., Dudin, S. (eds.) BWWQT 2013. CCIS, vol. 356, pp. 50–58. Springer, Heidelberg (2013). https://doi.org/10.1007/978-3-642-35980-4_7

6. Domańska, J., Domański, A., Czachórski, T., Klamka, J.: Fluid flow approximation of time-limited TCP/UDP/XCP streams. Bull. Pol. Acad. Sci. Tech. Sci. **62**(2), 217–225 (2014)
7. Domańska, J., Domański, A., Czachórski, T., Klamka, J.: Use of a non integer order PI controller to active queue management mechanism. Int. J. Appl. Math. Comput. Sci. **26**(4), 777–789 (2016)
8. Domańska, J., Domański, A., Czachórski, T., Klamka, J.: Self-similarity traffic and AQM mechanism based on non-integer order $PI^\alpha D^\beta$ controller. In: Proceedings of 24th International Conference on Computer Networks, CN 2017, Ladek Zdroj (2017)
9. Domańska, J., Domański, A., Czachórski, T., Klamka, J., Szyguła, J.: The AQM dropping packet probability function based on non-integer order $PI^\alpha D^\beta$ controller. In: International Conference on Non-Integer Order Calculus and its Applications (2017)
10. Domański, A., Domańska, J., Czachórski, T.: Comparison of AQM control systems with the use of fluid flow approximation. In: Kwiecień, A., Gaj, P., Stera, P. (eds.) CN 2012. CCIS, vol. 291, pp. 82–90. Springer, Heidelberg (2012). https://doi.org/10.1007/978-3-642-31217-5_9
11. Floyd, S., Jacobson, V.: Random early detection gateways for congestion avoidance. IEEE/ACM Trans. Netw. **1**(4), 397–413 (1993)
12. Hooke, R., Jeeves, T.: Direct search solution of numerical and statistical problems. J. ACM **8**(2), 212–229 (1961). (USA)
13. Karagiannis, T., Molle, M., Faloutsos, M.: Long-range dependence: ten years of internet traffic modeling. IEEE Internet Comput. **8**(5), 57–64 (2004)
14. Kelley, C.: Iterative methods for optimization. Front. Appl. Math. (18) (1999) (SIAM, Philadelphia)
15. Latawiec, K., Stanisławski, R., Łukaniszyn, M., Czuczwara, W., Rydel, M.: Fractional-order modeling of electric circuits: modern empiricism vs. classical science. In: Progress in Applied Electrical Engineering (PAEE) (2017)
16. Lopez-Ardao, J., Lopez-Garcia, C., Suarez-Gonzalez, A., Fernandez-Veiga, M., Rodriguez-Rubio, R.: On the use of self-similar processes in network simulation. ACM Trans. Model. Comput. Simul. **10**(2), 125–151 (2000)
17. Mandelbrot, B., Ness, J.: Fractional brownian motions, fractional noises and applications. SIAM Rev. **10**, 422–437 (1968)
18. Miller, K., Ross, B.: An Introduction to the Fractional Calculus and Fractional Differential Equations. Wiley, New York (1993)
19. Podlubny, I.: Fractional Differential Equations. Academic Press, San Diego, USA (1999)
20. Samorodnitsky, G., Taqqu, M.: Stable Non-Gaussian Random Processes: Stochastic Models with Infinite Variance. Chapman and Hall, New York (1994)

Data Analysis and Algorithms

Modified Graph-Based Algorithm for Efficient Hyperspectral Feature Extraction

Asma Fejjari[1]($\boxtimes$), Karim Saheb Ettabaa[2], and Ouajdi Korbaa[1]

[1] MARS (Modeling of Automated Reasoning Systems) Research Laboratory. ISITCom, University of Sousse, Sousse, Tunisia
asmafejjari@gmail.com,
Ouajdi.Korbaa@centraliens-lille.org
[2] IMT Atlantique, Iti Department, Telecom Bretagne, Brest, France
karim.sahebettabaa@riadi.rnu.tn

Abstract. Since the Laplacian Eigenmaps (LE) algorithm suffers from a spectral uncertainty problem for the adjacency weighted matrix construction, it may not be adequate for the hyperspectral dimension reduction (DR), classification or detection process. Moreover, only local neighboring data point's properties are conserved in the LE method. To resolve these limitations, an improved feature extraction technique called modified Laplacian Eigenmaps (MLE) for hyperspectral images is suggested in this paper. The proposed approach determines the similarity between pixel and endmember for the purpose of building a more precise weighted matrix. Then, based on the obtained weighted matrix, the DR data are derived as the Laplacian eigenvectors of the Laplacian matrix, constructed from the weighted matrix. Furthermore, the novel proposed approach focuses on maximizing the distance between no nearby neighboring points, which raises the separability among ground objects. Compared to the original LE method, experiment results, for hyperspectral images classification and detection tasks, have proved an enhanced accuracy.

Keywords: Laplacian eigenmaps · Hyperspectral dimension reduction
Endmember extraction · Hyperspectral images

1 Introduction

Hyperspectral images (HSI) [1], picked up from remote sensing airborne satellites, provide a very detailed information about the collected scenes; which results a various level of challenge during data processing. Practically, dimension reduction is a fundamental issue of the HSI high dimension problem. While keeping the important data properties, the dimension reduction concept is aimed to get a set of points $Y = \{y_1, y_2, \ldots, y_l\}$ in R^d, from the original data set $X = \{x_1, x_2, \ldots, x_l\} \in R^n$ where $d \ll n$. Therefore, a great set of dimension reduction techniques has been proposed in the last decade. These techniques can be categorized into two main branches: global methods, such like Isometric Mapping (ISOMAP) and Diffusion Maps (DM), and local methods as Locally Linear Embedding (LLE) and Laplacian Eigenmaps (LE) [2, 3].

© Springer Nature Switzerland AG 2018
T. Czachórski et al. (Eds.): ISCIS 2018, CCIS 935, pp. 87–95, 2018.
https://doi.org/10.1007/978-3-030-00840-6_10

The global approaches seek to keep the global data properties, while local approaches aim to preserve the local criteria of the manifold.

In this paper, our main focus is to improve the existing Laplacian Eigenmaps (LE) technique [3]. In fact, LE is a local dimension reduction method where the original data is constructed from a graph. The construction of the low dimensional space is achieved by minimizing the distance between data points and its neighbors. Consequently, the choice of the distance metric, used during adjacency graph construction, is an essential element due to its direct impact on the performance of dimensionality reduction. Euclidean distance, employed by the original LE algorithm, is susceptible to variations in the spectrum magnitudes, which can be generated by different factors such as illuminations, atmospheric changes, and sensor noise [11]. Subsequently, the selection of the neighbor pixels based on the Euclidean distance generates errors during the adjacency graph construction.

In this paper, we propose spectral angle based LE method that uses the similarity between pixels and endmembers [10] instead of the Euclidian distance, measures the similarity between two pixels. Additionally, this attempt serves to increase the separability between the different classes of the scene by maximizing the distance between non-nearest neighboring points.

The rest of this paper is organized as follows: The next section presents the LE algorithm, followed by a detailed description of the MLE method. Section 4 describes the experiment process and results followed by conclusions and future works.

2 Laplacian Eigenmaps (LE)

LE [3] is a well-known local feature extraction technique which is based on the spectral graph theory. Using Laplacian graph concept, the LE technique builds a dataset neighborhood graph and computes a transformation matrix that maps data points to the low dimension subspace. The LE algorithm includes three main steps:

1. Constructing a weighted graph G: G is built by looking for the k nearest neighbors of each point, using the Euclidian distance metric.
2. Defining the weighted matrix: Based on the graph G, weights may be computed as follows:

$$\omega_{ij} = \begin{cases} e^{-\frac{||x_i - x_j||^2}{\sigma}}, & \text{if } i \text{ and } j \text{ are connected} \\ 0, & \text{otherwise} \end{cases} \tag{1}$$

σ is a defined spectral scale parameter.
3. Deriving the Laplacian eigenvalues and eigenvectors: LE tends to preserve the local data properties, in the low-dimensional subspace, by optimizing the following objective function:

$$\arg\min \sum_{ij} ||\mathbf{y}_i - \mathbf{y}_j||^2 \omega_{ij} \tag{2}$$

Eigenvalues and eigenvectors, describing the dimension reduction data, can be obtained from the following generalized eigenvector problem:

$$\mathbf{YL} = \lambda \mathbf{YD} \tag{3}$$

D is a diagonal weighted matrix where $D_{i,i} = \sum_j \omega_{i,j}$, $\mathbf{L} = \mathbf{D} - \boldsymbol{\omega}$ represents the Laplacian matrix and λ accords to the d-smallest nonzero eigenvalues of (3).

3 Proposed Approach

The LE algorithm attempts to minimize the distance between data points and its neighbors, adopting the Euclidian distance. However, for hyperspectral images, LE often fails. This is caused by changes in spectrum magnitudes, particularly for a data points from small size classes [11]. To address this issue, we proposed a new approach, called modified LE (MLE), to construct an adjacency graph in which, for a given data point $\mathbf{x}_i$, its nearest neighbors appertained to the same ground object of $\mathbf{x}_i$ while others do not. In the MLE, a spectral-based distance, derived from the similarity between pixel and endmember [10], is used to define the neighbors of each data point. Furthermore, the proposed MLE interested more in widening the distances among the non-closest neighbors. The MLE algorithm can be summarized as follows:

1. Extract endmember spectra from hyperspectral image using the vertex component analysis (VCA) method [8]; then, based on the spectral angle distance, the similarity between pixel spectra and the endmember spectra can be computed. Extracted endmembers can be represented as a matrix $M = (\mathbf{m}_1, \mathbf{m}_2, \ldots, \mathbf{m}_E)$, where $\mathbf{m}_i (i = 1, 2, \ldots, E)$ is a $n \times 1$ vector that represents the ith endmember, n is the spectral bands' number and E is the endmembers' number.
2. Build the adjacency graph: Adopting the spectral angle distance metric can more indeed reduce the error produced by the spectral amplitude variations. The spectral angle distance, between each pixel and endmember, can be computed as bellow:

$$D_j^i = d(\mathbf{m}_i, \mathbf{x}_j) = arc \cos \left[\sum_{k=1}^{n} \frac{m_{ik} - x_{jk}}{\left(\sum_{k=1}^{n} m_{ik}^2\right)^{1/2} \left(\sum_{k=1}^{n} x_{jk}^2\right)^{1/2}} \right] \tag{4}$$

The k nearest neighbors of each pixel can be selected, referred to (5):

$$d'(x_i, x_j) = \sum_k \left| \left(\frac{D_i^k - D_{min}^k}{D_{max}^k - D_{min}^k} \right) - \left(\frac{D_j^k - D_{min}^k}{D_{max}^k - D_{min}^k} \right) \right| \tag{5}$$

Hence, we can construct an adjacency graph G' and calculate the adjacency weighted matrix ω' based on (6) and (7).

$$G'_{ij} = \begin{cases} 1 & , \quad \text{if } x_i \text{ and } x_j \text{ are nearest neighbors} \\ 0 & , \quad \text{otherwise} \end{cases} \tag{6}$$

$$\omega'_{ij} = \begin{cases} e^{-d'(\mathbf{x}_i, \mathbf{x}_j)\sigma^2}, & \text{if } \mathbf{x}_j \in N(\mathbf{x}_i) \\ 0 &, \quad \text{otherwise} \end{cases} \tag{7}$$

While D^i_j represents the spectral angle distance between the jth pixel and i^{th} endmember, D^k_{min} and D^k_{max} show the minimum and maximum distances between all pixels and the kth endmember, respectively, and $N(\mathbf{x}_i)$ determines the k nearest neighbor set of $(\mathbf{x}_i)$.

3. Solve the optimization problem: The novel Laplacian Eigenmaps (MLE) technique tends to project data point from the original space to the low-dimensional space in such a way that, the distances between nearest neighbors is reserved, i.e., local properties and the distances between non-neighboring points is maximized. This is reflected to optimize the following objective function:

$$\arg \max \sum_{ij} ||\mathbf{y}_i - \mathbf{y}_j||^2 \omega'_{ij} \tag{8}$$

Maximum eigenvalues and eigenvectors are calculated from the next eigendecomposition problem:

$$\mathbf{YL}' = \lambda \mathbf{YD}' \tag{9}$$

$\mathbf{D}'$ represents the diagonal weighted matrix, defined by $D'_{ii} = \sum_j \omega'_{ij}$, $\mathbf{L}' = \mathbf{D}' - \omega'$ corresponds to the Laplacian matrix and $\{\lambda_i\}^d_{i=1}$ conforms to the d-smallest eigenvalues of (9).

4   Experiment Process and Results

This section is dedicated to examine the suggested method efficiency. The modified LE approach was assessed during hyperspectral images classification and detection tasks; then compared according to the original LE accuracy results. The architecture of the suggested technique is shown in Fig. 1.

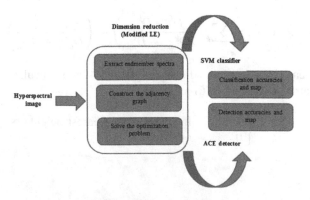

Fig. 1. The flowchart of the proposed approach.

4.1   Classification Tasks

For the classification tasks, the Indian Pines hyperspectral data set, collected in the north of Indiana (United States of America) in 1992 by the Airborne Visible/Infrared Imaging Spectrometer (AVIRIS) sensor system, was adopted. The used scene covers 204 spectral bands of size 145 × 145 pixels, in the spectral range 0.4–2.5 μm; it includes 16 classes as shown in Fig. 2. The Indian Pines image and its reference map were downloaded from [4]. As the SVM (Support Vector Machine) classifier [5] was performed to classify test data set, only 10% of each class pixels, picked randomly, were implemented as the input training samples. Each classification script was iterated ten times and the mean of the classification accuracies was used to judge classification performance. Overall accuracy (OA), average accuracy (AA) and kappa coefficient [9] were used to assess the proposed technique yield. We took $k = 20, n = 20$ and $\sigma = 1$ for the LE technique and the proposed feature extraction method. Table 1 summarizes classification results of the proposed MLE and the original LE technique, and Fig. 3 gives their classification maps. The best overall accuracy (OA) was obtained from the MLE approach as it provided 79,60%, while the kappa coefficient was 77,20%. The OA of original LE was 68,92% and the kappa coefficient was 65,17%. The proposed technique is characterized by its capability of improving the classification accuracies of the original LE technique by about 11% of overall accuracy. To more understand the novel suggested approach, we selected samples from the four first classes, C1, C2, C3 and C4. Figure 4 represents spectral curves of the four exploited classes, in which each spectrum represents one ground object. We selected 100 samples for each class and the reduced dimensionality of the MLE was two bands (band 21 and 50).

Figure 5 displays the projected data obtained by LE and the proposed approach. The results obtained by LE showed that this method is incapable of preserving the global structure of data properties. In fact, LE has a weak effect in terms of classes' separation; i.e. not all of the nearest neighbors come from the same ground object. The proposed MLE algorithm can separate widely the four selected classes.

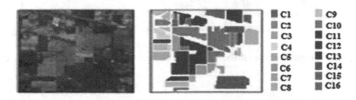

Fig. 2. Pseudo-color image, ground truth map and labels of the used hyperspectral scene.

(a)   (b)

Fig. 3. Classification maps obtained by (a) the original LE and (b) the proposed approach.

Table 1. Classification results obtained by the LE and the MLE techniques.

Classes	No. of samples	LE	MLE
C1	46	99,98	99,99
C2	1428	89,00	93,51
C3	830	94,03	95,49
C4	237	98,44	99,25
C5	483	98,83	99,47
C6	730	96,48	97,92
C7	28	99,92	99,89
C8	478	99,21	99,92
C9	20	99,48	99,79
C10	972	95,27	96,89
C11	2455	84,09	92,27
C12	593	94,82	96,40
C13	205	99,38	99,54
C14	1265	96,28	99,14
C15	386	96,39	99,14
C16	93	99,89	99,89
OA (%)		68,92	79,60
AA (%)		96,37	97,95
Kappa (%)		65,17	77,20

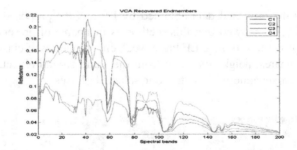

Fig. 4. Spectral curves of the first four classes in the Indian Pines data set.

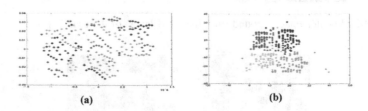

(a)   (b)

Fig. 5. Projected data produced by (a) LE and (b) MLE.

4.2 Detection Tasks

Urban-1 hyperspectral scene, selected from the Airport-Beach-Urban (ABU) hyperspectral data set, was used for target detection tasks. The adopted image contains 204 bands, each band is of size 100 × 100 pixels and a spatial resolution of 17,2 m per pixel. The Urban-1 scene, captured in Texas Coast in August of 2010, was collected by the AVIRIS sensor system and downloaded from [6]. Figure 6 shows the Urban-1 image and its detection map. The Adaptive Cosine/Coherence Estimator (ACE) detector [7] and the Receiver Operating Characteristic (ROC) curve metric were adopted to evaluate the qualitative results. The ROC curve is computed from probability of detection (PD) versus false alarm rate (FAR), at different values of threshold. Experimentally, $k = 200, n = 15$ and $\sigma = 1$, were chosen as optimal parameters for the MLE technique. The threshold was fixed from 0 to 255, and the ROC curves of LE and MLE techniques are presented in Fig. 7. When the false alarm rate varies from 0 to 1, the proposed method permits higher detection accuracy. In comparison with the original LE method, the proposed technique enhanced the true positive detection rate. The detection maps of the original LE and the suggested approach are shown in Fig. 8. By visualizing the two maps, we find that our proposed approach tends to be less attracted by false detection. Moreover, the MLE can detect the target objects clearly, especially the small ones.

Fig. 6. Color composites of the Urban-1 hyperspectral scene and its detection map.

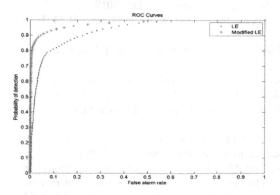

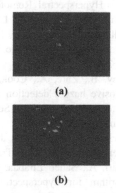

Fig. 7. ROC curves of LE and modified LE methods.

Fig. 8. Detection maps of (a) LE and (b) MLE techniques.

5   Conclusions and Future Works

This study is aimed to resolve the spectral uncertainty problem for the adjacency weighted matrix construction, for the Laplacian Eigenmaps (LE) approach. In this light, we proposed a modified version of LE, titled modified LE, for hyperspectral image classification and target detection. In a different way to the original LE, a spectral based distance derives from the similarity between pixel and endmember is used to define the neighbors of each data point. Besides to preserving local properties, the proposed approach tends to keep the global structure of original data. Experiments, during classification and detection tasks, demonstrated that MLE is characterized by a superior outstanding capacity compared to the original LE. In addition to spectral elements, spatial components are paramount to improve the MLE yield, which is seen very encouraging for future works.

Acknowledgment. This work was supported and financed by the Ministry of Higher Education and Scientific Research of Tunisia.

References

1. Camps-Valls, G., Tuia, D., Bruzzone, L., Benediktsson, J.A.: Advances in hyperspectral image classification: earth monitoring with statistical learning methods. IEEE Signal Process. Mag. **31**(1), 45–54 (2014)
2. Khodr, J., Younes, R.: Dimensionality reduction on hyperspectral images: a comparative review based on artificial datas. In: 2011 4th International Congress on Image and Signal Processing, pp. 1875–1883. IEEE, Shanghai, China (2011)
3. Hou, B., Zhang, X., Ye, Q., Zheng, Y.: A novel method for hyperspectral image classification based on laplacian eigenmap pixels distribution-flow. IEEE J. Sel. Top. Appl. Earth Obs. Remote Sens. **6**(3), 1602–1618 (2013)
4. Computational Intelligence search group site. http://www.ehu.eus/ccwintco/index.php?title = Hyperspectral_Remote_Sensing_Scenes. Last accessed 05 Dec 2017
5. Chang, C.-C., Lin, C.-J.: LIBSVM: a library for support vector machines. ACM Trans. Intell. Syst. Technol. **2**(3), 1–27 (2011)
6. Xudong Kang's home page. http://xudongkang.weebly.com/data-sets.html. Last accessed 24 Dec 2017
7. Alvey, B., Zare, A., Cook, M., Ho, D.K.C.: Adaptive coherence estimator (ACE) for explosive hazard detection using wideband electromagnetic induction (WEMI). In: SPIE Conference Detection and Sensing of Mines, Explosive Objects, and Obscured Targets XXI, Baltimore (2016)
8. Nascimento, J.M.P., Dias, J.M.B.: Vertex component analysis: a fast algorithm to unmix hyperspectral data. IEEE Trans. Geosci. Remote Sens. **43**(4), 898–910 (2005)
9. Fejjari, A., Saheb Ettabaa, K., Korbaa, O.: Modified schroedinger eigenmap projections algorithm for hyperspectral imagery classification. In: IEEE/ACS 14th International Conference on Computer Systems and Applications (AICCSA), pp. 809–814. IEEE, Hamammet, Tunisia (2017)

10. Wang, Y., Huang, S., Liu, Z., Wang, H., Liu, D.: Locality preserving projection based on endmember extraction for hyperspectral image dimensionality reduction and target detection. Appl. Spectrosc. **70**(9), 1573–1581 (2016)
11. Yan, L., Niu, X.: Spectral-angle-based laplacian eigenmaps for nonlinear dimensionality reduction of hyperspectral imagery. Photogramm. Eng. Remote Sens. **80**(9), 849–861 (2014)

The Competitiveness of Randomized Strategies for Canadians via Systems of Linear Inequalities

Pierre Bergé[1]($^{\boxtimes}$), Julien Hemery[2], Arpad Rimmel[2], and Joanna Tomasik[2]

[1] LRI, Université Paris-Sud, Université Paris-Saclay, Orsay, France
`Pierre.Berge@lri.fr`
[2] LRI, CentraleSupélec, Université Paris-Saclay, Orsay, France
`Julien.Hemery@supelec.fr`, `{Arpad.Rimmel,Joanna.Tomasik}@lri.fr`

Abstract. The Canadian Traveller Problem is a PSPACE-complete optimization problem where a traveller traverses an undirected weighted graph G from source s to target t where some edges E_* are blocked. At the beginning, the traveller does not know which edges are blocked. He discovers them when arriving at one of their endpoints. The objective is to minimize the distance traversed to reach t.

Westphal proved that no randomized strategy has a competitive ratio smaller than $|E_*|+1$. We show, using linear algebra techniques, that this bound cannot be attained, especially on a specific class of graphs: apex trees. Indeed, no randomized strategy can be $(|E_*|+1)$-competitive, even on apex trees with only three simple (s, t)-paths.

1 Introduction

The *Canadian Traveller Problem* (CTP) generalizes the *Shortest Path Problem* [8]. Given an undirected weighted graph $G = (V, E, \omega)$ and two nodes $s, t \in V$, the objective is to design a strategy which makes a traveller walk from s to t through G on the shortest path possible. However, edges in set $E_* \neq \emptyset$, $E_* \subset E$, are blocked. The traveller does not know which edges are blocked when starting his walk. He discovers a blocked edge, also called blockage, when arriving at one of its endpoints. We work on feasible instances: blocked edges E_* never disconnect s and t in G, so the traveller is ensured to reach t with a finite distance. The CTP has been proven PSPACE-complete [1,8]. This result is due to uncertainty over blockages. Solutions to the CTP are online algorithms, commonly called strategies. In one of its variants, the *k-Canadian Traveller Problem* (*k*-CTP), $1 \leq |E_*| \leq k$ for a positive integer k.

State-of-the-Art. The competitive ratio of a strategy, which evaluates its quality, is the maximum of the ratio of the distance traversed by the traveller following the strategy and the *optimal offline cost* [4]. The optimal offline cost designates the distance the traveller would traverse if he knew blocked edges from the beginning. It can also be seen as the cost of the shortest path in graph $G \backslash E_*$ which is graph G deprived of blocked edges E_*.

© Springer Nature Switzerland AG 2018
T. Czachórski et al. (Eds.): ISCIS 2018, CCIS 935, pp. 96–103, 2018.
https://doi.org/10.1007/978-3-030-00840-6_11

There are two classes of strategies: deterministic and randomized. West-phal [9] proved for the k-CTP that no deterministic strategy achieves a competitive ratio better than $2k + 1$. This ratio is obtained by considering graphs made of $k + 1$ simple node-disjoint (s, t)-paths of similar cost, and where k of them are blocked. In such an instance, the traveller potentially traverses the open path last, which produces the ratio $2k + 1$. In fact, as these instances verify $|E_*| = k$, this also proves that no deterministic strategy drops below competitive ratio $2|E_*| + 1$ for CTP. The REPOSITION strategy [9], which repeats an attempt to reach t through the shortest (s, t)-path and goes back to s after the discovery of a blockage attains this ratio and is optimal.

The competitiveness of the randomized strategies is evaluated as the maximal ratio of the mean distance traversed by the traveller following the strategy and the optimal offline cost. Westphal [9] proved that no randomized algorithm can attain a ratio smaller than $k + 1$ for k-CTP. As the proof consists in studying the same instance as in the deterministic case, it implies that any randomized strategy is at best $(|E_*| + 1)$-competitive for CTP. However, the identification of an $(|E_*| + 1)$-competitive randomized strategy for CTP (and a $k + 1$-competitive randomized strategy for k-CTP) has not been achieved yet. The randomized strategies proposed in the literature [2,5] are dedicated to two particular cases, so no conclusion on their competitiveness in general can be raised. Table 1 summarizes the state-of-the-art of CTP and k-CTP and formulates two open questions.

Table 1. State-of-the-art [2,9] and open questions for the CTP and k-CTP

	Deterministic strategies	
	CTP	k-CTP
Result	REPOSITION strategy is optimal and $(2(|E_*|) + 1)$-competitive	REPOSITION strategy is optimal and $(2k + 1)$-competitive
	Randomized strategies	
	CTP	k-CTP
Result	Any randomized strategy A is c_A-competitive with $c_A \geq |E_*| + 1$	Any randomized strategy A is c_A-competitive with $c_A \geq k + 1$
Open question	Can we find a strategy which is $(|E_*| + 1)$-competitive?	Can we find a strategy which is $(k + 1)$-competitive?

Contributions and Paper Organization. In Sect. 2, we introduce the notation and give the definition of the CTP and the competitive ratio. In Sect. 3, we put in place ε-apex trees which are a subfamily of apex trees, already evoked in [5]. We explain why the optimal randomized strategy over these instances consists in a randomized variant of the REPOSITION strategy. This restrains the study of randomized strategies over ε-apex trees to the randomized REPOSITION strategy, where the distribution used to select paths needs to be defined.

In Sect. 4, we determine the competitiveness of randomized strategies over a set $\mathscr{R}$ of road maps (G_α, E_*) containing an ε-apex tree G_α we designed. Farkas' lemma [6] enables to prove that the competitive ratio of any strategy cannot be smaller or equal to $|E_*| + 1$ on all road maps of set $\mathscr{R}$. Finally, no randomized strategy can drop below ratio $|E_*|+1$, even on ε-apex trees with only three simple paths (as graph G_α). This gives an answer to the open question on the CTP in Table 1. In Sect. 5, we conclude by presenting directions for future research.

2   Preliminaries

The traveller traverses an undirected weighted graph $G = (V, E, \omega)$, $n = |V|$ and $m = |E|$. He starts his walk at source $s \in V$. His objective is to reach target $t \in V$ with a minimum cost (also called distance), which is the sum of the weights of edges traversed. Set E_* contains blocked edges, which means that when the traveller reaches an endpoint of one of these edges, he discovers that he cannot pass through it. A pair (G, E_*) is called a *road map*. From now on, we focus on feasible road maps (G, E_*), *i.e.* s and t are always connected in graph $G \backslash E_*$. We study the competitiveness of randomized strategies for the CTP, in other words $|E_*|$ is unbounded.

We remind the definition of the competitive ratio introduced in [4]. Let $\omega_A (G, E_*)$ be the distance traversed by the traveller from s to t guided by a given strategy A on graph G with blocked edges E_*. The shortest (s, t)-path in $G \backslash E_*$ is called the *optimal offline path* of map (G, E_*) and its cost, noted $\omega_{\min} (G, E_*)$, is the optimal offline cost of map (G, E_*). Strategy A is c_A-competitive if, for any road map (G, E_*):

$$\omega_A (G, E_*) \le c_A \omega_{\min} (G, E_*) + \eta,$$

where η is constant. For randomized strategies: $\mathbb{E}\left[\omega_A (G, E_*)\right] \le c_A \omega_{\min} (G, E_*) + \eta$.

Eventually, we recall the description of REPOSITION, as we work on its randomized variants. REPOSITION is the optimal deterministic strategy from the competitive analysis point of view because its competitive ratio is $2|E_*| + 1$. Starting at source s, the traveller computes the shortest (s, t)-path in G and traverses it. If he is blocked on this path, he returns to s and restarts the process over graph G deprived of discovered blocked edges as many times as necessary until reaching t. REPOSITION can be randomized by the use of a certain probability distribution to select an (s, t)-path to be traversed. Bender *et al.* [2] built a randomized REPOSITION which is $(k + 1)$-competitive over graphs made up uniquely of node-disjoint (s, t)-paths.

3   Randomized Strategies for Apex Trees

Recent works studied the competitiveness of randomized strategies over apex trees [3,5]. An apex tree is a graph composed of a tree rooted in t and node-disjoint paths that connect s to nodes of the tree. As optimal strategies have been established for graphs with exclusively node-disjoint (s,t)-paths[2,9], the question of the competitiveness of randomized strategies over apex trees, which represent a more general family of graphs, is of interest. Demaine *et al.* [5] proved that for apex trees in which all simple (s,t)-paths have the same cost, there is an $(|E_*|+1)$-competitive randomized strategy. The open question is whether such a strategy exists for apex trees with arbitrary costs. A weaker but also significant result consists in finding a randomized strategy with competitive ratio $k+1$ for the k-CTP targeting apex trees.

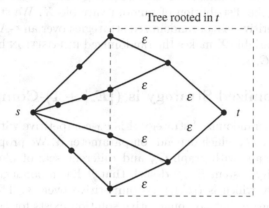

Fig. 1. An example of ε-AT with four simple (s,t)-paths

We specify a subfamily of apex trees called ε-apex trees (ε-ATs). An ε-AT is composed of a tree rooted in t whose all edges are of weight ε. Starting point s is connected to leaves of this tree with node-disjoint paths of arbitrary cost (Fig. 1). We suppose that the traveller traverses an ε-AT G with blocked edges in E_* which all belong to the tree rooted in t (their weight is thus ε). Let $\mathscr{P}$ be the set of simple (s,t)-paths of G. There is a bijective relation between paths in $\mathscr{P}$ and the leaves of the tree: for any leaf of the tree, there is exactly one simple (s,t)-path passing through it. We call the *memory* of the traveller the ordered set:

$$\mathscr{M} = \{(e_a^*, Q_a), (e_b^*, Q_b), \ldots, (e_z^*, Q_z)\},$$

which indicates the blocked edges that the traveller discovered successively (e_a^* then e_b^*, etc.) and the simple (s,t)-path he was traversing at these moments (he was traversing Q_a when he discovered blockage e_a^*). The most competitive manner to traverse an ε-AT is to follow the randomized REPOSITION strategy guided by the distribution of the adequate discrete random variable X which, given the traveller memory $\mathscr{M}$, assigns a probability to remaining open paths in $\mathscr{P}$. In short:

1. Draw an open (s,t)-path $Q \in \mathscr{P}$ according to the distribution of X.
2. If the traveller discovers at node v of Q a blocked edge e^*, append pair (e^*, Q) to memory $\mathscr{M}$, go back to s on the shortest (v,s)-path and restart the process, otherwise terminate.

Indeed, the traveller has no alternative because of the structure of an ε-AT: each time the traveller meets a blockage, the only manner to reach t with minimum distance is to make a detour via node s. For this reason, the randomized REPOSITION strategy is the best for ε-ATs.

Consequently, the optimal randomized strategy over ε-ATs is determined by the optimality of the distribution of random variable X. We study in the next section the competitiveness of randomized strategies over an ε-AT G_α. We prove that no random variable X makes the randomized REPOSITION have competitive ratio $|E_*| + 1$ on G_α.

4   No Randomized Strategy is $(|E_*| + 1)$-Competitive

We prove that any randomized strategy A is c_A-competitive with $c_A > |E_*| + 1$. We design an ε-AT G_α which depends on parameter α. We propose a road atlas $\mathscr{R}$ composed of maps with graph G_α and different sets of blocked edges. We build the inequality system $B\mathbf{x} \le \mathbf{d}$ such that it has a nonnegative solution iff there is a strategy which is $(|E_*| + 1)$-competitive over $\mathscr{R}$. Thanks to Farkas' lemma [6,7], we prove that no nonnegative solution exists for this system.

Proposition 1 (Farkas' lemma, Proposition 6.4.3 in [7]).
   Let $B \in \mathbb{R}^{m \times l}$ be a matrix and $\mathbf{d} \in \mathbb{R}^m$ be a vector. The system $B\mathbf{x} \le \mathbf{d}$ has a nonnegative solution iff every nonnegative vector $\mathbf{y} \in \mathbb{R}^m$ with $\mathbf{y}^T B \ge \mathbf{0}^T$ also satisfies $\mathbf{y}^T \mathbf{d} \ge 0$.

Keeping this lemma in mind, we build a system of linear inequalities such that if there is a nonnegative $\mathbf{y} \in \mathbb{R}^m$ satisfying $\mathbf{y}^T B \ge 0$ and $\mathbf{y}^T \mathbf{d} < 0$, then there is no nonnegative vector $\mathbf{x}$ such that $B\mathbf{x} \le \mathbf{d}$.

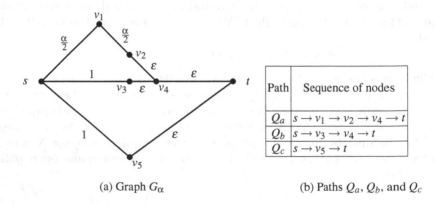

Path	Sequence of nodes
Q_a	$s \to v_1 \to v_2 \to v_4 \to t$
Q_b	$s \to v_3 \to v_4 \to t$
Q_c	$s \to v_5 \to t$

(a) Graph G_α (b) Paths Q_a, Q_b, and Q_c

Fig. 2. Graph G_α and its three simple paths Q_a, Q_b, and Q_c

Theorem 1. *There is no randomized strategy with competitive ratio* $|E_*|+1$ *on* ε-*ATs even with three simple* (s,t)-*paths.*

Proof. We start by introducing in Fig. 2 graph G_α which is an ε-AT composed of three simple (s,t)-paths, noted Q_a, Q_b, and Q_c. We focus on a road atlas $\mathcal{R}$ made for G_α composed of all feasible road maps, where only edges with weight $\varepsilon \ll 1$ can be blocked. First, we put two road maps into set $\mathcal{R}$, each one containing one blocked edge which is either (v_4,t) or (v_5,t).

$$\{(G_\alpha, E_*) : |E_*| = 1, E_* \subset \{((v_4,t),(v_5,t)\}\} \subset \mathcal{R},$$

Second, we put three road maps into $\mathcal{R}$, where two blocked edges are taken among (v_2,v_4), (v_3,v_4), and (v_5,t):

$$\{(G_\alpha, E_*) : |E_*| = 2, E_* \subset \{(v_2,v_4),(v_3,v_4),(v_5,t)\}\} \subset \mathcal{R}.$$

In the remainder of the proof, we neglect $\varepsilon \ll 1$ involved in calculations (weights in a CTP instance must be positive, this is why ε replaces zero). We make parameter α be in the interval $\left[\sqrt{2}, \frac{3}{2}\right[$.

Let A be a randomized REPOSITION strategy. We note p_a, p_b, and p_c the probabilities for the traveller to choose path Q_a, Q_b, and Q_c at the departure from s with strategy A, respectively. They obviously fulfil $p_a + p_b + p_c = 1$. Let $p(Q_b|(v_2,v_4),Q_a)$ be the probability to select path Q_b after discovering blockage (v_2,v_4) on path Q_a. In other words, set $\{(v_2,v_4),Q_a\}$ is the memory of the traveller. We define similarly probabilities $p(Q_c|(v_2,v_4),Q_a)$, $p(Q_a|(v_3,v_4),Q_b)$, $p(Q_c|(v_3,v_4),Q_b)$, $p(Q_a|(v_5,t),Q_c)$, and $p(Q_b|(v_5,t),Q_c)$. The sum of probabilities with the same condition is equal to 1, for example: $p(Q_b|(v_2,v_4),Q_a) + p(Q_c|(v_2,v_4),Q_a) = 1$.

In Table 2, we define six variables $x_{\cdot,\cdot}$ resulting from the conditional probabilities presented above, arranged in a vector $\mathbf{x}_A = [x_{a,b}\ x_{a,c}\ x_{b,a}\ x_{b,c}\ x_{c,a}\ x_{c,b}]^T$.

Table 2. Definition of coordinates of $\mathbf{x}_A$

Variable	Definition
$x_{a,b}$	$p(Q_b|(v_2,v_4),Q_a)\,p_a$
$x_{a,c}$	$p(Q_c|(v_2,v_4),Q_a)\,p_a$
$x_{b,a}$	$p(Q_a|(v_3,v_4),Q_b)\,p_b$
$x_{b,c}$	$p(Q_c|(v_3,v_4),Q_b)\,p_b$
$x_{c,a}$	$p(Q_a|(v_5,t),Q_c)\,p_c$
$x_{c,b}$	$p(Q_b|(v_5,t),Q_c)\,p_c$

We suppose that the competitive ratio of strategy A is $|E_*|+1$ and produce the consequence of this assumption for each road map from $\mathcal{R}$. For road map $(G_\alpha, \{(v_2,v_4),(v_3,v_4)\})$, the optimal offline path is Q_a with cost α. If the traveller chooses Q_a (he does this with the probability $x_{a,b} + x_{a,c}$), he reaches t without discovering any blockage so the competitive ratio is 1. If he first chooses path Q_b or Q_c and then Q_a (probability $x_{b,a} + x_{c,a}$), the competitive ratio is $\frac{2+\alpha}{\alpha}$. If the traveller traverses path Q_a after trying both Q_b, and Q_c (probability $x_{b,c} + x_{c,b}$), the competitive ratio is $\frac{4+\alpha}{\alpha}$. Vector $\mathbf{x}_A$ thus fulfils:

$$(x_{a,b} + x_{a,c}) + (x_{b,a} + x_{c,a})\frac{2+\alpha}{\alpha} + (x_{b,c} + x_{c,b})\frac{4+\alpha}{\alpha} \le 3.$$

Similar linear inequalities can be written for all other road maps in $\mathscr{R}$ and vector $\mathbf{x}_A$ is a solution of an inequality system $B'\mathbf{x} \le \mathbf{d}'$, with $\mathbf{x} \ge \mathbf{0}$:

$$\begin{bmatrix} 1 & 1 & \frac{2+\alpha}{\alpha} & \frac{4+\alpha}{\alpha} & \frac{2+\alpha}{\alpha} & \frac{4+\alpha}{\alpha} \\ 2\alpha+1 & 2\alpha+3 & 1 & 1 & 2\alpha+3 & 3 \\ 2\alpha+3 & 2\alpha+1 & 2\alpha+3 & 3 & 1 & 1 \\ \alpha+2 & \alpha+2 & 3 & 3 & 1 & 1 \\ \alpha & \alpha & 1 & 1 & 2+\alpha & 3 \end{bmatrix} \begin{bmatrix} x_{a,b} \\ x_{a,c} \\ x_{b,a} \\ x_{b,c} \\ x_{c,a} \\ x_{c,b} \end{bmatrix} \le \begin{bmatrix} 3 \\ 3 \\ 3 \\ 2 \\ 2 \end{bmatrix}.$$

Then, we write this system of inequalities in the canonical form and eliminate one redundant variable: we take $x_{c,b} = 1 - \sum_{i,j \ne c,b} x_{i,j}$. However, we must preserve the condition $x_{c,b} \ge 0$ which is equivalent to $\sum_{i,j \ne c,b} x_{i,j} \le 1$. Finally, as strategy A is $(|E_*| + 1)$-competitive on road atlas $\mathscr{R}$, vector $\mathbf{x}_A^c = [x_{a,b}\ x_{a,c}\ x_{b,a}\ x_{b,c}\ x_{c,a}]^T$ is a solution of the canonical system $B\mathbf{x} \le \mathbf{d}$, $\mathbf{x} \ge \mathbf{0}$ (with $B \in \mathbb{R}^{6\times 5}$, $\mathbf{d} \in \mathbb{R}^6$):

$$\begin{bmatrix} -\frac{4}{\alpha} & -\frac{4}{\alpha} & -\frac{2}{\alpha} & 0 & -\frac{2}{\alpha} \\ 2(\alpha-1) & 2\alpha & -2 & -2 & 2\alpha \\ 2(\alpha+1) & 2\alpha & 2(\alpha+1) & 2 & 0 \\ \alpha+1 & \alpha+1 & 2 & 2 & 0 \\ \alpha-3 & \alpha-3 & -2 & -2 & \alpha-1 \\ 1 & 1 & 1 & 1 & 1 \end{bmatrix} \begin{bmatrix} x_{a,b} \\ x_{a,c} \\ x_{b,a} \\ x_{b,c} \\ x_{c,a} \end{bmatrix} \le \begin{bmatrix} 2-\frac{4}{\alpha} \\ 0 \\ 2 \\ 1 \\ -1 \\ 1 \end{bmatrix}.$$

We define vector $\mathbf{y}$ such that $\mathbf{y}^T = [\alpha(\alpha-1), 0, 0, \alpha+1, 2, F(\alpha,\delta)]$, where $F(\alpha,\delta) = -2\alpha^2 + 5\alpha - 3 - \delta(\alpha-1)$. Polynomial $-2\alpha^2 + 5\alpha - 3$ is positive for any $1 < \alpha < \frac{3}{2}$. We set $\delta > 0$ small enough to guarantee $F(\alpha,\delta) > 0$. Therefore, vector $\mathbf{y}$ is nonnegative. We check that $\mathbf{y}^T B \ge \mathbf{0}^T$. For this purpose, we note as $\mathbf{b}_1, \ldots, \mathbf{b}_5$ the column vectors of matrix B. We have, indeed

$$\begin{cases} \mathbf{y}^T \mathbf{b}_1 = -\frac{4}{\alpha}\alpha(\alpha-1) + (1+\alpha)^2 + 2(\alpha-3) + F(\alpha,\delta) = \alpha^2 - 2 + F(\alpha,\delta) \ge 0 \\ \mathbf{y}^T \mathbf{b}_2 = -\frac{4}{\alpha}\alpha(\alpha-1) + (1+\alpha)^2 + 2(\alpha-3) + F(\alpha,\delta) = \alpha^2 - 2 + F(\alpha,\delta) \ge 0 \\ \mathbf{y}^T \mathbf{b}_3 = -\frac{2}{\alpha}\alpha(\alpha-1) + 2\alpha(1+\alpha) - 4 + F(\alpha,\delta) = F(\alpha,\delta) \ge 0 \\ \mathbf{y}^T \mathbf{b}_4 = 2(1+\alpha) - 4 + F(\alpha,\delta) = 2(\alpha-1) + F(\alpha,\delta) \ge 0 \\ \mathbf{y}^T \mathbf{b}_5 = -\frac{2}{\alpha}\alpha(\alpha-1) + 2(\alpha-1) + F(\alpha,\delta) = F(\alpha,\delta) \ge 0 \end{cases}$$

Eventually, we obtain that $\mathbf{y}^T \mathbf{d} < 0$, as:

$$\mathbf{y}^T \mathbf{d} = \alpha(\alpha - 1)(2 - \tfrac{4}{\alpha}) + 1 + \alpha - 2 + F(\alpha, \delta)$$
$$= 2\alpha^2 - 6\alpha + 4 + 1 + \alpha - 2 - 2\alpha^2 + 5\alpha - 3 - \delta(\alpha - 1) = -\delta(\alpha - 1).$$

Farkas' lemma yields a contradiction: no vector $\mathbf{x}_A$ is a solution of our system $B\mathbf{x} \leq \mathbf{d}$. So, no randomized strategy is $(|E_*| + 1)$-competitive.

5   Conclusion

Apex trees, particularly ε-ATs, represent a family of graphs for which the competitiveness of randomized strategies is a challenging question. We proved, by constructing a system of linear inequalities and applying Farkas' lemma, that even on a very small ε-AT G_α with three simple (s, t)-paths, there is no randomized strategy with competitive ratio $|E_*| + 1$. More generally, this leads to the conclusion that no randomized strategy has a competitive ratio $|E_*| + 1$, which is the lower bound established by Westphal.

Even if we know now that no randomized strategy can be $(|E_*| + 1)$-competitive, the open question for the parameterized variant k-CTP in Table 1 remains unanswered. Our technique seems appropriate to determine whether there is (or not) a $(k + 1)$-competitive strategy over ε-ATs. Future research could also focus on the evolution of the optimal competitive ratio, as function of $|E_*|$, on ε-ATs. Identifying a new lower bound of the competitive ratio, larger than $|E_*| + 1$, would be a significant breakthrough.

References

1. Bar-Noy, A., Schieber, B.: The Canadian Traveller Problem. In: Proceedings of ACM/SIAM SODA, pp. 261–270 (1991)
2. Bender, M., Westphal, S.: An optimal randomized online algorithm for the k-Canadian Traveller Problem on node-disjoint paths. J. Comb. Optim. **30**(1), 87–96 (2015)
3. Bergé, P., Hemery, J., Rimmel, A., Tomasik, J.: On the competitiveness of memoryless strategies for the k-Canadian Traveller Problem. Inform. Proces. Lett. (submitted)
4. Borodin, A., El-Yaniv, R.: Online Computation and Competitive Analysis. Cambridge University Press, New York, USA (1998)
5. Demaine, E.D., Huang, Y., Liao, C.-S., Sadakane, K.: Canadians should travel randomly. In: Proceedings of ICALP, pp. 380–391 (2014)
6. Farkas, J.: Uber die Theorie der Einfachen Ungleichungen. J. fur die Reine und Angewandte Math. **124**, 1–27 (1902)
7. Matousek, J., Gärtner, B.: Understanding and Using Linear Programming. Springer, New York, USA (2006)
8. Papadimitriou, C., Yannakakis, M.: Shortest paths without a map. Theor. Comput. Sci. **84**(1), 127–150 (1991)
9. Westphal, S.: A note on the k-Canadian Traveller Problem. Inform. Proces. Lett. **106**(3), 87–89 (2008)

Modelling and Designing Spatial and Temporal Big Data for Analytics

Sinan Keskin[1](✉) and Adnan Yazıcı[2](✉)

[1] Department of Computer Engineering, Middle East Technical University,
Ankara, Turkey
keskin.sinan@metu.edu.tr
[2] School of Science and Technology, Nazarbayev University,
Astana, Republic of Kazakhstan
adnan.yazici@nu.edu.k2

Abstract. The main purpose of this paper is to introduce a new approach with a new data model and architecture that supports spatial and temporal data analytics for meteorological big data applications. The architecture is designed with the recent advances in the field of spatial data warehousing (SDW) and spatial and temporal big data analytics. Measured meteorological data is stored in a big database (NoSQL database) and analyzed using Hadoop big data environment. SDW provides a structured approach for manipulating, analyzing and visualizing the huge volume of data. Therefore, the main focus of our study is to design a Spatial OLAP-based system to visualize the results of big data analytics for daily measured meteorological data by using the characteristic features of Spatial Online Analytical Processing (SOLAP), SDW, and the big data environment (Apache Hadoop). In this study we use daily collected real meteorological data from various stations distributed over the regions. Thus, we enable to do spatial and temporal data analytics by employing spatial data-mining tasks including spatial classification and prediction, spatial association rule mining, and spatial cluster analysis. Furthermore, a fuzzy logic extension for data analytics is injected to the big data environment.

Keywords: Meteorological big data analytics · DWH · SOLAP
Hadoop

1 Introduction

Data mining is the field of discovering novel and potentially useful information from large amounts of data [1]. Geospatial data mining is a sub-field of data mining that employs specialized techniques for dealing with geospatial data. There are two types of data mining tasks: (a) descriptive data mining tasks that describe the general properties of the existing data and (b) predictive data mining tasks that attempt to do predictions based on inference on available data. Predictive data mining tasks come up with a model from the available data set helpful in predicting unknown or future values of another data set of interest. Descriptive data mining tasks usually finds data describing patterns and comes up with new information or pattern from the available data set.

© Springer Nature Switzerland AG 2018
T. Czachórski et al. (Eds.): ISCIS 2018, CCIS 935, pp. 104–112, 2018.
https://doi.org/10.1007/978-3-030-00840-6_12

In this study, we design a spatial data warehousing (SDW) and do analytics on spatial for temporal big data. Daily measured meteorological data is stored in a NoSQL database and SDW that provides a structured approach for manipulating, analyzing and visualizing the huge volume of data. The Spatial OLAP-based system (SOLAP) is used to visualize the results of big data analytics using the big data environment (Apache Hadoop). The system learns the general features of the given data with descriptive data mining tasks and make predictions for the future with predictive data mining.

We propose a new model by designing SOLAP to visualize the trends for daily measured historical meteorological data. The daily meteorological data of different stations distributed over the regions is used as a case study. Also, recent theoretical and applied research in spatial data mining are studied. We also introduce fuzzy logic extension to our proposed system. Thus, fuzzy spatial temporal querying is supported by the system.

In this paper, the details of the study are described in the following sections, the related work on the topic is discussed in Sect. 2. The composite environment and the components of the architectural structure of the model (the proposed architecture) are briefly discussed in Sect. 3. A case study on the proposed architecture is given with examples in Sect. 4. In Sect. 5, conclusion and future works are given.

2 Related Works

Most of the meteorological data based prediction techniques and methods are based on statistical or widely used data mining techniques like clustering, classification, regression analysis, decision tree etc. Some of the related work is as follows:

Liang et al. [2] derived the sequence of ecological events using temporal association rule mining. Red tide phenomena occurred during 1991 and 1992 in Dapeng bay, South China Sea was taken as an example to validate T-Apriori algorithm which generated frequent itemsets and corresponding temporal association rules and K-means clustering analysis are used to map the quantitative association rule problem into the Boolean association rules.

Huang et al. [3] analyzed historic salinity-temperature data to make predictions about future variations in the ocean salinity and temperature relations in the water surrounding Taiwan. They use inter-dimensional association rules mining with fuzzy inference to discover salinity-temperature patterns with spatial-temporal relationships.

The other authors Kotsiantis et al. [4] proposed a hybrid data mining technique that can be used to predict the mean daily temperature values. Several experiments have been conducted with well-known regression algorithms using temperature data from the city of Patras in Greece. The methods used in their study needs be still validated by including temperature data with other meteorological parameters.

Kohail et al. [5] tried to extract useful knowledge from weather daily historical data collected locally at Gaza Strip city. The data include nine years period [1977–1985]. After data preprocessing, they apply basic algorithms of clustering, classification and association rules mining techniques. For each data mining technique, they present the extracted knowledge and describe its importance in meteorological field, which can be used to obtain useful prediction and support the decision making.

Sivaramakrishnan et al. [6] presented the method for prediction of daily rainfall. Meteorological data from 1961–2010 are used in their analysis. For the atmospheric parameters temperature, dew point, wind speed, visibility and precipitation (rainfall) are considered. They filter and discretize the raw data based on the best fit ranges and applied association mining on dataset using Apriori algorithm to find the hidden relationship between various atmospheric parameters to predict the rainfall.

3 Proposed Architecture

We designed a composite system to provide spatial and temporal data mining and analytics. This system consists of four layers structure. We can define the system from bottom to top as data sources, structured data, logic, and presentation layers. Multi-layer system architecture is represented in Fig. 1.

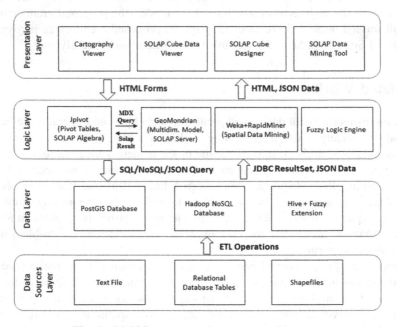

Fig. 1. Multi-layer composite system architecture.

At the bottom of the system we have text files, database tables and shape files that contain the pure data gathered from the meteorology service. Data in this layer is migrated to the structured data layer via Extract Transform and Load (ETL) operations.

Data layer is about semi-structured or structured data like relational database, Hive meta-store or Hadoop file system data nodes. Data in this layer is created by ETL operations. The upper logic layer requests data from data layer by using SQL, HiveQL or JSON request. Data layer returns the requested data via SQL tuples, JDBC result set or JSON response. Data layer also provide fuzzy querying on Hive which supported User Defined Functions to contribute the system.

Logic layer contains integrated systems which provide spatial, non-spatial, temporal and fuzzy data mining tools and function sets. It also contains data analytics and geovisualization platforms that helps visually pattern detection. Another integrated part is reporting tools which provides common reports on data. SOLAP server is another main part of this layer that provides SOLAP data cube operations and MDX querying. Weka [7], RapidMiner [8] and ArcMap [9] tools are integrated for spatial data mining. Fuzzy logic engine is integrated with the system for fuzzy operations such as membership calculation, fuzzy clustering and fuzzy class identification.

At the top of the proposed architecture we have representation layer which provides using all the system categorized and simplified structure. For instance, we can demonstrate the data in map with cartography viewer. The composite system architecture mainly consists of three environments and is explained in following sub sections.

3.1 PostGIS Environment

One part of the system is PostGIS [10] that provides spatial objects for the PostgreSQL database, allowing storage and query of information about location and mapping. ETL operations are handled on the text-based data. Also, we design the spatial hierarchy of the inserted data in database such as stations belongs to cities and cities belongs to regions. In the real data we have only station data that contains latitude and longitude values, but we do not have city and regions information. The city and region information were collected, transformed into polygon form and inserted to database tables. After this operation spatial queries can be done on hierarchical data.

3.2 SOLAP Environment

Designed SOLAP cube contains two hierarchies, one of them is temporal hierarchy and the other one is spatial hierarchy. Temporal hierarchy consists of year-month-day values for each measurement record. Spatial hierarchy is about region-city-station values. In addition to hierarchies we have ten measurements in our spatial OLAP cube as shown in Fig. 2.

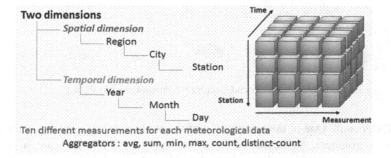

Fig. 2. Dimensions of the spatial OLAP cube.

After SOLAP cube is designed in Workbench [11] which provides SOLAP cube design, it is used as meta-data and feed the cube with data which was inserted in PostGIS database. The region-city-station spatial hierarchy and individual measurement data tables are used in cube definition. After providing SOLAP cube to PostGIS connection, MDX querying can be done and retrieved the SOLAP query result in Mondrian [12] system which is the main SOLAP server. System also provides geovisualization that show the query result in map after the integration of Spatialytics [13] which is a geovisualization tool. This tool also connected with the designed PostGIS database. Flow of the whole system including geovisualization is shown in Fig. 3.

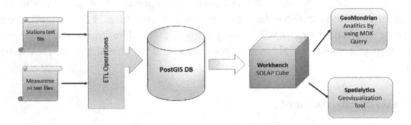

Fig. 3. SOLAP environment.

3.3 Big Data Environment

In big data environment, Apache Hadoop [14], which is an open-source software framework used for distributed storage and processing of dataset of big data is used. Another Apache product Hive [15] is selected to use above the Hadoop. Hive is a data warehouse infrastructure tool to process structured data in Hadoop. It resides on top of Hadoop to summarize Big Data and makes querying and analyzing easy.

The text base data is loaded to Hadoop HDFS by using Hive interface. Hadoop data nodes allocate the data in clusters. After the data is loaded to HDFS, we can do HQL queries on Hive for data analytics. After we load the data, apply analytics queries and fetch the result, we transform the result set into shape file. Created shape file can be load to geovisualization tool as map feature. Visual analyses can be done by importing features in to map. End to end data transformation is represented in Fig. 4.

Fig. 4. End to end data transformation in big data.

Fuzzy Extension. One of the contribution of the study is fuzzy querying extension on big data environment. As mentioned that Hive supports UDFs which provides custom built function for querying. To achieve this, FuzzyValue UDF is implemented and takes column value as parameter and return the fuzzy class name of the value. In this operation firstly, Fuzzy C-Means (FCM) [16, 17] is applied for clustering on whole data and determines the membership values. Each membership value according to their clusters is stored. For example, FCM is applied on temperature values and 3 clusters are determined such as cold, normal and hot. Temperature value 7.2 has membership like 0.1 cold, 0.8 normal and 0.1 hot. When we want to query hot days in a city, we can look up for the data which has hot membership is greater than 0.5. After we execute our fuzzy query, fuzzy spatial query or fuzzy spatial temporal query, we can fetch the result and transform them into shape file then load it to the map to do visual analytics. Fuzzy extension part of the study can be viewed as in Fig. 5.

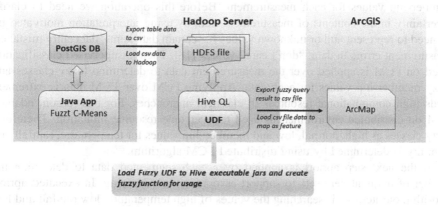

Fig. 5. Fuzzy extension part of study.

4 Case Study: Spatial Data Mining Tasks on Meteorological Big Data

In this section composed system is used with the following spatial data mining tasks that contains unsupervised classification, frequent item set mining, association rule learning and pattern discovery.

In this study, we have text files containing the results of 10 meteorological measurement types. The meteorological measurement types including the measurements of stations are as follows: daily vapor pressure, daily hours of sunshine, daily max speed and direction of the wind, daily average actual pressure, daily average cloudiness, daily average relative humidity, daily average speed of the wind, daily average temperature, daily total rainfall - manual and daily total rainfall - omgi.

These files contain daily measurements between 01.01.1970 to 01.01.2017. For each file there are records that are about station number, measurement type, and measurement date and measurement value data. Sample data in daily average speed of wind (m/s) is given in Table 1.

Table 1. Sample data of daily average wind speed file.

Station no	Station name	Year	Month	Day	Daily average speed of wind
8541	HASSA	1977	1	1	1.3
8541	HASSA	1977	1	2	1.1
8541	HASSA	1977	1	3	3.1
8541	HASSA	1977	1	4	3.4
8541	HASSA	1977	1	1	1.3

Firstly, we have crisp values of measurements and need to determine fuzzy membership values for each measurement. Before this operation we need to clarify uncertainty in the contents of measurement data by using interpretation motivated by the need to represent null or unknown values for certain data items, data entry mistakes, measurement errors in data, "don't care" values [18]. Then unsupervised classification based on FCM is applied over the measurement data to determine fuzzy classes and fuzzy membership values for each data. Applying FCM over 15 M data is extremely needs high computational resources in classical approaches. For this reason, adapted FCM on distributed environment is used to overcome resource limitation. Therefore, fuzzy classes as high, normal, low and membership values for temperature, rainfall and humidity is determined by using distributed FCM algorithm.

In the next step apriori is applied over each segmented data to determine the number of frequent item sets to support association rule learning. In executed apriori algorithm our item set is searching the values of high temperature, low rainfall and low humidity. At the end of execution, we have the support values for each winter partition.

Calculated support values are used for pattern discovery. Here we find meaningful pattern on these values. Using these patterns, it is possible to make prediction about the future meteorological events. Pattern discovery is studied on the data as Fig. 6.

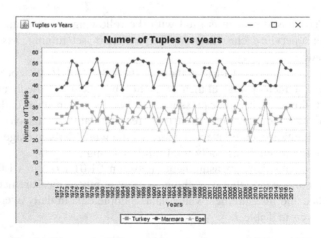

Fig. 6. The result of frequent item set between 1970 to 2017.

Geospatial data mining is employed on real data set, meteorological measurement data, of Turkey. 1161 different stations and 10 different measurement data types are used in the scope of this study. Each stations are chosen from different geographic regions of Turkey and used on text base data. Then the structured form of data set is built from that.

5 Conclusion and Future Works

The prosed approach introduces several common spatial data-mining tasks, including spatial classification, spatial association rule mining, spatial cluster analysis, frequent item set mining, pattern discovery and prediction. After using spatial data mining techniques to analyze the historical spatial meteorological data, make prediction about future meteorological measurement over Turkey climate by using geospatial predictive modelling is the primary target of this study. There are a number of possible future studies, such as developing a more efficient predictive model for meteorological data applications.

References

1. Han, J., Kamber, M.: Data Mining: Concepts and Techniques, 2nd edn. Morgan Kaufmann Publishers, USA (2012)
2. Liang, Z., Xinming, T., Wenliang, J.: Temporal association rule mining based on t-Apriori algorithm and its typical application. In: International Symposium on Spatial-Temporal Modeling Analysis, vol. 5, issue 2 (2005)
3. Huang, Y.P., Kao, L.J., Sandnes, F.E.: Predicting ocean salinity and temperature variations using data mining and fuzzy inference. Int. J. Fuzzy Syst. 9(3), 143–151 (2007)
4. Kotsiantis, S., Kostoulas, A., Lykoudis, S., Argiriou, A., Menagias, K.: A hybrid data mining technique for estimating mean daily temperature values. IJICT 1(5), 54–59 (2007)
5. Kohail, S.N., El-Halees, A.M.: Implementation of data mining techniques for meteorological data analysis. Int. J. Inf. Commun. Technol. Res. (JICT) 1(3) (2011)
6. Sivaramakrishnan, T.R., Meganathan, S.: Association rule mining and classifier approach for quantitative spot rainfall prediction. J. Theor. Appl. Inf. Technol. 34(2), 173–177 (2011)
7. Weka is a collection of machine learning algorithms for data mining tasks. https://www.cs.waikato.ac.nz/ml/weka/
8. RapidMiner is a software platform for data science teams that unites data prep, machine learning, and predictive model deployment. https://rapidminer.com
9. ArcMap is the main component of Esri's ArcGIS suite of geospatial processing programs. http://desktop.arcgis.com/en/arcmap/
10. PostGIS is a spatial database extender for PostgreSQL object-relational database. It adds support for geographic objects allowing location queries to be run in SQL. https://postgis.net/
11. Mondrian Schema Workbench is a designer interface that creates and tests Mondrian OLAP cube schemas visually. https://mondrian.pentaho.com/documentation/workbench.php
12. GeoMondrian is an open source Spatial OnLine Analytical Processing (Spatial OLAP or SOLAP) server, a spatially-enabled version of Pentaho Analysis Services. http://www.spatialytics.org/blog/geomondrian-1-0-is-available-for-download/

13. Geovisualization tool for spatial data. http://www.spatialytics.org/
14. The Apache Hadoop project develops open-source software for reliable, scalable, distributed computing. http://hadoop.apache.org/
15. The Apache Hive data warehouse software facilitates reading, writing, and managing large datasets residing in distributed storage using SQL. https://hive.apache.org/
16. Dunn, J.C.: A fuzzy relative of the ISODATA process and its use in detecting compact well-separated clusters. J. Cybern. **3,** 32–57 (1973)
17. Bezdek, J.C.: Pattern Recognition with Fuzzy Objective Function Algorithms, Plenum Press, New York (1981)
18. Gelenbe, E., Hebrail, G.: A probability model of uncertainty in data bases. In: ICDE, pp. 328–333 (1986)

Adaptive, Hubness-Aware Nearest Neighbour Classifier with Application to Hyperspectral Data

Michał Romaszewski[(⊠)], Przemysław Głomb, and Michał Cholewa

Institute of Theoretical and Applied Informatics, Polish Academy of Sciences,
Bałtycka 5, 44-100 Gliwice, Poland
{michal,przemg,mcholewa}@iitis.pl

Abstract. We present an extension of the Nearest Neighbour classifier
that can adapt to sample imbalances in local regions of the dataset. Our
approach uses the hubness statistic as a measure of a relation between
new samples and the existing training set. This allows to estimate the
upper limit of neighbours that vote for the label of the new instance. This
estimation improves the classifier performance in situations where some
classes are locally under-represented. The main focus of our method is
to solve the problem of local undersampling that exists in hyperspectral data classification. Using several well-known Machine Learning and
hyperspectral datasets, we show that our approach outperforms standard
and distance-weighted kNN, especially for high values of k.

Keywords: Nearest neighbour · Hyperspectral classification · Hubness

1 Introduction

The k-nearest neighbour classifier (kNN) [1] is one of the most popular methods
for statistical pattern recognition. It has been shown to successfully compete
with many complex models [2]. Its simplicity and predictability make it useful
as a component of other methods e.g. [3]. Its performance depends on a number
of factors: distance measure, voting strategy and the number of neighbours k
considered in voting. The choice of k usually has significant impact on classifier
performance [4]. When there is no class overlap, 1-nearest neighbour (k = 1) is
asymptotically optimal [5]. On the other hand, under strong assumptions that
$k \to \infty$ and $k/N \to 0$ the error rate converges to the Bayes' error rate [6]. In
general, smaller values of k may result in classifier overfitting and larger values
may capture only global tendencies in data.

Strategies of global (i.e. fixed for the whole dataset) selection of distance
measure and k value estimation [4,7] are commonly used, but may be suboptimal
if the characteristic of data is distinctly different between regions of the dataset.
To answer this problem NN classifiers may adapt their parameters to varying
characteristics of different regions in data as e.g. in [8]. In [9] a family of hubness-
aware NN classifiers is described, designed to cope with the high dimensionality

© Springer Nature Switzerland AG 2018
T. Czachórski et al. (Eds.): ISCIS 2018, CCIS 935, pp. 113–120, 2018.
https://doi.org/10.1007/978-3-030-00840-6_13

of data and the presence of label noise, effects of which are further explained in [10]. These methods consider the existence of instances that frequently appear as neighbours of other samples, called hubs. The presence of hubs may led to misclassification of neighbouring instances, and so the hubness statistics may be used for weighting data points, reducing their bad influence and improving the classifier accuracy [10]. An example of nonparametric NN classifier is presented in [11], where authors estimate k value for each test point, based on construction of locally informative hypersphere.

Classification of hyperspectral images [12] presents a particularly challenging problem due to their high dimensionality, class imbalance, and spectral mixing. In addition, hyperspectral classification considers scenarios when the number of training samples is very limited e.g. 10% or less, sometimes even as low as 5 samples per class [13]. While typically more complex classifiers such as Support Vector Machines (SVM) [14] are used for this task, in some scenarios kNN can be successfully applied, thanks to its predictability, simplicity of parameter choice and high computational performance in both classification and retraining e.g. in [3]. However, in case of unequal spatial distribution of training samples, such use may lead to local class imbalance. This results in some classes being under-represented in the extended training set, which may have a significant influence on the final accuracy.

In this paper we describe the locality sensitive hubness-aware classifier, that can adapt to the imbalance of training instances in local data region. Our approach considers the change in data hubness, caused by an introduction of the new sample, as a measure of uncertainty, limiting the number of k neighbours voting for the label of this sample. We compare the results of this approach with a standard and distance-weighted kNN, as well as classifier based on Hubness-aware weighting for k-Nearest Neighbor (hw-kNN) [15] and show its advantages, especially for high values of k, both for standard and hyperspectral test datasets.

2   Method

Let the $\mathfrak{D}_{train} = \{(\mathbf{x}_i, y_i) : i = 1, \ldots, L_{train}\}$ denote the dataset of training samples, where $\mathbf{x}_i \in \mathbb{R}^d$ are d-dimensional feature vectors and $y_i \in \{c_j, j = 1, \ldots, C\} = \mathcal{C}$ are class labels. By $\mathfrak{D}_{train}^{c_j} = \{(\mathbf{x}, y) : (\mathbf{x}, y) \in \mathfrak{D}_{train}, y = c_j\}$ we denote the subset of $\mathfrak{D}_{train}$ with $y_i = c_j$. By $\mathfrak{D}_{test} = \{\mathbf{x}_j : j = 1, \ldots, L_{test}\}$ we denote the test set where $\mathbf{x}_j \in \mathbb{R}^d$. Our goal is to assign labels $y_j \in \mathcal{C}$ for each instance from $\mathfrak{D}_{test}$, based on the information available in $\mathfrak{D}_{train}$. By $\mathfrak{N}_k(\mathbf{x}_j) \subset \mathfrak{D}_{train}$ we will denote the set of k nearest neighbours of $\mathbf{x}_j$ from $\mathfrak{D}_{train}$ according to Euclidean distance. By $H_k(\mathbf{x}_j)$ we denote the number of samples from $\mathfrak{D}_{train}$ that would have $\mathbf{x}_j$ among their k nearest neighbours. $H_k(\mathbf{x}_j)$ may be therefore treated as k-degree hubness of a sample $\mathbf{x}_j$ measured in $\mathfrak{D}_{train}$, similarly to the statistics used in hubness-aware classifiers such as hw-kNN or h-FNN [9]. Note, however, that these methods consider the hubness of the whole training set, therefore they know the labels of samples and can distinguish between scenarios when a sample is in the neighbourhood of instances

from the same class ('good' hubness) or different class ('bad' hubness). Not
knowing the label of $\mathbf{x}_j$ for the test set, we can only consider the total hubness
of a sample.

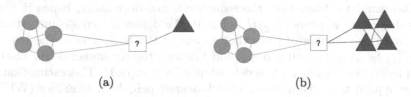

(a)   (b)

Fig. 1. An example for hubness-based estimation of neighbourhood stability. For kNN
with $k = 3$, more numerous samples from class 'circle' will determine the label of considered ('square') instance $\mathbf{x}$. Hubness of this instance $H_1(\mathbf{x}) = 1$ indicates imbalance
in local neighbourhood, resulting from underrepresentation of the class 'triangle'. In
panel (b) $H_1(\mathbf{x}) = H_2(\mathbf{x}) = H_3(\mathbf{x}) = 0$ so both classes are sufficiently represented in
$N_3(\mathbf{x})$.

2.1   Locality Sensitive Hubness-Aware Classifier

Consider the toy example presented in Fig. 1(a). In the presence of local imbalance in class sizes, the kNN classifier with $k = 3$ will assign the new instance
to the more numerous class even if its closer to the other one. In a self-learning
scheme, where classified samples extend the training set, this majority voting
would prevent the smaller class from gaining new samples. Now, lets consider
the hubness $H(\mathbf{x}_i)$ for the queried test sample $\mathbf{x}_i$, in scenarios presented on pan-
els (a) and (b). We can see that in panel (a) $H_1(\mathbf{x}_i) = 1$, while in panel (b)
$H_1(\mathbf{x}_i), H_2(\mathbf{x}_i), H_3(\mathbf{x}_i) = 0$, and $H_4(\mathbf{x}_i) = 2$. We can treat $H_j(\mathbf{x}_i)$ as an estimator of influence that this sample would have on instances from the training
set. In other words, if this sample was the part of the training set and its neighbours were classified, its vote could change their labelling. We observe that if
$H_j(\mathbf{x}_i) = 0$, it is safe to assign a label of $\mathbf{x}_i$ based on $\mathfrak{N}_k(\mathbf{x}_i)$. On the other hand,
$H_j(\mathbf{x}_i) > 0$ may indicate instability in the form of locally underrepresented class,
that will be penalized by voting from $\mathfrak{N}_j(\mathbf{x}_i)$. The decision on k value may be
based on the boundary between the $H_j(\mathbf{x}_i) = 0$ and $H_{j+1}(\mathbf{x}_i) > 0$. As we show
below, there is only one point with this characteristics.

Theorem 1. $k \geq n \rightarrow \forall_x H_k(\mathbf{x}) \geq H_n(\mathbf{x})$.

Proof. Let $\mathfrak{M}_n(\mathbf{x})$ be the set of instances from $\mathfrak{D}_{train}$ that would have $\mathbf{x}$ among
their n nearest neighbours, so $H_n(\mathbf{x}) = |\mathfrak{M}_n(\mathbf{x})|$. Let us assume by contradiction
that

$$\exists_x \exists_{k>n} H_k(\mathbf{x}) < H_n(\mathbf{x}). \tag{1}$$

We than have $|\mathfrak{M}_k(\mathbf{x})| < |\mathfrak{M}_n(\mathbf{x})|$, so $\exists_y \mathbf{y} \in \mathfrak{M}_n(\mathbf{x}) \wedge \mathbf{y} \notin \mathfrak{M}_k(\mathbf{x})$. Therefore,

$$x \in \mathfrak{N}_n(\mathbf{y}) \wedge \mathbf{x} \notin \mathfrak{N}_k(\mathbf{y}), \tag{2}$$

but $\mathfrak{N}_n(\mathbf{y}) \subset \mathfrak{N}_k(\mathbf{y})$, which contradicts Eq. (2).

Considering the above theorem, we can see that if $H_1(\mathbf{x}_i) = 0$ and $H_k(\mathbf{x}_i) > 0$, then there exists exactly one boundary point. Based on this observation we can describe the proposed solution as follows. Given a test sample $\mathbf{x}$, we can construct a sequence of hubness statistics $H_i(\mathbf{x})$, $i = 1, 2, \ldots, k$. From the Theorem 1 we know that the sequence is non-decreasing, hence if a non-zero value $H_i(\mathbf{x})$ appears, $\forall_{j \geq i} H_j(\mathbf{x}) > 0$. We define a 'zeros-count' statistic by counting the number of zeros that appear at the beginning of the sequence $\alpha = \sum_{i=1}^{k} \delta_{H_i(\mathbf{x})=0}$ where $0 \leq \alpha \leq k$ and δ denotes the Kronecker delta. The estimated individual k value for $\mathbf{x}$ is defined as $k_x = \max(\alpha, 1)$. This estimation can also be applied to a distance-weighted k-nearest neighbour classifier (WKNN) [16], created e.g. by assuming that the probability that $\mathbf{x}_i$ belongs to class c_j is equal to: $P_{c_j}(\mathbf{x}_i) = \dfrac{\sum_{\mathbf{x}_s \in \mathfrak{N}_k^{c_j}(\mathbf{x}_i)} \|\mathbf{x}_i - \mathbf{x}_s\|^{-1}}{\sum_{\mathbf{x}_s \in \mathfrak{N}_k(\mathbf{x}_i)} \|\mathbf{x}_i - \mathbf{x}_s\|^{-1}}$ where $\mathfrak{N}_k^{c_j}(\mathbf{x}_i) = \mathfrak{N}_k(\mathbf{x}_i) \cap \mathfrak{D}_{train}^{c_j}$.

3   Experiments

We compared our approach with the standard and distance-weighted kNN classifier, as well as hw-kNN [15]. The values of k (which are also the maximum values of k_i for each single test instance) were selected as $k \in [5, 9, 13]$ and also $k = \sqrt{N}$ where N is the number of training samples. Experiments were performed on publicly available datasets from the University of California, Irvine and mldata repositories[1]: *breast-cancer, glass, ionosphere, iris, segment, sonar, vehicle, wine*. Additionally, three hyperspectral datasets described in Sect. 3.1 were used.

Small dataset size is a common requirement in hyperspectral classification and datasets consisting of only a few training samples are often considered, e.g. [13]. Therefore, in our scenarios for both classic and hyperspectral datasets, the ratio of train and test data $\lambda \approx 0.1$ (we use ~10% data for training). The dataset was randomly shuffled and splitted into the test and training sets in a stratified way - maintaining the proportion of training samples for each class, with a minimum of $n = 3$ samples. This process was repeated 50 times. Internal parameters of hw-kNN used as a reference method were selected through a stratified cross-validation.

Our results include an additional statistical analysis to test if the advantage of our method is statistically significant, compared with the reference approaches. To do this, for each dataset D we computed $S(D)$ as the number of times our methods obtained higher accuracy than the mean accuracy of the best reference algorithm. We then considered the confidence interval of probability that $S(D) > 0$. The statistical inference is performed for significance levels of $\alpha = 0.05$.

3.1   Hyperspectral Datasets

The *Indian Pines* dataset[2] is the 145×145 image with 220 spectral bands and spatial resolution of 20m per pixel, collected with the AVIRIS sensor. It contains

---

[1] https://archive.ics.uci.edu/ml/datasets.html and http://mldata.org.
[2] https://engineering.purdue.edu/~biehl/MultiSpec/hyperspectral.html.

16 classes corresponding to different types of crops. The *Salinas* dataset[3] is 217×512 image with with 224 spectral bands and spatial resolution of 3.7m per pixel, also collected with the AVIRIS sensor. It contains 16 classes representing different bare soil, vegetables and vineyard fields. The *Pavia University* datasets is the 610×340 image (the original size is 610×610 but large part of the image is empty), with 115 spectral bands and spatial resolution of 1.3m per pixel, collected with the ROSIS sensor. It contains 9 classes representing gravel, trees, metal, bare soil, bricks and shadows.

3.2   Results

Comparison of results for non-hyperspectral machine learning test datasets is presented in Table 1. Our adaptive approach performs better in almost all scenarios. Its advantage is particularly visible in scenarios when k value is high. The advantage of our approach is even more apparent for hyperspectral data classification. The results for three spectral datasets are presented in Table 2. It should be noted that while low values of k may sometimes achieve better accuracy in test scenarios, the obtained classifier is at risk of being overtrained. In addition complicate the estimation of probability based on neighbour majority voting. The set value of k may also be imposed by the algorithm like e.g. in [3] where it is set to the number of classes. Histograms of estimated values of k_i for a sample run of the algorithm for the *Indian Pines* and *wine* datasets are presented in Fig. 2. We can observe that lower values of k are chosen for significant number of samples in spectral datasets, which results probably from the significant imbalances of class lengths.

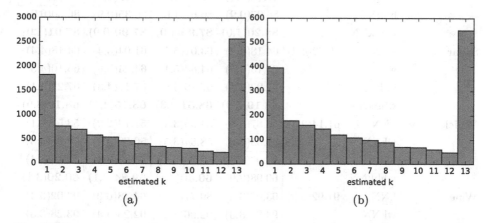

Fig. 2. Histograms of estimated values of k_i for the *Indian Pines* (a) and *segment* (b) datasets, with $\lambda \approx 0.1$ and $k = 13$.

---

[3] http://www.ehu.eus/ccwintco/index.php?title=Hyperspectral_Remote_Sensing_Scenes.

Table 1. Comparison between our approach denoted hbkNN, its distance-weighted implementation denoted whbkNN and reference approaches (kNN and wkNN) on publicly available datasets. The ratio between training and testing sets is $\lambda = 0.1$. Values in bold denote statistical significance of the advantage for our method in comparison with the best reference result.

Dataset	Classifier	$k = 1$	$k = 5$	$k = 9$	$k = 13$	$k = \sqrt{N}$
Breast-cancer	kNN	95.40(1.3)	96.15(0.7)	95.65(0.8)	95.02(0.8)	95.65(0.8)
	wkNN		96.18(0.7)	95.72(0.8)	95.17(0.7)	95.72(0.8)
	hbkNN		95.91(0.9)	95.58(0.9)	95.31(0.9)	95.58(0.9)
	whbkNN		96.03(0.7)	**95.77**(0.8)	**95.56**(0.8)	**95.77**(0.8)
Glass	kNN	58.17(5.1)	48.19(7.0)	41.60(4.6)	37.55(3.0)	48.19(7.0)
	wkNN		55.40(4.8)	54.06(5.1)	52.67(5.0)	55.40(4.8)
	hbkNN		53.39(5.4)	51.73(4.8)	51.55(5.1)	53.39(5.4)
	whbkNN		56.36(4.7)	55.90(5.0)	**55.80**(5.1)	56.36(4.7)
Ionosphere	kNN	79.33(5.6)	72.95(6.2)	68.96(4.9)	66.08(3.1)	74.07(5.7)
	wkNN		73.61(6.2)	69.99(5.4)	67.09(3.8)	74.50(6.5)
	hbkNN		74.46(5.7)	71.39(4.4)	69.11(2.8)	75.49(5.5)
	whbkNN		74.67(5.9)	71.87(5.0)	**69.72**(3.6)	75.50(6.2)
Iris	kNN	90.01(3.8)	86.86(3.4)	83.44(2.3)	64.67(3.4)	86.00(4.1)
	wkNN		88.74(3.2)	88.87(3.9)	89.53(3.6)	90.07(3.5)
	hbkNN		88.13(3.4)	86.50(3.6)	81.78(3.4)	87.39(3.4)
	whbkNN		89.02(3.2)	88.93(3.7)	89.32(3.6)	90.06(3.5)
Segment	kNN	88.96(1.2)	85.61(1.0)	84.25(1.3)	83.19(1.4)	82.55(1.5)
	wkNN		87.77(1.0)	87.04(1.0)	86.53(1.0)	86.29(1.0)
	hbkNN		86.97(0.9)	86.61(1.0)	86.35(0.9)	86.30(0.9)
	whbkNN		**88.20**(1.0)	**87.99**(1.0)	**87.90**(0.9)	**87.91**(1.0)
Sonar	kNN	69.29(4.4)	64.18(4.4)	63.01(5.1)	61.04(5.4)	64.18(4.4)
	wkNN		65.10(4.5)	64.83(5.1)	64.24(5.6)	65.10(4.5)
	hbkNN		67.22(4.1)	67.19(4.6)	67.17(4.3)	67.22(4.1)
	whbkNN		**68.19**(3.9)	**68.51**(4.3)	**68.75**(4.1)	**68.19**(3.9)
Vehicle	kNN	61.14(2.3)	56.87(3.5)	54.55(3.4)	51.73(2.9)	53.57(3.1)
	wkNN		60.33(3.0)	58.54(3.5)	56.70(3.4)	58.05(3.3)
	hbkNN		58.07(3.3)	57.73(3.4)	57.06(3.1)	57.49(3.4)
	whbkNN		60.98(2.9)	**60.40**(3.1)	**59.84**(3.1)	**60.20**(3.1)
Wine	kNN	91.92(2.9)	93.02(3.4)	89.77(4.8)	64.48(6.0)	93.02(3.4)
	wkNN		93.28(3.3)	92.96(3.4)	92.25(4.4)	93.28(3.3)
	hbkNN		92.93(3.4)	91.32(3.8)	86.49(3.5)	92.93(3.4)
	whbkNN		93.23(3.2)	**93.01**(3.4)	**93.51**(3.2)	93.23(3.2)

Table 2. Comparison between our approach denoted hbkNN, its distance-weighted implementation denoted whbkNN and reference approaches (kNN, wkNN and hw-kNN) on hyperspectral datasets. The ratio between the training and testing sets is $\lambda = 0.1$. Values in bold denote statistical significance of the advantage for our method in comparison with the best reference result.

Dataset	Classifier	$k = 1$	$k = 5$	$k = 9$	$k = 13$	$k = \sqrt{N}$
Indian	kNN	72.99(0.7)	70.75(0.6)	68.79(0.7)	66.78(0.8)	59.10(1.0)
	wkNN		72.37(0.5)	70.61(0.7)	68.96(0.7)	63.40(1.0)
	hw-kNN		70.98(0.5)	69.07(0.6)	67.30(0.6)	59.49(1.0)
	hbkNN		71.89(0.6)	71.28(0.6)	70.79(0.7)	69.97(0.8)
	whbkNN		**73.16**(0.5)	**72.58**(0.5)	**72.16**(0.6)	**71.49**(0.7)
Salinas	kNN	89.24(0.2)	89.42(0.2)	89.15(0.1)	88.76(0.2)	85.04(0.2)
	wkNN		89.84(0.2)	89.70(0.1)	89.46(0.2)	86.62(0.2)
	hw-kNN		89.44(0.2)	89.17(0.2)	88.83(0.2)	85.29(0.3)
	hbkNN		89.65(0.2)	89.58(0.2)	89.47(0.2)	89.25(0.2)
	whbkNN		89.77(0.2)	89.73(0.2)	**89.66**(0.2)	**89.49**(0.2)
Pavia	kNN	86.17(0.2)	86.69(0.2)	86.04(0.3)	85.35(0.3)	80.00(0.4)
	wkNN		86.77(0.2)	86.20(0.3)	85.61(0.3)	81.17(0.4)
	hw-kNN		86.76(0.2)	86.35(0.2)	85.86(0.2)	81.10(0.4)
	hbkNN		86.60(0.2)	86.30(0.2)	86.08(0.2)	85.58(0.2)
	whbkNN		86.76(0.2)	**86.56**(0.2)	**86.39**(0.2)	**85.99**(0.2)

4   Conclusion

Our results indicate that the proposed adaptive approach to parametrization of kNN classifier successfully limits the negative impact of locally underrepresented classes on classification accuracy. This allows to achieve significantly better classification results, especially for higher values of k. Since the kNN is often used as an element of a more complex algorithm, the value of k may be a subject to external constraints. For example, a commonly used hyperspectral segmentation step with Markov Random Fields (MRF) requires estimating probability of each class, for which a high k value is preferable. In such scenarios, our proposal allows to capture both local and global characteristics of data.

A promising research direction could involve including the proposed approach into the semi-supervised classification problem in order to limit imbalance in classes in the extended dataset.

Acknowledgments. This work has been supported by the project 'Representation of dynamic 3D scenes using the Atomic Shapes Network model' financed by National Science Centre, decision DEC-2011/03/D/ST6/03753. Authors would like to thank Marcin Blachnik for extended discussion on the first version of the paper and Krisztian Buza for his insightful comments and for making available the PyHubs (http://www.biointelligence.hu/pyhubs.) library.

References

1. Fix, E., Hodges, J.L., Jr.: Discriminatory analysis-nonparametric discrimination: consistency properties. Technical Report, DTIC Document (1951)
2. Ding, H., Trajcevski, G., Scheuermann, P., Wang, X., Keogh, E.: Querying and mining of time series data: experimental comparison of representations and distance measures. Proc. VLDB Endow. **1**(2), 1542–1552 (2008)
3. Romaszewski, M., Głomb, P., Cholewa, M.: Semi-supervised hyperspectral classification from a small number of training samples using a co-training approach. ISPRS J. Photogramm. Remote Sens. **121**, 60–76 (2016)
4. Ghosh, A.K.: On optimum choice of k in nearest neighbor classification. Comput. Stat. Data Anal. **50**(11), 3113–3123 (2006)
5. Cover, T.M., Hart, P.E.: Nearest neighbor pattern classification. IEEE Trans. Inf. Theory **13**(1), 21–27 (1967)
6. Devroye, L., Gyorfi, L., Krzyzak, A., Lugosi, G.: On the strong universal consistency of nearest neighbor regression function estimates. Ann. Stat. 1371–1385 (1994)
7. Ouyang, D., Li, D., Li, Q.: Cross-validation and non-parametric k nearest-neighbour estimation. Econom. J. **9**(3), 448–471 (2006)
8. Buza, K., Nanopoulos, A., Schmidt-Thieme, L.: Time-series classification based on individualised error prediction. In: 2010 IEEE 13th International Conference on Computational Science and Engineering (CSE), pp. 48–54. IEEE (2010)
9. Tomašev, N., Mladenić, D.: Nearest neighbor voting in high-dimensional data: Learning from past occurrences. In: 2011 IEEE 11th International Conference on Data Mining Workshops (ICDMW), pp. 1215–1218. IEEE (2011)
10. Tomašev, N., Buza, K.: Hubness-aware kNN classification of high-dimensional data in presence of label noise. Neurocomputing **160**, 157–172 (2015)
11. Bhattacharya, G., Ghosh, K., Chowdhury, A.S.: Test point specific k estimation for kNN classifier. In: 2014 22nd International Conference on Pattern Recognition (ICPR), pp. 1478–1483. IEEE (2014)
12. Bioucas-Dias, J.M., Plaza, A., Camps-Valls, G., Scheunders, P., Nasrabadi, N.M., Chanussot, J.: Hyperspectral remote sensing data analysis and future challenges. IEEE Geosci. Remote Sens. Mag. **1**(2), 6–36 (2013)
13. Li, J., Reddy Marpu, P., Plaza, A., Bioucas-Dias, J.M., Atli Benediktsson, J.: Generalized composite kernel framework for hyperspectral image classification. IEEE Trans. Geosci. Remote Sens. **51**(9), 4816–4829 (2013)
14. Melgani, F., Bruzzone, L.: Classification of hyperspectral remote sensing images with support vector machines. IEEE Trans. Geosci. Remote Sens. **42**(8), 1778–1790 (2004)
15. Tomašev, N., Buza, K., Marussy, K., Kis, P.B.: Hubness-aware classification, instance selection and feature construction: survey and extensions to time-series. In: Stańczyk, U., Jain, L.C. (eds.) Feature Selection for Data and Pattern Recognition. SCI, vol. 584, pp. 231–262. Springer, Heidelberg (2015). https://doi.org/10.1007/978-3-662-45620-0_11
16. Biau, G., Devroye, L.: Weighted k-nearest neighbor density estimates. Lectures on the Nearest Neighbor Method. SSDS, pp. 43–51. Springer, Cham (2015). https://doi.org/10.1007/978-3-319-25388-6_5

Graph Representation and Semi-clustering Approach for Label Space Reduction in Multi-label Classification of Documents

Rafał Woźniak[✉] and Danuta Zakrzewska

Institute of Information Technology, Lodz University of Technology,
Wólczańska 215, 90-924 Łódź, Poland
rafal.wozniak@edu.p.lodz.pl, danuta.zakrzewska@p.lodz.pl

Abstract. An increasing number of large online text repositories require effective techniques of document classification. In many cases, more than one class label should be assigned to documents. When the number of labels is big, it is difficult to obtain required multi-label classification accuracy. Efficient label space dimension reduction may significantly improve classification performance. In the paper, we consider applying graph-based semi-clustering algorithm, where documents are represented by vertices with edge weights calculated according to the similarity of associated texts. Semi-clusters are used for finding patterns of labels that occur together. Such approach enables reducing label dimensionality. The performance of the method is examined by experiments conducted on real medical documents. The assessment of classification results, in terms of Classification Accuracy, F-Measure and Hamming Loss, obtained for the most popular multi-label classifiers: Binary Relevance, Classifier Chains and Label Powerset showed good potential of the proposed methodology.

Keywords: Multi-label classification · Label space reduction
Text mining

1 Introduction

Nowadays, there have been appeared large repositories of documents that need to be automatically classified. Many of those documents require assigning more than one class label, thus using multi-label classification technique is necessary. Additionally, in many cases big dimensionality of label space makes it difficult to obtain the required accuracy of multi-label classification results.

There exist different approaches to handle the problem of reducing the amount of labels in multi-label classification tasks. Tsoumakas et al. [1] considered reducing label sets by using hierarchical algorithm for multi-label classification. Balasubramanian and Lebanon [2] proposed the method which is based on the assumption that for multidimensional variables there exists a small subset

© Springer Nature Switzerland AG 2018
T. Czachórski et al. (Eds.): ISCIS 2018, CCIS 935, pp. 121–129, 2018.
https://doi.org/10.1007/978-3-030-00840-6_14

of dimensions, such that all the remaining ones may be expressed by their linear combination. Read et al. [3] eliminated rare label sets. Bi and Kwok [4] proposed randomized sampling with the probability of class labels reflecting their importance. Hsu et al. [5] used compressed sensing technique, regarding sparsity of the label space and projecting it into a compressed space of lower dimensionality. Herrera et al. [6] pointed out that performing label selection tends to improve classification results. They indicated that methods based on sparseness and dependencies among labels are the most often used. Zhang and Zhou [7] mentioned using label dependency information in dimensionality reduction as one of the challenges in multi-label classification.

In the presented paper, the method of reducing label dimensionality by using semi-clustering is investigated. In the considered approach the documents represented by vertices comprise a social network with edges pointing out their mutual similarities. The documents are assigned to semi-clusters to find groups of labels which occur together the most often. Such approach has been introduced in [8]. Presented there qualitative analysis of the results, obtained by experiments conducted on real medical texts, showed a potential of the proposed method in indicating groups of labels. In the current research, we use such groups for building patterns of labels occuring together and then replacing them by single labels. We validate the proposed method by experiments conducted on real medical datasets. The performance of the proposed approach is checked by using three multi-label-classifiers: Binary Relevance, Classifier Chains and Label Powerset and three metrics: Classification Accuracy, F-Measure and Hamming Loss.

The remainder of the paper is organized as follows. The methodology including all its steps is described in the next section. Then the experiments conducted on datasets are depicted and comparison of the performance metrics values for different multi-label classification methods is presented. Finally, concluding remarks and future research are shortly described.

2   Methodology

The considered methodology aims at reducing the number of labels in the tasks of multi-label classification of text documents. The semi-clustering algorithm based on the graph representation is used to identify labels that mostly occur together and thus dimensionality reduction can be performed. An overview of the method is presented in Fig. 1, the main steps of the solution are described in the following subsections.

2.1   Text Pre-processing

Firstly documents should be prepared by using pre-processing techniques, these techniques were previously considered and described in [9]. There were applied software based on the Natural Language Tool Kit (NLTK) [10].

In the first step, all the documents in the corpus were converted to lowercase and punctuation marks were removed. Afterward, the stop words were eliminated

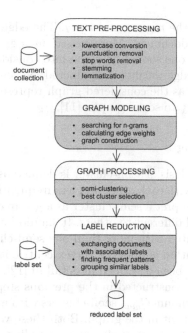

Fig. 1. A scheme of the proposed method.

from the texts. Finally, word stemming and lemmatization were carried out with the help of the Porter Stemmer and the WordNet Lemmatizer. Such prepared text corpus was provided as the input for the next step of the proposed algorithm.

2.2   Graph Modeling

The original idea of considering the text corpus as a social network was described in detail in [8]. In the graph, vertices represent text documents and edges indicate n-grams appearing in pairs of linked documents. Every edge has its own value that reflects the similarity degree of the two associated texts.

The process of building a graph representation is divided into three substeps. First, the list of all the n-grams which appear in the text corpus is constructed, while both upper and lower values of n are user-specified. As default, the minimal value of n is set to 2, thus bigrams are the shortest n-grams taken into account. If user does not define the maximum n, the algorithm will find out n for which no more new n-grams can be indicated. If there are no similar sequences of length of n, there will not be any of length of $n + 1$. Subsequently, we explore the text documents and an edge is created if the sequence is present in both of them. The weight w of the edge that connects documents d_i and d_j can be calculated according to the formula (1):

$$w(d_i, d_j) = \frac{(n - 0.5)^2}{max\{|d_i|, |d_j|\}} \tag{1}$$

where n is the length of the n-gram and $i \neq j$. The edge score is normalized by the length of the bigger document. Moreover, if an n-gram is a part of another n-gram, only the longest one should be taken into consideration. Afterward, the aggregation of multiple edge weights is conducted. Nevertheless, the elimination of loops can be omitted, as the considered graph representation precludes their existence, on the contrary to social graphs [11].

2.3   Graph Processing

In the social network analysis, a semi-cluster is defined as a group of individuals who interact frequently with each other and less frequently with people from the outside. However, we interpret a semi-cluster as a group of documents which are similar to each other and different to others. It should be stressed that the same document can be associated with more than one semi-cluster.

The considered algorithm adopts the vertex-centric iterative model from the Pregel system, which has been described in detail in [12]. Its input is a weighted, undirected graph that is constructed in the previous step of our solution, while the output is a list of maximum C_{max} semi-clusters with maximum V_{max} vertices, generated for each document in the graph. Both these values are user-specified. The score S_c is assigned to the semi-cluster c according to the Eq. (2):

$$S_c = \frac{I_c - f_B B_c}{V_c(V_c - 1)/2} \tag{2}$$

where I_c is the sum of all the weights of internal edges, B_c is the sum of all the weights of boundary edges, V_c is the number of vertices in the semi-cluster c and f_B is the user-specified boundary edge score factor (between 0 and 1). To avoid favoring only large semi-clusters, the value of the score S_c is normalized by the number of edges in a clique of size V_c.

Every iteration of the semi-clustering algorithm, that is named a super-step, deals with the results of the previous phase. First, each vertex creates an empty semi-cluster and adds itself in it. Next, vertices send a message about themselves to the neighbors that check if they are already included in the semi-clusters and if they are not, a new vertex is added and a semi-cluster score is calculated again. If it is higher than any score included in the list, a new semi-cluster is added or replaces the one with the lowest score. The maximum size of the list is managed by the parameter C_{max}. Moreover, vertex will not be added to the semi-cluster if its size is already equal to V_{max}. Finally, lists are sorted by semi-cluster scores and sent to the other neighbors. A stop condition of the semi-clustering algorithm can be either reaching the user-defined number of iterations or not receiving any improvement of the semi-cluster scores.

2.4   Label Reduction

The input for the final step of the considered method is a group of semi-clusters. Nevertheless, for each vertex we choose only the one with the highest score. From then on, the attention is focused on the labels assigned to the vertices, since the main objective is to reduce the number of labels.

First, for each semi-cluster a list of documents is converted to a list of labels. Next, the Apriori algorithm is performed to find the frequent labelsets and groups of labels that mostly occur together are transformed into the single ones. Then each occurrence of the grouped labels should be replaced with a new one, what results in the label space dimensionality reduction (LSDR).

3 Experiments

The aim of the experiments was to evaluate the proposed technique as the one improving multi-label classification tasks. There was considered Ohsumed corpus of medical documents [13]. Three classifiers and three performance metrics were applied.

3.1 Data Description

The Ohsumed dataset [13] consists of the first 20,000 documents from the 50,216 medical abstracts of the year 1991. In [14] the task was to categorize them into 23 Medical Subject Headings (MeSH) categories of cardiovascular diseases, thus the number of text documents was decreased to 13,929.

3.2 Multi-label Stratification

In order to assess the performance of the proposed method, the dataset was split into 10 folds and the first one was chosen to the further investigation. Since the task of sampling of multi-label data is not a simple one, the stratification is used. The software implemented for this part of experiments was based on Weka Open Source [15] and open-source Mulan Java library [16].

A stratified sampling divides the entire population into disjoint groups and provides samples which preserve the proportion of these groups. However, in the multi-label classification tasks, groups are separated based on the value of many target variables, what is the main difficulty. The solution that we applied during the experiments is the labelsets-based stratification which is recommended if the ratio of labelsets to examples is low (≤ 0.1) [17]. Considering the chosen dataset, this value equals about 0.08.

3.3 Graph Construction

For building a graph representation, the software implemented in Java programming language was applied. We also used the open-source Okapi library [18] for the purpose of the graph processing and analysis. The user-specified parameters were set to the following, experimentally chosen, values:

- the maximum number of iterations k is 1000,
- the maximum number of semi-clusters C_{max} is 10,
- the maximum number of vertices V_{max} is 10,
- the boundary edge score factor f_B is 0.5 (default).

Additionally, each undirected edge in the graph was processed twice, since the Okapi library only accepts directed edges.

The constructed graph consists of 462 vertices that represent documents and 316 edges (after the aggregation process), meaning that between 316 pairs of the abstracts some similarities were detected. However, another disadvantage of the Okapi library is performing poor when the graph is disconnected. To avoid such a situation, the software which finds all the subgraphs in the original graph was implemented using the open-source NetworkX Python package [19]. Afterward, the set of 192 distinct subgraphs of sizes from 2 to 7 was given as the input for the semi-clustering algorithm.

3.4   Frequent Labelsets

In the next step, frequent labelsets were found. Weka Open Source [15] Apriori implementation was used for this part of the experiments. The minimal values of support and confidence were experimentally chosen, then set to 0.04 and 0.7 respectively. Since for the considered confidence every itemset has support lower than 0.09, the decision to decrease its value was made. Two groups of labels which mostly occur together were discovered. The first labelset consists of three categories, i.e. C12, C14 and C18, while the second one contains two of them, i.e. C06 and C23. Both labelsets were transformed to the new categories which were named C24 and C25 respectively.

3.5   Evaluation

The performance of the method was evaluated using three datasets, three multi-label classifiers and three metrics. The original (baseline) Ohsumed collection is referred to as D1, the second dataset, that is called D2, includes the category C24 instead of three eliminated ones, and the last one, that is referred to as D3, incorporates both new categories which are C24 and C25.

There were three multi-label classifiers examined, i.e. Binary Relevance (BR), Classifier Chains (CC) and Label Powerset (LP). All of them were combined with the single-label Naive Bayes classifier. The assessment of classification results was made in terms of Classification Accuracy (CA), F-Measure (FM) and Hamming Loss (HL). All the obtained values are presented in Table 1.

The considered method of the label space dimensionality reduction obtained better results, in terms of CA and FM, than the ones collected on the baseline dataset. The highest values were achieved by LP classifier, BR took the second place and CC performed worstly. In cases of CC and LP, the dataset with more eliminated labels always attained bigger values than the less reduced one. There were some exceptions for BR classifier, since the higher label reduction did not

Table 1. Classification results

Metric	Dataset	Classifier		
		BR	CC	LP
CA	D1	0.299	0.293	0.385
	D2	0.317	0.313	0.396
	D3	0.317	0.319	0.402
FM	D1	0.415	0.396	0.451
	D2	0.428	0.408	0.466
	D3	0.426	0.410	0.474
HL	D1	0.085	0.137	0.074
	D2	0.090	0.139	0.079
	D3	0.093	0.142	0.081

improved the results of CA and FM. While the first one stayed at the same level, the second one got slightly worse, but still remained better than in the case of the initial dataset.

Although the considered method performs well in terms of CA and FM, the HL values tend to increase instead of decreasing. However, one should notice that HL value depends on the labelset length and its value is less for the bigger number of labels. Such situation takes place in the case of D1 dataset. Additionally, the presented results show that values of HL obtained for the baseline dataset by BR and CC are worse than the ones achieved by LP in all the cases, i.e. before and after label reduction.

4   Conclusions

In the paper the method of label space reduction in the pre-processing phase of multi-label classification is considered. A graph representation of text documents is used to create social network that enables building semi-clusters of documents and finding out frequent patterns of labels occuring together. Then, to reduce the dimensionality, patterns are replaced by single labels. The method has been evaluated by performance of multi-label classification algorithms for datasets of different label dimensionality. The experiments conducted on real medical documents showed the good potential of the proposed technique regarding the most commonly used metrics.

Future research will consist in further investigations of the considered method taking into consideration different document datasets, other multi-label classifiers as well as performance metrics.

References

1. Tsoumakas, G., Katakis, I., Vlahavas, I.: Effective and efficient multilabel classification in domains with large number of labels. In: Proceedings of the ECML/PKDD Workshop on Mining Multidimensional Data, Antwerp, Belgium, pp. 30–44 (2008)
2. Balasubramanian, K., Lebanon, G.: The landmark selection method for multiple output prediction. In: Proceedings of the 29th International Conference on Machine Learning, pp. 283–290. Omni Press, Edinburgh (2012)
3. Read, J., Pfahringer, B., Holmes, G.: Multi-label classification using ensembles of pruned sets. In: Proceedings of the 2008 8th IEEE International Conference on Data Mining, pp. 995–1000. IEEE Computer Society, Washington, DC (2008)
4. Bi, W., Kwok, J.: Efficient multi-label classification with many labels. In: Proceedings of the 30th International Conference on Machine Learning, Atlanta, GA, USA, vol. 28, pp. 405–413 (2013)
5. Hsu, D., Kakade, S.M., Langford, J., Zhang, T.: Multi-label prediction via compressed sensing. In: Bengio, Y., Schuurmans, D., Lafferty, J.D., Williams, C.K.I., Culotta, A. (eds.) Advances in Neural Information Processing Systems, vol. 22, pp. 772–780. Curran Associates Inc., Vancouver (2009)
6. Herrera, F., Charte, F., Rivera, A.J., del Jesus, M.J.: Multilabel Classification. Problem Analysis, Metrics and Techniques. Springer, Cham (2016). https://doi.org/10.1007/978-3-319-41111-8
7. Zhang, M., Zhou, Z.: A review on multi-label learning algorithms. IEEE Trans. Knowl. Data Eng. **26**(8), 1819–1837 (2014)
8. Woźniak, R., Ożdżyński, P., Zakrzewska, D.: Cluster analysis of medical text documents by using semi-clustering approach based on graph representation. Inf. Syst. Manag. **7**(3), 213–224 (2018)
9. Glinka, K., Woźniak, R., Zakrzewska, D.: Improving multi-label medical text classification by feature selection. In: Proceedings of the 2017 IEEE 26th International Conference on Enabling Technologies: Infrastructure for Collaborative Enterprises, pp. 176–181. IEEE Computer Society, Poznań (2017)
10. Bird, S., Klein, E., Loper, E.: Natural Language Processing with Python. O'Reilly Media Inc., Sebastopol (2009)
11. Andersen, J.S., Zukunft, O.: Semi-clustering that scales: an empirical evaluation of GraphX. In: Proceedings of the 2016 IEEE International Congress on Big Data, pp. 333–336. IEEE Computer Society, San Francisco (2016)
12. Malewicz, G., et al.: Pregel: a system for large-scale graph processing. In: Proceedings of the 2010 International Conference on Management of Data, pp. 135–146. ACM, Indianapolis (2010)
13. Ohsumed: text categorization corpus. http://disi.unitn.it/moschitti/corpora.htm. Accessed 6 June 2018
14. Joachims, T.: Text categorization with support vector machines: learning with many relevant features. In: Nédellec, C., Rouveirol, C. (eds.) ECML 1998. LNCS, vol. 1398, pp. 137–142. Springer, Heidelberg (1998). https://doi.org/10.1007/BFb0026683
15. Weka 3: data mining software in Java. https://www.cs.waikato.ac.nz/ml/weka/. Accessed 6 June 2018
16. Mulan: a Java library for multi-label learning. http://mulan.sourceforge.net/. Accessed 6 June 2018
17. Sechidis, K., Tsoumakas, G., Vlahavas, I.: On the stratification of multi-label data. In: Gunopulos, D., Hofmann, T., Malerba, D., Vazirgiannis, M. (eds.) ECML

PKDD 2011. LNCS (LNAI), vol. 6913, pp. 145–158. Springer, Heidelberg (2011). https://doi.org/10.1007/978-3-642-23808-6_10

18. Okapi: most advanced open-source machine learning library for Apache Giraph. http://grafos.ml/okapi.html. Accessed 6 June 2018

19. NetworkX: Python software for complex networks. https://networkx.github.io/. Accessed 6 June 2018

Online Principal Component Analysis
for Evolving Data Streams

Monika Grabowska[✉] and Wojciech Kotłowski

Institute of Computing Science, Poznan University of Technology, Poznań, Poland
{mgrabowska,wkotlowski}@cs.put.poznan.pl

Abstract. We consider an online version of the Principal Component Analysis (PCA), where the goal is to keep track of a subspace of small dimension which captures most of the variance of the data arriving sequentially in a stream. We assume the data stream is evolving and hence the target subspace is changing over time. We cast this problem as a prediction problem, where the goal is to minimize the total compression loss on the data sequence. We review the most popular methods for online PCA and show that the state-of-the-art IPCA algorithm is unable to track the best subspace in this setting. We then propose two modifications of this algorithm, and show that they exhibit a much better predictive performance than the original version of IPCA. Our algorithms are compared against other popular method for online PCA in a computational experiment on real data sets from computer vision.

Keywords: Incremental PCA · Online PCA · Evolving data streams

1 Introduction

Principal Component Analysis (PCA) [7] is a popular procedure for the analysis, compression, and visualization of the data. The goal is to find a low-dimensional representation of the data which captures most of the variance in the data. Formally, in (uncentered) PCA the goal is to project a set of T d-dimensional instance vectors $\boldsymbol{x}_1, \ldots, \boldsymbol{x}_T$ onto a k-dimensional subspace ($k \ll d$), represented by a rank k projection matrix $\boldsymbol{P}$, in order to maximize the total squared norm of the projected instances, $\sum_{t=1}^{T} \|\boldsymbol{P}\boldsymbol{x}_t\|^2$. This is equivalent to finding the *principal* eigenvectors $\boldsymbol{u}_1, \ldots, \boldsymbol{u}_k$ of the data covariance matrix $\sum_{t=1}^{T} \boldsymbol{x}_t \boldsymbol{x}_t^\top$, and setting the projection matrix to $\boldsymbol{P} = \sum_{i=1}^{k} \boldsymbol{u}_i \boldsymbol{u}_i^\top$.

This formulation of PCA can be limiting in cases when the data is observed *sequentially* (in a stream) and memory requirements forbid storing previously observed instances, a setting often called *online PCA* or *incremental PCA*. While one could just store and update the data covariance matrix, this requires $O(d^2)$

The authors acknowledge support from the Polish National Science Centre (grant no. 2016/22/E/ST6/00299).

T. Czachórski et al. (Eds.): ISCIS 2018, CCIS 935, pp. 130–137, 2018.
https://doi.org/10.1007/978-3-030-00840-6_15

time and memory per iteration, which is prohibitively expensive for real-life high-dimensional data. Therefore, there have been numerous research works dedicated to designing more efficient methods with $O(kd)$ space complexity, by only keeping track of the top k principal eigenvectors or maintaining a low-rank approximation of the covariance matrix [1,6,8,10,11,13]. These methods, however, mostly assume that the characteristic of the data does not change over time.

In this paper, we consider *evolving data streams*, where the data distribution (along with the target low-dimensional subspace) changes over time, a phenomenon referred to as *concept drift* [5]. The goal of an algorithm is then to track the target subspace by producing a sequence of rank k projection matrices $P_1, \ldots, P_T$. Since in the evolving streams it is often hard to determine the actual target subspace at any given time, we cast the online PCA as a *prediction problem* [12]: in each trial t, the projection matrix P_t is evaluated on the next instance x_t by means of a *compression loss* $\|x_t - P_t x_t\|^2$, the squared distance between the instance and its part captured within the subspace P_t. The algorithm is then evaluated by its cumulative loss over the whole data stream, without reference to some underlying target subspace.

We focus on a popular method for online PCA, simply called *Incremental PCA* (IPCA) [1,6]. The algorithm maintains a rank k approximation of the covariance matrix by keeping and efficiently updating its eigenvalue decomposition. IPCA has been shown to perform exceptionally well on the real-life data, outperforming all other methods in the experiments [1,2,4]. Unfortunately, IPCA fails in the presence of concept drift, unable to forget about the influence of the past instance. We thus propose two modifications of the IPCA algorithm suited for the evolving data streams. They introduce a forgetting mechanism by altering the eigenvalue update of IPCA. The first method, *Discounted IPCA (DIPCA)*, is based on gradually forgetting the stored eigenvalues by multiplying them by a discount factor $\gamma \in (0, 1)$ whenever the number of nonzero eigenvalues exceeds k. This effectively induces a soft time window over the recent past history taken into account by the algorithm. The second method, *Reduced IPCA (RIPCA)*, also reduces the stored eigenvalues, but the reduction depends on the accuracy of the currently stored low rank approximation with respect to the current instance x_t. In particular, if the algorithm incurs zero compression loss in a given trial, no reduction of eigenvalues is performed, while if the loss is large, the eigenvalues may be decreased substantially. We test our methods in a computational experiments involving several real-life data sets from computer vision, comparing them against three state-of-the-art algorithms for Online PCA: the original IPCA algorithm, Oja's method [10] and Matrix Stochastic Gradient (MSG) [2]. It turns out that toth DIPCA and RIPCA significantly improves on IPCA, and are superior or competitive to the other methods.

2   Problem Statement

We cast the online PCA as a prediction problem as follows [12]. In each trial $t = 1, \ldots, T$, the algorithm chooses a projection matrix $P_t \in \mathbb{R}^{d \times d}$ of rank k, based on the previously observed instance vectors $x_1, \ldots, x_{t-1}$. Then, a new instance $x_t \in \mathbb{R}^d$ appears, and the algorithm suffers compression loss $\|x_t - P_t x_t\|^2$, the squared Euclidean norm of the part of the instance orthogonal to the subspace defined by P_t. As P_t is chosen *before* observing instance x_t, the compression loss measures the quality of algorithm's prediction expressed by P_t. We evaluate the algorithm by means of its cumulative compression loss on the whole data sequence, $\sum_{t=1}^{T} \|x_t - P_t x_t\|^2$. To justify the use of compression loss as a performance metric, we note [12] that the projection matrix P^* minimizing the total compression loss on the whole sequence is exactly the solution of the *offline* PCA problem, i.e. $P^* = \sum_{i=1}^{k} u_i u_i^\top$, where $u_1, \ldots, u_k$ are the *principal* eigenvectors of the total data covariance matrix $\sum_{t=1}^{T} x_t x_t^\top$. For static data streams, the performance of an algorithm can be measured by the *regret*, which is the difference between the algorithm's cumulative loss and the cumulative loss of P^*. For evolving data stream, there is little sense in computing P^* over the entire stream, but one can sometimes still compute a sequence of optimal projections $P_1^*, \ldots, P_T^*$ and compare the total algorithm's loss to the loss of such sequence (as done in one of our experiments).

We focus on one of the most popular methods for online PCA, called *Incremental PCA* (IPCA) [1,3,6]. The algorithm maintains a rank k approximation of the covariance matrix, denoted C_t, and the prediction of the algorithm P_t is a projection matrix spanned by the eigenvectors of C_t. In each trial t, after observing new instance x_t, IPCA updates C_t to C_{t+1} by a two-step procedure:

$$(\text{update step}) \quad \widetilde{C}_{t+1} = C_t + x_t x_t^\top,$$
$$(\text{projection step}) \quad C_{t+1} = \operatorname*{argmin}_{\text{rank-}k \text{ matrix } C} \|\widetilde{C}_{t+1} - C\|_F,$$

where $\|\cdot\|_F$ denotes the Frobenious norm, while the minimum is over all matrices of rank k. Thus, C_t is first updated to an intermediate matrix $\widetilde{C}_{t+1}$ using a standard covariance matrix update. As the rank of $\widetilde{C}_{t+1}$ (number of nonzero eigenvalues) may exceed k, C_{t+1} is a rank k matrix closest to $\widetilde{C}_{t+1}$ in terms of Frobenius norm. This amounts to simply setting the smallest, i.e. $(k+1)$-th, eigenvalue of $\widetilde{C}_{t+1}$ to zero, while the remaining eigenvalues remain the same. While C_t has size $d \times d$, the algorithm never stores it explicitly, instead maintaining its eigenvalue decomposition $C_t = V_t \operatorname{diag}(\lambda_t) V_t^\top$, where $\lambda_t = (\lambda_{t,1}, \ldots, \lambda_{t,k})$ is a vector of k eigenvalues sorted in a decreasing order, and $V_t \in \mathbb{R}^{d \times k}$ stores the eigenvectors as its columns. The update step in the algorithm can be performed efficiently in time $O(dk^2)$ by using a rank-one update of the eigendecomposition [1,3]. Let $\widetilde{xC}_{t+1} = V_{t+1} \operatorname{diag}(\widetilde{\lambda}_{t+1}) V_{t+1}^\top$ be the eigendecomposition of $\widetilde{C}_{t+1}$ obtained in this way. The projection step then amounts to setting $C_{t+1} = V_{t+1} \operatorname{diag}(\lambda_{t+1}) V_{t+1}^\top$, where $\lambda_{t+1,i} = \widetilde{\lambda}_{t+1,i}$ for $i \leq k$ and $\lambda_{t+1,k+1} = 0$.

3 The Algorithms

While IPCA has been shown to perform very well on the real-life static data streams [1,2,4], our empirical analysis in the experiment section reveals that it fails in the presence of concept drift. This is because the stored eigenvalues λ_t can only increase in each trial, therefore the influence of the past instance is never forgotten, whereas the forgetting mechanism is crucial for the algorithm to account for the changes in the data distribution. Therefore, we propose two modifications of of the original IPCA algorithm suited for the evolving data streams, solely based on altering the eigenvalue update of IPCA.

The first method, called *Discounted IPCA (DIPCA)*, is based on decreasing the stored eigenvalues by multiplying them with a discount factor $\gamma \in (0, 1)$ whenever the number of eigenvalues exceeds k. Formally, let $\widetilde{\lambda}_{t+1}$ be the eigenvalue vector after the eigendecomposition update at trial t. If the length of $\widetilde{\lambda}_{t+1}$ is k, we set $\lambda_{t+1} = \widetilde{\lambda}_{t+1}$. If the length of $\widetilde{\lambda}_{t+1}$ is $k + 1$ (so that the current instance x_t is not in the span of C_t), we modify the projection step of IPCA to:

$$\lambda_{t+1,i} = \gamma\widetilde{\lambda}_{t+1,i}, \quad i \leq k, \qquad \lambda_{t+1,k+1} = 0.$$

It this way, the information stored in the covariance approximation C_t is reduced by γ. Therefore, the *effective* number of observations stored within C_t for large t is given by $1 + \gamma + \gamma^2 + \ldots = \frac{1}{1-\gamma}$, and thus can be thought of as a size of the soft time window of the past data on which the algorithm depends. Note that γ must be tuned for a particular data stream under consideration.

The second method, *Reduced IPCA (RIPCA)*, decreases the stored eigenvalues in a way, which depends on the accuracy of stored approximation C_t with respect to instance x_t. Formally, we perform the eigenvalue reduction as follows:

$$\lambda_{t+1,i} = \left(\widetilde{\lambda}_{t+1,i}^{1/\alpha} - \widetilde{\lambda}_{t+1,k+1}^{1/\alpha}\right)^\alpha, \quad i \leq k + 1,$$

where $\alpha \geq 1$ is a parameter. The smallest eigenvalue $\lambda_{t+1,k+1}$ thus becomes zero (and, along with its eigenvector, can be dropped), while the remaining eigenvalues decrease by the amount, which depends on $\lambda_{t+1,k+1}$ (large $\lambda_{t+1,k+1}$ implies large decrease), and on α (large α means more aggressive decrease). Note that if x_t is in the span of C_t (so that the compression loss is zero), $\widetilde{\lambda}_{t+1,k+1} = 0$, and no reduction is performed. On the other hand, it can be verified that if the algorithm suffers compression loss $\ell_t > 0$ on x_t, and all eigenvalues of C_t exceed ℓ_t, then $\widetilde{\lambda}_{t+1,k+1} = \ell_t$, i.e. the smallest eigenvalue equals the compression loss at trial t. Thus, the reduction of eigenvalues depends on the amount of loss suffered by the algorithm. Interestingly, when $\alpha = 1$, RIPCA becomes identical to the Frequent Directions algorithm introduced for matrix sketching [9].

4   Experimental Study

We test our methods in a computational experiment, comparing them against the state-of-the-art algorithms for online PCA: the original IPCA algorithm, Oja's method and Matrix Stochastic Gradient (MSG). Oja's algorithm [10] consists of the repeated update of stored eigenvectors followed by their orthonormalization:

$$\text{(update step) } \widetilde{V}_{t+1} = V_t + \eta_t x_t x_t^\top V_t,$$
$$\text{(normalization step) } V_{t+1} = \text{QR}(\widetilde{V}_{t+1}),$$

Table 1. Description of the movie data streams

Name	# instances (T)	# features (d)
David	537	4 800
David indoor	400	4 800
Dog	1 390	4 800
Ming Hsuan	1 804	4 800
Sylvester	1 344	4 800

where $V_t \in \mathbb{R}^{d \times k}$ stores k eigenvectors as columns, QR$(\cdot)$ is the QR decomposition, while η_t is a *learning rate*, which needs to be tuned. The MSG algorithm [2] works by a repeated application of updates and projections similarly to IPCA:

$$\text{(update step) } \widetilde{C}_{t+1} = C_t + \eta_t x_t x_t^\top,$$
$$\text{(projection step) } C_{t+1} = \underset{\text{rank-}\ell \text{ matrix } C \text{ with } \text{tr}(C)=k}{\text{argmin}} \|\widetilde{C}_{t+1} - C\|_F.$$

The main differences are: larger rank $\ell > k$ of the stored matrix, the trace constraint in the projection and the learning rate η_t in the update. Following [2], we set $\ell = k + 1$ in the experiment. We will show that the presence of learning rates makes both algorithms work quite well for evolving stream.

In the first experiment, we used five movies of different lengths[1] (see Table 1). We treat each frame in a movie as a data instance. As the scenes along with lightning conditions change over time in each movie, we thus get five evolving data streams. Every frame was downsampled to the resolution 80×60 with one channel, which gives 4800 features. The performance of the algorithms is measured in terms of the cumulative loss, but since this quantity increases in time, it is more illustrative to divide it by the number of trials and plot the *average loss per trial*. For each movie, we take the first 10% of the data, on which the algorithms are allowed to tune their parameters (fixed learning rate $\eta \in \{2^{-4}, 2^{-3}, \ldots, 2^5\}$ for MSG and Oja's method, $(1-\gamma) \in \{2^{-2}, 2^{-3}, \ldots, 2^{-10}\}$ for DIPCA, and $\alpha \in \{1, 1.5, 2, \ldots, 5\}$ for RIPCA). Then, the algorithms are run (from scratch) on the remaining 90% of the stream with selected learning rate, and their cumulative losses are measured. For each algorithm, we thus get a learning curve of the average loss per trial as a function of time. We tested each movie with the number of principal components $k \in \{5, 10\}$.

The results are presented in Fig. 1. They indicate that DIPCA and RIPCA are either competitive or superior to MSG and Oja's algorithms in terms of the average loss on all data sets, and the difference often gets even more pronounced at initial iterations. While MSG, Oja's, DIPCA and RIPCA generally decrease their average loss and thus are able to track the optimal subspace, IPCA gets stuck at a suboptimal solution and does not learn at all. The running times of each algorithm on each movie are given in Table 2. It follows that Oja's algorithm

---

[1] Obtained from: http://www.cs.toronto.edu/~dross/ivt/.

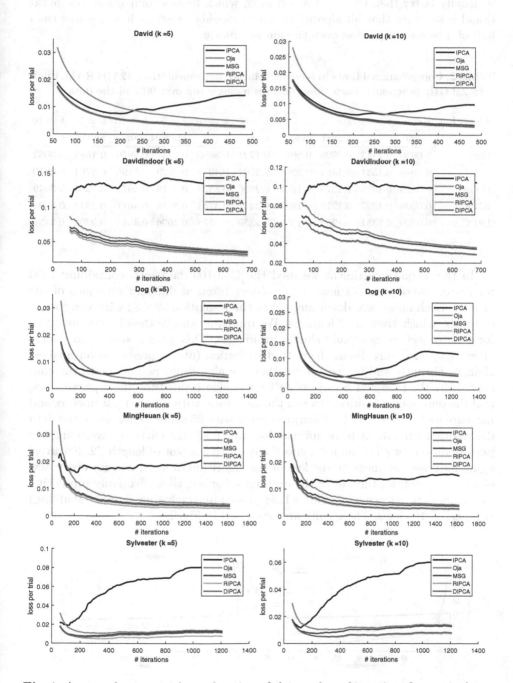

Fig. 1. Average loss per trial as a function of the number of iterations for movie data.

is usually faster than the other algorithms, which have a comparable computational cost. Note that all algorithms are reasonably fast, as it takes less than half of a second to process even the longest movie.

Table 2. Computational times in seconds (Matlab implementation, 12 GB RAM, dual-core 2.0 GHz processor). Each time concerns a single run over 90% of the data.

Algorithm	$k = 5$	$k = 10$	$k = 5$	$k = 10$	$k = 5$	$k = 10$	$k = 5$	$k = 10$	$k = 5$	$k = 10$
	David		David indoor		Dog		Ming Hsuan		Sylvester	
Oja	0.0650	0.1443	0.0929	0.2077	0.1721	0.3805	0.2284	0.4916	0.1685	0.3662
MSG	0.1040	0.1531	0.1484	0.2201	0.2761	0.4052	0.3629	0.5198	0.2701	0.3919
IPCA	0.0916	0.1386	0.1276	0.1967	0.2406	0.3626	0.3118	0.4671	0.2288	0.3449
RIPCA	0.0909	0.1397	0.1276	0.1967	0.2477	0.3704	0.3118	0.4671	0.2343	0.3598
DIPCA	0.0909	0.1351	0.1262	0.1939	0.2350	0.3578	0.3036	0.4584	0.2303	0.3427

In the second experiment we used the Coil-100 data set[2], containing 7200 images of 100 objects (72 images per object taken at different rotations of the object). Each image was downsampled to the resolution 32×32 with three color channels, which gives 3072 features. We randomly shuffle the objects and then for each object we randomly shuffle its images. This gives a stream in which, after every 72 observations, the data distribution (object presented on images) changes abruptly and let us test whether the algorithms can adapt to the concept drift. We take first 5 objects to let the algorithms tune their parameters, and the remaining 95 objects to run the algorithm with selected parameters and measure its loss. As the whole learning curve with 95 sudden changes of the data distribution turned out to be unreadable, we "fold" the curve by averaging the performance over all 95 objects, effectively getting a plot of length 72. For averaging purposes, we measure the loss of the algorithm from scratch for every new object and subtract the loss of the optimal subspace, thus effectively presenting the *average regret per trial*. This whole procedure (including random shuffling) is repeated 10 times. The results are presented in Fig. 2.

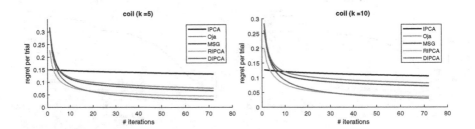

Fig. 2. Averaged regret per trial as a function of the iterations for coil data set.

As in the previous experiment, IPCA performs the worst, while the other methods are able adapt to the evolving stream, getting close to the optimal subspace for each object. Here, DIPCA and RIPCA work clearly better than MSG and Oja's method, and DIPCA has a slight advantage over RIPCA.

5   Conclusions

We considered an online version of the PCA problem for the evolving data streams. We cast this problem as a prediction problem, where the goal is to minimize the total compression loss on the data sequence. We then proposed two modifications of the popular IPCA algorithm, DIPCA and RIPCA, suited for the dealing with concept drift in the data stream. Our algorithms were shown to improve upon the original IPCA algorithm and to be competitive to other popular method for online PCA in a computational experiment on several real data streams with concept drift.

References

1. Arora, R., Cotter, A., Livescu, K., Srebro, N.: Stochastic optimization for PCA and PLS. In: 2012 50th Annual Allerton Conference on Communication, Control, and Computing, pp. 861–868 (2012)
2. Arora, R., Cotter, A., Srebro, N.: Stochastic optimization of PCA with capped MSG. In: NIPS, pp. 1815–1823 (2013)
3. Brand, M.: Incremental singular value decomposition of uncertain data with missing values. In: ECCV (2002)
4. Cardot, H., Degras, D.: Online principal component analysis in high dimension: which algorithm to choose? Int. Stat. Rev. (2017)
5. Gama, J.: Knowledge Discovery from Data Streams. Chapman & Hall/CRC, Boca Raton (2010)
6. Hall, P.M., Marshall, D., Martin, R.R.: Incremental eigenanalysis for classification. In: British Machine Vision Conference, pp. 286–295 (1998)
7. Hotelling, H.: Analysis of a complex of statistical variables into principal components. J. Educ. Psychol. **24**(417–441), 498–520 (1933)
8. Levy, A., Lindenbaum, M.: Sequential Karhunen-Loeve basis extraction and its application to images. IEEE Trans. Image Process. **9**(8), 1371–1374 (2000)
9. Liberty, E.: Simple and deterministic matrix sketching. In: International Conference on Knowledge Discovery and Data Mining, pp. 581–588. ACM (2013)
10. Oja, E., Karhunen, J.: On stochastic approximation of the eigenvectors and eigenvalues of the expectation of a random matrix. J. Math. Anal. Appl. **106**(1), 69–84 (1985)
11. Ross, D.A., Lim, J., Lin, R.S., Yang, M.H.: Incremental learning for robust visual tracking. Int. J. Comput. Vis. **77**(1–3), 125–141 (2008)
12. Warmuth, M.K., Kuzmin, D.: Randomized online PCA algorithms with regret bounds that are logarithmic in the dimension. J. Mach. Learn. Res. **9**, 2287–2320 (2008)
13. Zhao, H., Yuen, P.C., Kwok, J.T.: A novel incremental principal component analysis and its application for face recognition. IEEE Trans. Syst. Man Cybern. Part B **36**(4), 873–886 (2006)

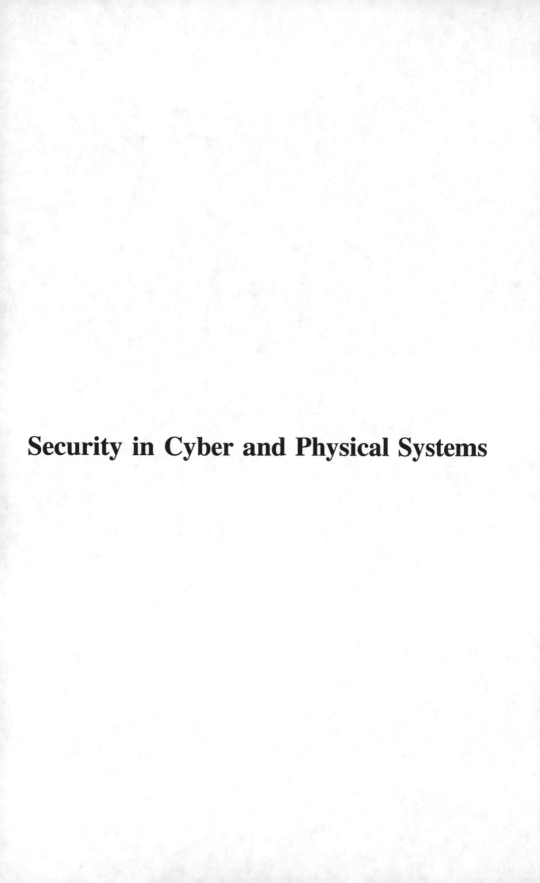

Security in Cyber and Physical Systems

Intrusion Detection with Comparative Analysis of Supervised Learning Techniques and Fisher Score Feature Selection Algorithm

Doğukan Aksu[1]([⊠]), Serpil Üstebay[2], Muhammed Ali Aydın[1], and Tülin Atmaca[3]

[1] Istanbul University, 34320 Istanbul, Turkey
{d.aksu,aydinali}@istanbul.edu.tr
[2] Istanbul Medeniyet University, 34000 Istanbul, Turkey
serpil.ustebay@medeniyet.edu.tr
[3] Université Paris-Saclay, 9 rue Charles Fourier, 91011 Paris, Evry, France
tulin.atmaca@telecom-sudparis.eu

Abstract. Rapid development of technologies not only makes life easier, but also reveals a lot of security problems. Developing and changing of attack types affect many people, organizations, companies etc. Therefore, intrusion detection systems have been developed to avoid financial and emotional loses. In this paper, we used CICIDS2017 dataset which consist of benign and the most cutting-edge common attacks. Best features are selected by using Fisher Score algorithm. Real world data extracted from the dataset are classified as DDoS or benign with using Support Vector Machine (SVM), K Nearest Neighbour (KNN) and Decision Tree (DT) algorithms. As a result of the study, 0,9997%, 0,5776%, 0,99% success rates were achieved respectively.

Keywords: IDS · Machine learning · CICIDS2017

1 Introduction

Network security is one of the major challenges in today's world. This challenge brings network security to a very important position in terms of research. Availability, confidentiality, and integrity of information have to be provided. If any of them is threatened by something or someone, this action can be identified as an intrusion. Intrusions can be classified as Active and Passive attacks. Passive attacks monitor and analyze the network traffic and usually based on eavesdropping. Active attacks disrupt and block the network normal s behavior. Denial of Service (DoS) attacks, Wormhole attacks, Distributed Denial of Service (DDoS) attacks, Modification, Spoofing attacks, Sybil attacks and Sinkhole are examples of active attacks.

Feature extraction can be made manually or various feature extraction algorithms can be applied to data for automated process. We use Fisher Score feature selection algorithm to select the best features.

© Springer Nature Switzerland AG 2018
T. Czachórski et al. (Eds.): ISCIS 2018, CCIS 935, pp. 141–149, 2018.
https://doi.org/10.1007/978-3-030-00840-6_16

Machine Learning algorithms can be classified as supervised and unsupervised learning algorithms. In this work, KNN, SVM and Decision Tree supervised machine learning algorithms are used to detect intrusions.

Remaining parts of the paper are organized as follows: Sect. 2 presents a literature review and provides a detailed explanation of IDS. Section 3 gives information about used Materials and methods. Section 4 introduces experimental results of the classification algorithms and highlights their performance measurements comparatively. Finally, outcome and our future works are placed in Sect. 5.

2   Literature Review

Intrusion detection is a process which analyses the behaviors that threaten the security of the system in order to disrupt accessibility, confidentiality, and integrity of the data on a network or computer system [7]. In addition to this definition, Intrusion Detection Systems have the various definitions in literature such as; they are designed to detect attacks on computer systems [8], they do not attempt to block the attack and gives a warning message (alarm) to the security specialist in case of possible security violation [9], they detect unauthorized access to the resources or to the data of computer systems [10], they are software tools used to detect unauthorized access to a network or computer system [11].

According to the usage and the learning methods, Intrusion Detection Systems are classified as below (Fig. 1).

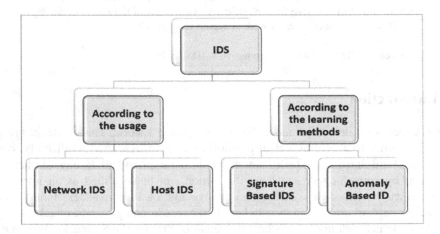

Fig. 1. Classification of IDS.

2.1   Network IDS

Network Intrusion Detection Systems (NIDS) monitor and analyze packet traffic on a network. Both Rule-based methods and Anomaly detection techniques can be used to detect intrusions. They usually work real time and when an intrusion is detected by NIDS, an alarm is generated. NIDS record all information about all intrusions as logs.

2.2   Host IDS

In spite of the fact that Network Intrusion Detection systems monitor all traffic on the network, Host-based Intrusion Detection systems only watch intrusions based on the system's configuration and application activity. Host-based IDS analyze abnormal behavior logs on a specific system. The term "host" is referred to a single computer, so a separate sensor for each machine will be required.

2.3   Signature-Based IDS

Firstly, rules are defined in this method. Therefore they can be called as Rule-Based or Misuse IDS. Then, Intrusions are detected with these rules and detected intrusions are stored in databases. Finally, Network traffics are monitored and at the same time packets are compared with stored intrusions. While they have high accuracy to detect known intrusion, they could not perform same results for new attack types. For this reason, they are preferred to common attacks.

2.4   Anomaly-Based IDS

In this method, a profile is determined for a user group or for each user separately. Profiles can be created dynamically or manually and can be used as baselines to define normal user activity. If an operation on the network is very different from the baseline, an alarm is triggered. They are very effective not only in detecting theft of the user account but also identifying internal attacks. They can identify new attacks with a better performance than Signature Based IDS.

Both Intrusion Detection Systems have some weaknesses. Therefore, Hybrid Intrusion Detection Systems are developed by using various Intrusion Detection Systems features together. Hybrid Systems aim to combine the strengths of each type and detection method while eliminating the weaknesses.

In literature, most of the studies on Intrusion Detection Systems use KDD99 dataset [1–5]. The KDD99 dataset consists of 41 features obtained by preprocessing from the DARPA dataset in 1999. Ibrahimi and Ouaddane applied Principal Component Analysis (PCA) and Linear Discriminant Analysis (LDA) to identify the intrusion with NSL-KDD dataset [1]. Moustafa and Slay show to comparative results of UNSW-NB15 and KDD99 datasets to analyze network intrusions [2]. In Liuying et al's paper, their experiments and analysis are performed based on the KDD99 dataset to detect and classify malicious patterns in network traffic [3]. Almansob and Lomte used Principal Component Analysis (PCA) feature extraction method and Naive Bayes classification algorithm with the KDD99 dataset [4]. In addition, Chithik and Rabbani used PCA, SVM, and KDD99 for IDS [5].

Our contribution is to use new and up to date CICIDS2017 dataset and presenting results of different machine learning algorithms comparatively. The CICIDS2017 dataset consists of benign and the most cutting-edge common attacks [6]. A detailed explanation of the dataset is in the Dataset Section.

3   Material and Method

3.1   Dataset

In this paper, the CICIDS2017 dataset is developed by Canadian Institute for Cybersecurity that is used to detect DDoS attacks. Benign and the most cutting-edge common attacks, such as real-world data (PCAPs), are included in CICIDS2017 dataset. Moreover, the dataset include es results of the network traffic analysis with using labeled flows based on the source and destination addresses of IPs protocols, source and destination ports, timestamp (CSV files).

There are 225,746 records of DDoS and Benign in the CICIDS2017 and each record has 80 features such as Protocol, Flow ID, Source IP, Destination IP, Source Port, Destination Port, Flow Duration, Total Fwd Packets, Total Backwards Packet etc. A part of features and records is as shown in Table 1.

Table 1. A sample set of records from dataset.

Source IP	Source port	Destination port		Flow duration	Total fwd packets	Total backward packets
192.168.10.16	41936	443		143347	47	60
192.168.10.16	42970	80		50905	1	1
192.168.10.16	41944	443	...	143899	46	58
192.168.10.17	12886	53		313	2	2
192.168.10.16	41942	443		142605	45	58
192.168.10.17	33063	53		253	2	2
192.168.10.16	41940	443		142499	46	53
192.168.10.16	41938	443		23828	27	31

The data collection process started on Monday, July 3, 2017 at 9:00 am and ended on July 7, 2017, Friday at 5:00 pm. Monday only contains the benign traffic. The applied attacks are Brute Force SSH, Brute Force FTP, Infiltration, Heartbleed, Web Attack, DoS, Botnet, and DDoS. Attacks had been implemented on Tuesday, on Wednesday, on Thursday and on Friday morning and afternoon [6].

3.2   Methodology

Machine Learning is a collection of methods which provides various inferences from existing data using mathematical and statistical methods. Machine Learning has a wide application area and includes different learning methodologies such as artificial neural networks (ANN), naive bayes, deep learning, k nearest neighbor, k means, support vector machines (SVM), decision trees, genetic algorithms etc. Machine Learning is used for estimation, prediction and classification. It can be divided into 3 groups in terms of methodologies as unsupervised, semi-supervised and supervised methods.

Supervised methods; a model is created using some training data according to the algorithm used. Then, it is tested to see how successful this model is developed with the test data which is never used in the training. Contrary, unsupervised techniques do not have training data, the model learns by itself. Thus, unsupervised machine learning algorithms usually have lower accuracy rate than supervised techniques.

Finding the best features are very important for classification. However, high dimensions include all features and lead to an increase in the working time; hence it is not a good choice for classification algorithms. One of the most commonly used supervised feature selection technique is Fisher Score feature selection method. Fisher Score is used to reduce dimensions by selecting best features. With selected m features, $X \in R^{dxn}$ input data matrix reduces to $Z \in R^{mxn}$. Then the Fisher Score [14] is calculated as follows (1),

$$F(Z) = tr\left\{(\overline{s_b})(\overline{s_b} + \gamma I)^{-1}\right\} \tag{1}$$

where γ is a positive regularization parameter, $\overline{s_b}$ is between-class scatter matrix, and $\overline{s_t}$ is total scatter matrix.

Let and denote the mean and standard deviation of the whole data set corresponding to the j-th feature. Then the Fisher score of the j-th feature is computed below (2).

$$F(x^j) = \frac{\sum_{k=1}^{c} n_k (\mu_k^j - \mu^j)^2}{(\sigma^j)^2} \tag{2}$$

The top m-ranked features are selected by calculated Fisher score for each feature. The reduced dataset will be the subdataset containing the most significant m features in the original dataset consisting of m feature.

K-NN algorithm is a classification method proposed by T. M. Cover and P. E. Hart [33], where the class of the sample data point and the closest neighbor are determined by k value [12].

1. K value is determined.
2. Euclidean distances to the target object from other objects are calculated.
3. The distances are sorted and the closest neighbors are found depending on the minimum distance.
4. The nearest neighbor categories are collected.
5. The most appropriate neighbor category is selected.

Support Vector Machine algorithms are based on the statistical learning and convex optimization that work according to the principle of structural risk minimization. SVM was developed by Vapnik et al. for the solution of pattern recognition and classification problems [13]. Support vector machines can be classified as linear and non-linear support vector machines.

Decision Tree algorithm is based on the division of input data into groups repeatedly with the aid of a clustering algorithm. Clustering continues in depth until all elements of the group have the same class label.

Flowchart of the system is as shown in Fig. 2. Firstly, we divide the dataset into two parts as training data (90%) and test data (10%).

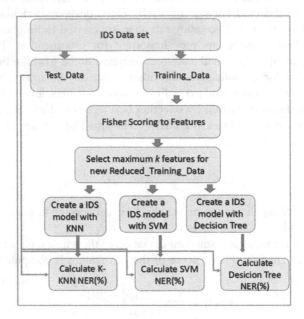

Fig. 2. Flowchart of the proposed system.

The effect of each feature in training dataset is determined by Fisher Score algorithm. Fisher Score creates a weight vector according to each feature's effect for classification. A subset of training data is obtained according to the k features which have maximum weights. Then, KNN, SVM and Decision Tree supervised machine learning algorithms are used to classify logs as benign or DDoS. Finally, Test data is used to measure the accuracy of learning algorithms.

4   Results

We used 26.167 DDos and 26.805 benign examples to train learning algorithms. KNN's k value was selected as 1, the linear kernel was used for SVM and Gini's diversity index was used for the split criterion for Decision Tree algorithm.

The number of features is reduced from 80 to 10 by tens and accuracy rates are calculated for all learning algorithms separately. Learning methods were tested for 100 iterations and the average results were calculated.

Results are shown in Fig. 3. Optimum feature number is 30 for KNN and Decision Tree. A large number of features in KNN cause noise and reduce accuracy. KNN accuracy rate is 99% with the most effective 30 features, while the accuracy is 95% with 80 features. On the other hand, reducing the number of features from 80 to 30 did not change Decision Tree's accuracy rate of 99%.

Beside accuracy rate, recall, precision and F-score metrics are used for performance evaluation in binary classifications. Performance measurements of classifiers are shown in below (Table 2).

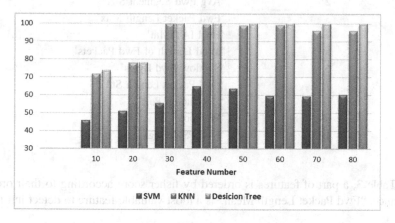

Fig. 3. Feature reduction accuracy results.

Table 2. Classifier performance.

Algorithm	Number of features	Accuracy	Recall	Precision	F1
KNN	80	0.9572	0.9589	0.9566	0.9577
	30	0,9997	0.9985	0.9968	0,9997
SVM	80	0,6069	0,7142	0.5956	0.6463
	30	0,5776	0,8097	0,5654	0,6564
DT	80	0,99	0,99	0,99	0,99
	30	0,99	0,99	0,99	0,99

Table 2 shows performance measurements of the classifiers with 80 and 30 features. Accuracy, recall, precision and F1 score are calculated separately for these learning algorithms. While KNN performed better results with 30 features, evaluation scores did not change for Decision Tree algorithm. On the other hand, SVM's results did not satisfy with both 80 and 30 features.

Finally, most effective 10 features information to detect attacks according to the Fisher score method is listed in Table 3.

Table 3. The most effective 10 features according to the Fisher Scoring.

Order of importance	Feature name
1	'Fwd Packet Length Mean'
2	'Avg Fwd Segment Size'
3	'Fwd Packet Length Max'
4	'Bwd IAT Min'
5	'Total Length of Fwd Packets'
6	'Subflow Fwd Bytes'
7	'Fwd Packet Length Std'
8	'Destination Port'
9	'Protocol'
10	'Fwd PSH Flags'

In Table 3, a part of features is ordered by fisher score according to their order of importance. "Fwd Packet Length Mean" is a most valuable feature to detect intrusions.

5 Conclusion and Future Works

We presented performance measurements of Support Vector Machines, K Nearest Neighbor, and Decision Tree algorithms based on CICIDS2017 dataset comparatively. The best features are selected by using Fisher Score algorithm so non-related features are eliminated and dimension is reduced. Although the dataset was reduced 60% by selecting the best features, the success of KNN increased, the accuracy of DT did not change and SVM's accuracy decreased. Results show that Decision Tree algorithm performed same consequences for both 80 features and 30 features. While SVM's accuracy is decreasing, the accuracy of KNN increased when the number of features was reduced from 80 to 30.

We are planning to use not only DDoS attacks but also all dataset with deep learning algorithms, Apache Spark, and Apache Hadoop technologies together to train and test the dataset as a future work.

Acknowledgement. This work is also a part of the M.Sc. thesis titled Performance Analysis of Log Based Intrusion Detection Systems Istanbul University, Institute of Physical Sciences.

References

1. Ibrahimi, K., Ouaddane, M.: Management of intrusion detection systems based-KDD99: analysis with LDA and PCA. In: 2017 International Conference on Wireless Networks and Mobile Communications (WINCOM), pp. 1–6. IEEE (2017)
2. Moustafa, N., Slay, J.: The significant features of the UNSW-NB15 and the KDD99 data sets for network intrusion detection systems. In: 2015 4th International Workshop on Building Analysis Datasets and Gathering Experience Returns for Security (BADGERS), pp. 25–31. IEEE (2015)

3. Sun, L., Anthony, T.S., Xia, H.Z., Chen, J., Huang, X., Zhang, Y.: Detection and classification of malicious patterns in network traffic using Benford's law. In: Asia-Pacific Signal and Information Processing Association Annual Summit and Conference (APSIPA ASC), pp. 864–872. IEEE (2017)
4. Almansob, S.M., Lomte, S.S.: Addressing challenges for intrusion detection system using naive Bayes and PCA algorithm. In: 2017 2nd International Conference for Convergence in Technology (I2CT), pp. 565–568. IEEE (2017)
5. Raja, M.C., Rabbani, M.M.A.: Combined analysis of support vector machine and principle component analysis for IDS. In: IEEE International Conference on Communication and Electronics Systems, pp. 1–5 (2016)
6. UNB Canadian Cyber Security, Intrusion Detection Evaluation Dataset (CICIDS2017). http://www.unb.ca/cic/datasets/ids-2017.html
7. Lunt, T.F.: Automated audit trail analysis and intrusion detection: a survey. In Proceedings of the 11th National Computer Security Conference, vol. 353 (1988)
8. Denning, D.E.: An intrusion-detection model. IEEE Trans. Softw. Eng. **2**, 222–232 (1987)
9. Crosbie, M., Spafford, E.H.: Defending a computer system using autonomous agents (1995)
10. Endler, D.: Intrusion detection. Applying machine learning to Solaris audit data. In: 1998 Proceedings of 14th Annual Computer Security Applications Conference, pp. 268–279. IEEE (1998)
11. Patcha, A., Park, J.M.: An overview of anomaly detection techniques: existing solutions and latest technological trends. Comput. Netw. **51**(12), 3448–3470 (2007)
12. Cover, T., Hart, P.: Nearest neighbor pattern classification. IEEE Trans. Inf. Theory **13**(1), 21–27 (1967)
13. Cortes, C., Vapnik, V.: Support-vector networks. Mach. Learn. **20**(3), 273–297 (1995)
14. Gu, Q., Li, Z., Han, J.: Generalized fisher score for feature selection (2012). arXiv preprint arXiv:1202.3725

A New Secure and Usable Captcha-Based Graphical Password Scheme

Altaf Khan[✉] and Alexander G. Chefranov

Department of Computer Engineering,
Eastern Mediterranean University, TRNC, Mersin 10, Turkey
{altaf.khan, alexander.chefranov}@emu.edu.tr

Abstract. CaRP are known graphical password schemes using Captcha visual objects for password setting. CaRP contains four schemes with different alphabet symbols used for password specification. We generalize CaRP schemes introducing Click Symbol-Alphanumeric (CS-A) scheme which as CaRP schemes, ClickText (CT), ClickAnimal (CA), AnimalGrid (AG), and ClickPoint (CP), uses a proper symbol selection on the screen by clicking, but does not specify a particular alphabet. In particular, we show that using together in one alphabet Alphanumeric (A) and Visual (V) symbols (CS-AV) improves its usability and users are more motivated towards making strong passwords. For the security analysis, we applied segmentation techniques to identify the symbols on CT and proposed CS-AV. The segmentation and symbols identification of CS-AV and CT scheme do not reveal sensitive information. This paper also studies the usability: Experiments on both schemes show that such usability feature as memorability of CS-AV is greater by 3.75% than that of CT scheme.

Keywords: Graphical password · Captcha · CaRP · Click symbol
Alphabet · Segmentation · Usability

1 Introduction

Graphical password systems use images instead of the textual password that is motivated by the fact that human can remember images easier than text [1]. Security (ability to withstand brute force and segmentation attacks) and memorability (ability to be easily memorized by people) are important for them. Zhu et al. [2] introduced a graphical password scheme, CaRP (Captcha as a gRaphical Password), consisting of CT (ClickText), CA (ClickAnimal), AnimalGrid (AG), and TextPoint (TP) schemes. CaRP is a click-based graphical password scheme based on Captcha technology while Captcha is used by many online services to distinguish the human users and bots (programs) by introducing a challenge [3, 4]. Contrary to Captcha challenges, in CaRP, users' task is to recognize and identify the locations of the password symbols in a proper order.

CT [2] is human-friendly and has low implementation cost but memorability is the same as of the Text password [5, 6]. CA [2] provides the weak password choices while AG has strong choices of password setting but grid-cells window shows poor response

© Springer Nature Switzerland AG 2018
T. Czachórski et al. (Eds.): ISCIS 2018, CCIS 935, pp. 150–157, 2018.
https://doi.org/10.1007/978-3-030-00840-6_17

on image segmentation. Meanwhile, TP [2] scheme can generate stronger password but user's memorability is lower than CT, CA, and AG.

In this paper, we introduce CaRP generalization, referred to hereafter as Click Symbol – Alphabet (CS-A). CS-A is a family of graphical password schemes differing by an alphabet used. In particular, if the alphabet, A is the union of alphanumeric and visual symbols, AV, we have a particular scheme, CS-AV. User's task is to set the graphical password by clicking on the sequence of objects. We found that memorability of CS-AV is better compared to the CT scheme. We conduct two experiments to analyse security (Sect. 4.1) and usability (Sect. 4.2) of CS-AV versus CT. CS-AV shows better than CT resistance to such attacks as segmentation, automatic guessing attacks, and password cracking using standard software tools. In the usability study, we conduct analysing memorability, ease of use, and authentication time showing that these features are better for CS-AV compared to CT.

2   CaRP Scheme Description

CaRP [2] schemes are click-based graphical passwords. According to memory task in memorizing and password setting, CaRP schemes can be classified into two categories: Recognition and a recognition-recall where the user is required to recognize an image and using the recognized objects as cues to enter the password. Recognition-recall combines the tasks of both recognition and cued-recall. Consequently, CaRP has four sub-schemes, CT, CA, AG, and TP described as follows:

The CT scheme is recognition based CaRP which uses 33-character alphabet: capital English letters and digits (excluding visually confusing characters such as I, J, O, and Z, and digits 0, 1), and three special characters, "#", "@", and "&". Characters are drawn in 5 rows with each character rotated randomly from −30 to 30 degrees, scaled from 60% to 120%, and overlapped up to 3 pixels in a 400 × 400 pixel image, shown in Fig. 1(a). CA is recognition based CaRP using 3D models to generate 2D animal images (bird, cow, horse, dog, giraffe, pig, rabbit, camel, and dinosaur) with different views, textures, colours, lighting effects, and optional distortion, e.g., in Fig. 1 (b). The disadvantage of this method is that the number of combinations of animal images is less than that of characters. AnimalGrid is a combination of CA and Click-A-Secret based graphical password scheme. The password space is increased by combining CA with a grid-based graphical password in AG scheme. The grid depends on the size of the selected animal. To set a password, a CA image appears first, then an animal is selected, and the image with $n \times n$ grid appears (shown in Fig. 1 (b)). Each grid-cell is indexed. A user can select from zero to multiple grid-cells to set his/her password. Hence, a password is a sequence of animals interleaving with grid-cells. In TextPoints (TP), that is a recognition-recall CaRP, a set of internal invariant points of the characters is selected to form a set of clickable points. Each point has fixed relative position in a different incarnation, e.g., the font of the character/object and uniquely clicked by users no matter how the object appears in CaRP image. To set the password, a user must identify the first object or character then click the invariant points matching her password. Identification of objects provides the cues with 3 pixels or less tolerance to locate the invariant point for setting the password but still, it is difficult to recall for

(a) CT scheme   (b) AG scheme   (c) CS-AV scheme

Fig. 1. Shows the Fig. (a) is a CT scheme, Fig. (b) is AG and Fig. (c) is proposed CS-AV scheme

human and memorability results significantly decrease compared to recognition based schemes. Nguyen et al. [4] assume that the Captcha image contains alphanumeric characters and a user has to drag-and-drop each challenge character onto the correct character in the image. Their main objective was to solve the Captcha challenge with colour and black-and-white versions, where they only examine solving Captcha challenge but they did not examine the graphical password.

3   Click Symbol – Alphanumeric and Visual (CS-AV) Scheme

Click Symbol – Alphanumeric generalizes CaRP by allowing any alphabet to be used for a graphical password, and CS-AV is a recognition-based graphical password built on a combination of letters, digits, visual symbols, and images as it is shown in Fig. 1 (c).

According to the recent Captcha security and research study [4, 7, 8], a two-layer Microsoft Captcha is broken with a success rate of 65.8% [7] and 44.6% [8]. Thus, instead of letters and digits only, CS-AV model is built on letters, digits, visual symbols and images which strongly oppose the text-based Captcha attacks. CS-AV follows the CaRP mechanism with a few additional characteristics. CS-AV alphabet objects (their number, N=143, in our settings), are mapped into the image in random sequence but with the same colour for each symbol in each attempt, each symbol is rotated from 30^0 to $-30°$, zoomed from 60% to 80%, overlapped up to (3-to-5) pixels randomly. In each attempt, each row contains r ($10 \leq r \leq 15$, depending on the number of input symbols) symbols which are drawn into the sine wave structure in a CS-AV image where the wave amplitude is varied (8 to 15 pixels) in each attempt. Like CaRP mechanism, our scheme excludes the boundary, corner and overlapped area with neighbours to maintain the security and ease of use for users. Each image name is assigned a unique string and instead of the image, the string is used for password setting. The CS-AV scheme is implemented in C#.Net. Each symbol is placed in a quadrilateral area and ground truth is stored; and the symbols are arranged on the CS-AV image as shown in Fig. 1(c). The quadrilateral area can be divided into two triangles to implement the proposed scheme in the response of user click. Furthermore, we applied the binary search algorithm to reduce computational cost with $O(\log_2 n)$

computational complexity. If it returns nothing, it means the click is located outside the symbols boundaries, or on the boundary, or on the overlapped area. To verify that a point lies inside a triangle, the following inequality [9] is used:

$$(P_X - B_X) \times (A_Y - B_Y) - (P_Y - B_Y) \times (A_X - B_X) \geq 0,$$

where P_x and P_y are coordinates of click point P, and A_x, A_y and B_x, B_y represent x and y-coordinates of vertices A and B corresponding to edge AB of a triangle, respectively.

CS-AV has three modes of operation:

- Add symbols
- Client registration
- Client authentication

In the first mode, admin of an Authentication Server (AS), adds alphanumeric characters, special symbols, and images to the dataset. In the registration mode, a client, C, is registered to AS securely and generates a graphical password by clicking on the sequence of visual symbols displayed on the CS-AV image to generate a graphical password, e.g., a user clicks on the following sequence of symbols: p=ABC@T98 🦓. An animal image will be replaced with its name and then 'p' will be hashed with salt 's' and then stored into AS database. In authentication mode, the client C will click the same sequence of objects and it will be hashed with s, then both the stored one and new hashed values will be compared, and if they are the same, the user will be accepted, otherwise, rejected.

4 Experimental Results on Security and Usability of CS-AV and CT Schemes

4.1 Security Analysis

Security analysis is conducted using advanced image segmentation technique, and automatic guessing attacks, and Captcha breakers test.

Image Segmentation Technique. Image segmentation Captcha attack can be used to break it at a high success rate ($\sim 100\%$ for simple Captcha) [2, 4, 7, 8, 10–12]. To analyse the Captcha segmentation results on CS-AV, CT, and AG schemes, we apply a top four best-ranked programs of Captcha breakers to obtain the characters information. The programs are built on advanced image processing technique which analyses and solves Captcha. GSA [11] version v2.97 and Captcha Sniper [12] version X3 are advanced Captcha breakers which are built on colour filling segmentation, and opportunistic segmentation techniques and character skeletonization. We use i2OCR [13], and OCR [14] as well to analyse segmentation results for the CT and CS-AV images.

Skeletonization is a process that is used in image processing to thin a shape of input symbol while preserving the general pattern of the shape which may potentially be used to identify geometric features of characters [4].

We apply the edge detection filter to CS-AV by applying GSA and Sniper [11, 12] with their adjustable parameters. Thus, the edge detection filter highlights the edges but doesn't facilitate the task of segmenting a character boundary.

For object identification, segmentation of image is a computationally hard combinatorial problem [6] but in brute force attack on AG scheme, in grid-cells window, the grid-cells are clearly recognized (98.5%) by [11–14]. Consequently, we applied the brute force attack to identify characters on the CT and CS-AV images by using [11, 12]. In this experiment, we obtained 16 images of CT and CS-AV schemes individually and then we applied Captcha breaker tools [11, 12] on each image. Therefore, the mean and standard deviation for CT and CS-AV scheme is recorded. In the result, mean, minimum, maximum, and standard deviation (SD) of character identification of CT and CS-AV schemes are shown in Table 1. Thus, Table 1 results indicate that CS-AV scheme provides less character identification information than CT scheme.

Table 1. Comparison of Captcha breaker attacks' on CT and CS-AV scheme

Methods	Mean	Min	Max	SD
CT	4.57	3.37	7.54	4.86
CS-AV	2.10	1.06	2.45	1.9

Automatic Guessing Attacks. In this attack, the trial process is performed automatically. A theoretical description of automatic guessing attacks is given in [2, section VI-B]. However, in this study, we applied a practical approach to finding out the number of characters which are accurately clicked. Thus, we applied an Automatic-Mouse Click attack. It is actually a type of brute force attack which uses random or designated clicks on a computer screen. Each mouse click defines x and y coordinates which represent a point location on the computer screen. This program takes input coordinates from a script (file) and clicks on the screen accordingly.

Automatic Mouse Click Setting. We generate the random coordinate values which lie inside the CS-AV images. We repeat this process and generate several files containing random sequences of coordinates. Then these files are used as input in the 'Auto Mouse Clicker' [15]. We try these settings in several attempts for CT and CS-AV to examine how many correct symbol locations are clicked on CS-AV and CT. Mean percentage of characters clicked correctly for CT and CS-AV images is 5.89% and 6.34%, respectively. Percentage for CT is lower than for CS-AV because the number of objects on CS-AV is much larger than on CT and they cover greater clickable space. However, the resultant string is not enough to guess the password. Additionally, only objects locations are clickable and login attempts are limited.

Password Cracker. We also analysed the security of the passwords by using a popular password-cracking tool: 'John the Ripper version 1.7.9' [16]. This cracker is used for a database with passwords of 40 participants engaged in our usability study (see Sect. 4.2). John the Ripper has three operation modes: "Single crack", "wordlist", and "incremental". In our study, the default setting is used of John the Ripper and taking wordlist "password.lst" from [17], which was used in the "wordlist" mode. Operating in "single crack", "wordlist", and "incremental" modes for 24 h for each scheme, John the Ripper did not find any password of CT or CS-AV schemes. This experiment was conducted using SAMSUNG (Core i5, 2.53 GHz, RAM 4 GB) portable PC.

4.2 Usability Analysis

Usability can be characterized by the following features according to [2, section VII-B].

- Successful attempts of participants (memorability study)
- Ease of use
- Time of authentication

Experiment Setting. We conducted the usability analysis to compare memorability of CS-AV and CT schemes. We recruited 40 participants (36 males, 4 females, and the average age was 25.5) including 5 PhD and 12 Master's students, 5 job holders, and remaining were undergraduate students.

All participants were trained for each scheme as they were not familiar with the graphical password before. Each participant was trained in: using a login form to interact with an authentication server, and creating a password. To maintain the same security level, each participant was required to enter at least 8 alphanumeric characters or symbols, and password must contain at least two not repeated digits, letters, or symbols, and should not be a dictionary word. Our system motivates the users by providing the guidance and alternative forms of feedback (emoji-based approach) [18]. The time required for each participant authentication in each trial was recorded. During three week evaluation of each scheme, each participant was required to login with particular intervals between two regular logins: after the creation of a password, one, two, and three weeks later. In each attempt, a participant was allowed three attempts to log in. Additionally, at the end of the survey, we also conducted a survey asking for participants' opinions about the graphical password schemes.

Experimental Results. Table 2 shows the memorability results of CT and CS-AV schemes. For both schemes, nobody forgets the password in the first week. For CT, in the second-week, one participant forgot a full password, and two persons forgot half passwords (95%), for the third-week, two users forgot full passwords and two of them remembered just 2 to 3 characters only (93.5%). For CS-AV scheme, in the second week study, one user forgot half password (98.75%) and in the third week, two users forgot the half passwords 97.25%. Consequently, the CS-AV memorability result is 3.75% better than the CT scheme in the last two-weeks of a usability study. To measure ease of use, each participant was required to compare CS-AV versus CT, on ease of use answering yes or no on the questions of the type "CS-AV is much easier than CT"; Table 3 shows the distribution of participants' answers.

Table 2. Memorability results of CT and CS-AV schemes (percentage of correct authentications on the 1-st, 2-nd, and 3-rd weeks)

Methods	1st week (%)	2nd week (%)	3rd week (%)
CT	100	95	93.50
CS-AV	100	98.75	97.25

Table 3. Comparing CS-AV versus CT on ease of use

	CS-AV vs. CT
Much Easier (%)	12.50
Easier (%)	22.50
Same (%)	50
More Difficult (%)	12.50
Much more Difficult (%)	2.50

Table 4. Mean, standard deviation (SD), maximum, and minimum time (s) of authentication using CT and CS-AV schemes

Method	Mean	SD	Max	Min
CT	38.05	8.38	60.40	25.30
CS-AV	42.16	7.85	71.50	23.70

Time of Authentication. Authentication time of 40 participants is shown in Table 4 for CT and CS-AV. In this study, CS-AV has longer by 4.11 s mean time compared to CT scheme due to a large number of symbols embedded into the example CS-AV image but its minimum time is less than that of CT.

Server Load. The average time of generating the Captcha image was ~ 40 ms and ~ 26 ms for CS-AV and CT scheme respectively.

5   Conclusion

We generalize CaRP scheme introducing CS-AV scheme based on CaRP that uses a proper symbol selection on the screen by clicking, but does not specify a particular alphabet. In particular, we find that using together in one alphabet alphanumeric and visual symbols can improve its usability (CS-AV). Text-based Captcha can easily be identified by [7, 8] techniques but a graphical password can be found only probabilistically by automatic brute force attack. We see that AG and TP schemes have some drawback as described in Sect. 1. Therefore, we study the CT and CS-AV schemes, and show that the CS-AV memorability is greater by 3.75% compared to CT scheme and it is much easier for human memory as compared to CT schemes.

References

1. Shepard, R.N.: Recognition memory for words, sentences, and pictures. J. Verbal Learn. Verbal Behav. **6**(1), 156–163 (1967)
2. Zhu, B.B., Yan, J.D., Bao, G., Yang, M., Xu, N.: Captcha as graphical passwords - a new security primitive based on hard AI problems. IEEE Trans. Inf. Forensics Secur. **9**(6), 891–904 (2014)
3. von Ahn, L., Blum, M., Hopper, N.J., Langford, J.: CAPTCHA: using hard AI problems for security. In: Biham, E. (ed.) EUROCRYPT 2003. LNCS, vol. 2656, pp. 294–311. Springer, Heidelberg (2003). https://doi.org/10.1007/3-540-39200-9_18
4. Nguyen, V.D., Chow, Y.-W., Susilo, W.: A CAPTCHA scheme based on the identification of character locations. In: Huang, X., Zhou, J. (eds.) ISPEC 2014. LNCS, vol. 8434, pp. 60–74. Springer, Cham (2014). https://doi.org/10.1007/978-3-319-06320-1_6
5. Biddle, R., Sonia, C., van Oorschot, P.C.: Graphical passwords: learning from the first twelve years. ACM Comput. Surv. **44**(4) (2012)
6. Chellapilla, K., Larson, K., Simard, P., Czerwinski, M.: Designing human friendly human interaction proofs (HIPs). In: Proceedings of the SIGCHI Conference on Human Factors in Computing Systems, pp. 711–720. ACM (2005)
7. Tang, M., Gao, H., Zhang, Y., Liu, Y., Zhang, P., Wang, P.: Research on deep learning techniques in breaking text-based Captchas and designing image-based Captcha. IEEE Trans. Inf. Forensics Secur. **13**(10), 2522–2537 (2018)
8. Gao, H., Tang, M., Liu, Y., Zhang, P., Liu, X.: Research on the security of Microsoft's two-layer Captcha. IEEE Trans. Inf. Forensics Secur. **12**(7), 1671–1685 (2017)
9. Anton, H., Rorres, C.: Elementary linear algebra: application version - 7th editition, Howard, Drexel Unversity, ISSBN 0471-58741-9, Theorem 11.1.1, pp. 571–572 (1994)
10. El Ahmad, A.S., Yan, J., Tayara, M., The robustness of Google CAPTCHAs University of Newcastle, UK, Technical Report 1278, 1–15 (2011)
11. GSA Captcha segmentation. http://www.gsa-online.de/
12. Captcha Sniper available. http://www.Captchasniper.com/
13. Free online OCR [online]. http://www.i2ocr.com/
14. Free online OCR [online]. http://www.free-ocr.com/
15. Auto mouse clicker. http://www.murgee.com/auto-clicker/
16. John the Ripper Password Cracker [Online]. http://www.openwall.com/john/
17. Openwall Wordlists Collection [Online]. http://www.openwall.com/wordlists/
18. Furnel, S., Esmael, R., Yang, W., Li, N.: Enhancing security behaviour by supporting the user. Comput. Secur. Jan **31** (2018)

An IT Tool to Support Anti-crisis Training in WAZkA System: A Case Study

Wojciech Kulas(ID) and Zbigniew Tarapata$^{(\boxtimes)}$ (ID)

Faculty of Cybernetics, Military University of Technology, Warsaw, Poland
{wojciech.kulas,zbigniew.tarapata}@wat.edu.pl

Abstract. In the paper, the authors presented the concept and elements of implementation of the subsystem to support the training process of operators of the anti-crisis system. It was made in the form of emulators of hazard monitoring systems for the needs of an IT system supporting the analysis of threats in the form of CBRN (Chemical, Biological, Radiation, Nuclear) contamination, forecasting their effects and alerting the population (WAZkA).

The genesis of building the emulator subsystem is the need to provide a tool to support the training process of people involved in the activities of the National System of Detection of Contamination and Alarming (KSWSiA) in Poland. However, the emulators designed in this way can also be used as a tool to support the development of emergency procedures.

Emulators were proposed as IT tools. A constructive simulation was chosen as the emulation method, but reduced to a simple, determined data delivery in accordance with the previously prepared scenario.

Keywords: Emulators · Support of anti-crisis training · Software development WAZkA system

1 Introduction

The work is based on our experiences resulting from developing IT system supporting analyses of threats related to contamination and alarming (WAZkA) [10] for the purpose of the National System for Detection of Contamination and Alarming (pol. *Krajowy System Wykrywania Skażeń i Alarmowania, KSWSiA* [1]) in Poland. The implementation of the WAZkA system made it necessary to implement the subsystem to support the training process of operators. It was one of the main the WAZkA software requirements.

The purpose of the constructed the WAZkA system was to support the anti-crisis management system, mainly in terms of passing the information, coordinating actions and forecasting the development of threats. The WAZkA system is aimed at collecting information obtained from various sources: starting from sensors [3, 7] and single observers, through particular levels of the anti-crisis management system and ending with national centers [7]. The information is collected and supplemented with the results of the analyses conducted in the system environment. The so prepared data are made available to all interested parties: population, elements of the anti-crisis management system, other information media. The data are made available in different

© Springer Nature Switzerland AG 2018
T. Czachórski et al. (Eds.): ISCIS 2018, CCIS 935, pp. 158–165, 2018.
https://doi.org/10.1007/978-3-030-00840-6_18

forms: tabular, descriptive, graphic on a background map, text and voice notifications. Alerts and notifications, which confirm the development of threats and which constitute direct instruction to undertake preventive actions, are of special significance.

To allow the designed system work in the training mode, it must be possible to replace the current environment with the training environment. The replaceable elements of the environment shall be as follows: databases, information sources and recipients of alerts and notifications (see Fig. 1a). The sources and data recipients may be replaced with specialized operators and automatic machines. The logic of the information recipients is usually very simple. It is much more complex in case of the information sources. They need to deliver notifications in accordance with the principles effective while observing the phenomena and in accordance with the physics of the development of threats. Therefore, the information sources were chosen as the most suitable for automating the IT system.

Replacement of the actual information sources with automatic machines makes it necessary to build emulators. The easiest way of emulation is the computer simulation method. The behavior of the information sources suggests that the construction of the simulation software shall be a good way to provide IT support. That is how the IT tool to support the training process was created.

In general, emulators are used in different applications and contexts. For example, the paper [5] presents test results using EM (real-time hazard monitor, historically termed an error monitor (EM)) in conjunction with a Flight Management System (FMS) emulator. In the paper [2] authors develop methodology for the two thin-plate spline, with application to atmospheric dispersion using emulators. Authors of the book [11] write about emulators approach to automatic malware analysis. In the paper [8] authors demonstrate the potential of the proposed simulation-driven WSN emulation approach by using it to estimate how communication and energy costs scale with the network's size when implementing a collaborative algorithm for tracking the spatiotemporal evolution of a progressing environmental hazard.

Although, the presented solution was designed for the anti-crisis system, however, the outlined problems occur in the majority of the constructed IT systems, in particular class C2 (Command and Control) [9]. It is important to emphasize that the presented solution is dedicated to replace personnel on different levels during anti-crisis CBRN threats training (see Fig. 1a), not during anti-crisis management (like human evacuation and rescue [3], sanitary inspection simulation exercises [11]) or anti-crisis decision support [6, 9].

The paper is organized as follows. In Sect. 2 we present requirements on the WAZkA system, especially from the training role point of view. Section 3 contains description of the architecture of the emulator and its ultimate role in the WAZKA.

2 Requirements on the WAZkA System

The expectations of shareholders with respect to the presented anti-crisis system (WAZkA) may be summarized in the following points: (1) The basic result shall be in the form of the IT tool, (2) It should reduce the time between detection of a CBRN threat and passing of the information to the public, (3) The tool shall be intended for the bodies responsible for undertaking particular actions, (4) It should optimize the decision-making processes of the public administration bodies and coordinate activities of the rescue entities, (5) It should also be the system ready to react to new threats, (6) The tool must be a platform for organizing training sessions.

On the basis of such expectations, the requirements for the software were formulated. The requirements may be summarized in the following points [10, 13]:

1. Exchange of information.
2. Assessment and analysis of threats.
3. Coordination of activities.
4. Access to the threat knowledge base.
5. Training session. The purpose of the requirement is to allow training of the public administration entities, using the created products.
6. Emulation of the monitoring systems. The purpose of the requirement is to feed the system with the generated test, user-controlled data on threats. It facilitates the training process and allows to verify cooperation between the system and services in case of unusual threats. Furthermore, the requirement is aimed at supporting the training system by generating the data on threats to implement the predefined scenario of development and consequences of such threats.

The two last requirements are related to the training function of the system. The training sessions are usually conducted in a non-automatic manner, using operators. The preparation of exercises requires development of a plan for sending notifications, including the following information: operating and astronomical time of sending notifications, content of notifications, source or sender, recipient, manner of sending notifications.

The exercises are performed in the form of sending the notifications by the properly instructed operators in accordance with the developed plan, without any significant deviations.

The concept of using the constructed the WAZkA system for the training purposes is based on applying exactly the same system as in case of typical work (see Fig. 1a). Therefore, it is necessary to change the entire environment, in which such system is supposed to be operating during the training session. The environment elements are as follows:

- sources of data on contamination,
- recipients of notifications and alerts,
- databases.

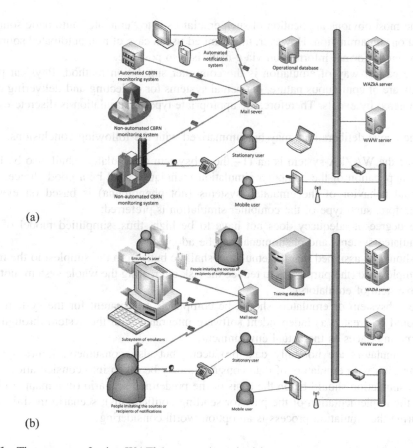

(a)

(b)

Fig. 1. The concept of using WAZkA system in anti-crisis management (with CBRN threats): (a) during operational work, (b) during personnel training, source: own elaboration.

The exchange of sources and recipients usually comes down to replacing the actual elements with training services (see Fig. 1b). It is often troublesome and costly to organize the training, as it requires a large number of operators. Therefore, it becomes necessary to substitute a part of the personnel (or even all of them) for the specialized IT subsystem. It is easiest to do it in the area of automatic or automated data sources.

3 Description of the Architecture of the Emulator and Its Ultimate Role in the WAZKA

3.1 Localization of Emulator in WAZkA and Its Training Role

The emulator, in general, is the system which behaves like another computer system, but which was designed in a different technology and environment. The emulator behaves like the actual system only from a certain point of view, depending on the purpose of application of such emulator. Since the emulator is "seen" only by the constructed IT system, it has to be compatible with the system replaced at the interface level.

The most obvious application of such emulators is to "emulate" automatic sources of data on contamination. However, their limited use in case of non-automated sources, e.g. to send informal information via e-mail, is also possible.

The easiest way of emulation is the computer simulation method. Physical phenomena are of continuous nature, but actual systems for collecting and delivering data are triggered by events. Therefore, the appropriate type of simulation is discrete-event ones.

The above deliberations may be summarized with the following conclusions:

- since the WAZkA system is an IT– the subsystem of emulators shall also be IT;
- the application of the computer simulation techniques shall be a good choice;
- actual behavior of the emulated systems (not phenomena) is based on events, therefore, such type of the computer simulation is preferred;
- the degree of adequacy does not have to be high, thus, simplified model of the emulated systems and phenomena may be adopted;
- it should be assumed that the emulators shall be built from the simplest to the most complex one (the purpose is to reduce the risk of creating the whole system, not the subsystem of emulators);
- the subsystem of emulators should be completely transparent for the system – it should be created as independent software integrated with the system through the same interfaces as the actual environment;
- the emulators are not only data producers, but also consumers; future system extension with emulators of data consumers may be taken into consideration;
- the simulation should be on the basis of the predefined scenario (in a manner close to the implementation of the plan for sending notifications); scenario modification during the emulation process is an option worth considering.

3.2   Layered Software Concept of the Emulator Subsystem

The analysis of the expected behavior of the emulator subsystem conducted based on the specification of requirements led to the development of the layer software concept. It was shown in Fig. 2.

The key component of the developed concept is the component of emulators. It appears in such a number of copies that corresponds to the developed types of emulators. For the purpose of the constructed system, three types of emulators were developed:

- simple generation of data as defined in the scenario,
- simple determination of the environment status as defined in the scenario and automatic data generation,
- data generation using the behavior model of the phenomenon with the parameters as defined in the scenario and automatic data generation.

The emulators differ in the level of technological advancement, hence, complexity of performance. The adopted solutions for particular types of emulators have been described below.

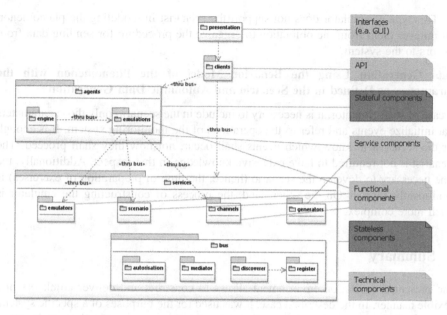

Fig. 2. Layered software concept of the emulator subsystem, source: own elaboration.

Simple Generation of Data as Defined in the Scenario

This concept of emulation is the simplest, but also the most flexible. It means that the information to be passed in the notifications for the system was expressly defined in the scenario. Therefore, the emulation scenario must include: expected time of sending the notification, contents of the notification.

The difficulty in using such emulator is that the model of spreading the phenomenon and operations of the monitoring system must exist "in the mind" of a person creating the scenario (scenarist, analyst or training manager). The emulator does not provide any support in that respect. A person with a specialist knowledge may develop the scenario, which is also labor-intensive.

Simple Determination of the Environment Status as Defined in the Scenario and Automatic Data Generation

This type of scenario has an in-built model of operations of the monitoring system. Such system is usually fully automatic and the algorithm of its operations relatively simple. The model of such system is simple thus, the emulator is easy to implement. The model of spreading the phenomenon must still exist "in the mind" of a scenarist. However, creation of the scenario comes down to the definition of the instructions, which shall appear in sensors. Therefore, the scenario needs to include: expected time of changing the value read by the sensor, identifier (location) of the sensor, value which needs to be read, parameters of reading the value from the sensors by the monitoring system (frequency of reading the value, frequency of sending data to the system).

This type of emulator does not support the scenarist in modeling the phenomenon but relieves them from the obligation to organize the procedure for sending data from sensors to the system.

Data Generation Using the Behavior Model of the Phenomenon with the Parameters as Defined in the Scenario and Automatic Data Generation

In case of such emulator, it is necessary to include in the scenario only those parameters that initialize events and refer to the operations of the monitoring system. It is enough for the scenarist to know which events shall occur, not how they shall proceed. The scenarist is not required to have extensive knowledge in that respect. Additionally, the time necessary to develop the scenario (hence, the time of preparation of exercises) is significantly shorter. On the other hand, the process of constructing the emulator is much more complex.

4 Summary

The presented emulation environment allows to construct and deliver emulators in a flexible manner. In the described case, it was used for the purposes of a specific system, but potentially it may be also applied in any other system. In the article, three implemented emulators were described, but it is possible to extend the environment with other emulators as well - designed both for a specific system and for general application.

The main objective of providing the emulators was a possibility of easy use of the system for the training purposes. However, the emulators also proved useful in the process of designing the software. They allowed quick provision of the environment for testing the designed product.

In case of large systems, it is usually required to deliver the emulators together with the training environment. Extensive training sessions require substantial funds and time. It is indispensable to develop the exercise scenario and train personnel. The main personnel consist of people imitating the sources or recipients of notifications. In both cases, the emulators contribute to the reduction of costs and time necessary to prepare the exercises by: providing tools for building scenarios, simplifying the construction of scenarios by delivering the implemented models, providing tools for automatic generation of events, without the help of personnel.

The concept of emulators may be extended. One of the possibilities is to deliver the consumer emulators apart from the source emulator. Once initiated, the outlined emulators operate in accordance with the scenario, without a possibility of interference. In some cases, it may prove useful to influence the emulation process during its course. It is the second possible direction of development of the presented emulators.

Acknowledgements. This work was partially supported by grant N^{oo} DOB-BIO7/12/01/2015 of Polish National Center for Research and Development (NCBiR) titled "Integration and support of information management processes and decision optimization in warning and alarm system" [13] and Statutory Research Work of Institute of Computer and Information Systems, Cybernetics Faculty, Military University of Technology in Warsaw, Poland.

References

1. Binek, T., Czepiel, J.: The national system of contamination detection and alarm. Curr. Oper. Pol. BiTP **36**(4), 15–24 (2014)
2. Bowman, W., Woods, D.: Emulation of multivariate simulators using thin-plate splines with application to atmospheric dispersion. SIAM/ASA J. Uncertain. Quantif. **4**, 1323–1344 (2016)
3. Gelenbe, E., Wu, F.-J.: Large scale simulation for human evacuation and rescue. Comput. Math. Appl. **64**(12), 3869–3880 (2012)
4. Grabowski, D., Kurowski, W., Muszynski, W., Rubel, B., Smagala, G., Swietochowska, J.: Radiation monitoring network in Poland. Nukleonika **46**(4), 147–149 (2001)
5. Greenberg, A., Small, R., Zenyuh, J., Skidmore, M.: Monitoring for hazard in flight management systems. Eur. J. Oper. Res. **84**(1), 5–24 (1995)
6. Li, X.L., et al.: Framework for emergency decision exercise system of urban crisis based on Wargaming. Appl. Mech. Mater. **373–375**, 1139–1143 (2013)
7. Lipiński, P., Isajenko, K., Biernacka, M., Żak, A.: Integration of polish monitoring networks (ASS-500 and PMS systems). Nukleonika **46**(4), 143–146 (2001)
8. Manatakis, D., Nennes, M., Bakas, I., Manolakos, E.: Simulation-driven emulation of collaborative algorithms to assess their requirements for a large-scale WSN implementation. In: Proceedings of the 2014 IEEE International Conference on Acoustics, Speech and Signal Processing (ICASSP), IEEE Explore (2014)
9. Tarapata, Z.: Models and algorithms for knowledge-based decision support and simulation in defense and transport applications. Military University of Technology, Warsaw (2011)
10. Tarapata, Z., Antkiewicz, R., Chmielewski, M., Dyk, M., Kasprzyk, R., Kulas, W., Najgebauer, A., Pierzchała, D., Rulka, J.: A computer system for CBRN contamination threats analysis support, prediction their effects and alarming the population: polish case study. MATEC Web Conf. **125**, 02012 (2017). https://doi.org/10.1051/matecconf/201712502012
11. Waszkowski, R., Nowicki, T., Saniuk, A.: Human-computer interaction in sanitary inspection simulation exercises. In: Soares, M., Falcão, C., Ahram, T. (eds.) Advances in Ergonomics Modeling, Usability & Special Populations. Advances in Intelligent Systems and Computing, vol. 486. Springer, Cham (2017)
12. Yin, H., Song, D.: Automatic Malware Analysis. An Emulator Based Approach. Springer, New York (2013)
13. WAZkA Project Homepage, http://wazka.wat.edu.pl/. Accessed 5 June 2018

European Cybersecurity Research
and the SerIoT Project

Joanna Domańska, Mateusz Nowak,
Sawomir Nowak, and Tadeusz Czachórski[✉]

IITIS Polish Academy of Science, Gliwice, Poland
tadek@iitis.pl

Abstract. This paper briefly reviews some recent research in Cybersecurity in Europe funded by the European Commission in areas such as mobile telephony, networked health systems, the Internet of Things. We then outline the objectives of the SerIoT Project which started in 2018 to address the security needs of fields such as Smart Cities, Smart Transportation Systems, Supply Chains and Industrial Informatics.

Keywords: Cybersecurity · European Commission · E-Health
Smart Cities · IoT · Network attacks · Random Neural Network
Cognitive packet routing

1 Introduction

Viewed for a long time as a peripheral issue, Cybersecurity is now at the forefront of everyday computer system and network operations, and of research in Computer Science and Engineering. Indeed cyberattacks, even when they are detected and mitigated, have a very large cost to systems operations including the degradation of the commercial image or trust of the and in 2017 the European Union published its recommendation for security and privacy. In addition, the organisations that operate systems that come under cyberattack can not only lose market share and lose the trust of the end users, but they also have to increase their operating costs both in terms of means to defend themselves but also in increased energy consumption and operating costs [31] and CO^2 impact [17,60].

The SerIoT Project [14] finds its origins in early work started over a decade ago on Distributed Denial of Service (DDoS) Attacks [25,44] and on using routing with the Cognitive Packet Network protocol (CPN) [38] to detect DDoS, and trace the attacking traffic so as to use CPN's ACK packets to drop the attacking traffic packets at upstream routers that carry the attacking traffic, and also detect worm attacks [65,69–71]. More recently, the EU FP7 Project NEMESYS [3,33,34] provided the opportunity to examine the cybersecurity of mobile networks including the control plane which is used to establish and keep track of calls. Since the control plane is a critical element that enables the mobile network to function, some attacks aim in particular at this part of the system [2,58].

© Springer Nature Switzerland AG 2018
T. Czachórski et al. (Eds.): ISCIS 2018, CCIS 935, pp. 166–173, 2018.
https://doi.org/10.1007/978-3-030-00840-6_19

Further work on the security of cyber-physical systems has considered vulnerabilities that address the physical infrastructure, the decision algorithms that manage the system when it operates normally or under threat, and the communication system used to convey data, information and commands between different system components [1,4,12,26,28,53].

2   European Research in Cybersecurity in Recent Years

In [20], some recent research on cybersecurity in Europe has been summarised regarding the several projects funded by the European Commission. A core issue that diffuses through all layers of information technology concerns cybersecurity for mobile telephony. Because most modern mobile phones offer opportunistic access [57] to WIFI and other wireless networks, the resulting security vulnerabilities should be constantly monitored both at the network and control plane levels, and in the mobile device. Thus recent [55] has investigated the use of neural network and machine learning methods to discuss this issue. The research in [56,66], addresses attacks that manipulate the signalling plane of the backbone network and directly concerns the mobile network operator as well as the end user, and the project NEMESYS addressed many of these issues [67,68] using techniques from Queuing Theory [11,49].

KONFIDO [73] concentrates on the security of communications and data transfers for interconnected European national or regional health services. Since travellers from European countries must often access health services in another European country, the health informatics systems will have to access remote patient data in a secure manner [73] and the related technical and ethical issues are addressed in a series of recent papers [5,8,16].

The GHOST project [9] addresses security in the IoT system market [59] for homes, and focuses on the design of a secure home IoT gateway including the attack detection techniques [7], and the analysis of attack methods that try to bring down the energy supply of the devices by draining their batteries [35]. The detection techniques that are proposed are based on Deep Learning [54] and recurrent Random Neural Neworks [22,23] that have been used previously in a variety of applications [10,51]. GHOST also investigates blockchain based methods to track and improve the security of the home IoT system [61].

3   The SerIoT Project

The SerIoT project started in January of 2018 [14], and further details regarding can also be found in a forthcoming paper [32]. The project's Technical Objectives include means to understand the threats to a IoT based economy and understand how distributed ledgers (Blockchain) may improve IoT based systems. It will design and implement virtualised self-aware honeypots to attract and analyse attacks.

The project will design SerCPN [13], a network that manages specific distributed IoT devices based on the Cognitive Packet Network (CPN). It will use the implementation of Software Defined Networks (SDN) based on CPN [18,19,29] using measurements that create the system self-awareness [37–40,42]. These SDNs will use "Smart" Packets (SP) to search [1,27] for secure multi-hop routes having good quality of service (QoS) and measure their security and performance, and will use Reinforcement Learning with Random Neural Networks [21] to improve the network overall performance, including all three criteria of high security, good QoS and low energy consumption [36,41]. It may be possible to extend these schemes with genetic algorithms which use an analogy between network paths and genotypes [24,43,63]. Several SerCPN network clusters may be interconnected via end overlay network [6], with adaptive connections to Cloud and Fog servers [74,75] for network data analysis and visualisation.

Combining energy aware routing and QoS [45,46] with security, we can also address network admission [50] to enhance security. Wireless IoT device traffic may also be specifically monitored and adaptively routed in a similar manner as it accesses SerCPN [47,48,64].

The project will deliver a number of platforms that comprise the main technical outputs of the project, including Platforms for (i) IoT Data Acquisition, (ii) Ad-hoc Anomaly Detection, (iii) Interactive Visual Analytics and Decision Support Tools, and (iv) Mitigation and Counteraction that will orchestrate, synchronise and implement the decisions taken by the various components.

4   SerIoT: Use Cases and Future Work of the Project

The SerIoT project's outcomes will be evaluated in a number of significant use cases. These include four main areas. The first one is Surveillance, where physical security in bus depots will be monitored through the infrastructure of OASA which is the largest transport authority in Greece. The second one involves Intelligent Transport Systems in Smart Cities, in particular in areas such as collision avoidance, where we will demonstrate how SerIoT can enhance the cybersecurity of such systems with infrastructures proveded by OASA, Austria-Tech (ATECH), and TECNALIA for vehicle safety. The third use case will involve Flexible Manufacturing Systems (Industry 4.0), which will monitor physical attacks to wireless sensor networks in Industry 4.0 with the help of DT/T-Sys., for situations related to automated warehouses where different attack vectors may be used for breaking or jamming communication lines. The fourth use case will address Food Chains which require end-to-end security through multiple communication channels, including device authentication, detection and avoidance of DDoS and replication attacks, and detection of functionality anomalies and disabling of IoT devices. In the food chain, IoT devices may be critical to notify perishability of food items that use visually readable labels by IoT devices to trigger indicators for shop managers and customers, offering "on board sensing and communications" for food. This Use Case will be supported by third parties. We take into account diverse, numerous and powerful cyber attacks.

Thus the confrontation in SerIoT of the physical world with issues of Cybersecurity, creates a rich opportunity to move forward from traditional work in this area that focuses on cryptography and the management of cryptographic keys [15,62,76,77], or the security of software [72] and physical structures [30,52], to broad issues regarding security and system efficiency in the presence of cyberattacks to the integrated cyber and physical infrastructure.

References

1. Abdelrahman, O.H., Gelenbe, E.: Time and energy in team-based search. Phys. Rev. E **87**(3), 032125 (2013)
2. Abdelrahman, O.H., Gelenbe, E.: Signalling storms in 3G mobile networks. In: IEEE International Conference on Communications, ICC 2014, Sydney, Australia, 10–14 June 2014, pp. 1017–1022. IEEE (2014). https://doi.org/10.1109/ICC.2014. 6883453
3. Abdelrahman, O.H., Gelenbe, E., Görbil, G., Oklander, B.: Mobile network anomaly detection and mitigation: The nemesys approach. In: Gelenbe E., Lent R. (eds.) Information Sciences and Systems 2013, pp. 429–438. Springer International Publishing, Cham (2013)
4. Akinwande, O.J., Bi, H., Gelenbe, E.: Managing crowds in hazards with dynamic grouping. IEEE Access **3**, 1060–1070 (2015)
5. Akriotou, M., Mesaritakis, C., Grivas, E., Chaintoutis, C., Fragkos, A., Syvridis, D.: Random number generation from a secure photonic physical unclonable hardware module. In: Gelenbe, E., et al. (eds.) Recent Cybersecurity Research in Europe: Proceedings of the 2018 ISCIS Security Workshop. CCIS, vol. 821. Springer, Cham (2018)
6. Brun, O., Wang, L., Gelenbe, E.: Big data for autonomic intercontinental communications. IEEE Trans. Sel. Areas Commun. **34**(3), 575–583 (2016)
7. Brun, O., Yin, Y., Gelenbe, E., Kadioglu, Y.M., Augusto-Gonzalez, J., Ramos, M.: Deep learning with dense random neural networks for detecting attacks against IoT-connected home environments. In: Gelenbe, E. (ed.) Recent Cybersecurity Research in Europe: Proceedings of the 2018 ISCIS Security Workshop. CCIS, vol. 821. Springer, Cham (2018)
8. Castaldo, L., Cinque, V.: Blockchain based logging for the cross-border exchange of ehealth data in Europe. Recent Cybersecurity Research in Europe: Proceedings of the 2018 ISCIS Security Workshop. CCIS, vol. 821. Springer, Cham (2018)
9. Collen, A., et al.: Ghost - safe-guarding home IoT environments with personalised real-time risk control. In: Gelenbe, E., et al. (eds.) Recent Cyber security Research in Europe: Proceedings of the 2018 ISCIS Security Workshop, Imperial College London. Communications in Computer and Information Science, vol. 821. Springer, Cham (2018)
10. Cramer, C.E., Gelenbe, E.: Video quality and traffic QoS in learning-based subsampled and receiver-interpolated video sequences. IEEE J. Sel. Areas Commun. **18**(2), 150–167 (2000)
11. Czachórski, T., Gelenbe, E., Lent, R.: Information Sciences and Systems. Springer International Publishing, Cham (2014)
12. Desmet, A., Gelenbe, E.: Graph and analytical models for emergency evacuation. In: 2013 IEEE International Conference on Pervasive Computing and Communications Workshops, PERCOM 2013 Workshops, San Diego, CA, USA, 18–22 March 2013, pp. 523–527 (2013). https://doi.org/10.1109/PerComW.2013.6529552

13. Domanska, J., Czachòrski, T., Nowak, M., Nowak, S., Gelenbe, E.: Sercpn: smart software defined network for IoT (2018). (To appear)
14. Domanska, J., Gelenbe, E., Czachorski, T., Drosou, A., Tzovaras, D.: Research and innovation action for the security of the internet of things: the SerIoT project. In: Gelenbe, E. (eds.) Recent Cybersecurity Research in Europe: Proceedings of the 2018 ISCIS Security Workshop, Imperial College London. Communications in Computer and Information Science, vol. 821. Springer, Cham (2018)
15. Ermis, O., Bahtiyar, S., Anarim, E., Çaglayan, M.U.: A key agreement protocol with partial backward confidentiality. Comput. Netw. **129**, 159–177 (2017). https://doi.org/10.1016/j.comnet.2017.09.008
16. Faiella, G., et al.: Building an ethical framework for cross-border applications: the konfido project. In: Gelenbe, E., et al. (eds.) Recent Cyber security Research in Europe: Proceedings of the 2018 ISCIS Security Workshop, Imperial College London. Communications in Computer and Information Science, vol. 821. Springer, Cham (2018)
17. François, F., Abdelrahman, O.H., Gelenbe, E.: Impact of signaling storms on energy consumption and latency of LTE user equipment. In: 17th IEEE International Conference on High Performance Computing and Communications, HPCC 2015, 7th IEEE International Symposium on Cyberspace Safety and Security, CSS 2015, and 12th IEEE International Conference on Embedded Software and Systems, ICESS 2015, New York, NY, USA, 24–26 Aug 2015, pp. 1248–1255 (2015). https://doi.org/10.1109/HPCC-CSS-ICESS.2015.84
18. François, F., Gelenbe, E.: Optimizing secure sdn-enabled inter-data centre overlay networks through cognitive routing. In: 24th IEEE International Symposium on Modeling, Analysis and Simulation of Computer and Telecommunication Systems, MASCOTS 2016, London, United Kingdom, 19–21 Sept 2016, pp. 283–288 (2016). https://doi.org/10.1109/MASCOTS.2016.26
19. François, F., Gelenbe, E.: Towards a cognitive routing engine for software defined networks. In: 2016 IEEE International Conference on Communications, ICC 2016, Kuala Lumpur, Malaysia, 22–27 May 2016, pp. 1–6 (2016). https://doi.org/10.1109/ICC.2016.7511138
20. Gelenbe, E. et al. (eds.): Proceedings of the 2018 ISCIS Security Workshop: Recent Cybersecurity Research in Europe, vol. 821. Lecture Notes CCIS, Springer (2018)
21. Gelenbe, E.: Random neural networks with negative and positive signals and product form solution. Neural Comput. **1**(4), 502–510 (1989)
22. Gelenbe, E.: Réseaux neuronaux aléatoires stables. Comptes Rendus de l'Académie des sciences. Série 2 **310**(3), 177–180 (1990)
23. Gelenbe, E.: Learning in the recurrent random neural network. Neural Comput. **5**(1), 154–164 (1993)
24. Gelenbe, E.: Genetic algorithms with analytical solution. In: Proceedings of the 1st Annual Conference on Genetic Programming, pp. 437–443. MIT Press (1996)
25. Gelenbe, E.: Dealing with software viruses: a biological paradigm. Inf. Sec. Tech. Rep. **12**(4), 242–250 (2007)
26. Gelenbe, E.: Steady-state solution of probabilistic gene regulatory networks. Phys. Rev. E **76**(1), 031903 (2007)
27. Gelenbe, E.: Steps toward self-aware networks. Commun. ACM **52**(7), 66–75 (2009)
28. Gelenbe, E.: Search in unknown random environments. Phys. Rev. E **82**, 061112 (2010)
29. Gelenbe, E.: A software defined self-aware network: the cognitive packet network. In: IEEE 3rd Symposium on Network Cloud Computing and Applications, NCCA

2014, Rome, Italy, 5–7 Feb 2014, pp. 9–14 (2014). https://doi.org/10.1109/NCCA. 2014.9

30. Gelenbe, E., Bi, H.: Emergency navigation without an infrastructure. Sensors **14**(8), 15142–15162 (2014)
31. Gelenbe, E., Caseau, Y.: The impact of information technology on energy consumption and carbon emissions. Ubiquity **2015**(June), 1 (2015)
32. Gelenbe, E., Domanska, J., Czachorski, T., Drosou, A., Tzovaras, D.: Security for internet of things: the seriot project. In: Proceedings of the International Symposium on Networks, Computers and Communications. IEEE (2018)
33. Gelenbe, E. et al.: Nemesys: Enhanced network security for seamless service provisioning in the smart mobile ecosystem. In: Gelenbe E., Lent R. (eds.) Information Sciences and Systems 2013, pp. 369–378. Lecture Notes in Electrical Engineering, vol 264. Springer International Publishing, Cham (2013)
34. Gelenbe, E. et al.: Security for smart mobile networks: the nemesys approach. In: 2013 International Conference on Privacy and Security in Mobile Systems (PRISMS), pp. 1–8. IEEE (2013)
35. Gelenbe, E., Kadioglu, Y.M.: Energy life-time of wireless nodes with network attacks and mitigation. In: Proceedings of ICC 2018, 20–24 May 2018, W04: IEEE Workshop on Energy Harvesting Wireless Communications. IEEE
36. Gelenbe, E., Lent, R.: Power-aware ad hoc cognitive packet networks. Ad Hoc Netw. **2**(3), 205–216 (2004)
37. Gelenbe, E., Lent, R., Montuori, A., Xu, Z.: Cognitive packet networks: Qos and performance. In: Proceedings of 10th IEEE International Symposium on Modeling, Analysis and Simulation of Computer and Telecommunications Systems, MASCOTS 2002, pp. 3–9. IEEE (2002)
38. Gelenbe, E., Lent, R., Nunez, A.: Self-aware networks and qos. Proc. IEEE **92**(9), 1478–1489 (2004)
39. Gelenbe, E., Lent, R., Xu, Z.: Design and performance of cognitive packet networks. Perform. Eval. **46**(2), 155–176 (2001)
40. Gelenbe, E., Lent, R., Xu, Z.: Measurement and performance of a cognitive packet network. Comput. Netw. **37**(6), 691–701 (2001)
41. Gelenbe, E., Lent, R., Xu, Z.: Towards networks with cognitive packets. In: Goto K., Hasegawa T., Takagi H., Takahashi Y. (eds.) Performance and QoS of Next Generation Networking, pp. 3–17. Springer, Cham (2001)
42. Gelenbe, E., Liu, P.: Qos and routing in the cognitive packet network. In: Sixth IEEE International Symposium on World of Wireless Mobile and Multimedia Networks, WoWMoM 2005, pp. 517–521. IEEE (2005)
43. Gelenbe, E., Liu, P., Laine, J.: Genetic algorithms for route discovery. IEEE Trans. Syst. Man Cybern. Part B (Cybernetics) **36**(6), 1247–1254 (2006)
44. Gelenbe, E., Loukas, G.: A self-aware approach to denial of service defence. Comput. Netw. **51**(5), 1299–1314 (2007)
45. Gelenbe, E., Mahmoodi, T.: Energy-aware routing in the cognitive packet network. Energy, pp. 7–12 (2011)
46. Gelenbe, E., Mahmoodi, T.: Distributed energy-aware routing protocol. In: Computer and Information Sciences II, pp. 149–154. Springer, London (2012)
47. Gelenbe, E., Ngai, E.C.H.: Adaptive qos routing for significant events in wireless sensor networks. In: 5th IEEE International Conference on Mobile Ad Hoc and Sensor Systems, 2008. MASS 2008, pp. 410–415. IEEE (2008)
48. Gelenbe, E., Ngai, E.C., Yadav, P.: Routing of high-priority packets in wireless sensor networks. In: IEEE Second International Conference on Computer and Network Technology, IEEE (2010)

49. Gelenbe, E., Pujolle, G.: Introduction aux réseaux de files d'attente. Edition Hommes et Techniques et Techniques, Eyrolles (1982)
50. Gelenbe, E., Sakellari, G., D'arienzo, M.: Admission of qos aware users in a smart network. ACM Trans. Auton. Adapt. Syst. (TAAS) **3**(1), 4 (2008)
51. Gelenbe, E., Sungur, M., Cramer, C., Gelenbe, P.: Traffic and video quality with adaptive neural compression. Multimed. Syst. **4**(6), 357–369 (1996). https://doi.org/10.1007/s005300050037
52. Gelenbe, E., Wu, F.J.: Large scale simulation for human evacuation and rescue. Comput. Math. Appl. **64**(12), 3869–3880 (2012)
53. Gelenbe, E., Wu, F.J.: Future research on cyber-physical emergency management systems. Future Internet **5**(3), 336–354 (2013)
54. Gelenbe, E., Yin, Y.: Deep learning with random neural networks. In: 2016 International Joint Conference on Neural Networks (IJCNN). IEEE, July 2016
55. Geneiatakis, D., Baldini, G., Fovino, I.N., Vakalis, I.: Towards a mobile malware detection framework with the support of machine learning. In: Gelenbe, E., et al. (eds.) Recent Cybersecurity Research in Europe: Proceedings of the 2018 ISCIS Security Workshop, Imperial College London. Lecture Notes CCIS, vol. 821, Springer (2018)
56. Gorbil, G., Abdelrahman, A.H., Pavloski, M., Gelenbe, E.: Modeling and analysis of rrc-based signaling storms in 3g networks. IEEE Trans. Emerg. Topics Comput. **4**(1), 113–127 (2016)
57. Gorbil, G., Gelenbe, E.: Opportunistic communications for emergency support systems. Procedia Comput. Sci. **5**, 39–47 (2011)
58. Görbil, G., Abdelrahman, O.H., Gelenbe, E.: Storms in mobile networks. In: Mueller, P., Foschini, L., Yu, R. (eds.) Q2SWinet'14, Proceedings of the 10th ACM Symposium on QoS and Security for Wireless and Mobile Networks, Montreal, QC, Canada, September 21–22, 2014. pp. 119–126. ACM (2014). https://doi.org/10.1145/2642687.2642688
59. Horváth, M., Buttyán, L.: Problem domain analysis of iot-driven secure data markets. In: Gelenbe, E. et al., (eds.) Recent Cybersecurity Research in Europe: Proceedings of the 2018 ISCIS Security Workshop, Imperial College London. Lecture Notes CCIS, vol. 821, Springer (2018)
60. Jiang, H., Liu, F., Thulasiram, R.K., Gelenbe, E.: Guest editorial: Special issue on green pervasive and ubiquitous systems. IEEE Syst. J. **11**(2), 806–812 (2017). https://doi.org/10.1109/JSYST.2017.2673218
61. Kouzinopoulos, C.S. et al.: Using blockchains to strengthen the security of internet of things. In: Gelenbe, E. et al., (eds.) Recent Cybersecurity Research in Europe: Proceedings of the 2018 ISCIS Security Workshop, Imperial College London. Lecture Notes CCIS. vol. 821, Springer (2018)
62. Levi, A., Çaglayan, M.U., Koç, Ç.K.: Use of nested certificates for efficient, dynamic, and trust preserving public key infrastructure. ACM Trans. Inf. Syst. Secur. **7**(1), 21–59 (2004). https://doi.org/10.1145/984334.984336
63. Liu, P., Gelenbe, E.: Recursive routing in the cognitive packet network. In: 3rd International Conference on Testbeds and Research Infrastructure for the Development of Networks and Communities, 2007. TridentCom 2007, pp. 1–6. IEEE (2007)
64. Ngai, E.C., Gelenbe, E., Humber, G.: Information-aware traffic reduction for wireless sensor networks. In: IEEE 34th Conference on Local Computer Networks, 2009. LCN 2009, pp. 451–458. IEEE (2009)

65. Oke, G., Loukas, G., Gelenbe, E.: Detecting denial of service attacks with bayesian classifiers and the random neural network. In: IEEE International Fuzzy Systems Conference, 2007. FUZZ-IEEE 2007, pp. 1–6. IEEE (2007)
66. Pavloski, M.: Signalling attacks in mobile telephony. In: Gelenbe, E. et al., (eds.) Recent Cybersecurity Research in Europe: Proceedings of the 2018 ISCIS Security Workshop, Imperial College London. Lecture Notes CCIS No. 821, Springer (2018)
67. Pavloski, M., Gelenbe, E.: Mitigating for signalling attacks in umts networks. In: Information Sciences and Systems 2014, pp. 159–165. Springer International Publishing (2014)
68. Pavloski, M., Gelenbe, E.: Signaling attacks in mobile telephony. In: SECRYPT 2014 - Proceedings of the 11th International Conference on Security and Cryptography, Vienna, Austria, 28–30 August, 2014. pp. 206–212 (2014). https://doi.org/10.5220/0005019802060212
69. Sakellari, G., Gelenbe, E.: Adaptive resilience of the cognitive packet network in the presence of network worms. In: Proceedings of the NATO Symposium on C3I for Crisis, Emergency and Consequence Management, pp. 11–12 (2009)
70. Sakellari, G., Gelenbe, E.: Demonstrating cognitive packet network resilience to worm attacks. In: Proceedings of the 17th ACM Conference on Computer and Communications Security, pp. 636–638. ACM (2010)
71. Sakellari, G., Hey, L., Gelenbe, E.: Adaptability and failure resilience of the cognitive packet network. In: Demo Session of the 27th IEEE Conference on Computer Communications (INFOCOM2008), Phoenix, Arizona, USA (2008)
72. Siavvas, M., Gelenbe, E., Kehagias, D., Tzovaras, D.: Static analysis-based approaches for secure software development. In: Gelenbe, E. et al., (eds.) Proceedings of the 2018 ISCIS Security Workshop: Recent Cybersecurity Research in Europe. vol. 821. Lecture Notes CCIS, Springer (2018)
73. Staffa, M. et al.: An openncp-based secure ehealth data exchange system. In: Gelenbe, E. et al., (eds.) Recent Cybersecurity Research in Europe: Proceedings of the 2018 ISCIS Security Workshop, Imperial College London. Lecture Notes CCIS No. 821, Springer (2018)
74. Wang, L., Brun, O., Gelenbe, E.: Adaptive workload distribution for local and remote clouds. In: 2016 IEEE International Conference on Systems, Man, and Cybernetics (SMC), pp. 003984–003988. IEEE (2016)
75. Wang, L., Gelenbe, E.: Adaptive dispatching of tasks in the cloud. IEEE Trans. Cloud Comput. **6**(1), 33–45 (2018)
76. Yu, C., Ni, G., Chen, I., Gelenbe, E., Kuo, S.: Top-k query result completeness verification in tiered sensor networks. IEEE Trans. Inf. Forensics Secur. **9**(1), 109–124 (2014). https://doi.org/10.1109/TIFS.2013.2291326
77. Yu, C.M., Ni, G.K., Chen, Y., Gelenbe, E., Kuo, S.Y.: Top-k query result completeness verification in sensor networks. In: 2013 IEEE International Conference on Communications Workshops (ICC), pp. 1026–1030. IEEE (2013)

Machine Learning and Applications

FTScMES: A New Mutation Execution Strategy Based on Failed Tests' Mutation Score for Fault Localization

André Assis Lôbo de Oliveira[1,2]([⊠]) [iD], Celso G. Camilo Jr[1],
Eduardo Noronha de Andrade Freitas[3], and Auri Marcelo Rizzo Vincenzi[4]

[1] Instituto de Informática (UFG), Goiânia, GO, Brazil
andre.assis.lobo@gmail.com, celsocamilo@gmail.com
[2] Instituto Federal de Mato Grosso (IFMT), Sorriso, MT, Brazil
[3] Instituto Federal de Goiás (IFG), Goiânia, GO, Brazil
eduardonaf@gmail.com
[4] Universidade Federal de São Carlos - UFSCAR, São Carlos, SP, Brazil
auri@dc.ufscar.br

Abstract. Fault localization has been one of the most expensive activity in the whole debugging process. The spectrum-based fault localization (SBFL) is the most studied and evaluated technique. Other approach is the mutation-based fault localization technique (MBFL) that needs to execute the test suite on a large amount of mutants increasing its cost. Efforts from research community have been performed in order to achieve solutions reducing such cost and keeping a minimum quality. Current mutation execution strategies are evaluated considering artificial faults. However, recent researches show that some MBFL techniques exhibit low efficacy fault localization when evaluated on real faults. In this paper, we propose a new mutation execution strategy based on failed tests' mutation score, called (FTScMES), aiming to increase the efficacy on fault localization reducing the cost of mutants execution. FTScMES uses only the set of failed test cases to execute mutants and bases on mutation score concept to compute the suspiciousness statements. The experiments were conducted considering 221 real faults, comparing the efficacy of localization of FTScMES against 5 baselines from the literature. We found that FTScMES outperforms the baselines reducing the cost in 90% on average with a high efficacy of ranking defective code.

Keywords: Fault localization · Mutation analysis
Mutation-based fault localization · Debugging
Mutation execution strategy

1 Introduction

According to National Institute of Standards and Technology (NIST), faults on softwares incurs in annual economic losses to U.S. users higher than $ 59 billion [1] increasing annualy [9]. Besides that, fault localization is one of the most

© Springer Nature Switzerland AG 2018
T. Czachórski et al. (Eds.): ISCIS 2018, CCIS 935, pp. 177–187, 2018.
https://doi.org/10.1007/978-3-030-00840-6_20

expensive, tedious and time-consuming process in the whole debugging activity, driving some efforts of the research community to automation of these activities. Amongst Fault Localization (FL) techniques, the spectrum-based (SBFL) [3,6,17] is the most studied and evaluated. Mostly FL techniques generate a suspiciousness score $S(s)$ for each statement s. Based on this score, a decreasing list is generated from software statements. The technique is more *efficacy* when faulty statements lies on the top of this ranking, aiming to minimize programmer work which may uses the list as a suggestion to detect and repair the faults. In this paper, we consider *efficacy* (benefit) as the technique capacity to rank the faulty statements in the first positions of program statements list.

Mutation-based fault localization techniques (MBFL) aims to improve the efficacy of ranked list, based on the hypothesis that the Mutation Testing (or Mutation Analysis - MA) performed on a faulty software can contribute on fault localization, highlighting in this context the pioneers MUSE [10] and Metallaxis [12]. Research in this area showed that Metallaxis overcomes MUSE on efficacy [12,13] and *efficiency* to obtain the rank of statements. For this reason, we choose Metallaxis as MBFL baseline although it present problems, for instance, when a fault is located on immutable places of the software. When it happens, MBFL loss effectiveness on fault localization. Hybrid approaches combining MBFL and SBFL techniques were proposed aiming at mitigating this shortcoming, as MCBFL-hybrid-avg and MRSBFL-hybrid-max, whose results surpassed traditional MBFL techniques in real faults [14]. Despite this overcoming, authors report high computational cost, with some versions requiring Mutation Analysis (MA) lasting from 32 to 168 hours. Thus, the effectiveness on localization of an MBFL technique must be higher to justify its utilization cost. In this paper, we consider *efficiency* (cost) as the technique capacity to reduce the number of executions between test cases and mutants.

Several cost reduction techniques were proposed aiming at improving MBFL applicability. Such approaches present variations in distinct steps of the localization process when using mutants: (i) the strategy of reducing mutation operators [13]; (ii) the strategy of reducing mutants [12]; (iii) the strategy of statement-oriented mutant reduction [9], and (iv) the dynamic mutation execution strategy [5]. The dynamic execution strategy (DMES or Faster-MBFL) is an approach that aims to make MBFL more efficient by optimizing the way in which mutatns are executed. All these approaches measure the cost by the amount of execution of the mutants (Mutant Test Pair values - MTP). However, DMES was validated in software with artificial faults. Our approach lies on mutation execution strategies since other approaches can be used in earlier stages.

Therefore, we propose a new Mutation Execution Strategy based on Failed Tests' Mutation Score (FTScMES) aiming at obtaining efficacy of ranked list in the more efficient way. Empirical studies are conducted to evaluate FTScMES as a mutation execution strategy and compare our approach with DMES, as well as the best current MBFL techniques [14]. We used the Defects4J benchmark [8] to evaluate the solutions of all techniques. Following, we highlight some contributions of our study:

1. A novel mutant execution strategy with two objectives: (i) reduction of mutants executions and (ii) a high efficacy of ranked list.
2. Proposition of MBFL approach which considers real faults.
3. Comparison of FTScMES with current mutation execution strategy and best MBFL techniques.
4. Experimental studies reveal that FTScMES presented the best quality in the rank of faulty statements, in terms of cost-benefit.

This paper is structured as follows: Sect. 2 presents the FTScMES approach. The experiments and its configurations are presented in Sect. 3 and the Sect. 4 summarizes the proposed ideas and suggest future works.

2 FTScMES: A Mutation Execution Strategy Based on Failed Tests' Mutation Score for Fault Localization

In MBFL context, T executes P, where P is a Program Under Test (PUT) and T its set of test. Next, the coverage information and test results (FAIL or PASS) are collected. Then, T is divided in two sets: T_p and T_f, where T_p are the passed test cases and T_f are the failed test cases. Besides that, $cov(T_f)$ is the set of covered statements by T_f. After, the mutation operators inserts artificial faults to generate mutant programs considering only statements in $cov(T_f)$. In general, a statement s has a set of mutants with more than one associated element, denoted by $M(s)$. The test cases are executed against each mutant, and the killing information are stored. Then, T is divided in two groups: T_n and T_k, where T_n is the set that *does not kill m*, and T_k *kills m*. Ochiai [2] formula (Eq. 1) is a example of SBFL technique. The suspiciousness of a mutant m can be computed considering different spectrum-based (SBFL) formulas [2,11,17], but after a transformation of killing information. This transformation can be performed considering four main metrics: $a_{np} = |T_n \cap T_p|$, $a_{kp} = |T_k \cap T_p|$, $a_{nf} = |T_n \cap T_f|$ and $a_{kf} = |T_k \cap T_f|$. These metrics also satisfy: $a_{np} + a_{kp} = total passed = |T_p|$ and $a_{nf} + a_{kf} = total failed = |T_f|$. The Eq. 2 is an adaptation of Ochiai formula for mutant suspiciousness calculation [5,13]. Finally, the mutant m with max $Susp(m)$ value signs the statement suspiciousness $Susp(s)$. The MBFL techniques run all T set against all generated mutants set $M(s)$. The mutation execution strategies [5] aiming to reduce the number of mutant executions that increases the computational cost in fault localization process. However, such reduction also can decrease the localization efficacy when incorporated to some MBFL technique. Thus, the challenge is to achieve two conflicting objectives: (i) reduces the number of mutant executions and (ii) obtains a high efficacy of localization.

$$Susp(s)_{SBFL} = \frac{failed(s)}{\sqrt{total failed * (failed(s) + passed(s))}} \tag{1}$$

$$Susp(m) = \frac{ak_f}{\sqrt{|T_f| * (ak_f + ak_p)}} \tag{2}$$

$$Susp_{FTMES}(m) = \frac{ak_f}{\sqrt{|T_f| * (ak_f + aCov_p)}} \tag{3}$$

$$Sc_m = \frac{ak_f}{|T_f|} * Susp_{FTMES}(m) \tag{4}$$

$$Sc_s = \frac{KM}{|M(s)|} * max(Sc_{M(s)}) \tag{5}$$

$$Susp(s)_{FTScMES} = avg(Sc_s, Susp(s)_{SBFL}) \tag{6}$$

Algorithm 1 Algorithm of FTScMES Approach

Input: PUT P; test suite T; test result R; statement s covered by failed test cases; coverage information C of s and the MBFL suspicious formula $Susp_{FTMES}(m)$. The formula $Susp_{FTMES}(m)$ can be a transformation with Ochiai [2], Dstar [17], or other suspiciousness formula. We use Dstar with *=2 in the experiments.

Output: $Sus(s)$

1: $M(s) \leftarrow Mutate(s)$ //Mutants Generation
2: $Tf, Tp \leftarrow$ Partition T using R //Splitting T from previous P execution
3: **for** $m \in M(s)$ **do**
4:    **for** $t_f \in T_f \&\& C(t_f) ==$ *Covered* **do**
5:       *Execute* $< m, t_f >$ // Execution only with T_f subset - part of FTMES strategy
6:       Count $\underline{ak_f}$ and $\underline{an_f}$
7:    **end for**
8:    **for** $t_p \in T_p \&\& C(t_p) ==$ *Covered* **do**
9:       Count $\underline{aCov_p}$ and $\underline{anCov_p}$
10:    **end for**
11:    Calculates $\underline{Susp_{FTMES}(m)}$ //Using data of T_f execution and T_p coverage - FTMES strategy (Equation 3)
12:    Calculates $\underline{Sc_m}$ //Sc strategy - mutant level score (Equation 4)
13: **end for**
14: Calculates $\underline{Sc_s}$ // Sc strategy - statement level score (Equation 5)
15: **return** $Susp(s)_{FTScMES}$ (Equation 6)

In this context, we propose the FTScMES approach consisting of **two strategies**: (i) the failed-test-oriented mutation execution strategy (FTMES) and (ii) the mutation score strategy (Sc). Algorithm 1 shows FTScMES framework which is composed by FTMES and Sc strategies. The **first strategy** aims to reduce the number of mutants executions running only the failed test set T_f to count the ak_f and an_f metrics. Moreover, FTMES does not execute the passed test set T_p replacing the killing by coverage data of previous runs of P avoiding additional executions. Thus, $ak_p = aCov_p$, where $aCov_p$ is the number of test cases in T_p that cover a mutant $m \in M(s)$. Similarly, $an_p = anCov_p$, where $anCov_p$ is the number of test cases in T_p that do not

Table 1. Subject programs

Subject program	Number of faulty version	KLOC	$|T_f|$	$|T_p|$	Average number of mutants
Chart	26 (24)	50	3,8	235,9	5284
Lang	65 (49)	6	1,8	169,8	2153
Math	106 (93)	19	3,5	186,0	9664
Mockito	38 (29)	22	3,9	661,5	2353
Time	27 (26)	53	3,5	2541,4	11031

cover a mutant $m \in M(s)$. The Eq. 3 shows the FTMES strategy with Ochiai formula replacing ak_p by $aCov_p$.

The **second strategy** aims to improve the efficacy of rank. The mutation score strategy of FTScMES calculates scores at mutant and statement level. The mutant level score (Sc_m - Eq. 4) is a fine ground because calculates the $Susp_{FTMES}(m)$ value for each mutant $m \in M(s)$ multiplied per the rate of T_f that kill m. The statement level score (Sc_s - Eq. 5) the mutant $m \in M(s)$ with the highest Sc_m has its value Sc_m multiplied per mutants rate killed by T_f. Similarly to Mutation Analysis (MA), such rate is the *mutation score* of statement, where KM is the number of killed mutants by T_f and $|M(s)|$ is the number of generated mutants from s. Finally, the suspiciousness value of statement s (Eq. 6) is calculated from average between Sc_s (Eq. 5) and $Susp(s)_{SBFL}$ (Eq. 1). This last stage is important because it's common the existence of immutable statements in P that decrease the efficacy of MBFL techniques when them contain the fault. Thus, the $Susp(s) = Susp(s)_{SBFL}$ when s is immutable.

3 Experiments

3.1 Setup

Coverage and Mutation Framework Tools: The Major mutation framework tool [7] provides the MA data to techniques evaluation. Major generates mutants considering all available mutation operators. GZoltar tool is frequently used in FL context [4]. Such tool provides the coverage data needed by our research.

Subject Programs: Defects4J is a database and extensible framework providing real bugs to enable reproducible studies in software testing research [8]. Our experiments consider the programs in the Defects4J dataset (v1.1.0). The Table 1 shows relevant information. The column 2 is the *Number of Faulty Versions*. Such column has two numbers: the total provides by Defects4J and the total considered in the experiments. We did not find the following information after running the scripts to get the coverage data in some programs versions: (i) the bugged lines after generation of spectra file; (ii) faulty lines without candidates lines to

Table 2. Fault localization techniques

Short name	Mutation execution strategy	Technique
B1	-	SBFL (Dstar using variable* = 2)
B2	-	MRSBFL-hybrid-max
B3	-	MBFL (killing a mutant like Metallaxis)
B4	-	MCBFL-hybrid-avg
B5	DMES	Faster-MBFL (applied to MCBFL-hybrid-avg)
B6	FTMES	FTScMES

correction and; (iii) versions with only failed test cases. We exclude the versions without such informations. For this reason, we did not use all versions.

Techniques of Investigation: The Table 2 presents the configuration of the classes of techniques considered, as well as the mutation execution strategies used. The SBFL technique named B1 is Dstar [17] (the best SBFL technique validated in real faults [14]). Dstar (with * = 2) was considered in all our experiments including it as the formula of MBFL and Hybrid techniques following the transformation explained in Sect. 2. MRSBFL-hybrid-max (B2) [14] is other considered technique. Both techniques do not run mutants, so the mutation execution strategies do not apply to them. The MBFL technique named (B3) runs mutants and considers the mutant killing mechanism of the Metallaxis technique. The MCBFL-Hybrid-avg named (B4) also runs mutants [14] and is other baseline technique. The mutation strategy DMES (Faster-MBFL) [5] operates on two distinct MBFL techniques: MBFL (B3) and MCBFL-Hybrid-avg (B4). The best interaction in real defects was between DMES and MCBFL-Hybrid-avg (B4). We show only this interaction due space limitation. Finally, our approach is FTScMES (B6) incorporating the FTMES as the mutation execution strategy.

In addition to all MBFL techniques that run mutants (B3, B4, B5 and B6), we apply an optimization to make MBFL more efficient: skipping execution of T_p on mutants that remained *alive* (not killed) after being executed by T_f. Without such optimization, DMES works very inefficiently in real defects and does not compete with our approach.

Evaluation Metrics: In this paper, we consider *efficiency* (cost) as the technique capacity to reduce the amount of mutant test cases executions. Similarly, we consider *efficacy* (benefit) as the technique capacity to rank the faulty statements in the fist positions of program statements list.

Mutation Execution Strategies Efficiency (**Cost**): A MTP value counts the number of mutant runs for test cases. This metric has been used to measure the cost of cost reduction techniques for MBFL [5,9]. The idea of the metric is that the number of executions of mutants is linked to the computational cost demanded to obtain the rank of statements. Thus, the lower MTP value of a MBFL technique, the greater its efficiency. We use this metric to evaluate the techniques that run mutants.

Efficacy of Ranked List (**Benefit**): Considering the importance of the efficacy of ranked list, the techniques studied were evaluated taking 3 metrics: (i) *EXAM score* [16]; (ii) Accuracy (acc@n) and; (iii) *wef* (Wasted Effort) [15]. The EXAM score is n/N, n denotes the number of statements that need to be inspected before finding the faulty statement of PUT and N is the number of statements in the program. The score ranges between 0 and 1, and *smaller* numbers are better. We consider the best case debugging scenario and tie-breaking by average [18]. The *acc@n* counts the number of faults that have been localized within *top n places* of the ranking [15]. We use to evaluate the techniques 1, 3, 5, 10 and 20 for number n, and count the number of corresponding faults per project and also overall. *Higher acc@n* values are better. The *wef* measures the amount of effort wasted looking at non-faulty program elements.

3.2 Results and Analysis

In order to evaluate the quality of FTScMES solutions and other FL techniques, we consider the following research questions:

(RQ1) Which mutation execution strategy produces the least number of mutant runs?

(RQ2) What is the cost-benefit of different fault localization techniques?

RQ1 uses the Mutant Test Pair (MTP) value of each technique for efficiency evaluation. The Table 3 shows the performance of FTScMES and Faster-MBFL. The first column describes the considered programs. The second column shows the average number of runs of the mutant executing techniques (B3 and B4) without applying a mutant execution strategy. The third column shows the mean MTP value for the Faster-MBFL technique (B5). The fourth column consists of the reduction percentage of Faster-MBFL (B5) compared to techniques B3 and B4. Similarly, the performance of FTScMES is presented in columns 5 and 6. For example, considering the program *Chart*, Faster-MBFL (B5) performs a 30% reduction in mutant runs while FTScMES performs a reduction of 88%. In general, FTScMES (B6) performs a greater reduction of executions than Faster-MBFL (B5) for all studied programs. On average, FTScMES (B6) reduces the number of executions by 90% while Faster-MBFL (B5) reduces by only 34%. Therefore, our approach overcomes the current mutation execution strategy of literature ranking statements at a lower computational cost. Reducing the computational cost can reduce the effectiveness of the solutions obtained. The RQ2 suggests the investigation of the impact of the cost (MTP Executions) of the different techniques on the effectiveness of the ranking represented by the 3 evaluation metrics: (i) *Percentage of Located Faults* (Exam Score), *Accuracy* (acc@n) and *Wasted Effort* (wef). The idea is to evaluate the techniques always considering two objectives, similarly the multi-objective evaluation [19]. For this reason, we used the Pareto front to demonstrate the dominance relationship between the techniques considering the *cost-benefit* relationship. So, one solution dominates another when it has lower cost and better benefit at the same time. It is worth noting that the SBFL (B1) and MRSBFL-hybrid-max (B2) techniques do not perform mutants and therefore always present lower cost (MTP = 0). Despite this, we insert them in the charts to evaluate if the benefit of the approaches that execute mutants justifies a greater computational cost demanded.

Table 3. Average execution ratios reduced by mutation execution

Programs	B3 and B4	B5		B6	
	MTP (Baseline)	MTP	% Reduction	MTP	% Reduction
Chart	91185,88	64004,25	30%	10794,54	88%
Lang	13205,27	7343,29	44%	507,88	96%
Math	54471,91	27796,41	49%	17221,10	68%
Mockito	266467,03	212336,28	20%	3477,48	99%
Time	1692594,35	1234955,35	27%	10452,31	99%
Average	423584,89	309287,11	34%	8490,66	90%

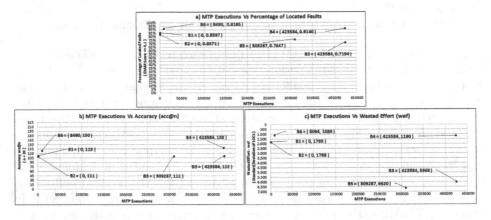

Fig. 1. Cost-Benefit Comparison: (a) *MTP Executions* vs *Percentage of Located Faults* (EXAM Score ≤ 0.1), (b) *MTP Executions* vs *Accuracy* (acc@n with $n = 20$), and (c) *MTP Executions* Vs *Wasted Effort* (wef average).

The **(a) chart** of the Fig. 1 relates the average of *Percentage of Located Faults* when the techniques reported Exam Score ≤ 0.1 and their respective costs. FTScMES (B6) dominates all the techniques that execute mutants (B3, B4 and B5) in the two objectives considered. It is worth noting that SBFL (B1) and MRSBFL-hybrid-max (B2) dominate MBFL (B3) and Faster-MBFL (B5), that is, localize defects with lower cost and greater efficiency. **The (b) chart** of the Fig. 1 relates the cost to the number of defects found up to the 20th position in the ranking (*Accuracy* - acc@n com n = 20). FTScMES dominates MBFL (B3) and Faster-MBFL (B5) in both objectives but does not dominate MCBFL-hybrid-avg (B4) in Accuracy. SBFL (B1) and MRSBFL-hybrid-max (B2) continue to dominate MBFL (B3) and Faster-MBFL (B5) also in this regard. The **(c) chart** of Fig. 1 relates the cost to the *Wasted Effort* (standard deviation of wef). Again, FTScMES (B6) dominate all the techniques that perform mutants (B3, B4 and B5) on the two objectives considered and SBFL (B1) and MRSBFL-hybrid-max (B2) dominates MBFL (B3) and Faster-MBFL (B5). The fact that SBFL (B1) and MRSBFL-hybrid-max (B2) dominate MBFL (B3) and Faster-MBFL (B5) in all objectives demonstrates that B3 and B4 are not good alternatives due to the high cost with low location efficacy. Differently from the MCBFL-hybrid-avg (B4) and FTScMES (B6) techniques that demonstrate better benefits than B1 and B2, justifying a higher application cost. Thus, our approach is the best alternative among those that perform mutants because it presents high localization efficiency with a cost closer to the approaches that do not perform mutants.

4   Conclusion and Future Works

This paper presented a new mutation execution strategy based on failed tests' mutation score for fault localization (FTScMES). FTScMES works aiming a high efficacy of the ranked list and reduction of the execution cost of the mutants. The experiments comprised 221 real faults, 6 fault localization techniques and 4 metric for evaluation of the quality of solutions. Moreover, our study compares FTScMES with Faster-MBFL, the current mutation execution strategy. FTScMES achieving 90% of reduction on quantity of the execution of mutants against 34% of Faster-MBFL. Moreover, FTScMES surpassed all the other techniques considering the cost-benefit relationship of each studied technique. As future works we pretend expand FTScMES evaluation with other subject programs.

Acknowledgments. This study was financed in part by the Coordenação de Aperfeiçoamento de Pessoal de Nível Superior - Brasil (CAPES) - Finance Code 001, Universidade Federal de Mato Grosso do Sul (UFMS) and, the Instituo Federal de Educação, Ciência e Tecnologia de Mato Grosso (IFMT) for their financial support.

References

1. National institute of standards and technology. http://www.abeacha.com/nist_press_release_bugs_cost.htm
2. Abreu, R., Zoeteweij, P., c. Van Gemund, A.J.: An evaluation of similarity coefficients for software fault localization. In: 2006 12th Pacific Rim International Symposium on Dependable Computing (PRDC 2006), pp. 39–46, December 2006

3. Abreu, R., Zoeteweij, P., van Gemund, A.J.C.: On the accuracy of spectrum-based fault localization. In: Proceedings of the Testing: Academic and Industrial Conference Practice and Research Techniques - MUTATION, pp. 89–98. TAICPART-MUTATION 2007. IEEE Computer Society, Washington, DC, USA (2007)
4. Campos, J., Riboira, A., Perez, A., Abreu, R.: Gzoltar: an eclipse plug-in for testing and debugging. In: 2012 Proceedings of the 27th IEEE/ACM International Conference on Automated Software Engineering, pp. 378–381, September 2012. https://doi.org/10.1145/2351676.2351752
5. Gong, P., Zhao, R., Li, Z.: Faster mutation-based fault localization with a novel mutation execution strategy. In: 2015 IEEE Eighth International Conference on Software Testing, Verification and Validation Workshops (ICSTW), pp. 1–10, April 2015
6. Jones, J.A., Harrold, M.J.: Empirical evaluation of the tarantula automatic fault-localization technique. In: Proceedings of the IEEE/ACM International Conference on Automated Software Engineering, pp. 273–282 (2005)
7. Just, R.: The major mutation framework: efficient and scalable mutation analysis for java. In: Proceedings of the 2014 International Symposium on Software Testing and Analysis, ISSTA 2014, pp. 433–436. ACM, New York (2014). https://doi.org/10.1145/2610384.2628053
8. Just, R., Jalali, D., Ernst, M.D.: Defects4J: a database of existing faults to enable controlled testing studies for Java programs. In: Proceedings of the 2014 International Symposium on Software Testing and Analysis, ISSTA 2014, pp. 437–440. San Jose, CA, USA, July 2014. (tool demo)
9. Liu, Y., Li, Z., Wang, L., Hu, Z., Zhao, R.: Statement-oriented mutant reduction strategy for mutation based fault localization. In: 2017 IEEE International Conference on Software Quality, Reliability and Security (QRS), pp. 126–137, July 2017
10. Moon, S., Kim, Y., Kim, M., Yoo, S.: Ask the mutants: mutating faulty programs for fault localization. In: Proceedings of the 2014 IEEE International Conference on Software Testing, Verification, and Validation, ICST 2014, pp. 153–162. IEEE Computer Society, Washington, DC, USA (2014)
11. Naish, L., Lee, H.J., Ramamohanarao, K.: A model for spectra-based software diagnosis. ACM Trans. Softw. Eng. Methodol. **20**(3), 11:1–11:32 (2011). https://doi.org/10.1145/2000791.2000795
12. Papadakis, M., Traon, Y.L.: Using mutants to locate "unknown" faults. In: 2012 IEEE Fifth International Conference on Software Testing, Verification and Validation (ICST), pp. 691–700, April 2012
13. Papadakis, M., Le Traon, Y.: Effective fault localization via mutation analysis: a selective mutation approach. In: Proceedings of the 29th Annual ACM Symposium on Applied Computing, SAC 2014, pp. 1293–1300. ACM, New York (2014)
14. Pearson, S., et al.: Evaluating and improving fault localization. In: Proceedings of the 39th International Conference on Software Engineering, pp. 609–620. IEEE Press, Piscataway (2017). https://doi.org/10.1109/ICSE.2017.62
15. Sohn, J., Yoo, S.: FLUCCS: Using code and change metrics to improve fault localization. In: Proceedings of the 26th ACM SIGSOFT International Symposium on Software Testing and Analysis, ISSTA 2017, pp. 273–283. ACM, New York (2017). https://doi.org/10.1145/3092703.3092717
16. Wong, E., Wei, T., Qi, Y., Zhao, L.: A crosstab-based statistical method for effective fault localization. In: 2008 1st International Conference on Software Testing, Verification, and Validation, pp. 42–51, April 2008. https://doi.org/10.1109/ICST.2008.65

17. Wong, W.E., Debroy, V., Gao, R., Li, Y.: The dstar method for effective software fault localization. IEEE Trans. Reliability **63**(1), 290–308 (2014). https://doi.org/10.1109/TR.2013.2285319

18. Wong, W.E., Gao, R., Li, Y., Abreu, R., Wotawa, F.: A survey on software fault localization. IEEE Trans. Softw. Eng. **42**(8), 707–740 (2016)

19. Yoo, S., Harman, M.: Using hybrid algorithm for pareto efficient multi-objective test suite minimisation. J. Syst. Softw. **83**(4), 689–701 (2010). https://doi.org/10.1016/j.jss.2009.11.706

Use of Neural Networks in Q-Learning Algorithm

Nataliya Boyko$^{(\boxtimes)}$ (ID), Volodymyr Korkishko (ID),
Bohdan Dohnyak (ID), and Olena Vovk (ID)

Lviv Polytechnic National University, Lviv 79013, Ukraine
{nataliya.i.boyko,Olena.B.Vovk}@lpnu.ua,korkisvolodimir@gmail.com,
bogdan270398@gmail.com
http://www.lp.edu.ua/gp/computer-science/lncs

Abstract. This article is devoted to the algorithm of training with reinforcement (reinforcement learning). This article will cover various modifications of the Q-Learning algorithm, along with its techniques, which can accelerate learning through the use of neural networks. We also talk about different ways of approximating the tables of this algorithm, consider its implementation in the code and analyze its behavior in different environments. We set the optimal parameters for its implementation, and we will evaluate its performance in two parameters: the number of necessary neural network weight corrections and quality of training.

Keywords: Training with reinforcement · Q-Learning
Neural networks · Markov environment

1 Introduction

The problem of reinforcement learning in general formed as follows. For each transition from one state to another appointed some scalar value "reward". The system receives a "reward" when making transition. The purpose of the system is a management policy that maximizes the expected amount of compensation known as a return. The function of the value is the prediction value of all states

$$V_{(xt)} \leftarrow E \sum_{k=0} y^k r_{t+k} \tag{1}$$

where r_t - the award received during transition from the system in state x_t to x_{t+1} and y - discount factor ($0 \leq y \leq 1$). Thus, $V(x_t)$ represents the discount amount of rewards system can get at time t. This amount depends on the selected sequence of actions defined by policy management. The system needs to find a management policy that maximizes $V(x_t)$ for each state [1].

Q-Learning Algorithm is not working with the function of value and uses instead of it Q-function argument which is not only the state but also action.

© Springer Nature Switzerland AG 2018
T. Czachórski et al. (Eds.): ISCIS 2018, CCIS 935, pp. 188–195, 2018.
https://doi.org/10.1007/978-3-030-00840-6_21

It is possible to present Q-function and thereby find the optimal management policy (policy). This statement looks like [5,6]:

$$Q(x_t, a_t) \leftarrow r_t + y * V(x_{t+1}) \tag{2}$$

where a_t - action selected a_t time t from the set of all possible actions A. Since the aim of the system is the total reward maximization, we create replacement max and then we get the following:

$$Q(x_t, a_t) \leftarrow r_t + y * maxQ(x_{t+1}, a_t) \tag{3}$$

Values are stored in a 2-dimensional table, the entry submitted by states and actions. The tabular representation of Q-function and Markov environment creates an element of convergence of the algorithm Q-Learning [4].

Systems that use this algorithm, usually combined with a time difference $(TD(\lambda))$, which was suggested by Sutton. If the time difference method (λ) is equal to zero, it means that the upgrade involves only the current and the following values forecast Q-values. Therefore, in this case, a method is called one-step Q-Learning. Expression of this algorithm is as follows:

$$Q(x_t, a_t) \leftarrow Q(x_t, a_t) + a(r_t + y * maxQ(x_{t+1}, a_t) - Q(x_t, a_t)) \tag{4}$$

Analyzing expression of the Q-update function can conclude that the maximum use of this function is not good usually. In the early stages of learning algorithm Q-value table contains estimates that are not ideal, and even in the later stages usage of maximum could lead to a revaluation of Q-values. Moreover rule of updating algorithm Q-Learning in combination with the time difference needs zero value for λ in choosing actions based on "not greedy" policy (policy action in which selected from some probability that depends on the value Q-functions for the state, as opposed to "greedy" when the selected action with the largest Q-value). These deficiencies have caused modification algorithm Q-Learning, which is one of the sources called SARSA (State-Action-Reward-State-Action), the other - modified Q-Learning. The main difference between these algorithms is that updates the rules Q-max " or not, without having to reset the time difference. If the action will be selected in accordance with the "greedy politics", then this rule will fully comply update updates the formula above [13].

2   Methods Approximation Q - Values

One of the easiest ways of dealing with a large volume dimension which will run the agent is sampling, i.e. partitioning state space for small area each table entry field is Q - values. Using this approach received a gross generalization states.

Approximation CMAC structure consists of several layers. Each layer is divided into intervals of equal length ("tiles") using the quantization. As each layer has a quantum function, the "tiles" layers are shifted relative to each other. Thus, system status, filed at the entrance CMAC, is associated with a set that overlap shifted tiles. The weighted sum of the indices of tiles and gives the output value.

SMAS had success in solving difficult problems with continual space values, including the task of robot control. But nevertheless, despite the successful use, this algorithm requires quite difficult settings. The accuracy of functions that approximates is limited expansion of quantization. High precision requires a larger number of quantization scales and a long-term study environment [6,7].

RBF networks (Radial Bases Functions) closely related to the CMAC and conventional tables. When using this method of approximation table instead of the table of Q - values stored Gaussian table of functions or quadratic function. Rolling systems passed through all the functions of the function then summed and as a result, we obtain approximate values [2]. The work of Linis one of the first works in which in order for table to approximate and table with Q - values is used multilayer perceptron [2,3]. Using a neural network to approximate Q - function has the following advantages: 1. Effective scaling for space has more dimensions; 2. Generalization for large and continuous state space; 3. The possibility of implementation of parallel hardware.

3   Connectable Q-Learning

When using connect - approach in the Q-Learning algorithm tabular representation of Q-functions become replaced by neural network. The input of the network is fed by conditions, and initial data is estimated by Q-values. Thus, no major changes in the classic Q-Learning are not included, except mechanism of changes in estimates storage of Q-values. This article uses a method of neural network offered by Lin which consists of applying a separate neural network for each action [8,9]. Q value of an action (see Fig. 1 a).

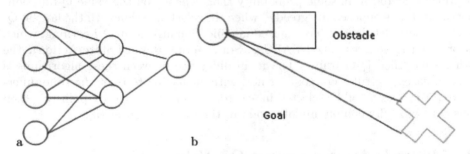

Fig. 1. (a) Q-approximation function using a plurality of neural networks; (b) Recognition Scheme interference

At each iteration of the algorithm current state is fed to the inputs of each neural network, but updating the weights is performed only for one neural network, whose actions were selected. When using a one-step Q-Learning, error correcting network weights is

$$r_t + y * maxQ(x_{t+1}, a_{t+1}) - Q(x_t, a_t) \tag{5}$$

It is worth noting that Lin in his work used a special method of correction weights of the neural network, named backward replay. When using this method, the weights of the neural network are updated only when you reach absorbing system state (final state, for example, when reached any purpose). Using this technique provides storing all pairs of state - action that meets the system before reaching the absorbing state. Algorithm updates using the classic method of Q-values from reverse repetition: To reverse repetition:

$$(x_0, a_0, x_1, r_0) \ldots (x_n, a_n, x_{n+1}, r_n) \tag{6}$$

Perform

1. $t \leftarrow n$
2. $e_t \leftarrow Q(x_t, a_t)$
3. $u_{t+1} \leftarrow (maxQ(x_{t+1}, k)|kA)$
4. $\acute{e}_t \leftarrow r_t + \gamma[(1 - \lambda) * u_{t+1} + \lambda * e_t]$

Then, you configure the network that implements the algorithm using reverse distribution, where the error is approximately equal

$$(x_t, a_t)\acute{e}_t - e_t \tag{7}$$

If $t = 0$ output, otherwise $t \leftarrow t - 1$; transition to step 2.

The idea of the methodology used Lin, lies in the fact that a correct assessment Q- values is known only at achieving system absorbing state. In this case, the Q-rating values equal prize. When removing from absorbing state evaluation Q-value is reduced by using discount factor. Scrolling the list of state - in reverse allows you to perform studies with a more precise estimate. However, the sequence of steps performed by the system may be sub-optimal and therefore assess which training will be carried out, as will be optimum. To address this shortcoming in their methods Lin used a weighted sum consisting of two components:

1. Current grades of Q-function
2. Grade obtained using the recursive expression in step 4 of the algorithm.

Parameter λ, used in step 4 determines which of these two components need to be provided with more benefits.

When using modified Q- Learning expression in step 3 to be replaced.

$Q(u_{t+1} \leftarrow Q(x_{t+1}, a_{t+1})\lambda)$. Algorithm requires making more serious changes that can be implemented as follows: Add steps 2a and 4a, which are as follows

2a: $e2_t \leftarrow max\{Q(x_t, k)|k\epsilon|A|\}$
4a: $e2_t \leftarrow r_t + \gamma * u_{t+1}$
Error in step 5 will be as follows:
$\acute{e}_t - e2_t + e2_t - e_t$

The obvious drawback of reverse repetition technique is the need to store information about all the passages that have been implemented the system before reaching the absorbing state. Version of this algorithm adapted and modified for Q-Learning and $Q(\lambda)$ below [10, 11]:

Modified Connectable Q-Learning
Set "tracks matching" zero, $e_0 = 0$
$t = 0$
Choose action, at
If $t > 0$, we correct weights:

$$w_t = w_{t-1} + a(r_{t-1} + \gamma Q_t - Q_{t-1})e_{t-1} \tag{8}$$

Calculate initial gradient ∇wQt only for that network whose actions were selected.

$$e_t = \nabla_w Q_t + \gamma\lambda * e_{t-1} \tag{9}$$

Take action and get at "award" rt
If the absorbing state is reached, then we end; otherwise
$t \leftarrow t + 1$ and transition to step 3.

Connectable Q-Learning for $Q(\lambda)$
Set "tracks matching" zero, $e_0 = 0$
$t = 0$
Choose action, at
If $t > 0$, then be corrected weights:
$w_t = w_{t-1} + a([r_{t-1} + \gamma maxQ_t - Q_{t-1}] * \nabla_w Q_{t-1} + [r_{t-1} + \gamma maxQ_t - Q_{t-1}] * e_{t-1}$
$e_t = \nabla_w Q_t + \gamma\lambda * e_{t-1}$

Calculate the input ingredients ∇wQt only for one network, the effect of which has been selected. Take action at and "to receive the award" rt.

If the absorbing state is reached - we end, and if not,
$t \leftarrow t + 1$ and transition to the 3rd step.

When using MCQ-L should be stored neural networks weight "footprints matching" last mentioned Q-function Q and reward r. For $Q(\lambda)$ storage costs more, as addition is necessary to keep the output gradients between steps neural network algorithm. Despite this it costs significantly less than those costs which are necessary for keeping the list of state-action methods using reverse repetition. Overview of tasks for robot control. The problem of robot control in 2-dimensional space has been solving at different times by different methods. Most work in this area dedicated to planning routes, which analyzed the environment with the aim of finding the most convenient way. One of the first works in this field is the work of Wilson. This work led to the birth of a whole class of problems dealing animates (ANIMAT = ANIMAL + ROBOT), that works enrolled using an algorithm of reinforcement. Classic animat of Wilson works in the discrete world and continually trains in the same environment. Animata's purpose - is to learn how to achieve the goals of any training position for a minimum number of steps. All these works are characterized by the fact that tuition is always done in the same environment, so the warranty is only that the robot can only operate effectively in this environment and it is unknown how effective will be his behavior with the little change of the environment. In our work, the experiments with the robot, which learns many pretty typical examples, robot can function effectively, got a completely unfamiliar environment. Task management robot. Efficiency of described algorithms in this work analyzed using developed software simulator, operating in the 2-dimensional continuous medium. There was a task for a robot - to reach the goal, not facing any obstacles. Approximate scheme of sensors and work: (see Fig. 1 b)

The learning process has been divided into trials. At each stage of education robot and goal were moved to a new access point, which took place after the generation of the new location of obstacles. Robot received award only in the end of the stages, in all other cases, the reward was zero. The stage ended in achieving the goals robot and receiving awards in the form of units. In this article, we reviewed the case where the robot could not reach the goal because of the location of obstacles. This case will be described and listed below. We generated 26 randomly placed on the map, and there is a way in which the robot reaches the target (as shown below) (see Fig. 2 a).

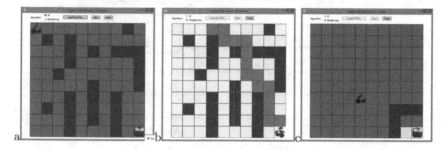

Fig. 2. (a) Generated Map interference; (b) Successful implementation of the algorithm (c) The case when the target is protected

Processes of exploration and exploitation are important in the algorithms of reinforcement learning. The first step is to explore how you can set the environment by choosing less priority action. The final step is to go directly to the operation embodied in this article using the Boltzmann distribution:

$$P(a_t|x_t) = \frac{exp(Q(x_t, a_t)/T)}{\sum_{a \in A} exp(Q(x_t, a_t)/T)} \tag{10}$$

where T - the temperature that regulates the degree of randomness of selection with the largest Q- value.

4   Results

In an experiment with systems, the main component, neural network consists of, the problem is related to the fact that reducing the error rate networks strongly depends on init weights. Therefore, before conducting our experiments, we have carefully studied all the possible distribution of weights for better performance of our neural network. Besides using Q-Learning algorithm we should pay attention to changes in temperature interval T and the speed of change, because algorithm depends on these parameters convergence. Because these parameters and the "cornerstones" were considered (see Fig. 2 b):

As we see in the picture above, the algorithm remembers the way from any cell on the map to the target and then just executes it. However, we should also consider the case when the target will be "locked" by obstacles, such as the unpredictable situation behave neural network of reinforcement (see Fig. 2 c).

In this case, the neural network and the algorithm simply loop. The algorithm tries to sort through all the possible admission to the goal, but each time facing one and the same obstacles. Since our robot stops only when the target is reached, program simply loops (see Fig. 3)

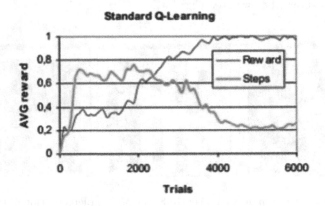

Fig. 3. Charts comparing two methods: interactive update and feedback repetition

5   Conclusions and Perspectives of Further Scientific Developments

We presented a description of the algorithm Q-Learning and its various options (such as modification Q-Learning $IQ(\lambda)$. Each of the above-mentioned algorithms was presented separately from two sides (direct correction weights and reverse playback). Experiments and practical application can be seen in the work and in our created environment. The researchers created the optimal conditions of algorithm parameters and compared their effectiveness. So, after all that is said and analyzed above, we can conclude that the best and most effective algorithm was modified Q-Learning method with an immediate change of scale. This algorithm makes gains in many criteria such as quality, speed and memory cost. It is also worth noting that the use of the algorithm $Q(\lambda)$ of reverse repetition.

This combination shows the fastest convergence algorithm $Q(\lambda)$ of reverse repetition of the initial stages of training and high enough value of the average reward at the end of training. If we take into account only those parameters $Q(\lambda)$, it is much better than other algorithms using reverse repetition. In summary, I would like to point out that the use of immediate correction of weights provides a better solution and requires fewer resources. The advantage of immediate correction weights also lies in the fact that it can be used to solve problems that are not absorbing state.

References

1. Leskovec J., Rajaraman, A., Ullman, J.D.: Mining of Massive Datasets, p. 470. Cambridge University Press, Massachusetts (2014)
2. Mayer-Schoenberger V., Cukier, K.: A Revolution That Will Transform How We Live, Work, and Think, p. 230. Houghton Mifflin Harcourt, Boston, New York (2013)
3. Boyko N., Shakhovska N., Sviridova N.: Use of machine learning in the forecast of clinical consequences of cancer diseases. In: 7th Mediterranean Conference on Embedded Computing - MECO 2018, pp. 531–536. IEEE (2018)
4. Maass, W., Natschger, T., Markram, H.: Real-time computing without stable states: a new framework for neural computations based on perturbations. In: Neural Computation: Proceedings, Institute for Theoretical Computer Science, Switzerland, vol. 11, pp. 2531–2560 (2002)
5. Schrauwen, B., Verstraeten, D., Campenhout, J.V.: An overview of reservoir computing theory, applications and implementations. In: Proceedings of the 15th European Symposium on Artificial Neural Networks, Belgium, Bruges, pp. 471–482 (2007)
6. Coombes, S.: Waves, bumps, and patterns in neural field theories. Biol. Cybern. **93**(2), 91–108 (2005). Proceedings. University of Nottingham, Nottingham
7. Antonopoulos, N., Gillam, L (eds).: Cloud Computing: Principles, Systems and Applications, p. 379. Springer, London (2010)
8. Gosavi, N., Shinde, S.S., Dhakulkar, B.: Use of cloud computing in library and information science field. Int. J. Digital Library Serv. **2**(3), 51–60 (2012)
9. Dhamdhere, S.N. (ed.).: Cloud Computing and Virtualization, p. 385 (2013)
10. Monirul Islam, M.: Necessity of cloud computing for digital libraries: Bangladesh perspective. In: International Conference on Digital Libraries (ICDL) Vision 2020: Looking Back 10 Years and Forging New Frontiers, pp. 513–524 (2013)
11. Mell, P., Grance, T.: The NIST Definition of Cloud Computing: Recommendations of the National Institute of Standards and Technology (2011)
12. Boyko, N.I.: Perspective technologies of study of large data in distributed information systems. Radioelectronics, Computer Science, Management, vol. 4, pp. 66–77. Zaporizhzhya National Technical University, Zaporozhye (2017)
13. Shakhovska, N., Vovk, O., Hasko, R., Kryvenchuk, Y.: The method of big data processing for distance educational system. In: Shakhovska, N., Stepashko, V. (eds.) CSIT 2017. AISC, vol. 689, pp. 461–473. Springer, Cham (2018). https://doi.org/10.1007/978-3-319-70581-1_33

The Random Neural Network
with a BlockChain Configuration in Digital
Documentation

Will Serrano[(✉)]

Intelligent Systems and Networks Group, Electrical and Electronic Engineering,
Imperial College London, Kensington, UK
g.serranoll@imperial.ac.uk

Abstract. This paper presents the Random Neural Network in BlockChain configuration where neurons are gradually incremented as user information increases. The additional neurons codify both the new information to be added to the "neural block" and previous neurons potential to form the "neural chain". This configuration provides the proposed algorithm the same properties as the BlockChain: security and decentralization with the same validation process: mining the input neurons until the neural network solution is found. The Random Neural Network in BlockChain configuration is applied to a digital documentation application that avoids the use of physical papers. Experimental results are presented with optimistic conclusions; this paper provides a digital step forward to avoid physical currencies, documentation and contracts.

Keywords: Random neural network · BlockChain · Digital documentation
Smart contracts

1 Introduction

BlockChain enables the digitalization of contracts as it provides authentication between parties and information encryption of data that gradually increments and it is processed in a decentralized network. Due to these properties BlockChain has been already applied in Cryptocurrency [1], Smart Contracts [2], Intelligent Transport Systems [3], Smart Cities [4] and Internet of Things [5]. Applications are based on the digitalizing physical or paper based agreements.

Neural Networks have analogy biological properties as BlockChain where neurons are chained connected through synapses and information is stored and processed in decentralized clusters of neurons that perform specialized functions [6, 7]. Neural Network weights are increased to store or codified variable user information emulating the human Genome [8].

This paper proposes a neural network solution equivalent to BlockChain with the same properties: user authentication, data encryption and decentralization where user information is gradually incremented and learned. The presented algorithm is based on the Random Neural Network with feedforward configuration [9–12]. The innovative solution is applied to a digital documentation application based on biometrics that will

© Springer Nature Switzerland AG 2018
T. Czachórski et al. (Eds.): ISCIS 2018, CCIS 935, pp. 196–210, 2018.
https://doi.org/10.1007/978-3-030-00840-6_22

be attached to the user during its lifetime and it will never have to be renewed. User own biometrics represent the Private Key whereas there is no need for a Public Key; therefore proposing a truly decentralized solution.

Section 2 presents BlockChain and Neural Networks applications to cryptography related work. Section 3 describes the mathematical model the proposed Random Neural Network in BlockChain configuration. Section 4 defines the Digital Documentation in Block Chain Model whereas Sect. 5 presents the validation and experimental results. Finally, conclusions are presented on Sect. 6.

2 Related Work

Neural Networks have been already applied to Cryptography; Pointcheval [13] presents a linear scheme based on the Perceptron problem or N-P problem suited for smart cards applications. Kinzel et al. [14] train two multilayer neural networks on their mutual output bits with discrete weights to achieve a synchronization that can be applied to secret key exchange over a public channel. Klimov et al. [15] propose three cryptanalytic attacks (genetic, geometric and probabilistic) to the above neural network. Volna et al. [16] apply feed forward neural networks as an encryption and decryption algorithm with a permanently changing key. Yayık et al. [17] present a two stage cryptography multilayered neural network where the first stage generates neural network-based pseudo random numbers and the second stage, a neural network encrypts information based on the non-linearity of the model. Schmidt et al. [18] present a review of the use of artificial neural networks in cryptography.

Presently; there is a great research effort in BlockChain Algorithms. Peters et al. [19] provide an overview of the BlockChain technology and its potential to disrupt the world of banking through enabling global money transfers, smart contracts, automated banking records and digital assets. Zyskind et al. [20] describe a decentralized personal data management system that ensures users own control of their data where a protocol turns BlockChain into an automated access-control manager. Kishigami et al. [21] develop a BlockChain based digital content distribution system operated by the user rights. Watanabe et al. [22] propose a new mechanism that includes a consensus method using a credibility score for securing a BlockChain applied to contracts management such as digital rights management. Kosba et al. [2] propose a framework for building privacy preserving smart contracts formalizing the BlockChain model of cryptography. Aitzhan et al. [23] address the issue of providing transaction security in decentralized smart grid energy trading using BlockChain technology. Yuan et al. [3] study a BlockChain Intelligent Transport System on a seven layer conceptual model that emulates the OSI model. Biswaset et al. [4] propose a security framework that integrates the BlockChain Technology with Smart Devices to provide a secure communication platform in a smart city. Huh et al. [5] propose to use BlockChain to control and configure devices in Internet of Things where public RSA keys are stored in Ethereum and private keys are saved in individual devices. Dorri et al. [24] present BlockChain for Internet of Things security and privacy applied in Smart Homes. Kraft [25] models mining as a Poison process with tine dependent intensity and uses this model to derive predictions about block times for various hash rate scenarios. Beck et al. [26] develop a prototype to replace a coffee shop payment solution based on an analogue prepaid punch solution. Heilman et al. [27] present solutions to the anonymity problem for both transactions on Bitcoin BlockChain and off the BlockChain.

3 The Random Neural Network with BlockChain Configuration

BlockChain is based on several key concepts and components that also can be applied by the use of Neural Networks. Information in the BlockChain is contained in blocks that also include a timestamp, the number of attempts to mine the block and the previous block hash. Decentralized miners then calculate the hash of the current block to validate it. Information contained in the BlockChain consists of transactions which are authenticated by a signature that uses the user private key, transaction origin, destination and value [1] as represented on Fig. 1.

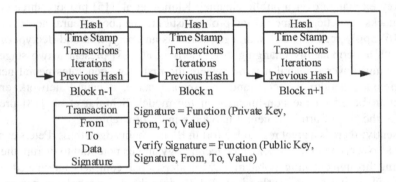

Fig. 1. BlockChain model

3.1 The Random Neural Network

The proposed BlockChain configuration is based on the Random Neural Network (RNN) [9–12] which is a spiking neuronal model that represents the signals transmitted in biological neural networks, where they travel as spikes or impulses, rather than as analogue signal levels. The RNN is a spiking recurrent stochastic model for neural networks where its main analytical properties are the "product form" and the existence of the unique network steady state solution.

The RNN is composed of M neurons each of which receives excitatory (positive) and inhibitory (negative) spike signals from external sources which may be sensory sources or other neurons. These spike signals occur following independent Poisson processes of rates $\lambda^+(m)$ for the excitatory spike signal and $\lambda^-(m)$ for the inhibitory spike signal respectively, to neuron m in $\{1, ..., M\}$ as shown on Fig. 2. In this model, each neuron is represented at time $t \geq 0$ by its internal state $k_m(t)$ which is a non-negative integer and q_m as the probability a neuron is excited.

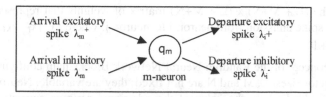

Fig. 2. The random neural network model

If $k_m(t) \geq 0$, then the arrival of a negative spike to neuron m at time t results in the reduction of the internal state by one unit: $k_m(t^+) = k_m(t) - 1$. The arrival of a negative spike to a neuron has no effect if $k_m(t) = 0$. On the other hand, the arrival of an excitatory spike always increases the neuron's internal state by 1; $k_m(t^+) = k_m(t) + 1$. Neuron m can fire when $k_m(t) > 0$.

3.2   The Random Neural Network with BlockChain Configuration

The Random Neural Network with BlockChain configuration consists of L Input Neurons, M hidden neurons and N output neuros Network as represented on Fig. 3. Information in this model is contained networks weights $w^+(j, i)$ and $w^-(j, i)$ rather than neurons x_L, z_M, y_N.

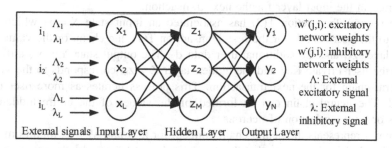

Fig. 3. The random neural network structure

- $I = (\Lambda_L, \lambda_L)$, a variable L-dimensional input vector $I \in [-1,1]^L$ represents the pair of excitatory and inhibitory signals entering each input neuron respectively; where scalar L values range $1 < L < \infty$;
- $X = (x_1, x_2, ..., x_L)$, a variable L-dimensional vector $X \in [0,1]^L$ represents the input state q_L for the neuron L; where scalar L values range $1 < L < \infty$;
- $Z = (z_1, z_2, ..., z_M)$, a M-dimensional vector $Z \in [0,1]^M$ that represents the hidden neuron state q_M for the neuron M; where scalar M values range $1 < M < \infty$
- $Y = (y_1, y_2, ..., y_N)$, a N-dimensional vector $Y \in [0,1]^N$ that represents the neuron output state q_N for the neuron N; where scalar N values range $1 < N < \infty$;
- $w^+(j,i)$ is the $(L + M+N) \times (L + M+N)$ matrix of weights that represents from the excitatory spike emission from neuron i to neuron j; where $i \in [x_L, z_M, y_N]$ and $j \in [x_L, z_M, y_N]$;

- w⁻(j,i) is the (L + M+N) x (L + M+N) matrix of weights that represents from the inhibitory spike emission from neuron i to neuron j; where i $\in$ [x_L, z_M, y_N] and j $\in$ [x_L, z_M, y_N].

The key concept of the Random Neural Network BlockChain configuration is that the neuron vector sizes, L, M and N are not fixed; they are variable. Neurons or blocks are iteratively added where the value of the additional neurons consists on both the value of the additional information and the value of previous neurons therefore forming a neural chain.

Information in this model is transmitted in the matrixes of network weighs, w^+(j, i) and w⁻(j, i) rather than in the neurons. The input layer X represents the user's incremental data; the hidden layer Z represents the values of the chain and the output layer Y represents the user Private Key.

Let's define Transaction and Data as:

- Transactions, T(t) = {T(1), T(2), ... T(t)} as a variable accumulative vector where t is the transaction number;
- Data, D = {d_1, d_2, ... d_t} as a set of is a set of t I-vectors where e_t = (e_{o1}, e_{o2}, ... e_{oI}) and e_{oI} are the I different dimensions for o = 1, 2, ... t.

The first Transaction T(1) has associated an input state X = x_I which corresponds d_1 representing the user data. The output state Y = y_N corresponds to the user Private Key and the hidden layer Z = z_M corresponds to the value of the neural chain that will be inserted in the input layer for the next transaction.

The second Transaction T(2) has associated an input state X = x_I which corresponds to the user data d_1 for the first Transaction T(1), the chain, or the value of the hidden layer z_M and the additional user data d_2. The output state Y = y_N still corresponds the user Private Key and the hidden layer Z = z_M corresponds to the value of the neural chain for the next transaction. This process iterates as more user data is inserted. The neural chain can be formed of the values of the entire hidden layer neurons or only a selection of neurons.

Figure 4 represents the neural chain concept for I, N and M = 2; minimum values chosen for clarity, please note that these values do not have to be the same or fixed.

Data is validated or mined by calculating the outputs of the Random Neural Network using the transmitted network weighs, w^+(j, i) and w⁻(j, i) at variable random inputs i, or following any other method. The solution is found or mined when quadratic error function E_k is lesser than determined minimum error or threshold T.

$$E_k = \frac{1}{2} \sum_{n=1}^{N} (y'_n - y_n)^2 < T \tag{1}$$

where E_k is the minimum error or threshold, y' is the output of the Random Neural Network with mining or random input i and y is the user Private Key. The mining complexity can be tuned by adjusting E_k or the truncated neuron resolution.

Once the solution is found or mined, the values of the hidden layer are used in the input of the next transaction, along with the new data; where the Random Neural

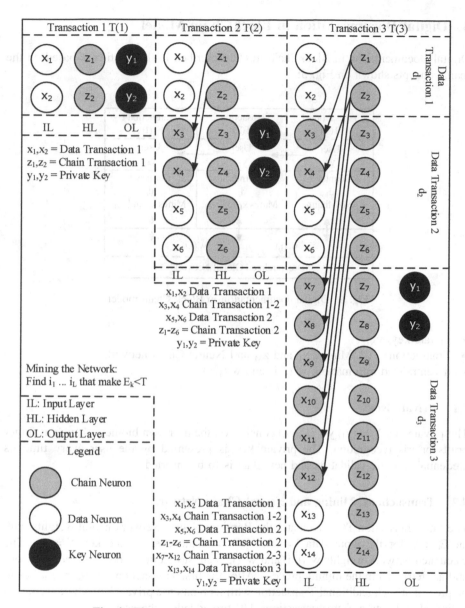

Fig. 4. The random neural network BlockChain structure

Network with gradient descent learning algorithm is calculated again to generate the new network matrixes $w^+(j, i)$ and $w^-(j, i)$. The more transactions and the more data; the validation or mining process increases on complexity.

4 Digital Documentation in BlockChain Model

Digital Documentation in BlockChain model described in this section is based on the main concepts shown on Fig. 5:

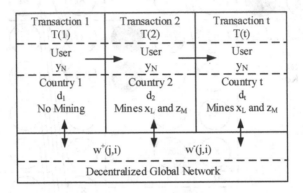

Fig. 5. Digital documentation in Block Chain model

- private key, y_N;
- Transactions $T(t)$, Mining x_L and z_M and Neural Chain network;
- decentralized information; $w^+(j, i)$ and $w^-(j, i)$.

4.1 Private Key

The private key $Y = (y_1, y_2, ..., y_N)$ consists on the user own biometrics such as finger prints or iris recognition. The private key is presented by the user every time its credentials require validation and new data is to be inserted.

4.2 Transactions, Mining and Neural Chain Network

The first Transaction $T(1)$ calculates the Random Neural Network neural weights with an $E_k < Y$ for the input data $I = (\Lambda_L, \lambda_L)$, and the user private key $Y = y_N$. The calculated network weights $w^+(j, i)$ and $w^-(j, i)$ are stored in the decentralized network and are retrieved in the mining process. After the first Transaction; the user requires to be present at each additional Transaction with its biometric private key where its data is validated and data d_t from transactions $T(t)$ are added to the user.

The Random Neural Network with BlockChain configuration is mined when an Input I is found that delivers an output Y with an Error E_k lesser than a threshold T for the retrieved user network weights $w^+(j, i)$ and $w^-(j, i)$. When the solution is found, the user data can be processed, the potential value of the neural hidden layer $Z = z_M$ is added to form the Neural Chain where more user data is added.

Finally, the system calculates the Random Neural Network with Gradient descent algorithm for the new pair (I, Y) where the new calculated network weights $w^+(j, i)$ and $w^-(j, i)$ are stored in the decentralized network.

4.3 Decentralized Information

The user network weights $w^+(j, i)$ and $w^-(j, i)$ are stored in the decentralized network rather than its data I directly from which are calculated. The network weights expand as more data is inserted, therefore creating an adaptable method. In addition; only the user Data can be extracted when the user presents its biometric key therefore making secure to store information in a decentralized system.

5 Digital Documentation Validation

This section proposes a practical validation of the Digital Documentation in Block-Chain model as a Digital Passport application. The user is assigned a four neuron private key and each country is assigned a four neuron code. When the user travels between countries; the biometric private key is presented at the passport control; the decentralized system retrieves the neural weights associated to the private key; mines the block, adds the country code and stores back the network weights in the decentralized system. Mining for this validation is considered as the selection of random neuron values until $E_k < T$.

In the experiments; the user travels to five different countries where neurons in the input, and output layer are truncated to $\Delta = 1E-2$, $\Delta = 1E-4$, $\Delta = 1E-6$ and $\Delta = 1E-8$ resolution respectively. The Country Code (I) and Biometric key (Y) for the different resolutions are represented on Table 1.

Table 1. Digital passport validation configuration

Trip	Country code (I)			
	$\Delta = 1E-2$	$\Delta = 1E-4$	$\Delta = 1E-6$	$\Delta = 1E-8$
1	(0.28, 0225, 0.22 0.29)	(0.2228, 0.2225, 0.2222 0.2229)	(0.222228, 0.222225, 0.222222 0.222229)	(0.22222228, 0.22222225, 0.22222222 0.22222229)
2	(0.42, 0.48, 0.44, 0.41)	(0.4442, 0.4448, 0.4444, 0.4441)	(0.444442, 0.444448, 0.444444, 0.444441)	(0.44444442, 0.44444448, 0.44444444, 0.44444441)
3	(0.62, 0.68, 0.65, 0.67)	(0.6662, 0.6668, 0.6665, 0.6667)	(0.666662, 0.666668, 0.666665, 0.666667)	(0.66666662, 0.66666668, 0.66666665, 0.66666667)
4	(0.78, 0.75, 0.73, 0.71)	(0.7778, 0.7775, 0.7773, 0.7771)	(0.777778, 0.777775, 0.777773, 0.777771)	(0.77777778, 0.77777775, 0.77777773, 0.77777771)
5	(0.82, 0.88, 0.85, 0.84)	(0.8882, 0.8888, 0.8885, 0.8884)	(0.888882, 0.888888, 0.888885, 0.888884)	(0.88888882, 0.88888888, 0.88888885, 0.88888884)
	Biometric (Y)			
All	(0.24, 0.46, 0.68, 0.82)	(0.2224, 0.4446, 0.6668, 0.8882)	(0.222224, 0.444446, 0.666668, 0.888882)	(0.22222224, 0.44444446, 0.66666668, 0.88888882)

Table 2. Digital passport validation values

User trip	Iteration number	Error E_k	Mining threshold	Mining iteration	Mining error	Number of neurons (x_L, z_M, y_N)
$\Delta = 1E\text{-}2$						
1	143.000	7.53E-31	1E-5	1235.525	3.41E-06	04-04-04
2	251.067	8.74E-31	1E-5	5252.959	3.37E-06	12-12-04
3	316.158	8.55E-31	1E-5	4592.880	3.52E-06	20-20-04
4	478.818	8.63E-31	1E-5	3646.378	3.45E-06	28-28-04
5	659.329	7.36E-31	1E-5	1416.612	3.28E-06	36-36-04
$\Delta = 1E\text{-}4$						
1	144.000	8.67E-31	1E-5	1294.436	3.43E-06	04-04-04
2	251.851	8.70E-31	1E-5	5451.931	3.28E-06	12-12-04
3	316.625	8.55E-31	1E-5	4763.359	3.45E-06	20-20-04
4	480.909	8.64E-31	1E-5	3615.913	3.20E-06	28-28-04
5	660.525	7.50E-31	1E-5	1361.162	3.55E-06	36-36-04
$\Delta = 1E\text{-}6$						
1	145.000	7.55E-31	1E-5	1328.892	3.27E-06	04-04-04
2	251.914	8.74E-31	1E-5	5473.929	3.22E-06	12-12-04
3	316.614	8.57E-31	1E-5	4929.567	3.42E-06	20-20-04
4	480.924	8.60E-31	1E-5	3624.507	3.51E-06	28-28-04
5	660.692	7.53E-31	1E-5	1408.170	3.28E-06	36-36-04
$\Delta = 1E\text{-}8$						
1	144.000	9.43E-31	1E-5	1326.848	3.26E-06	04-04-04
2	251.909	8.74E-31	1E-5	5594.360	3.29E-06	12-12-04
3	316.608	8.52E-31	1E-5	4991.639	3.49E-06	20-20-04
4	482.756	8.59E-31	1E-5	3646.790	3.39E-06	28-28-04
5	660.740	7.52E-31	1E-5	1349.107	3.39E-06	36-36-04

The algorithm is run 1000 times for each truncated resolution where the averaged validation results are represented on Table 2. The information shown is the number of iterations the Random Neuron Network with BlockChain configuartion requires to achieve an $E_k < 1.0E\text{-}30$; the error E_k, the number of iterations to mine the BlockChain and the number of neurons for each layer; input x_L, hidden z_M and output y_N.

As expected; The Random Neural Network requires more iterations following the increase of user data because the number of neurons expands; the number of iterations are independent to the truncated neuron resolution as the algorithm fills the decimal values with zeros as shown on Fig. 6. The Random Neural Network in BlockChain configuration achieves rather easily very minor error thresholds E_k 1E-30 due its main analytical properties based on the "product form" and the existence of the unique network steady state solution.

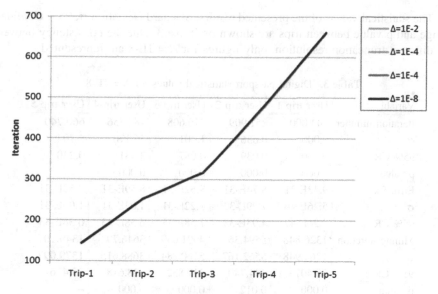

Fig. 6. Learning iteration versus Trip – 5 Trips

On the other side; the truncated neuron resolution does not affect the number of iterations when mining the network. Because mining is performed using random values, the results are not as linear as expected as shown on Fig. 7. Unexpectedly; the later user trips are mined easier in all resolutions when actually mining shall be harder or longer as the number of neurons increases.

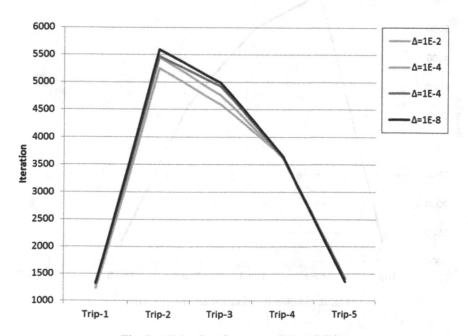

Fig. 7. Mining iteration versus Trip – 5 Trips

The statistical values of the presented results; Standard Deviation σ, 95% Confident Range and p value between trips are shown on Table 3. Due the consistency between the different truncation resolution, only figures for Δ = 1E-8 are represented.

Table 3. Digital passport statistical values for Δ = 1E-8

Variable	User trip 1	User trip 2	User trip 3	User trip 4	User trip 5
Iteration number	144.000	251.909	316.608	482.756	660.740
σ	0.000	0.636	1.401	56.170	3.704
95% CR	0.000	0.039	0.087	3.481	0.230
p value	0.000	0.000	0.000	0.000	–
Error Ek	9.43E-31	8.74E-31	8.52E-31	8.59E-31	7.52E-31
σ	5.26E-46	7.99E-32	1.22E-31	1.03E-31	1.03E-31
95% CR	3.26E-47	4.95E-33	7.58E-33	6.38E-33	6.38E-33
Mining iteration	1326.848	5594.36	4991.639	3646.79	1349.107
σ	1264.948	5562.167	5160.284	3688.615	1379.097
95% CR	78.401	344.740	319.832	228.618	85.476
p value	0.000	0.012	0.000	0.000	–
Mining error	3.26E-06	3.29E-06	3.49E-06	3.39E-06	3.39E-06
σ	2.98E-06	2.99E-06	3.02E-06	2.99E-06	2.92E-06
95% CR	1.85E-07	1.85E-07	1.87E-07	1.85E-07	1.81E-07

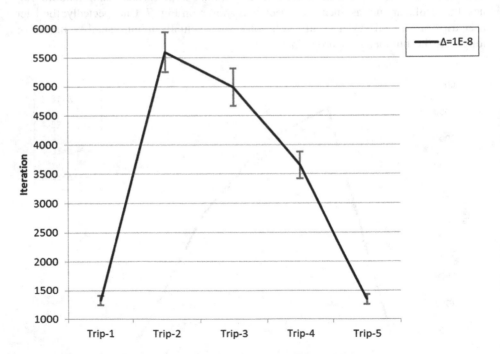

Fig. 8. Mining iteration versus Trip – 5 Trips

The Validation presents statistically significant results with a minor mining iteration overlap between Trip 2 and Trip 3; as shown on Fig. 8.

6   Conclusions

This paper has presented the Random Neural Network in BlockChain configuration where neurons are gradually incremented as user information increases. This configuration provides the proposed algorithm the same properties as the BlockChain: security and decentralization with the same validation process: mining the input neurons until the neural network solution is found.

The Random Neural Network in BlockChain configuration has been applied to a Digital Documentation application that avoids the use of physical paper. Experimental results show that BlockChain applications can be successfully implemented using neural networks where mining effort can be gradually increased, user authentication and data encryption in a decentralized network therefore removing centralized validation mechanisms.

This paper has provided a digital step forward to avoid physical currencies, documentation and contracts. Future wok will include additional validations to the BlockChain configuration with an increase of resolution, trips, further analyze the mining process and the development of new applications in cryptocurrency and Internet of Things.

Appendix: RNN – BlockChain Schematic

Trip 1
04-04-04

Trip 2
12-12-04

Trip 3
20-20-04

Trip 4
28-28-04

Trip 5
36-36-04

Trip 6
44-44-04

Trip 7
52-52-04

Trip 8
60-60-04

Trip 9
68-68-04

Trip 10
76-76-04

● Key Neuron
◉ Link Neuron
○ Data Neuron

References

1. Nakamoto, S.: Bitcoin: A Peer-to-Peer Electronic Cash System-Bitcoin.org. (2008)
2. Kosba, A., Miller, A., Shi, E., Wen, Z., Papamanthou, C.: Hawk: the Blockchain model of cryptography and privacy-preserving smart contracts. In: IEEE Symposium on Security and Privacy, pp. 839–858 (2016)
3. Yuan, Y., Wang, F.-Y.: Towards Blockchain-based intelligent transportation systems. In: International Conference on Intelligent Transportation Systems, pp. 2663–2668 (2016)
4. Biswas, K., Muthukkumarasamy, V.: Securing smart cities using Blockchain technology. International Conference High Performance Computing and Communications/Smart City/Data Science and Systems, pp. 1392–1393 (2016)
5. Huh, S., Cho, S., Kim, S.: Managing IoT devices using BlockChain platform. In: International Conference on Advanced Communication Technology, pp. 464–467 (2017)
6. Serrano, W., Yin, Y., Gelenbe, E.: The random neural network with deep learning clusters in smart search. Neurocomputing (2018) (To be published)
7. Serrano, W, Gelenbe, E.: Deep learning clusters in the cognitive packet network. Neurocomputing (2018) (To be published)
8. Serrano, W.: The random neural network with a genetic algorithm and deep learning clusters in fintech: smart investment. In: Iliadis, L., Maglogiannis, I., Plagianakos, V. (eds.) AIAI 2018. IAICT, vol. 519, pp. 297–310. Springer, Cham (2018). https://doi.org/10.1007/978-3-319-92007-8_26
9. Gelenbe, E.: Random neural networks with negative and positive signals and product form solution. Neural Comput. **1**, 502–510 (1989)
10. Gelenbe, E.: Learning in the recurrent random neural network. Neural Comput. **5**, 154–164 (1993)
11. Gelenbe, E.: G-networks with triggered customer movement. J. Appl. Probab. **30**, 742–748 (1993)
12. Gelenbe, E., Hussain, K.F.: Learning in the multiple class random neural network. IEEE Trans. Neural Netw. **13**(6), 1257–1267 (2002)
13. Pointcheval, D.: Neural Networks and their Cryptographic Applications. Livre des resumes Eurocode Institute for Research in Computer Science and Automation, pp. 1–7 (1994)
14. Kinzel, W., Kanter, I.: Interacting Neural Networks and Cryptography Secure exchange of information by synchronization of neural networks. Adv. Solid State Phys. **42**, 383–391 (2002)
15. Klimov, A., Mityagin, A., Shamir, A.: Analysis of neural cryptography. In: Zheng, Y. (ed.) ASIACRYPT 2002. LNCS, vol. 2501, pp. 288–298. Springer, Heidelberg (2002). https://doi.org/10.1007/3-540-36178-2_18
16. Volna, E., Kotyrba, M., Kocian, V., Janosek, M.: Cryptography based on the neural network. In: European Conference on Modelling and Simulation, pp. 1–6 (2012)
17. Yayık, A., Kutlu, Y.: Neural network based cryptography. Int. J. Neural Mass Parallel Comput. Inf. Syst. **24**(2), 177–192 (2014)
18. Schmidt, T., Rahnama, H., Sadeghian, A.: A review of applications of artificial neural networks in cryptosystems. In: World Automation Congress, pp. 1–6 (2008)
19. Peters, Gareth W., Panayi, E.: Understanding modern banking ledgers through Blockchain technologies: future of transaction processing and smart contracts on the internet of money. In: Tasca, P., Aste, T., Pelizzon, L., Perony, N. (eds.) Banking Beyond Banks and Money. NEW, pp. 239–278. Springer, Cham (2016). https://doi.org/10.1007/978-3-319-42448-4_13
20. Zyskind, G., Nathan, O., Pentland, A.: Decentralizing privacy: using Blockchain to protect personal data. Security and Privacy Workshops, pp. 180–184 (2015)

21. Kishigami, J., Fujimura, S., Watanabe, H., Nakadaira, A., Akutsu, A.: The Blockchain-based digital content distribution system. Big Data Cloud Comput. 187–190 (2015)
22. Watanabe, H., Fujimura, S., Nakadaira, A., Miyazaki, Y., Akutsu, A., Kishigami, J.: Blockchain contract: Securing a Blockchain applied to smart contracts. In: International Conference on Consumer Electronics, pp. 467–468 (2016)
23. Aitzhan, N.Z., Svetinovic, D.: Security and privacy in decentralized energy trading through multi-signatures, Blockchain and anonymous messaging streams. IEEE Trans. Dependable Secur. Comput. 1–14 (2016)
24. Dorri, A., Kanhere, S.S., Jurdak, R., Gauravaram, P.: Blockchain for IoT security and privacy: The case study of a smart home. In: Pervasive Computing and Communications Workshops, pp. 1–6 (2017)
25. Kraft, D.: Difficulty control for Blockchain-based consensus systems. Peer-to-Peer Netw. Appl. 9(2), 397–413 (2016)
26. Beck, R., Stenum, J., Lollike, N., Malone, S.: Blockchain-the gateway to trust-free cryptographic transactions. In: European Conference on Information Systems, pp. 1–14 (2016)
27. Heilman, E., Baldimtsi, F., Goldberg, S.: Blindly signed contracts: anonymous on-Blockchain and off-Blockchain bitcoin transactions. In: Clark, J., Meiklejohn, S., Ryan, Peter Y.A., Wallach, D., Brenner, M., Rohloff, K. (eds.) FC 2016. LNCS, vol. 9604, pp. 43–60. Springer, Heidelberg (2016). https://doi.org/10.1007/978-3-662-53357-4_4

A Reinforcement Learning Approach to Adaptive Forwarding in Named Data Networking

Olumide Akinwande[✉] and Erol Gelenbe

Department of Electrical and Electronic Engineering,
Imperial College London, London, UK
olumide.akinwande13@imperical.ac.uk

Abstract. This paper addresses Information Centric Networks, and considers in-network caching for Named Data Networking (NDN) architectures. We depart from forwarding algorithms which primarily use links that have been selected by the routing protocol for probing and forwarding, and propose an adaptive forwarding strategy using reinforcement learning with the random neural network (NDNFS-RLRNN), to leverage the routing information and actively seek possible deliveries outside these paths in a controlled way. Our simulations show that NDNFS-RLRNN achieves more efficient delivery performance than a strategy that strictly follows the routing layer or a strategy that retrieves contents from the nearest caches by flooding requests.

1 Introduction

Information-Centric Networking (ICN) treats content as fundamental by naming and addressing data objects at the network level, which is a significant departure from the Internet's host-centic architecture. This enables ICN to naturally support features like in-network caching and many-to-many communication which can be essential in meeting the current predominant use of the Internet [1,2]. This paper focuses on *Named Data Networking* (NDN) [3], one of the prominent ICN approaches. In NDN, where requests are sent in *Interest packets*, while *Data packets* carry the requested contents; both packets carry the name or identification of the desired data object. An Interest is uniquely identified by its name and nonce values, where the nonce is randomly generated by the requesting application. A NDN node maintains three main data structures for implementing the forwarding plane: a *content store* (CS) which acts as a cache for Data packets, a *pending interest table* (PIT) which keeps track of unanswered requests, and a *forwarding information base* (FIB) which maps reachable name prefixes to outgoing interfaces. The FIB is updated by a name-based routing protocol.

NDN differs significantly from most of the other ICN proposals because it incorporates an intelligent forwarding plane through its *strategy module*. The strategy module is a program or algorithm, defined for each prefix in the FIB, for making Interest forwarding decisions. It is expected to leverage on both the

© Springer Nature Switzerland AG 2018
T. Czachórski et al. (Eds.): ISCIS 2018, CCIS 935, pp. 211–219, 2018.
https://doi.org/10.1007/978-3-030-00840-6_23

routing information in the FIB and the observed packet delivery measurements in making adaptive decisions. An important benefit of this layer is that it can relax the stringent convergence and correctness demands on the routing layer [4]. A NDN node matches an Interest, using the content name, in the CS, PIT and FIB, in that order. A match in the FIB results in the strategy being called upon to decide the Interest's next hop. Data packets are sent along the reverse paths used by their corresponding Interest packets, following the states in the PITs. For scalability and practicality reasons, the name-based routing protocol in NDN can only announce and monitor paths leading to the actual content sources and designated repositories, thus leaving the responsibility of exploiting the in-network caching capability, which is important for delivering the design goals of NDN, entirely to the forwarding strategy. However, most of the proposals for the strategy layer, including the algorithm currently adopted by the NDN project, follow a "monitor-the-routing-paths" approach, whereby their forwarding and probing actions are restricted to the links suggested by the routing layer [5–8]. This approach limits the strategy from exploiting local caches closer but outside the routing paths. Our goal is to follow a more dynamic self-aware [9] approach for the strategy layer of the NDN architecture which actively seeks faster content delivery offered by the local content stores, while retaining the guarantees offered by the routing layer. Towards these objectives, we present a design for the strategy module of the NDN that uses the Random Neural Network (RNN) [10] based adaptive learning algorithm, inspired by the Cognitive Packet Network (CPN) [11,12].

The rest of this paper report is organised as follows. Section 1.1 reviews the related literature, focusing on the NDN strategy. We introduce our proposed strategy, the *NDN forwarding strategy using reinforcement learning with the RNN* (NDNFS-RLRNN) in Sect. 2. Simulation results are presented in Sect. 2.1, and conclusions and future work are presented in Sect. 3.

1.1   Related Work

In [13] it is shown that coupling caching and forwarding is essential in ICN to significantly benefit from ubiquitous caching. An ideal policy *ideal Nearest Replica Routing* (iNRR), forwards requests to the nearest possible replica with the help of an "oracle" that keeps track of a network's caching state, before proposing practical implementations that regularly explore a given neighbourhood in the network through scoped flooding of requests. In the NDN context, Jacobson et al. [5] proposed forwarding an Interest along all the interfaces suggested by the routing layer excluding the interface the Interest arrives on, also called the *multicast strategy*. The *best route strategy* [6] forwards interests using the available upstream with the lowest routing costs. The current NDN strategy [3,7,14] combines interface ranking and colour classification in order to decide where to forward Interests. Interfaces suggested by the routing protocol are first classified using a colour scheme according to how well they are known to return Data, then the interfaces are ranked in each class using some metric, usually the SRTT. The forwarding logic is to use the highest ranked available interface in the best possible classification. Interest NACKs were introduced in NDN to address the inefficiencies that result from the dangling states in the PIT caused by unsatisfied Interests. When it cannot forward nor satisfy an Interest, an NDN router responds with an Interest NACK; the Interest NACK also carries a code describing the reasons. Therefore, Interest NACKs can help the network to quickly and informedly detect faults and, when possible, try other forwarding options. To eliminate undetected loops in NDN, the *Strategy for Interest Forwarding and Aggregation with Hop-Counts* (SIFAH) was proposed in [8]. In SIFAH, a node accepts to forward an Interest packet only if there exists, based on distance information to the content source, a neighbour node that moves the packet closer to the content. The distance information used in SIFAH is the number of hops to the content repository and it is provided to the forwarding plane by the routing protocol. The multipath forwarding strategies [15–17] dynamically assign to each interface of an NDN router, a forwarding weight or probability per name prefix, which determines the proportion of request traffic sent on each interface, so as to achieve good load balancing and manage network congestion. *INFORM* as presented in [18] and inspired by the Q-routing [19]. INFORM alternates between exploration and exploitation phases when making forwarding decisions. In the initial exploration phase when no learning has occurred, a received Interest is sent using the best interface according to the information in the FIB and a copy of the Interest is also sent on a randomly selected interface. The same actions are repeated in subsequent exploration phases except that the best interface is the one learnt by the Q-learning algorithm. Only the best interface computed after an exploration phase is used during the subsequent exploitation phase. The authors do not address the possible inefficiencies that could be introduced by the dangling states in the PIT and the handling of Interest NACKs.

Our approach uses the CPN routing protocol [20] which employs reinforcement learning using the RNN [21] to establish and maintain connections between network nodes. The algorithm used has been shown to possess fast convergence properties during an initial learning phase and good sensitivity to environmental changes [22]. Other work on CPN can be found in [23–26].

2 NDN Forwarding Using Reinforcement Learning with the RNN

In this section, we present NDNFS-RLRNN where we use this reinforcement learning with RNN algorithm to realize the strategy module per prefix in the NDN architecture. The learning algorithm is expected to be supported by a name-based routing protocol and the online measurements from the state recorded in the PIT. In NDNFS-RLRNN, an RNN is created for each prefix announced into the FIB by the routing protocol. The RNN has as many neurons as the number of outgoing interfaces at the NDN router. An RNN in the initial state only knows of the routing preferences for its prefix and is yet to be updated by packet delivery measurements. In this state, NDNFS-RLRNN's forwarding decisions will be to use the best interface according to the routing layer.

On the arrival of a Data packet, a reward value is computed for the arrival interface and used to update the RNN. The goal of our distributed reinforcement learning is to minimise the delay for retrieving contents, so we estimate reward using the RTT values. Let $T^j{}_I$ be the time an NDN router forwards an Interest along an interface j and $T^j{}_D$ be the arrival time of the Data packet satisfying the Interest which also arrives on the same interface, we can estimate the reward, R^j as the inverse of the RTT using

$$R^j = (T^j{}_D - T^j{}_I)^{-1} \tag{1}$$

In applying the reinforcement learning algorithm, it is important to consider in this application that the links suggested by the routing protocol offer better assurances on content delivery. Therefore, only positive reinforcements are applied to the neurons corresponding to these interfaces, ensuring that alternative interfaces will be used only when they are known to improve delivery. Also, whenever an entry in the PIT expires without any response or the RNN receives no updates for T_r time units, the learning algorithm reinitializes, thereby falling back to the routing layer preferences.

For an updated RNN, the forwarding decision of NDNFS-RLRNN is, excluding the arrival interface, with a high probability p only the interface corresponding to the most excited neuron is used or with probability $(1 - p)$ a probing decision is made. Before explaining the probing process, we first introduce the idea of marking an Interest packet for probing. This means an Interest can be identified at the NDN routers as either a "normal" Interest or a probe Interest. The probing process involves sending two packets: the original Interest which is sent along the best known interface and a copy which is sent as a probe Interest on a randomly selected interface. We impose that an NDN router only forwards a probe Interest along the best known interface. The motivation for this probing process is to control exploration in order to reduce the possibility of unnecessarily using longer paths to retrieve contents and to manage overhead.

In NDNFS-RLRNN, we have also adopted the use of NACKS as in the current NDN. Clearly, the reward computation is explicit when the Interest is satisfied; but, this is not the case when a NACK is returned or no response is received before the Interest times out. In such cases, the reward can be estimated as

$$R^j = [c(T - T^j{}_I)]^{-1} \tag{2}$$

where T is the current time and c is a constant large enough such that a negative reinforcement is applied.

2.1 Performance Evaluation

In this section, we present initial evaluations of the performance of NDNFS-RLRNN through extensive simulations using the *ndnSim* [27], an NS-3 based simulator which already exists for NDN. For the simulations, we consider an NDN-based network connecting users to content servers. We use the real topology *Elibackbone* shown in Fig. 1 according to the dataset in [28]. Each node

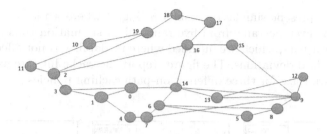

Fig. 1. *Elibackbone* topology. The network consists of 20 nodes and 30 links.

receives external requests for contents at an average of 5 request packets per second with a Poisson distribution. We model the requests according to the Mandelbrot-Zipf (MZipf) distribution. The plateau parameter for the distribution is fixed at $p = 5.0$ while the skew parameter, α at each node is randomly chosen in the range [0.6, 1.2]. The cache capacity is fixed for each node at 10 data units and we investigate performances under different catalogue sizes. The simulations begin with empty caches at the nodes. We consider a single access router for the network through which requests are served from the content servers. Furthermore, we compare NDNFS-RLRNN with the *Adaptive SRTT-based Forwarding Strategy* (ASF) [4] and a Nearest Replica Routing (NRR) strategy [13]. The ASF strategy uses the upstream with the lowest measured SRTT and probes alternative interfaces suggested in the FIB at intervals. The length of a probing interval is chosen to be 3 s and we install all possible routes in the FIB such that no loop exists in the forwarding. We have considered a small probing interval for ASF in comparison with a probing probability of 0.3 for NDNFS-RLRNN. For the NRR strategy, we implement a multicast algorithm that sends each request on all the interfaces of a node except the arrival interface, which guarantees that the requested data objects are retrieved from the closest caches. The strategies are implemented per content in the catalogue. Also, since the cache states in the network will influence performance, the strategies are compared under three different cache policies from the literature:

- Leave copy everywhere combined with LRU replacement policy (*LCE*).
- In the "Betweenness centrality policy and LRU (*Betw*)" [29], only the routers with the highest betweenness centrality values along the delivery path, cache the content.
- In *ProbCache and LRU* routers cache content based on some probability. *ProbCache* [30], computed by weighing the caching capacity of the delivery path with the relative position of the router along the path.

Finally, we measure athe *cache hit rate* and the *network load per request*. The cache hit rate is the proportion of the requests arriving into the network which are satisfied from the local caches. The network load or overhead is the total number of hops traversed by the network packets, which includes Interests, Data and NACK packets, per request sent into the network.

Results. We present simulation results in Fig. 2 where a plot on each graph represents the average value from five randomised simulation runs each lasting 400 s; the error bars, which are included where readability is not affected, represent the standard deviations. The figures report the cache hit rate as a function of the catalogue size for three different on-path caching policies.

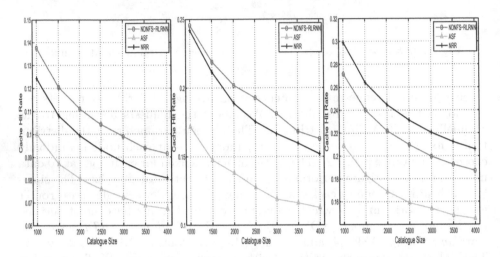

Fig. 2. Cache hit rate performance comparison of NDNFS-RLRNN, ASF and NRR under the (i) LCE and LRU cache policy (Left), (ii) *Betw* and LRU cache policy (Centre), and (iii) *ProbCache* and LRU cache policy, with different catalogue sizes. The cache size of each node is fixed at 10 data objects. Content popularity is modelled according to the Mandelbrot-Zipf (MZipf) distribution with settings $p = 5.0$ and $\alpha \in [0.6, 1.2]$. The results reported are the average of 5 randomized simulation runs.

We observe that NDNFS-RLRNN delivers a better hit rate performance than both ASF and NRR under the LCE cache policy. It provides an average improvement of about 37% compared with ASF, and an improvement between 10–13% in comparison with NRR for the considered catalogue sizes. The cache pollution caused by the flooding of requests in NRR combined with the characteristic high eviction rate of the LCE policy offsets the gains of content retrieval from the closest cache. Improved results are obtained generally as the cache policy tries to cache packets at the most "central" nodes along the delivery paths. Under the *Betw* policy, compared with ASF, NDNFS-RLRNN provides an improvement between 40–53% in terms of the cache hit rate While, compared with NRR, we see an improvement between 1–10%. The *ProbCache* policy produces the best hit results for the strategies as observed in because it uses the cache space more efficiently than the other policies. The reduced eviction rate suits the NRR as it produces the best performance in terms of the cache hit rate. NDNFS-RLRNN still provides an average performance improvement of about 30% over ASF for the considered catalogue sizes. These results suggest that when caching is effective, NDNFS-RLRNN can take better advantage compared with ASF which restricts its forwarding decisions to the delivery paths according to the FIB. Finally, Fig. 3, reports the overhead per request as a function of the catalogue size for the different on-path caching policies. Generally, we have observed NDNFS-RLRNN generates about one-fifth of the overhead produced in NRR under all the scenarios. Also, the results show that NDNFS-RLRNN achieves better hit rates compared with ASF under all the cache policies with less overhead.

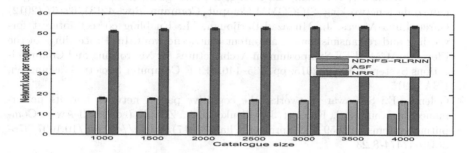

Fig. 3. Network load performance of NDNFS-RLRNN, ASF and NRR under the LCE and LRU cache policy and different catalogue sizes. The cache size of each node is fixed at 10 data objects. Content popularity is modelled according to the Mandelbrot-Zipf (MZipf) distribution with settings, $p = 5.0$ and $\alpha \in [0.6, 1.2]$. The results are averages of 5 randomized simulation runs.

3   Conclusions

This paper has proposed an adaptive forwarding strategy, NDNFS-RLRNN for the NDN architecture. The approach is dynamic and does not persist on the links put forward by the routing protocol, so that it may better recognize the role of the forwarding plane to take advantage of the in-network caching capability of NDN. Our experiments suggest that when in-network caching is effective, NDNFS-RLRNN achieves better delivery than a strategy that persists with existing static routing layer preferences.

References

1. Xylomenos, G., et al.: A survey of information-centric networking research. IEEE Commun. Surv. Tutor. **16**(2), 1024–1049 (2014)
2. Cisco, V.: Cisco visual networking index: forecast and methodology, 2016–2021 (2017)
3. Zhang, L., et al.: Named data networking. SIGCOMM Comput. Commun. Rev. **44**(3), 66–73 (2014)

4. Lehman, V., et al.: An experimental investigation of hyperbolic routing with a smart forwarding plane in NDN. In: 2016 IEEE/ACM 24th International Symposium on Quality of Service (IWQoS), pp. 1–10 (2016)
5. Jacobson, V., Smetters, D.K., Thornton, J.D., Plass, M.F., Briggs, N.H., Braynard, R.L.: Networking named content. In: Proceedings of the 5th International Conference on Emerging Networking Experiments and Technologies, CoNEXT 2009, pp. 1–12. ACM, New York, USA (2009)
6. Afanasyev, A., et al.: NFD developer's guide. Technical Report NDN-0021, Department of Computer Science, University of California, Los Angeles, USA (2014)
7. Yi, C., Afanasyev, A., Wang, L., Zhang, B., Zhang, L.: Adaptive forwarding in named data networking. SIGCOMM Comput. Commun. Rev. **42**(3), 62–67 (2012)
8. Garcia-Luna-Aceves, J., Mirzazad-Barijough, M.: Enabling correct interest forwarding and retransmissions in a content centric network. In: Proceedings of the Eleventh ACM/IEEE Symposium on Architectures for Networking and Communications Systems, ANCS 2015, pp. 135–146. IEEE Computer Society, Washington, USA (2015)
9. Gelenbe, E.: Self-aware networks: the cognitive packet network and its performance. In: Kounev, S., Kephart, J., Milenkoski, A., Zhu, X. (eds.) Self-Aware Computing Systems, pp. 659–668. Springer, Cham (2017). https://doi.org/10.1007/978-3-319-47474-8_23
10. Gelenbe, E., Fourneau, J.M.: Random neural networks with multiple classes of signals. Neural Comput. **11**(4), 953–963 (1999)
11. Gelenbe, E.: Steps toward self-aware networks. Commun. ACM **52**(7), 66–75 (2009)
12. Birke, R.: Self-aware computing systems: open challenges and future research directions. In: Kounev, S., Kephart, J., Milenkoski, A., Zhu, X. (eds.) Self-Aware Computing Systems, pp. 709–722. Springer, Cham (2017). https://doi.org/10.1007/978-3-319-47474-8_26
13. Rossini, G., Rossi, D.: Coupling caching and forwarding: benefits, analysis, and implementation. In: Proceedings of the 1st ACM Conference on Information-Centric Networking, ACM-ICN 2014, pp. 127–136. ACM, New York, USA (2014)
14. Yi, C., Afanasyev, A., Moiseenko, I., Wang, L., Zhang, B., Zhang, L.: A case for stateful forwarding plane. Comput. Commun. **36**(7), 779–791 (2013)
15. Qian, H., Ravindran, R., Wang, G.Q., Medhi, D.: Probability-based adaptive forwarding strategy in named data networking. In: 2013 IFIP/IEEE International Symposium on Integrated Network Management (IM 2013), pp. 1094–1101 (2013)
16. Nguyen, D., Fukushima, M., Sugiyama, K., Tagami, A.: Efficient multipath forwarding and congestion control without route-labeling in CCN. In: 2015 IEEE International Conference on Communication Workshop (ICCW), pp. 1533–1538 (2015)
17. Posch, D., Rainer, B., Hellwagner, H.: SAF: stochastic adaptive forwarding in named data networking. IEEE/ACM Trans. Netw. **25**(2), 1089–1102 (2017)
18. Chiocchetti, R., Perino, D., Carofiglio, G., Rossi, D., Rossini, G.: Inform: a dynamic interest forwarding mechanism for information centric networking. In: Proceedings of the 3rd ACM SIGCOMM Workshop on Information-Centric Networking, ICN 2013, pp. 9–14. ACM, New York, USA (2013)
19. Boyan, J.A., Littman, M.L.: Packet routing in dynamically changing networks: a reinforcement learning approach. In: Proceedings of the 6th International Conference on Neural Information Processing Systems, NIPS 1993, pp. 671–678. Morgan Kaufmann Publishers Inc., San Francisco, USA (1993)
20. Gelenbe, S.E.: Cognitive packet network. US Patent No. 6804201 (2004)

21. Gelenbe, E.: Réseaux neuronaux aléatoires stables. Comptes-rendus de l'Académie des Sciences. Série 2, Mécanique, Physique, Chimie, Sciences de l'Univers. Sciences de la Terre 310(3), 177–180 (1990)
22. Halici, U.: Reinforcement learning with internal expectation for the random neural network. Eur. J. Oper. Res. 126(2), 288–307 (2000)
23. Gelenbe, E., Lent, R.: Power-aware ad hoc cognitive packet networks. Ad Hoc Netw. 2(3), 205–216 (2004)
24. Sakellari, G.: The cognitive packet network: a survey. Comput. J. 53(3), 268 (2010)
25. Gelenbe, E., Liu, P., Lainé, J.: Genetic algorithms for route discovery. IEEE Trans. Syst. Man Cybern. Part B (Cybern.) 36(6), 1247–1254 (2006)
26. Wang, L., Gelenbe, E.: Adaptive dispatching of tasks in the cloud. IEEE Trans. Cloud Comput. 6(1), 33–45 (2018)
27. Mastorakis, S., Afanasyev, A., Moiseenko, I., Zhang, L.: ndnSIM 2: an updated NDN simulator for NS-3. Technical Report NDN-0028, Revision 2, NDN (2016)
28. Knight, S., Nguyen, H., Falkner, N., Bowden, R., Roughan, M.: The internet topology zoo. IEEE J. Sel. Areas Commun. 29(9), 1765–1775 (2011)
29. Chai, W.K., He, D., Psaras, I., Pavlou, G.: Cache "less for more" in information-centric networks (extended version). Comput. Commun, 36(7), 758–770 (2013)
30. Psaras, I., Chai, W.K., Pavlou, G.: Probabilistic in-network caching for information-centric networks. In: Proceedings of the Second Edition of the ICN Workshop on Information-Centric Networking, ICN 2012, pp. 55–60. ACM, New York, USA (2012)

Bidirectional Action Rule Learning

Paweł Matyszok[1], Łukasz Wróbel[1,2](✉), and Marek Sikora[1,2]

[1] Institute of Informatics, Silesian University of Technology, ul. Akademicka 16,
44-100 Gliwice, Poland
{pawel.matyszok,lukasz.wrobel,marek.sikora}@polsl.pl
[2] Institute of Innovative Technologies EMAG, ul. Leopolda 31, 40-189 Katowice,
Poland

Abstract. Action rules specify recommendations which should be followed in order to transfer objects to the desired decision class. In this paper influence of employing information contained in source and target class examples in sequential covering based action rule induction method is examined. Results show that using source class for guiding the induction process produces best results.

Keywords: Action rules · Classification · Data mining

1 Introduction

Action rules are one of the ways to use rule-based representations to search for recommendations which indicate how the change of attribute values can cause the change in the assignment of examples to the given concept (decision class). There have been several proposals of algorithms for action rule induction, but neither presents one of the most popular and efficient approaches to the rule induction, which is the sequential covering (known also as separate-and-conquer) strategy [4]. The paper features a proposal of an algorithm for action rule induction by means of the sequential covering strategy.

The rule growing and pruning phases are guided by rule quality measures [4]. The possibility to use different quality measures allows generating more accurate or general rules, depending on the users' needs [17]. In comparison to other methods, the proposed algorithm is distinguishable by its possibility to generate action rules on the basis of numerical attributes without necessity of their previous discretization. The algorithm features two versions: the first approach builds action rules based on rules describing the examples in the source class (the class from which examples should be transferred out), while the second version is driven by rules selecting examples in the target class (the one to which the examples should be shifted).

The paper is organized as follows: Sect. 2 features related work on the action rule induction, Sect. 3 describes the proposed algorithm. Section 4 presents the results of the algorithm application in sample publicly available datasets with comparison to other action rule induction method, ARED. Section 5 gives the conclusions and presents the possible future work.

© Springer Nature Switzerland AG 2018
T. Czachórski et al. (Eds.): ISCIS 2018, CCIS 935, pp. 220–228, 2018.
https://doi.org/10.1007/978-3-030-00840-6_24

2   Related Work

First, the works in the field of action rule induction concentrate on generating action rules on the basis of the existing classification rules generated by means of algorithms based on the rough set theory [9,10]. Then algorithms for direct induction of action rules from data were proposed. Here it is worth to mention the algorithm of association action rule induction and the ARED algorithm [3,8]. All aforementioned approaches are based on the assumption that all possible rules which fulfill the condition of minimum support and confidence are generated. In [6] the authors proposed an algorithm which allowed to generate action rules from temporal decision tables.

Action rules present recommendations on the changes of attribute values but they do not indicate which operations cause the changes (e.g. recommendation "change blood sugar level from 95 to 80" does not show what kind of medicine should be taken to fulfill this recommendation). In this case the usability of action rules is understood as the analysis and identification of operations that must be done to change the values of the attributes occurring in the action rules premises. Such operations were called meta-actions, the analysis of dependencies between action rules and meta-actions was presented in [14,16]. Recently, Almardini et al. [1] have presented procedure paths as a sequence of procedures that a given patient undertakes to reach the desired treatment.

The action rule induction is part of a more general issue of the usability and actionability of the data exploration results. This issue has been raised more and more often [7]. In the case of rule-based representations, the issue of actions generation on the basis of classification rules, without necessity to generate action rules, was proposed in [15]. In other works [5,12,18], in turn, the authors discussed the methods of rule assessment from the point of view of their usability and actionability.

3   Approach Description

3.1   Basic Notion

An action rule [11] may be seen as the conjunction of two decision rules. To define the action rule, basic notions are presented in this section.

Let us consider that a finite set of examples T_r is given. Each example in this set can be described with a set of attributes $A \cup \{d\}$, where $a : T_r \rightarrow V_a$ for each $a \in A \cup \{d\}$. The set V_a is called *range* of attribute a. The elements of A are called conditional attributes, and the variable d is known as a decision attribute – its value is considered as an assignment of an example to a decision class. Conditional attributes can be of numeric or symbolic type. Symbolic attributes have discrete value. Numeric attributed are represented by real values or ranges. The decision attribute is always of symbolic type.

The conditional expression IF $w_1 \wedge w_2 \wedge \ldots \wedge w_k$ THEN $d = v$ is called decision rule. The conclusion of a decision rule is understood as an assignment of an example fulfilling the premise of this rule to the concept bound with the value of decision attribute d. The premise of the decision rule is a conjunction of elementary conditions w_i. The form of an elementary condition used in the presented approach is $w_i \equiv a_i \in Z_i$, where a_i is the name of the conditional attribute and Z_i is the interval in this attribute range V_{a_i}. For symbolic attributes the elementary condition is simple $a_i = v_j$, where $v_j \in V_{a_i}$.

Let us consider following formula: IF $w_{1_1} \rightarrow w_{2_1} \wedge \ldots \wedge w_{1_k} \rightarrow w_{2_k}$ THEN $d = v_1 \rightarrow v_2$ which may be seen as a composition of two decision rules $r1, r2$ having mutually exclusive conclusions (i.e. $v_1 \neq v_2$). We will refer to such expression as an action rule. An action rule shows possible transition of examples from one class to another in some example set T_r after a suggested action in premise of the rule are undertaken, i.e. attribute values are changed according to actions gathered. The class on the left of the action rule conclusion will be often referred to as *source class* or *source concept* of given rule, while the class on the right of the premise is being called *target class* or *target concept* of the rule. We will refer to the left side of action rule (the $r1$ part of the composition) as *source rule*, while the right side (the $r2$ part of the composition) will be called *target rule*. Such naming convention clearly expresses the ability of source and target rule to select source and target class examples in the dataset.

The formula of the action rule may be rewritten in simpler form which maintains clarity of connection between the value change and the attribute: $(a_1, v_{a_{1_1}} \rightarrow v_{a_{1_2}}) \wedge \ldots \wedge (a_k, v_{a_{k_1}} \rightarrow v_{a_{k_2}}) \rightarrow (d = v_1 \rightarrow v_2)$.

The elementary condition of the form $(a_i, v_{a_{i_1}} \rightarrow v_{a_{i_2}})$ is called an *elementary action* (simply – an *action*). In the context of action rules as described in this section, the action should be understood as demand to influence the examples from dataset T_r in a way that will change value of an attribute a_i of examples covered by condition $a_i \in v_{a_{i_1}}$ such they will now fulfill the other condition $a_i \in v_{a_{i_2}}$. The conclusion of the action rule is the expected effect of applying the action rule premise to examples in the dataset. It describes change of concept from source to target class. In the context of the action rule induction, attributes are divided into two types: *flexible* and *stable*. Stable attributes cannot be used in any of the action induced (e.g. the date of birth cannot be changed), while flexible attributes can be subject of change by some action.

3.2   Action Rule Induction

In this section a covering action rule induction algorithm is presented. The algorithm utilizes a well known separate-and-conquer framework [4] and classification rule quality measures [17] to induce action rules. The algorithm of rule induction is divided into two phases: growing and pruning. The action rule is added to the resulting rule set, and all source class examples covered by left side of newly created action rules are removed from the training set. The examples of the target class are never removed from the training set. Rules are inducted until all examples of the source class in the training set T_r are covered by left sides of action rules inducted.

To grow an action rule is a process beginning with a rule having empty premise and established conclusion with a source class on the left side and a target class on the right side. Two temporal classification rules are being maintained during action rule growing, one rule per class in conclusion. Iteratively (limited by the min_cov parameter), candidate for best elementary condition describing the source class is searched in the input dataset feature space and added to temporary rule responsible for selecting source class examples. The rule is assessed with quality measure q. After choosing the best elementary condition, attribute on which it is based on is extracted and new best elementary condition is being looked for, but this time with regard to target class and limited by attribute selected. Second temporary rule is used to choose the best condition. Both conditions are used to build an action, which is added to premise of action rule being build.

The process of pruning of the action rule begins when the rule is fully grown. Actions in the premise of the action rule are being iteratively trimmed or removed, as long as the quality of the rule measured by the function q does not decrease. To trim the action means that the action of the form $(a_i, v_{a_{i1}} \rightarrow v_{a_{i2}})$ becomes $(a, v_{a_{i1}})$. If the quality of the action rule after action trimming does not decrease, it is also checked if removal of whole action will have similar effect. The action rule premise is modified based on result of that test.

The proposed bidirectional algorithm of action rules induction covers the input dataset sequentially and simultaneously induces two action rules using sequential covering process described above. One action rule is induced according to the intention of the algorithm user: the rules are initialized with a conclusion having the source class on the left side and the target class on the right – we will refer to this rule as a *forward-rule*. The other rule starts with the conclusion constructed with the classes reverted – in the article text this rule will be described as *backward-rule*. Two copies of dataset are maintained during rule induction: one for the forward-rule, and one for the backward-rule. Both rules are sequentially grown, each on respective copy of input dataset.

After the rules are grown, the optional pruning step is performed. The examples covered by newly created action rules are removed from respective datasets, and the rules are collected in separate ruleset: *FAR* for forward-rules, and *BAR* for backward-rules. This procedure is repeated until both copies of input dataset are empty. Now the procedure of reverting the rules gathered in the *BAR* set is conducted. The goal of this procedure is to obtain action rules which are representing the transition of examples demand by the user of the method. The reverting procedure is quite simple: first, new conclusion for a rule is constructed by reversing the order of the classes in the original conclusion. Afterwards, the premise is traversed, and each action is reverted. If the action in the premise being reverted was trimmed, then new action is constructed with special symbol *ALL* on the left side, and the left value of the original action on the right side, i.e. reverting action of form $(a_i, v_{a_{i1}})$ will produce $(a_i, ALL \rightarrow v_{a_{i1}})$. In other cases, the reverting of the action is realized by switching places of attribute values on left and right side of the action. Both *FAR* and *BAR* rulesets are returned from the method.

The goal of the process of inducing rules with reverted conclusion is to steer the process of building the action rule by knowledge contained in examples representing the target class. Conceptually, the rules collected in the *FAR* ruleset are representing the idea of an example leaving the source class (because the attributes for the premise are selected based on the data assigned to the source class), while the reverted rules from the *BAR* ruleset represent concept of "achieving" the target class – because more emphasis in the premise of the backward-rule is put on the knowledge gathered in the target class examples.

4   Experiments

4.1   Experimental Setup

In the experimental part of the study, we compare Forward with the Backward method of action rule induction in order to determine which of these two approaches could be more beneficial for action rule learning. For both methods the pruning procedure is enabled and the *mincov* parameter is set to 5. During specialization and pruning of the rules the *Correlation* quality measure (q parameter) is used. The *Correlation* measure is defined as: $(pN - Pn)/\sqrt{PN(p+n)(P-p+N-n)}$ where: P (N) stands for the number of examples in the dataset that are covered (not covered) by the conclusion of r, p is the number of true positives, that is, the number of examples covered by both the premise and the conclusion of the rule r, and n is the number of false positives, that is, the number of examples covered by the premise, but not covered by the conclusion of the rule r. The measure evaluates the correlation coefficient between the predicted and the target labels. As empirical [4,17] studies show, it maintains a good balance between accuracy and comprehensibility of rules generated in covering schemas.

For comparison purposes, we also provide the results obtained with the custom implementation of the ARED algorithm [8]. The ARED method uses the concept of Pawlaks' information system [9] in which certain relationships between granules, defined by indiscernibility relation of objects, are identified. Some of these relationships are used to define the action rule. The ARED approach is based on the assumption that all possible rules are generated that meet the minimum support and minimum confidence constraints. For all examined datasets minimum support was set to 5 and the minimum confidence parameter was equal to 0.9.

Experiments were carried out on 11 publicly available datasets, mostly from the UCI repository. Although, the Forward and Backward methods are able to handle multi-class problems by employing the one-vs-all binarization schema, for simplicity we consider only two-class problems, choosing one of the class as the source and the second one as the target. As the ARED algorithm is not able to handle numerical attributes it was run on the discretized version of the datasets. The discretization was conducted using the entropy criterion. For the Forward, Backward and ARED methods all attributes of all tested datasets were marked as flexible.

Table 1. The characteristics of action rule sets generated by Forward, Backward and ARED algorithms: the total number of rules (#r), the average number of conditions (c̄) and actions (ā) per rule, the average precision (prec‾) and sensitivity (sens‾) of the left/right side of the rule in the set. The *pval* row shows the p-value of the Wilcoxon signed rank test confronting Forward method with other approaches. The *Me* row contains median value over all datasets.

Data	Forward					Backward					ARED				
	#r	c̄	ā	prec‾	sens‾	#r	c̄	ā	prec‾	sens‾	#r	c̄	ā	prec‾	sens‾
bre	11	3.3	0.4	.42/.80	.18/.77	10	3.1	2.6	.69/.81	.30/.42	75	1.0	1.0	.34/.72	.19/.24
cr-a	3	3.3	2.3	.81/.87	.85/.63	3	3.3	3.3	.82/.74	.72/.72	3344	3.6	3.1	.69/.86	.02/.05
cr-g	13	5.2	2.7	.50/.88	.47/.32	18	5.3	5.2	.67/.84	.18/.52	428	2.2	1.6	.34/.69	.07/.10
hun	5	3.6	1.2	.74/.92	.69/.38	4	2.2	2.2	.76/.82	.68/.88	18	1.2	1.1	.41/.70	.25/.40
lab	2	3.0	1.0	.94/.85	.62/.89	1	1.0	1.0	.82/.85	.45/.89	15	1.0	1.0	.68/.76	.42/.41
monk	7	1.7	1.1	.78/.95	.27/.41	6	1.5	1.3	.65/.73	.38/.41	25	1.3	1.2	.50/.62	.27/.32
pima	7	3.7	1.1	.55/.91	.80/.36	18	3.9	3.9	.56/.85	.62/.51	22	1.0	1.0	.37/.67	.30/.40
prnn	4	1.2	1.0	.79/.88	.76/.69	4	1.8	1.8	.85/.82	.83/.91	7	1.0	1.0	.71/.76	.34/.47
stat	6	5.7	2.5	.82/.80	.59/.70	6	3.8	3.8	.85/.84	.55/.73	13	1.0	1.0	.52/.59	.50/.61
tit	2	2.0	0.5	.66/.73	.49/.48	7	2.0	1.1	.79/.54	.92/.23	8	1.0	1.0	.45/.32	.09/.37
vot	3	1.3	1.0	.97/.89	.86/.93	1	1.0	1.0	.99/.92	.92/.97	110496	6.4	4.5	.90/.90	.04/.14
Me	5	3.3	1.1	.78/.88	.62/.63	6	2.2	2.2	.79/.82	.62/.72	22	1.0	1.0	.50/.70	.25/.37
pval						1.0	0.6	0.0	.45/.08	.95/.41	0.0	0.0	0.8	.02/.00	.00/.01

4.2   Results

In the experimental part of this study the examined algorithms are evaluated according to the: total number of action rules, average number of conditions per rule, average number of actions per rule, precision and sensitivity of the left and the right side of the rule. The precision of the rule r is defined as $\frac{p}{p+n}$ where p, n, P i N values have the same meaning as for *Correlation* measure. The higher precision of the left/right side of the action rule is, the more accurately rule covers examples from the source/target class. The sensitivity, expressed as $\frac{p}{P}$, estimates what part of the source/target class is covered by the left/right side of the action rule. The low value of the sensitivity usually reflects very specific rule which might not generalize well for new examples. The detailed characteristics of the action rule sets generated by the Forward, Backward and ARED algorithms are provided in Table 1.

According to the Wilcoxon signed rank test the only significant difference between the Forward and Backward methods is in the average number of actions per rule (the p-value is close to 0). On average, the number of action per rule for Backward is twice as large as for Forward – the median value for Backward is 2.2 whereas for Forward it equals 1.1.

In regard to remaining criteria the Forward and Backward behave very similarly, all the p-values of the Wilcoxon test are greater than 0.05. Both Forward and Backward are able to generate compact rule sets – for most datasets algorithms found less than 10 rules. The output rules usually contain 2–3 conditions among which 1–2 are actions.

Rules generated by Forward and Backward methods are characterized by relatively high values of precision and sensitivity of the left and the right side of the action rules. For most datasets, the average precision of rules is greater than 0.7. The sensitivity, on average, ranges from 0.2 to 0.9 with the median value over all datasets around 0.6. It can be also observed that for many datasets the precision of the right side of the action rule is higher than of the left side, indicating that action rules usually cover the target class more accurately than the source class.

Compared to the ARED algorithm, the Forward method seems to achieve better results according to the considered criteria. In most cases, the p-values of the Wilcoxon test are close to 0. The only exceptions are the average number of actions where both algorithms behave similarly and the average number of conditions where ARED tends to generate shorter rules. The greater number of rules for the ARED method results from the fact that ARED is based on the concept of learning all possible rules satisfying minimum confidence and support thresholds. As ARED usually generates very short rules, containing only one condition, the large number of rules often goes hand in hand with decreased average precision and sensitivity of rules.

5   Conclusions

In this paper two working action rule induction algorithms were presented. After analysis of the output of the presented methods, despite that the idea of employing knowledge gathered in target class examples embedded in Backward method is appealing, our recommendation is to use the Forward method. It was shown that both Forward and Backward method outperformed ARED method wherever number of resulting action rules or precision and sensitivity of source and target rule are considered. If the goal of using action rule induction method is to reach consistent and comprehensible ruleset, then approach presented in this paper is able to deliver demanded output.

Future work will focus on the development of measures and methods for assessing the quality of inducted action rules and sets. It is planned to adapt the measures dedicated to the quality evaluation of classification rules. Our work will focus on measures which assess the coverage and precision of a rule at the same time. In the case of large datasets or the necessity to reduce the number of rules, the methods of example selection, as well as rules filtering will be used [2, 13]. A very important next step is the preparation of datasets where successive decision tables will reflect successive moments of time (control points). The tables will contain information about the application of certain actions to specific examples. A part of the datasets will be generated synthetically (e.g. the inverted pendulum problem), another part will describe a real-life problem (PersonALL project – see acknowledgment).

Acknowledgement. This work was partially supported by Polish National Centre for Research and Development (NCBiR) within the programme Prevention and Treatment of Civilization Diseases – STRATEGMED III, grant number STRATEGMED3/304586/5/NCBR/2017 (PersonALL). A part of the work was carried out within the statutory research project of the Institute of Informatics, BK-213/RAU2/2018.

References

1. Almardini, M., et al.: Reduction of readmissions to hospitals based on actionable knowledge discovery and personalization. In: Kozielski, S., Mrozek, D., Kasprowski, P., Małysiak-Mrozek, B., Kostrzewa, D. (eds.) BDAS 2015-2016. CCIS, vol. 613, pp. 39–55. Springer, Cham (2016). https://doi.org/10.1007/978-3-319-34099-9_3
2. Blachnik, M.: Instance selection for classifier performance estimation in meta learning. Entropy **19**(11), 583 (2017)
3. Dardzinska, A.: Action Rules Mining, vol. 468. Springer, Cham (2012)
4. Fürnkranz, J., Gamberger, D., Lavrač, N.: Foundations of Rule Learning. Springer, Cham (2012)
5. Greco, S., Matarazzo, B., Pappalardo, N., Słowinski, R.: Measuring expected effects of interventions based on decision rules. J. Exp. Theor. Artif. Intell. **17**(1–2), 103–118 (2005)
6. Hajja, A., Raś, Z.W., Wieczorkowska, A.A.: Hierarchical object-driven action rules. J. Intell. Inf. Syst. **42**(2), 207–232 (2014)
7. He, Z., Xu, X., Deng, S.: Data mining for actionable knowledge: a survey (2005). arXiv preprint arXiv:cs/0501079
8. Im, S., Raś, Z.W.: Action rule extraction from a decision table: ARED. In: An, A., Matwin, S., Raś, Z.W., Ślęzak, D. (eds.) ISMIS 2008. LNCS (LNAI), vol. 4994, pp. 160–168. Springer, Heidelberg (2008). https://doi.org/10.1007/978-3-540-68123-6_18
9. Pawlak, Z.: Information systems theoretical foundations. Inf. Syst. **6**(3), 205–218 (1981)
10. Raś, Z.W., Tzacheva, A.A., Tsay, L.S., Giirdal, O.: Mining for interesting action rules. In: IEEE/WIC/ACM International Conference on Intelligent Agent Technology, pp. 187–193. IEEE (2005)
11. Ras, Z.W., Wieczorkowska, A.: Action-rules: how to increase profit of a company. In: Zighed, D.A., Komorowski, J., Żytkow, J. (eds.) PKDD 2000. LNCS (LNAI), vol. 1910, pp. 587–592. Springer, Heidelberg (2000). https://doi.org/10.1007/3-540-45372-5_70
12. Słowiński, R., Greco, S.: Measuring attractiveness of rules from the viewpoint of knowledge representation, prediction and efficiency of intervention. In: Szczepaniak, P.S., Kacprzyk, J., Niewiadomski, A. (eds.) AWIC 2005. LNCS (LNAI), vol. 3528, pp. 11–22. Springer, Heidelberg (2005). https://doi.org/10.1007/11495772_3
13. Stańczyk, U., Zielosko, B.: On combining discretisation parameters and attribute ranking for selection of decision rules. In: Polkowski, L., et al. (eds.) IJCRS 2017. LNCS (LNAI), vol. 10313, pp. 329–349. Springer, Cham (2017). https://doi.org/10.1007/978-3-319-60837-2_28
14. Touati, H., Raś, Z.W., Studnicki, J., Wieczorkowska, A.A.: Mining surgical meta-actions effects with variable diagnoses' number. In: Andreasen, T., Christiansen, H., Cubero, J.-C., Raś, Z.W. (eds.) ISMIS 2014. LNCS (LNAI), vol. 8502, pp. 254–263. Springer, Cham (2014). https://doi.org/10.1007/978-3-319-08326-1_26

15. Trépos, R., Salleb-Aouissi, A., Cordier, M.O., Masson, V., Gascuel-Odoux, C.: Building actions from classification rules. Knowl. Inf. Syst. **34**(2), 267–298 (2013)
16. Wang, K., Jiang, Y., Tuzhilin, A.: Mining actionable patterns by role models. In: 22nd International Conference on Data Engineering, pp. 16–16. IEEE (2006)
17. Wróbel, Ł., Sikora, M., Michalak, M.: Rule quality measures settings in classification, regression and survival rule induction-an empirical approach. Fundam. Inform. **149**(4), 419–449 (2016)
18. Zhu, H.M., Huang, W.D., Zheng, H.S.: Method for discovering actionable rule. In: Fourth International Conference on Fuzzy Systems and Knowledge Discovery, vol. 1, pp. 397–401. IEEE (2007)

Applications to Linguistics, Biology and Computer Vision

A Possibilistic Approach for Arabic Domain Terminology Extraction and Translation

Wiem Lahbib[1,2(✉)], Ibrahim Bounhas[1,2,3], and Yahya Slimani[1,2,4]

[1] LISI Laboratory of Computer Science for Industrial Systems,
Carthage University, Tunis, Tunisia
wiemlahbib88@hotmail.fr,
bounhas.ibrahim@gmail.com, yahya.slimani@gmail.com,
[2] JARIR: Joint Group for Artificial Reasoning and Information Retrieval,
Manouba, Tunisia
[3] Higher Institute of Documentation, La Manouba University, Manouba, Tunisia
[4] Higher Institute of Multimedia Arts, La Manouba University,
Manouba, Tunisia
http://www.jarir.tn

Abstract. This paper proposes a hybrid possibilistic approach for bilingual terminology extraction using possibility and necessity measures. On the one hand, we extract domain-relevant terms from the source language, and on the other hand, we build a co-occurrence-based translation graph, which is mined to translate terms in the target language. We compare our approach with different state-of-the art approaches. Experimental results show that the possibilistic approach reaches better results in terms of Recall, Precision and Mean Average Precision (MAP). The differences between the compared approaches show that our contribution is significant in terms of p-value.

Keywords: Arabic bilingual terminology · Possibility theory · Graph-mining

1 Introduction

Terminology extraction is an important task in the general area of knowledge engineering [1]. A specific task consists in extracting bilingual pairs of terms which may be useful for several applications like Machine Translation (MT), Cross-Language Information Retrieval (CLIR) and Dictionary Building (DB). However, most of state-of-art approaches are applied for languages of Latin origin (e.g. English, French and Italian) [2], while Arabic is a low-resourced language and not well investigated [3]. This may be explained by the complexity of this language being highly derivational, flectional and agglutinative [14, 15].

Bilingual Terminology Extraction (BTE) requires the existence of parallel[1] or comparable[2] corpora. Most of approaches using parallel corpora are based on alignment techniques or dictionaries [4]. Alignment-based approach is the most widespread in works interested by parallel texts. However, some dictionary-based approaches reach

---

[1] In parallel corpora, documents are translated sentence-by- sentence.
[2] In comparable corpora, documents are dealing with same topics and subjects.

© Springer Nature Switzerland AG 2018
T. Czachórski et al. (Eds.): ISCIS 2018, CCIS 935, pp. 231–238, 2018.
https://doi.org/10.1007/978-3-030-00840-6_25

successful results. For example, Hazem and Morin (2016) [4] assume source and target terms are likely to appear in similar contexts. This approach seems to be theoretically more advantageous compared to alignment-based method, since it exploits better contextual information to determine the correct translation.

This paper proposes a corpus-based possibilistic approach for BTE. We opt for a corpus-based approach as bilingual dictionaries are hard to build and are not available for all domains. Otherwise, Arabic language is low-resourced and lacks specialized corpora with good coverage. Morphological ambiguities make hard to obtain precise contextual information. Possibility theory [5, 12] is naturally adapted to this kind of problems i.e. when training data are incomplete or imprecise.

The remainder of the paper is organized as follows: Sect. 2 reviews previous works in BTE. In Sect. 3, we present our approach which exploits possibilistic similarity. Experimental results and interpretation are presented in Sect. 4. Lastly, we conclude this paper in Sect. 5 by evaluating our approach and providing some perspectives for future research.

2 Related Works

We distinguish three categories of approaches to BTE, namely resource-based, alignment-based and statistical approaches [2, 16]. In the following, we present these three categories.

Resource-Based Approaches. This kind of approach exploits external resources such as dictionaries or Wikipedia. In this context, Hazem and Morin (2013) [2] presented a French-English dictionary-based approach which uses contextual representation to identify translations. Indeed, they combine graphic context with syntactic context to produce a merged list of candidate translations. Bouamor et al. (2013) [6] used Wikipedia to create a bilingual dictionary. They derived similar Wikipedia concepts, then they used a translation graph to locate the corresponding concepts in target language.

Alignment-Based Approaches. Zhao and Xing (2008) [7] used bilingual topic models for parallel texts with word-to-word alignment. Authors assume that topics of English and foreign language share similar meanings. The sub-sentential alignment proposed by Lefever et al. (2009) [8] is rather at sentence level. Similarities are calculated between anchor and non-anchor chunks. However, this approach is language-dependent. Linking identical strings can easily improve results but may produce poor results for some languages such as Arabic. Sellami et al. (2012) [3] employed cross-language links in Arabic Wikipedia and Giza++[3] for alignment to extract French-Arabic and French-Yoruba terminologies.

Statistical Approaches. Statistical approaches are based on contextual vectors and co-occurrence matrices. For example, Okita (2014) [9] used monolingual embedded models to translate terminologies. Vulic and Moens (2016) [10] proposed a new word

---

[3] http://www.statmt.org/moses/giza/GIZA++.html.

embedding model for bilingual word representations called merge and shuffle, based on a length-Ration shuffle. Gaussier et al. (2017) [11] combined the standard approach based on context vectors with formal closed concepts vectors.

In the rest of this paper, we study the performance of these categories of approaches. However, our prior hypothesis is that possibility theory [12], which is naturally adapted to imprecise and incomplete data, may contribute in extracting bilingual terminologies from a low-resourced and ambiguous language like Arabic. This theory was successfully applied to MT by Menacer et al. (2016) who proposed a word-sequence possibilistic measure [13]. They used weights estimated from a training corpus to reinforce the possibility of a word-sequence that contains a subsequence.

In the following, we detail our hybrid approach, which combines linguistic analysis with semantic representation and possibilistic similarity.

3   A Possibilistic Approach for Bilingual Terminology Extraction

Possibility theory, which was introduced by Zadeh (1978) [5], deals with uncertain information and incomplete knowledge. Unlike probability theory, possibility theory employs two measures, namely possibility (Π) necessity (N). While the latter represents the degree of certainty of an event, the former expresses to which degree an event is possible. If e denotes an event, the possibility distribution will be a function in the closed interval [0, 1] with $\Pi(e) = 1$ means that the event e is possible and $\Pi(e) = 0$ means that the event se is more likely to be impossible.

The performance of the possibilistic model has been showed in many applications including Arabic morphological disambiguation [14, 15]. In our case, it consists on building a possibilistic graph where nodes are terms and edges are weighted by possibility distributions. Given a term (or a set of terms) as input, the model is able to mine the graph and infer the most plausible nodes, which are more likely to be similar to the input.

Figure 1 presents the different resources and steps of our approach. These steps, which include possibilistic graph construction and querying for term translation, are detailed in the following subsections.

3.1   Morphological Analysis and Disambiguation

This step allows to recognize morphological variations of Arabic words. It consists in studying the form and recognizing several features such as the Part-Of-Speech (POS), the lemma, etc. For English texts, we integrated TreeTagger[4] tool to recognize the lemma and the POS of each word. However, this task is more challenging with Arabic language due to some specificities and characteristics illustrated in Table 1 through examples. To resolve such ambiguities, we used MADAMIRA[5], which is a current state of the-art tool for Arabic morphological analysis and disambiguation.

---

[4] http://www.cis.uni-muenchen.de/ ~ schmid/tools/TreeTagger/.
[5] https://camel.abudhabi.nyu.edu/madamira/.

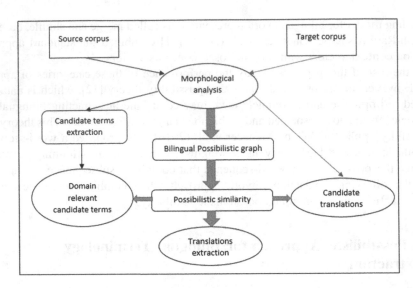

Fig. 1. Bilingual terminology extraction process

Table 1. Arabic language morphological characteristics

Phenomenon	Description	Example
Vocalization	Words are written using symbols, placed under and above letters. The absence of short vowels generates several ambiguities.	Non-vocalized word "كتب" (ktb) has numerous potential vocalizations (كَتَبَ; kataba : write/Verb, كُتُب; kutuba: books/Noun, etc.),
Orthographic variation	Similarly spelled characters are confusing in scripting.	These letters have many variations: (ي،ى), (ة،ت), (ا،إ،أ)).
Agglutination	Some articles, prepositions and pronouns are attached to adjectives, nouns, verbs and particles.	The expression "ورد" (wrd) has three interpretations: "وَ;wa/CONJ رَد~;rad~/VB" (and response), "وَرَدَ; warada/NOUN" (come) or "وَرْد; warodN/NOUN" (flowers).

3.2   Candidate Terms Extraction

We start by extracting domain relevant terms from the source language using possibilistic similarity in a monolingual context. This task applies, first, TF-IDF to extract a set of terms called *minimal terminology* (T_m) from corpus titles, which are more likely to contain domain relevant terms. Then, we enrich T_m with similar terms from the remaining parts of the corpus to obtain a final specific-domain terminology. In [16], we showed that this approach reaches better results than extracting terminologies from the integral texts in one swoop.

Let T_m be the minimal terminology of a specific domain: $T_m = \{t_1, t_2, \ldots, t_m\}$; and let Cs be the source corpus containing n terms tc: $Cs = \{tc_1, tc_2, \ldots, tc_n\}$. We model this corpus as a graph where nodes are terms and edges are non-oriented and weighted by the number of co-occurrence of the corresponding nodes. The weights of edges are normalized to obtain possibility distributions. We use T_m to mine the graph and retrieve all the similar terms t_c in the corpus. This is modeled as an Information Retrieval (IR) task where T_m is considered as a query and candidate terms are documents.

The possibilistic similarity between a candidate term from the corpus t_c and T_m is equal to the degree of possibilistic relevance (DPR), given by the sum of two measures. Possibility and necessity are defined as follows [12, 15–17]:

$$\text{DPR}(t_c|T_m) = \prod (t_c|T_m) + \text{N}(t_c|T_m) \qquad (1)$$

In this model, Possibility is estimated by:

$$\prod (t_c|T_m) = \prod_{i=1}^{n} weight(t_i, t_c) \qquad (2)$$

The Necessity is computed as follows:

$$\text{N}(t_c|T_m) = 1 - \prod_{i=1}^{n} (1 - \varnothing_{ic}) \qquad (3)$$

where:

$$\varnothing_{ic} = log_{10}\left(\frac{N}{co(t_i)}\right) * weight(t_i, t_c) \qquad (4)$$

In these formulae, $weight(t_i, t_c)$, is the weight of the edge linking t_i and t_c. It is equal to the normalized number of co-occurrence of t_i and t_c in the corpus. This applies when we need to compute the similarity of terms in the same language or when we want to evaluate the similarity of a term with a given translation as explained in the following section.

3.3 Translation Extraction

The principle of the translation module is to build a bilingual graph to identify the most suitable translation. The edges reflect the normalized number of co-occurrence of both terms in the virtual corpora composed of pairs of documents in both languages. That is, we will be able to compute the degree of possibilistic relevance of a term t_t in the target language given a term t_c from the source language. We apply same possibility and necessity measures (see formula (1) to (4)) by replacing $t_c|T_m$ by $t_t|t_c$.

4 Experiments and Results

We evaluate our bilingual possibilistic approach on a classical Arabic corpus freely available for research purposes[6]. It is composed of 7031 documents translated into English and organized in 97 domains. Documents are structured into several hierarchical section levels which help extract T_m and obtain domain terminologies.

---

[6] http://www.jarir.tn/kunuzproject.

4.1 Baseline Approaches

It is difficult to make comparison with different state of the art bilingual extraction approaches, due to many differences in used corpora, languages, methods and tools. For this reason, we aim to develop different baseline approaches and use their results for comparison.

The first baseline is an alignment-based approach, which consists in extracting a list of pertinent terms from source language using TF-IDF and using Giza++ to align pairs of sentences and build translation matrices [18].

The second baseline is the standard approach presented by Hazem and Morin [4]. Its first step consists in building for each word in the source and target languages a context vector using deep learning-based word embedding [19]. In the second step, the vectors of the source language are translated using a bilingual dictionary. Finally, the cosine similarity is used to compute the similarities of the translated vectors and the vectors of the target terms.

The third baseline follows the same steps as the possibilistic approach (cf. Sect. 3). However, we use Skip-Gramm model of word embedding [19] to calculate cosine similarity between embedded vectors based on a length-Ration shuffle [10]. We adopt the default settings: a window size equal to 5, a sampling of $1e^{-3}$ and a minimal word frequency equal to 1.

4.2 Results and Discussion

Table 2 details Recall, Precision and F-score rates of our approach compared to the three baselines. The improvement rates of the possibilistic approach are computed compared to the alignment-based baseline approach. Results show that the possibilistic approach outperforms all baselines for both language pairs with an average amelioration rate of +12,01%. This reveals the power of the possibilistic model which is able to link terms to their translations even with poor contextual information. As a general second observation, we note that alignment approach reaches encouraging results. However, it does not success to beat possibilistic scores. In fact, we notice that alignment is hypersensitive to some specificities of the corpus, i.e. some Arabic words are translated by transliteration (e.g. "زكاة"; zkAp meaning "alms" is translated to "zakat"), while Giza++ tool is unable to deal with such cases.

In addition, Table 2 highlights the weakness of the dictionary-based approach despite it uses contextual embedded vectors. In fact, in specific domains, the use of a generic bilingual dictionary or Google Translate is not appropriate for context vectors translation [16].

Finally, word2vec appears to be ineffective in finding semantically coherent lists of bilingual words. In fact, deep learning needs large corpora to produce efficient results. This reveals that the size of the corpus impacts word embedding. Besides, our results show that the shuffling ratio strategy is not efficient for word2vec-based translation.

To refine our study about the possibilistic approach, we provide MAP values in Table 3 and we use student's paired test samples [20]. The given p-values are computed by comparing MAP results of the possibilistic approach to all the baselines. Results show that the improvement of the possibilistic approach is statistically significant (p-value < 0.05).

Table 2. Recall, Precision and F-score rates of BTE approaches.

Approach	Alignment		Word2vec		Dictionary		Possibilistic	
Language pairs	AR-EN	EN-AR	AR-EN	EN-AR	AR-EN	EN-AR	AR-EN	EN-AR
Recall	68.25	61.25	31.25	33.5	56.25	59.50	78.00 (+14.29%)	71.75 (+17.14%)
Precision	67.50	65.75	31.75	33.0	58.50	61.75	75.75 (+12.22%)	70.50 (+07.22%)
F-score	67.80	63.27	31.475	33.2	57.225	60.17	75.77 (+11.76%)	69.27 (+09.48%)

Table 3. MAP and p-values of BTE approaches.

	MAP	p-value
Possibilistic	0.655	–
Alignment	0.473	0.0070
Word2vec	0.301	0.0035
Dictionary-based	0.484	0,0066

We remark that possibilistic similarity seems to outperform word2vec, alignment and dictionary-based approaches. In fact, computing the possibilistic relevance allows to reject irrelevant translations, whereas the necessary relevance helps to reinforce the relevant translations which were not eliminated by the possibility measure.

5 Conclusion

In this paper, we proposed and evaluated a corpus-based hybrid possibilistic approach for Arabic BTE extraction. It uses standard possibilistic measures to extract domain-relevant terms and find their correct translations in the target language. Mining bilingual co-occurrence graphs enhances the performance of mapping between a candidate term and its translation. The experimentation of the proposed approach over different baselines reported encouraging results and reveals promising perspectives. As future work, we plan to investigate the performance of the possibility theory in multi-word term translation.

References

1. Shah, N.S.: Review of indexing techniques applied in information retrieval. Pak. J. Eng. Technol. Sci. 5(1) (2016)
2. Hazem, A., Morin, E.: Extraction de lexiques bilingues à partir de corpus comparables par combinaison de représentations contextuelles. In: Actes de la 20ème conférence sur le Traitement Automatique des Langues Naturelles (TALN), Sables d'Olonne, France, 17–21 June, pp. 243–256 (2013)
3. Sellami, R., Sadat, F., Belguith, L.H.: Extraction de lexiques bilingues à partir de Wikipédia. In: Atelier de Traitement Automatique des Langues Africaines, JEP (conférence Journées d'Études en Parole) -TALN-RECITAL, Grenoble, France, 4–8 June (2012)

4. Hazem, A., Morin, E.: Efficient data selection for bilingual terminology extraction from comparable corpora. In: Proceedings of the 26th International Conference on Computational Linguistics (COLING), Osaka, Japan, 11–16 Dec 2016. Technical Papers, pp. 3401–3411 (2016)
5. Zadeh, L.A.: Fuzzy sets as a basis for a theory of possibility. Fuzzy Sets Syst. 1(1), 3–28 (1978)
6. Bouamor, D., Popescu, A., Semmar, N., Zweigenbaum, P.: Building specialized bilingual lexicons using large scale background knowledge. In: Proceedings of the 2013 Conference on Empirical Methods in Natural Language Processing, Seattle, Washington, USA, 18–21 Oct, pp. 479–489 (2013)
7. Zhao, B., Xing, E.P.: HM-BiTAM: Bilingual topic exploration, word alignment, and translation. In: Advances in Neural Information Processing Systems (NIPS), Vancouver, Canada, 3–6 Dec, pp. 1689–1696 (2007)
8. Lefever, E., Macken, L., Hoste, V.: Language-independent bilingual terminology extraction from a multilingual parallel corpus. In: Proceedings of the 12th Conference of the European Chapter of the Association for Computational Linguistics, Athens, Greece, 03 Apr, pp. 496–504 (2009)
9. Okita, T., Hosseinzadeh Vahid, A., Way, A., Liu, Q.: The DCU terminology translation system for the medical query subtask at WMT 2014. In: Proceedings of the Ninth Workshop on Statistical Machine Translation, Baltimore, USA, 26–27 June, pp. 239–245 (2014)
10. Vulic, I., Moens, M.F.: Bilingual distributed word representations from document-aligned comparable data. J. Artif. Intell. Res. 55(1), 953–994 (2016)
11. Chebel, M., Latiri, C., Gaussier, E.: Bilingual lexicon extraction from comparable corpora based on closed concepts mining. In: Kim, J., Shim, K., Cao, L., Lee, J.-G., Lin, X., Moon, Y.-S. (eds.) PAKDD 2017. LNCS (LNAI), vol. 10234, pp. 586–598. Springer, Cham (2017). https://doi.org/10.1007/978-3-319-57454-7_46
12. Dubois, D., Prade, H.: Possibility theory and its application: where do we stand. Mathw. Soft Comput. 18(1), 18–31 (2011)
13. Menacer, M.A., Boumerdas, A., Zakaria, C., Smaili, K.: A new language model based on possibility theory. In: Gelbukh, A. (ed.) CICLing 2016. LNCS, vol. 9623, pp. 127–139. Springer, Cham (2018). https://doi.org/10.1007/978-3-319-75477-2_8
14. Bounhas, I., Ayed, R., Elayeb, B., Evrard, F., Saoud, N.B.B.: Experimenting a discriminative possibilistic classifier with reweighting model for Arabic morphological disambiguation. Comput. Speech Lang. 33(1), 67–87 (2015)
15. Bounhas, I., Ayed, R., Elayeb, B., Saoud, N.B.B.: A hybrid possibilistic approach for Arabic full morphological disambiguation. Data Knowl. Eng. 100, 240–254 (2015)
16. Lahbib, W., Bounhas, I., Slimani, Y.: Arabic terminology extraction and enrichment based on domain-specific text mining. In: The 27th IEEE International Conference on Tools with Artificial Intelligence (ICTAI), Vietri sul Mare, Italy, 9–11 Nov, pp. 340–347 (2015)
17. Alguliyev, R.M., Aliguliyev, R.M., Isazade, N.R.: A new similarity measure and mathematical model for text summarization. Problems Inf. Technol. 6(1), 42–53 (2015)
18. Lahbib, W., Bounhas, I., Elayeb, B.: Arabic-English domain terminology extraction from aligned corpora. In: Meersman, R., et al. (eds.) OTM 2014. LNCS, vol. 8841, pp. 745–759. Springer, Heidelberg (2014). https://doi.org/10.1007/978-3-662-45563-0_46
19. Mikolov, T., Yih, W., Zweig, G.: Linguistic regularities in continuous space word representations. In: Proceedings of the Conference of the North American Chapter of the Association of Computational Linguistics on Human Language Technologies (HLT-NAACL), Atlanta, Georgia, 10–12 June, pp. 746–751 (2013)
20. Dem˘sar, J.: Statistical comparisons of classifiers over multiple data sets. J. Mach. Learn. Res. 7, 1–30 (2006)

Matrix and Tensor-Based Approximation of 3D Face Animations from Low-Cost Range Sensors

Michał Romaszewski[(✉)], Arkadiusz Sochan, and Krzysztof Skabek

Institute of Theoretical and Applied Informatics, Polish Academy of Sciences,
Bałtycka 5, 44-100 Gliwice, Poland
{michal,arek,kskabek}@iitis.pl

Abstract. Three-dimensional animation is often represented in the form of a sequence of 3D meshes, also called dynamic animation or Temporally Coherent Mesh Sequence (TCMS). Widespread availability of affordable range sensors makes capturing such data easy, however, its huge volume complicates both storage and further processing. One of the possible solutions is to approximate the data using matrix or tensor decomposition. However the quality the animation may have different impact on both approaches. In this work we use the Microsoft Kinect[TM] to crate sequences of human face models and compare the approximation error obtained from modelling animations using Principal component analysis (PCA) and Higher Order Singular Value Decomposition (HOSVD). We focus on distortion introduced by reconstruction of data from its truncated factorization. We show that while HOSVD may outperform PCA in terms of approximation error, it may be significantly affected by distortion in animation data.

Keywords: 3D face models · Approximation · HOSVD · PCA
Kinect

1 Introduction

Animation of a 3D object [1] is often represented in the form of a sequence of 3D meshes ordered in time, with a constant number of vertices, connectivity and topology [2]. Such a sequence is called the dynamic animation or the Temporally Coherent Mesh Sequence (TCMS) [3]. With the availability of affordable 3D range imaging equipment, such as Microsoft Kinect[TM], collection of dynamic animations is relatively easy. However, captured sequences usually require additional registration, smoothing and filtering [4], to limit the impact of range sensor limitations. In addition, large volume of acquired data complicates their storage and further use.

One of the approaches to address this problem may be to perform the decomposition of an animation and represent it as a model based on principal components. Since the original animation can be reconstructed from only a limited

© Springer Nature Switzerland AG 2018
T. Czachórski et al. (Eds.): ISCIS 2018, CCIS 935, pp. 239–246, 2018.
https://doi.org/10.1007/978-3-030-00840-6_26

number of components, such model allows to conserve storage space and memory at the expense of introducing error into the reconstruction. Linear methods, such as Principal Component Analysis (PCA) were commonly applied for both compression [5] and 3D modelling e.g. in [6]. Another promising approach lies in using the tensor-based methods such as the Higher Order Singular Value Decomposition (HOSVD), employed e.g. in [7] to describe the motion of human body and face.

While selection of parameters for HOSVD is more complicated [8], as there are multiple modes to consider, tensor-based approach may outperform matrix decomposition in regards to the estimation error, both for artificial animations and motion-capture sequences [9]. However, the quality of animations obtained from affordable range sensors may be lower than those obtained with skeleton animation or motion-capture, because of the noise in captured data and possible improper correspondence of vertices in consecutive frames. The question is, how the differences in these data types affect the estimation error of both approaches to animation decomposition?

In this paper we compare two decomposition algorithms: PCA and HOSVD, applied to sequences of 3D face images obtained using Kinect for Windows v2 Sensor. It allows not only to capture raw point clouds that can be registered into a dynamic sequence of human face models, but its SDK includes also the deformable face model parametrised with characteristic face points. This model has good correspondence between vertices in each frame and introduces minimal noise in vertex positions. This will allow us to show how each decomposition is affected by registration errors in comparison to 'ideal' scenario, that is similar to the ones presented in [9].

2   Tensor Decomposition

In our experiments we represent 3D face animation as a tensor. More detailed description of tensor processing can be found in [10]. Basic notions regarding tensor operations may be described as follows:

A tensor is denoted as

$$\mathcal{T} = \{t_{i_1,i_2,\dots,i_n}\}_{i_1,i_2,\dots,i_n=0}^{I_1-1,I_2-1,\dots,I_N-1} \in \mathbb{R}^{I_1,I_2,\dots,I_N}. \tag{1}$$

This tensor has n modes. Each of the indices corresponds to one of the modes *i.e.* i_l to mode l. By *multiplication* of tensor $\mathcal{T}$ by matrix $\mathbf{U} = \{u_{i_l d}\}_{i_l,d=0}^{I_l-1,D} \in \mathbb{R}^{I_l,D}$ in mode l we define a tensor $\mathcal{T}' \in \mathbb{R}^{I_1,\dots,I_{l-1},D,I_{l+1},\dots,I_N}$, such that:

$$\mathcal{T}' = (\mathcal{T} \times_l \mathbf{U})_{i_1\dots i_{l-1}d\,i_{l+1}\dots i_N} = \sum_{i_l=0}^{I_l-1} t_{i_1 i_2\dots i_l\dots i_N} u_{i_l d}. \tag{2}$$

By *unfolding* a tensor $\mathcal{T}$ in mode l we define a matrix $\mathbf{T}_{(l)}$ such that

$$(\mathbf{T}_{(l)})_{i,j} = t_{i_1\dots i_{l-1}j\,i_{l+1}\dots i_N}, \tag{3}$$

where $i = 1 + \sum_{\substack{k=1 \\ l \neq l}}^{N}(i_k - 1)J_k$ and $J_k = \prod_{\substack{m=1 \\ m \neq l}}^{k-1} I_m$. Given a tensor $\mathcal{T}$, defined as in the Eq. (1), a new *sub-tensor* $\mathcal{T}_{i_n = \alpha}$ can be created as follows:

$$\mathcal{T}_{i_l = \alpha} = \{t_{i_1 i_2 \ldots i_{l-1} i_l i_{l+1} \ldots i_n}\}_{i_1 = 0, i_2 = 0, \ldots, i_l = \alpha, \ldots, i_n = 0}^{I_1 - 1, I_2 - 1, \ldots, \alpha, \ldots, I_N - 1}$$
$$\in \mathbb{R}^{I_1, I_2, \ldots, 1, \ldots, I_N}. \tag{4}$$

The *scalar product* $\langle \mathcal{A}, \mathcal{B} \rangle$ of tensors $\mathcal{A}, \mathcal{B} \in \mathbb{R}^{I_1, I_2, \ldots, I_N}$ is defined as

$$\langle \mathcal{A}, \mathcal{B} \rangle = \sum_{i_1=0}^{I_1-1} \sum_{i_2=0}^{I_2-1} \cdots \sum_{i_N=0}^{I_N-1} b_{i_1, i_2, \ldots, i_n} a_{i_1, i_2, \ldots, i_n}. \tag{5}$$

We say that if scalar product of tensors equals 0, then they are orthogonal.
The *Frobenius norm* of a tensor $\mathcal{T}$ is given by $||\mathcal{T}|| = \sqrt{\langle \mathcal{T}, \mathcal{T} \rangle}$.

2.1 Higher Order Singular Value Decomposition

Higher Order Singular Value Decomposition, also called Tucker decomposition, is a generalisation of SVD from matrices to tensors. Given a tensor $\mathcal{T}$, in order to find its HO-SVD, in the form of the Tucker operator $[\![\mathcal{C}; \mathbf{U}^{(1)}, \ldots, \mathbf{U}^{(N)}]\!]$, such that $\mathcal{C} \in \mathbb{R}^{I_1, \ldots, I_N}$ and $\mathbf{U}^{(k)} \in \mathbb{R}^{I_k, I_k}$ are orthogonal matrices, Algorithm 4.3 from [10] can be used.

Tensor $\mathcal{C}$ is called the core tensor and has the following useful properties. Reconstruction: $\mathcal{T} = \mathcal{C} \times_1 \mathbf{U}^{(1)} \times_2 \mathbf{U}^{(2)} \times_3 \ldots \times_N \mathbf{U}^{(N)}$, where $\mathbf{U}^{(i)}$ are orthogonal matrices. Orthogonality: $\langle \mathcal{C}_{i_l = \alpha}, \mathcal{C}_{i_l = \beta} \rangle = 0$ for all possible values of l, α and β, such that $\alpha \neq \beta$. Order of sub-tensor norms: $||\mathcal{C}_{i_n = 1}|| \leq ||\mathcal{C}_{i_n = 2}|| \leq \cdots \leq ||\mathcal{C}_{i_n = I_n}||$ for all n.

HOSVD-based dimensionality reduction results from the useful property that larger magnitudes of a core tensor are denoted by low values of indices. Therefore $\tilde{\mathcal{T}} = \tilde{\mathcal{C}} \times_1 \tilde{\mathbf{U}}^{(1)} \times_2 \tilde{\mathbf{U}}^{(2)} \times_3 \ldots \times_N \tilde{\mathbf{U}}^{(N)}$, where

$$\tilde{\mathcal{C}} = \{c_{i_1, i_2, \ldots, i_n}\}_{i_1, i_2, \ldots, i_n = 0}^{R_1 - 1, R_2 - 1, \ldots, R_N - 1} \in \mathbb{R}^{R_1, R_2, \ldots, R_N} \tag{6}$$

is a truncated tensor in such a way that in each mode l indices span from 0 to $R_l - 1 \leq I_l - 1$ where matrices $\tilde{\mathbf{U}}^{(l)} \in \mathbb{R}^{R_l, I_l}$ have orthonormal columns and their rows form orthonormal basis in respective vector spaces.

Given $(R_l)_{l=1}^{N}$ one can form tensor $\tilde{\mathcal{T}}$ that approximates tensor $\mathcal{T}$ in the sense of their euclidean distance $||\tilde{\mathcal{T}} - \mathcal{T}||$.

2.2 Principal Component Analysis

Principal Component Analysis described e.g. in [11] may be defined as follows. Let $\mathbf{X} = [\mathbf{x}_1, \mathbf{x}_2 \ldots, \mathbf{x}_L]$ be a data matrix, where $\mathbf{x}_i \in \mathbb{R}^p$ are data vectors with zero empirical mean. The associated covariance matrix is given by $\mathbf{E} = \mathbf{X}\mathbf{X}^T$. By performing eigenvalue decomposition of $\mathbf{E} = \mathbf{O}\mathbf{D}\mathbf{O}^T$ such that eigenvalues $\lambda_i, i = 1, .., p$ of $\mathbf{D}$ are ordered in a descending order $\lambda_1 \geq \lambda_2 \geq \ldots \geq \lambda_p > 0$, one obtains the sequence of principal components $[\mathbf{o}_1, \mathbf{o}_2, \ldots, \mathbf{o}_p]$ which are columns of $\mathbf{O}$. One can form a feature vector $\mathbf{y}$ of dimension $p' \leq p$ by calculating $\mathbf{y} = [\mathbf{o}_1, \mathbf{o}_2, \ldots, \mathbf{o}_{p'}]^T \mathbf{x}$.

In order to apply PCA, tensor $\mathcal{T} = t_{i,j,k} \in \mathbb{R}^{K,3,F}$ must be unfolded according to the Eq. (3). We consider two unfoldings: a mode-0 (vertex) unfolding forms a matrix $\mathbf{X}_{\mathcal{T}(0)} \in \mathbb{R}^{K,3 \times J}$ and will be further called vertex-PCA, while a mode-3 (frame) unfolding forms $\mathbf{X}_{\mathcal{T}(3)} \in \mathbb{R}^{F,3 \times K}$ and will be called frame-PCA.

3   Method

The aim of our experiment is to find the reconstruction error of dynamic face sequences obtained from parametrized face model. We will now describe our experimental environment and method of measuring the approximation error.

3.1   Data Acquisition

Our dataset consist of digitized series of face expressions performed by six participants, who imitated selected expressions from the Bosphorus Face Database [12]. Kinect for Windows v2 Sensor was used to collect range data. This sensor uses regular RGB camera, infrared (IR) camera and IR projector to obtain depth images convertible to 3D point clouds. Resulting point cloud sequences are noisy and may contain holes and artefacts. They need to be aligned and correspondence of vertices must be found for obtained range images in the sequence. These problems may be mitigated by approximating range data with a deformable face model similarly to the approach presented e.g. in [13]. Such a deformable face model is implemented by the FaceModel in HighDefinitionFaceFrame class of the Kinect for Windows SDK 2.0.[1] It outputs a matrix $\mathbb{R}^{L \times 3}$ of $L = 1347$ vertices corresponding to characteristic points of a human face. We have verified that expressions performed by our participants are well represented by this model. By stacking obtained matrices $\mathbf{M}_l, l < L$ we formed a tensor $\mathcal{T} = t_{i,j,k} \in \mathbb{R}^{L,3,F}$ where $\mathbf{M}_l$, following the notation in [10], form frontal slices $\mathcal{T}_{::l}$.

To obtain a reference model from raw data we extracted feature points - particularly position of eyes and corners of the mouth to determine the face location. Raw spatial data within this area is a sequence of F 3D points and can be represented as a $K_f \times 3$ matrices $\mathbf{M}_f \in \mathbb{R}^{K_f \times 3}$. This data is converted into a tensor by obtaining correspondence of vertices for point clouds in the sequence. Since the difference between neighboring frames is small, we align consecutive matrices $\mathbf{M}_f$ using ICP algorithm [14]. We than perform 1-NN k-d tree search [15] starting from the reference point cloud with minimal K_f, denoted K. Finally, we obtain a tensor $\mathcal{T} = t_{i,j,k} \in \mathbb{R}^{K,3,F}$.

3.2   Experiment Scenario

Our experiments aim to compare methods of data decomposition used for modelling sequences of aligned point clouds. Our criterion is the distortion introduced by approximating data from the reduced representation. For HOSVD this

---

[1] http://www.microsoft.com/en-us/kinectforwindows/develop.

reduced representation results from truncating the Tucker operator $[\![\tilde{C}; \tilde{U}^{(1)}, \tilde{U}^{(2)}, \tilde{U}^{(3)}]\!]$. For PCA it results from using a limited number of principal components.

If we denote v as the number of mode-0 (vertex) components and f as mode-2 (frame) components, than for the sequence of K vertices and F frames we need $\nu_{hosvd} = v \times K + 9 + f \times F + v \times J \times f$ floating points to store truncated Tucker operator. For frame-PCA we need $\nu_{fpca} = (V \times 3 + F) \times N_f$ floating-points to store N_f components and for vertex-PCA $\nu_{vpca} = (F \times J + V) \times N_v$ floating-points to store N_v components. The size of original tensor T is $s = V \times J \times F$. We will present the rate of data reduction as $\phi = \frac{\nu}{s}$.

The approximation is lossy and introduces distortion into the reconstructed tensor T'. As a measure of distortion between tensors T and T' we use mean squared error (MSE) $\rho = \frac{1}{n} \sum_{i=1}^{n} (\mathbf{v}' - \mathbf{v})^2$, where $\mathbf{v}$ is the vector in original data and $\mathbf{v}'$ is its reconstruction.

4 Results

Plot (a) of the Fig. 2 presents reconstruction error for averaged sequences of morphable face models. These results are consistent with previous experiments for synthetic data, described in [9]. For these sequences HOSVD outperforms

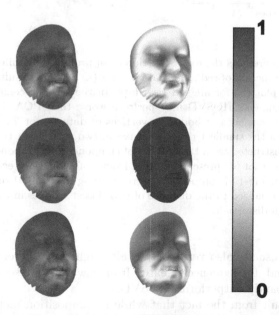

Fig. 1. The distortion between the original model and its approximation from approx. $\phi = 0.03$ (left) and $\phi = 0.01$ (right) original data size. Error value was normalized to the distance of two closest vertices in the sequence. Red color indicates high distortion. Top pair was approximated using vertex-PCA, middle one with frame-PCA and bottom one with HOSVD. Notice that for high reduction rate frame-PCA produces significantly worse reconstruction than other two methods.

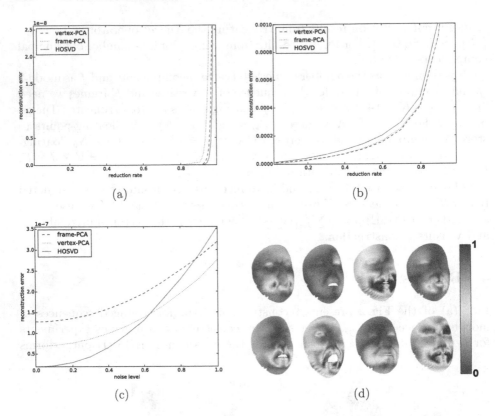

(a)   (b)

(c)   (d)

Fig. 2. Upper plots presents the reconstruction error produced by different decomposition methods as a function of reduction rate ϕ. Plot (a) presents results for deformable face model, while plot (b) for aligned raw data. In the second scenario due to noise and vertex misalignments HOSVD may perform worse than PCA. Plot (c) presents the impact of Gaussian noise σ added to vertices of data tensor $\mathcal{T}$. Maximum value of σ corresponds to the smallest distance between two vertices in the sequence. The sequence was reconstructed from the number of components corresponding to $\phi = 0.02$ of original data size. Plot (d) presents selected frames of animation reconstructed using HOSVD from the number of components corresponding to $\phi = 0.01$ original data size. Error value was normalized to the distance of two closest vertices in the sequence. Red color indicates high distortion.

frame-PCA and usually also vertex-PCA, although this difference is not large. On the other hand, for sequences created from raw data, presented on the plot (b), PCA significantly outperforms HOSVD.

This may result from the fact that while decomposition methods are moderately sensitive to noise, when HOSVD multiplies the core tensor by matrices $\mathbf{U}^{(i)T}$ associated with correlations of data in each mode i, errors are also multiplied. Therefore the method is affected more than a matrix-based approach. This tendency can be observed in the Fig. 2 plot (c), where the reconstruction of a sequence created with a deformable face model is performed, using the number of components corresponding to $\phi = 0.02$ of its original size. Gaussian noise σ is gradually added to the position of each vertex in the data tensor, with a maximum value equal to the distance between two closest vertices in the sequence. We can see that when no noise is present, HOSVD outperforms PCA-based decomposition while for noisy data the tendency is reversed. Selected frames of animation reconstructed using HOSVD with $\phi = 0.01$ are presented in Fig. 2 plot (d).

Reconstruction errors of deformable models are presented in the Fig. 1. Distortion is almost unnoticeable for sequences reconstructed from $\phi = 0.03$ of original data and for reconstruction from $\phi = 0.01$ only frame-PCA introduces significant error.

5 Conclusion

Tensor decomposition can be used for approximation of Temporally Coherent Mesh Sequences. The quality of reconstruction, however, is highly dependent on data characteristics. For artificial or motion-capture animations, HOSVD produces low reconstruction error even for high rate of data reduction. These results are consistent with experiments previously performed for well known test sequences [9]. On the other hand, noise and vertex misalignment present in Kinect-based raw spatial data proves to be challenging for tensor-based method. In such scenario matrix decomposition may be more suitable to minimize the reconstruction error. It should be noted that simplification of digitized face expression with a deformable model may, in some cases, disregard important features. Therefore requirements and limits of the point cloud registration process may determine the choice of a more robust decomposition.

Acknowledgements. This work is partially based on results of the National Science for Research and Development projects: INNOTECH-K2/IN2/50/182645/NCBR/12 and National Science Centre, decision 2011/03/D/ST6/03753. Authors would like to thank Sebastian Opozda for his help with data visualization and development of experimental environment.

References

1. De Aguiar, E., Theobalt, C., Thrun, S., Seidel, H.-P.: Automatic conversion of mesh animations into skeleton-based animations. In: Computer Graphics Forum, vol. 27, no. 2, pp. 389–397. Wiley Online Library (2008)
2. Starck, J., Hilton, A.: Surface capture for performance-based animation. Comput. Graph. Appl. IEEE **27**(3), 21–31 (2007)
3. Arcila, R., Cagniart, C., Hétroy, F., Boyer, E., Dupont, F.: Segmentation of temporal mesh sequences into rigidly moving components. Graph. Models **75**(1), 10–22 (2013)
4. Tong, J., Zhou, J., Liu, L., Pan, Z., Yan, H.: Scanning 3d full human bodies using kinects. IEEE Trans. Vis. Comput. Graph. **18**(4), 643–650 (2012)

5. Váša, L., Skala, V.: Cobra: compression of the basis for pca represented animations. In: Computer Graphics Forum, vol. 28, no. 6, pp. 1529–1540. Wiley Online Library (2009)
6. Breidt, M., Biilthoff, H.H., Curio, C.: Robust semantic analysis by synthesis of 3d facial motion. In: 2011 IEEE International Conference on Automatic Face and Gesture Recognition and Workshops (FG 2011), pp. 713–719. IEEE (2011)
7. Akhter, I., Simon, T., Khan, S., Matthews, I., Sheikh, Y.: Bilinear spatiotemporal basis models. ACM Trans. Graph. (TOG) 31(2), 17 (2012)
8. Romaszewski, M., Głomb, P.: Parameter estimation for hosvd-based approximation of temporally coherent mesh sequences. In: Proceedings of the 11th Joint Conference on Computer Vision, Imaging and Computer Graphics Theory and Applications, pp. 138–145 (2016)
9. Romaszewski, M., Gawron, P., Opozda, S.: Dimensionality reduction of dynamic animations using HO-SVD. In: Rutkowski, L., Korytkowski, M., Scherer, R., Tadeusiewicz, R., Zadeh, L.A., Zurada, J.M. (eds.) ICAISC 2014. LNCS (LNAI), vol. 8467, pp. 757–768. Springer, Cham (2014). https://doi.org/10.1007/978-3-319-07173-2_65
10. Kolda, T.G., Bader, B.W.: Tensor decompositions and applications. SIAM Rev. 51(3), 455–500 (2009)
11. Jolliffe, I.: Principal Component Analysis. Wiley Online Library (2005)
12. Savran, A., et al.: Bosphorus database for 3D face analysis. In: Schouten, B., Juul, N.C., Drygajlo, A., Tistarelli, M. (eds.) BioID 2008. LNCS, vol. 5372, pp. 47–56. Springer, Heidelberg (2008). https://doi.org/10.1007/978-3-540-89991-4_6
13. Zollhöfer, M., Martinek, M., Greiner, G., Stamminger, M., Süßmuth, J.: Automatic reconstruction of personalized avatars from 3D face scans. Comput. Animat. Virtual Worlds 22(2–3), 195–202 (2011). https://doi.org/10.1002/cav.405
14. Rusinkiewicz, S., Levoy, M.: Efficient variants of the ICP algorithm. In: Proceedings of the Third International Conference on 3-D Digital Imaging and Modeling 2001, pp. 145–152. IEEE (2001)
15. Shakhnarovich, G., Darrell, T., Indyk, P.: Nearest-Neighbor Methods in Learning and Vision: Theory and Practice (Neural Information Processing). The MIT press (2006)

Enhancing Hybrid Indexing for Arabic Information Retrieval

Souheila Ben Guirat[1,2,5], Ibrahim Bounhas[2,4,5(✉)],
and Yahya Slimani[2,3,5]

[1] Department of Computer Sciences, Prince Sattam Ibn Abdulaziz University,
Riayd, Saudi Arabia
benguirat.souheila@gmail.com
[2] LISI Laboratory of Computer Science for Industrial Systems,
Carthage University, Tunis, Tunisia
bounhas.ibrahim@gmail.com, yahya.slimani@gmail.com
[3] Higher Institute of Multimedia Arts of La Manouba, La Manouba University,
Manouba, Tunisia
[4] Higher Institute of Documentation, La Manouba University, Manouba, Tunisia
[5] JARIR: Joint Group for Artificial Reasoning and Information Retrieval,
Manouba, Tunisia
http://www.jarir.tn/

Abstract. Existent literature proposes several approaches to enhance Arabic
document retrieval using different indexing units. In anterior work [1, 2], we
proposed to combine multiple indexing units which improved retrieval performance. This paper develops this approach and suggests enhancing term
weighting through result aggregation and pseudo-relevance feedback techniques. We compare these approaches to three baselines to enhance the previous
results which showed the performance of hybrid indexing. To assess our
hypothesis, we run four experimental setups based on a larger corpus with
various query sets. Finally, we aim to compare all these methods using standard
information retrieval metrics.

Keywords: Arabic information retrieval · Hybrid indexing
Result aggregation · Pseudo-relevance feedback

1 Introduction and Related Work

Document indexing is the process of assigning and arranging index terms. Choosing
the best terms which are likely to represent documents has always been a challenge
since it systematically affects the retrieval effectiveness. For Arabic texts, many types
of indexing units were proposed using stemming algorithms [12], namely root-based
stemming [5, 6, 8] and light stemming [7, 9, 11]. Both approaches perform better than
using surface word-based indexing [7] and reduce storage size and processing time.
Therefore, for several years, Arabic stemming tools have been developed and
improved, while no comprehensive tool is available [12]. Indeed, comparative research
works [12] tried to determine the best stemming depth (root or stem) but until then,

© Springer Nature Switzerland AG 2018
T. Czachórski et al. (Eds.): ISCIS 2018, CCIS 935, pp. 247–254, 2018.
https://doi.org/10.1007/978-3-030-00840-6_27

none of the two indexing units widely overtook the other. In general, root-based techniques performed better in terms of recall where light stemming methods allowed better precision and each of the two indexing units performed better under different circumstances [1]. To overcome the shortcoming of both approaches and take advantage of their benefits, hybrid indexing was proposed in our previous work [1, 2].

In our method we combine 3 indexing units, namely the root, the stem and the verbed-pattern. For example, the root of the word "الانقسامات" ("alinkissamat"; the divisions) is "ق س م" (k s m), its stem is "انقسام" (inkissam; division) and its verbed pattern is "انقسم" (inkassama; was divided).

2 Proposed Approaches

As our previous work [1, 2] showed the effectiveness of hybrid indexing, our goal is no longer showing the evidence of the importance of combining, but goes further to find the best hybrid indexing method. In the following, we propose two main techniques, namely result aggregation and pseudo-relevance feedback.

2.1 Result Aggregation Approach

This approach is based on results resorting [3, 4]. The first step consists on running the retrieval process for each indexing unit. Let consider, S_k, P_k and R_k, the sorted lists of results obtained with indexes composed only of stems, verbed patterns and roots, respectively. These lists are combined and a common list of relevant documents noted *RES* is constituted. We compare the following aggregation methods. On the one hand, **random sampling** is inspired from the TREC standard sampling procedure [17]. It consists in adding to *RES* the top ranked document in a each result (i.e. S_k, then P_k and R_k). In the second iteration, we add documents which are ranked at the second position in each list. This process is iterated until all the documents in S_k, then P_k and R_k are added to *RES*. On the second hand, in intelligent sampling, which is inspired from [14], we stack the documents of S_k on the top of *RES*, then those of P_k and finally those of R_k. This approach is supposed to improve MAP, P@N and R@N, since stems are the most canonical forms.

2.2 Pseudo-Relevance Feedback-Based Approach

In this approach, we aim to estimate the weights of the three indexing units with a linear model, as follows:

$$I_j(W_i) = \alpha * TF_j(S_i) + \beta * TF_j(P_i) + \gamma * TF_j(R_i) \tag{1}$$

where $I_j(W_i)$ is the weight of the word W_i in the document d_j and $TF_j(S_i)$, (respectively $TF_j(P_i)$ and $TF_j(R_i)$) is the normalized frequency of S_i (respectively of P_i and R_i) in document d_j.

In the Pseudo-Relevance Feedback [13], we exploit the top N ranked documents for each indexing unit to estimate the parameters in linear combination. We compute optimal values α^*, β^* and γ^* as follows:

$$\alpha^* = \sum_{j=1}^{N} TF_j(S_i)/N \qquad (2)$$

We compute β^* and γ^* in the same way as α^*. Finally these values are normalized to obtain a sum equal to 1 ($\alpha + \beta + \gamma = 1$).

3   Experiments

The goal of this section is to study the effectiveness of the proposed approaches compared to three baselines using the three indexing units.

3.1   Experimental Setup

The test corpus used in all experiments (see Table 1) is the LDC2001T55 collection that is the only standard corpus available for Arabic. It consists of 383,872 articles from "Agence France Presse" Arabic newswire. As in our previous work [2], we use a modified version of Ghwanmeh stemmer [15] and PL2 (Poisson estimation for randomness), which is implemented in Terrier platform [16], as ranking model. We perform four experimental setups as detailed in Table 1.

Table 1. Experimental setups.

Designation	TREC version	# topics	Query type
T1	TREC 2001	25	Topic title
T2	TREC 2002	50	
TD1	TREC 2001	25	Topic title + description
TD2	TREC 2002	50	

3.2   Experimental Results

For each experimental setup, we perform six runs (see Table 3) which are compared based on standard information retrieval metrics. These runs are namely: stem-based approach (S1); pattern-based approach (S2); root-based approach (S3); intelligent sampling (H1); random sampling (H2); and pseudo-relevance feedback (H3).

PRF Parameters Tuning. Before presenting comparative studies, we start by tuning the parameters of the PRF-based approach (H3). The obtained parameters are illustrated in Table 2.

Table 2. PRF parameter tuning results

Test setup	Parameters		
	α	β	γ
T1	0,2760	0,4320	0,2920
T2	0,3010	0,4352	0,2638
TD1	0,3393	0,3587	0,3020
TD2	0,3330	0,3736	0,2934

Recall-Precision Curves. Figure 1 illustrates Recall-Precision curves for all the experimental configurations. Figure 1(a) shows that H1 improves the precision over recall variations. Besides, we note that all proposed combination methods outperform S1 which reaches better results compared to S2 and S3. In the other test setups (see Fig. 1(b), (c) and (d)) H1, H2 and H3 reach competitive results compared to S1, but widely outperform S2 and S3.

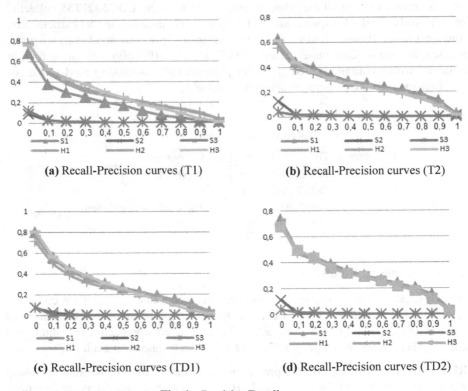

(a) Recall-Precision curves (T1)   (b) Recall-Precision curves (T2)

(c) Recall-Precision curves (TD1)   (d) Recall-Precision curves (TD2)

Fig. 1. Precision/Recall curves

Precision at N Curves. All the curves in Fig. 2 show that root and pattern based methods gave the worst precision rates. Besides, the precision after 100 clearly decreases for all approaches in all experimental configurations. This may be explained by the pool size which was 164.9 in TREC 2001 and did not exceed 118.2 in TREC 2002. Moreover, all tests show that the hybrid approaches widely overcome S2 and S3. S1 reaches the same and sometimes better results than the hybrid approaches (cf. Fig. 2 (b)). This may explained by the fact that the descriptions of queries contain variants of the words appearing in the title. That is, the hybrid indexing, which aims mainly to handle variants, may not enhance results. Besides, descriptions, which are longer than titles, are more exhaustive to reflect the search topic, thus reducing noise and enhancing precision.

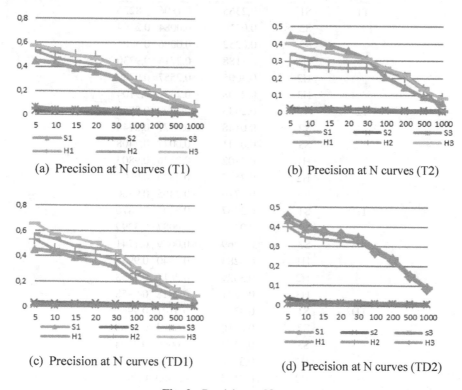

(a) Precision at N curves (T1)

(b) Precision at N curves (T2)

(c) Precision at N curves (TD1)

(d) Precision at N curves (TD2)

Fig. 2. Precision at N curves

R-Precision, Mean Average Precision and Recall Comparison. Table 3 indicates that stem-based indexing (S1) gives better results than S2 and S3 based respectively on pattern and root indexing units. Indeed, stems are the most canonical forms and thus more precise than roots or patterns. Moreover, we notice the improvement given by the hybrid approaches compared to baselines. In fact, proposed approaches always reach higher precision and recall results than S2 and S3, and usually better results than S1(in T1 and T2). In TD2, S1 gives competitive results with our proposed systems and slightly overcomes them in TD1. This is explained by the same reason (description effect) previously detailed in P@N variations. In addition, H1 outperforms H3 which usually achieves better results than H2. Furthermore, title+description configuration reaches usually better performance than title-based queries for all proposed methods. This could be explained by the nature of description which repeats the title words and extends the query with some derivatives of its original words. This increases the number of significant terms in the query and enlarges its scope.

Table 3. Results comparison based on R-precision, MAP and recall

Test setup	Approach	Criteria		
		R-Precision	*MAP*	*Recall*
T1	S1	0,2365	0,1806	0,8226
	S2	0,0210	0,0084	0,2794
	S3	0,0252	0,0096	0,3005
	H1	0,3188	0,2716	0,9730
	H2	0,3005	0,2557	0,9730
	H3	0,2908	0,2621	0,9704
T2	S1	0,2943	0,2698	0,9756
	S2	0,0148	0,0077	0,3144
	S3	0,0141	0,0077	0,2408
	H1	0,2802	0,2546	0,9803
	H2	0,2577	0,2320	0,9803
	H3	0,2716	0,2465	0,9800
TD1	S1	0,2967	0,3393	0,9876
	S2	0,0214	0,0087	0,3299
	S3	0,0069	0,0019	0,1741
	H1	0,3283	0,2840	0,9958
	H2	0,3029	0,2611	0,9958
	H3	0,3241	0,2818	0,9958
TD2	S1	0,3372	0,3101	0,9961
	S2	0,0110	0,0064	0,3885
	S3	0,0153	0,0066	0,2604
	H1	0,3314	0,3040	0,9977
	H2	0,3145	0,2860	0,9977
	H3	0,3142	0,2931	0,9976

Significance Analysis. We assess in Table 4 the significance of our results using student's paired test samples [10]. It allows checking whether the difference between the MAP values of different approaches is statistically significant. This table shows that usually (except one case) the improvement of MAP of all the proposed approaches versus the baselines is statically significant (P-value < 0.05) [18].

Table 4. Significance evaluation with student's paired test samples

Test setup	Approaches	P-values	Test setup	Approaches	P-values
T1	H1 vs S1	0.00008	TD1	H1 vs S1	0.00144
	H1 vs S2	0.000069		H1 vs S2	0.000029
	H1 vs S3	0.000041		H1 vs S3	0.000019
	H2 vs S1	0.000112		H2 vs S1	0.001248
	H2 vs S2	0.000098		H2 vs S2	0.00006
	H2 vs S3	0.000702		H2 vs S3	0.000038
	H3 vs S1	0.000018		H3 vs S1	0.532109
	H3 vs S2	0.000011		H3 vs S2	0.000002
	H3 vs S3	0.000833		H3 vs S3	0.000001
T2	H1 vs S1	0.001283	TD2	H1 vs S1	0.001277
	H1 vs S2	0.000001		H1 vs S2	0.000001
	H1 vs S3	0.000001		H1 vs S3	0.000001
	H2 vs S1	0.000002		H2 vs S1	0.000004
	H2 vs S2	0.000001		H2 vs S2	0.000001
	H2 vs S3	0.000001		H2 vs S3	0.000001
	H3 vs S1	0.015025		H3 vs S1	0.0064972
	H3 vs S2	0.000001		H3 vs S2	0.000001
	H3 vs S3	0.000001		H3 vs S3	0.000001

4 Conclusion

In this paper, we extended a previous work [2] which showed the contribution of hybrid indexing in Arabic information retrieval systems. It mainly aims to improve hybrid indexing using new approaches based on result aggregation and pseudo-relevance feedback. Our goal is to ensure better vocabulary coverage which will ensure a closer representation to the importance of each indexing unit in representing the word meaning.

Based on experimental results on a modern Arabic news collection, we conclude that the proposed approaches widely outperform the root-based and pattern-based approaches. Our results also show the contribution of aggregating results, while intelligent sampling reached the best performance. Besides, we note some differences between the 4 test setups mainly due to the variety of the query length. Furthermore, the low performance rates of S2 and S3 reveal the need for developing more efficient root and pattern extraction tools and to consider all words which have the same pattern or root.

Moreover, the application of random sampling strategy to hybrid indexing systems needs further improvement. We think that specifying the number of documents for each set when creating the aggregated list may be promising.

Overall, our experiments reveal that our proposed methods do not degrade and often improve the system performance. But a further research could focus on refining parameter tuning using more sophisticated techniques [13, 14].

References

1. Ben Guirat, S., Bounhas, I., Slimani, Y.: Combining indexing units for arabic information retrieval. Int. J. Softw. Innov. (IJSI) **4**(4), 1–14 (2016)
2. Ben Guirat, S., Bounhas, I., Slimani, Y.: A hybrid model for arabic document indexing. In: 17th IEEE/ACIS International Conference on Software Engineering, Artificial Intelligence, Networking and Parallel/Distributed Computing (SNPD), Shanghai, China, 30 May–1 June 2016
3. Kopliku, A., Pinel-Sauvagnat, K., Boughanem, M.: Aggregated search: a new information retrieval paradigm. ACM Comput. Surv. **46**(4) (2014)
4. Arguello, J., Diaz, F., Callan, J.: Learning to aggregate vertical results into web search results. In: CIKM 2011, Glasgow, Scotland, UK, 24–28 Oct, pp. 24–28 (2011)
5. Al-Kabi, M., Al-Radaideh, Q., Akawi, K.: Benchmarking and assessing the performance of Arabic Stemmers. J. Inf. Sci. **37**(2), 1–12 (2011)
6. Al-Shawakfa, E., Al-Badarneh, A., Shatnawi, S., Al-Rabab'ah, K., Bani-Ismail, B.: A comparison study of some Arabic root finding algorithms. J. Am. Soc. Inform. Sci. Technol. **6**(5), 1015–1024 (2010)
7. Aljlayl, M., Frieder, O.: On Arabic search: improving the retrieval effectiveness via a light stemming approach. In: Proceedings of the Eleventh International Conference on Information and Knowledge Management, McLean, Virginia, USA, 04–09 Nov 2002
8. Khoja, S., Garside, S.: Stemming arabic text. Technical report, Computing Department, Lancaster University, UK (1999)
9. Larkey, L., Connell, M.E.: Arabic information retrieval at UMass in TREC-10. In: Proceedings of Text Retrieval conference (TREC), Gaithersburg, USA (2001)
10. Sawilowsky Shlomo, S.: Misconceptions leading to choosing the t-Test over the wilcoxon mann-whitney test for shift in location parameter. J. Mod. Appl. Stat. Methods **4**(2), 598–600 (2005)
11. Chen, A., Gey, F.: Building an Arabic stemmer for information retrieval. In: Proceedings of the Text Retrieval Conference TREC-11, pp. 631–639 (2002)
12. Hadni, M., Lachkar, A., Alaoui Ouatik, S.: A new and efficient stemming technique for arabic text categorization. In: International Conference on Multimedia Computing and Systems (ICMCS), 10–12 May 2018, Tangier, Morocco, pp. 791–796 (2012)
13. Liu, T.Y.: Learning to rank for information retrieval. Found. Trends Inf. Retr. **3**(3), 225–331 (2009)
14. Hsu, D.F., Taksa, I.: Comparing rank and score combination methods for data fusion in information retrieval. Inf. Retr. **8**(3), 449–480 (2005)
15. Ghwanmeh, S., Rabab'ah, S., Al-Shalabi, R., Kanaan, G.: Enhanced algorithm for extracting the root of arabic words. In: Sixth International Conference on Computer Graphics, Imaging and Visualization, Tianjin, China, 11–14 Aug, pp. 388–391 (2009)
16. Ounis, I., Amati, G., Plachouras, V., He, B., Macdonald, C., Lioma, C.: Terrier: a high performance and scalable information retrieval platform. In: Proceedings of Open Source Information Retrieval (OSIR) Workshop, Seattle, USA, 10 Aug 2006
17. Aslam, J.A., Pavlu, V., Yilmaz, E.: A sampling technique for efficiently estimating measures of query retrieval performance using incomplete judgments. In: ICML Workshop on Learning with Partially Classified Training Data, Bonn, Germany, 7 Aug 2005
18. Biau, D.J., Jolles, B.M., Porcher, R.: P-value and the theory of hypothesis testing: an explanation for new researchers. Clin. Orthop. Relat. Res. **468**(3), 885–892 (2010)

Methods of Tooth Equator Estimation

Agnieszka Anna Tomaka, Dariusz Pojda$^{(\boxtimes)}$,
Leszek Luchowski, and Michał Tarnawski

Institute of Theoretical and Applied Informatics, Polish Academy of Sciences,
Bałtycka 5, Gliwice, Poland
{ines,dpojda,leszek.luchowski}@iitis.pl, dr.tarnawski@gmail.com

Abstract. Full automation of the designing process of an occlusal splint requires an algorithm to determine the boundary of the splint. For this purpose, the idea of tooth equator is frequently used. The task is to find the approximate level where the teeth are widest, and then cut off the shape of the splint there. The article presents methods for automatic estimation of the tooth equator, used to determine the splint boundary.

Keywords: Tooth equator · Occlusal splint · Mesh segmentation

1 Computerized Methods of Designing an Occlusal Splint

The occlusal splint is one of the methods of treatment of discrepancies between the centric relation and maximal intercuspation (CR/MI) [11], and other temporomandibular joint (TMJ) disorders [1]. Designing an occlusal splint involves: creating partial surfaces, integrating them, and producing the splint on a 3D printer. Some examples of computerized design of various kinds of splint are presented in [4,5,9]. Our previous work concentrated on the inner and outer splint surfaces. The solid was then closed with an arbitrary plane [12]. Full automation of the design process requires an algorithm of splint boundary estimation.

2 The Idea of Tooth Equator and its Application in Occlusal Splint Construction

A splint fully matching the teeth, which taper somewhat towards the collum, would be impossible to apply or to remove (Fig. 1), unless made from an elastic material. The problem of undercuts was solved in our previous work by the impression method of generating the inner surface of the splint [12]. The present task is to find the approximate level where the teeth are widest and then cut the shape of the splint off. To determine this level, we use the idea of tooth equator.

In dentistry, the equator of a tooth is a curve surrounding the tooth, consisting of the points of contact between the insertion direction lines and the tooth surface (Fig. 1). The tooth equator can be determined using the parallelometer [13] (Fig. 2). The tooth equator separates surfaces above, which support the

T. Czachórski et al. (Eds.): ISCIS 2018, CCIS 935, pp. 255–263, 2018.
https://doi.org/10.1007/978-3-030-00840-6_28

Fig. 1. Elimination of undercuts of the convex shaped tooth by the impression method (left). The Equator (middle) vs the tooth equator (right).

splint (supporting surface) from those underneath (undercuts) in which any contact with the splint results in locking. During manual splint forming the undercuts are covered with dental wax (Fig. 2), only supporting surfaces are further used.

The equator curve highly depends on the insertion direction, which can be fixed perpendicular to the Frankurt plane, or optimized for the greatest area of the supporting surfaces and the least changing splint depth. Depending on the tooth shape the curve can be irregular, can vanish or even be doubled (Fig. 2). It can therefore be treated as a rough approximation of the splint boundary.

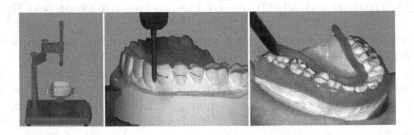

Fig. 2. The tooth equator estimation.

3   Proposed Algorithm

3.1   Patient Models

Automatic estimation of the tooth equator requires some geometric input. At this stage of processing 3D scans of dental models or intraoral scans are sufficient.

The data is represented by the triangular mesh $\mathcal{M}$, – a graph represented by sets of vertices: $\mathcal{V} = \{v_1, v_2, \ldots, v_V\}$ and faces $\mathcal{F} = \{f_1, \ldots, f_F\}$ [3]. Each vertex v_i is associated with its position in $\Re^3$: $\mathcal{P} = \{\mathbf{p}_1, \ldots, \mathbf{p}_V\}$, $\mathbf{p}_i = (x_{v_i}, y_{v_i}, z_{v_i})^T$ and each face represents a triangle specified by three vertex positions.

Additionally, the position of the reference plane π relative to the model is known. The normal to the plane: $\mathbf{n}_\pi = (\mathbf{n_x}, \mathbf{n_y}, \mathbf{n_z})^T$ is the direction of insertion.

3.2 Self–occlusions

The simplest way of determining the tooth equator seems to be the detection of boundaries of the set of faces visible from the $\mathbf{n}_\pi$ direction. This can be done by considering, for each vertex v_i, the set of all triangles in the mesh and determining which of them are crossed by the insertion line passing through v_i.

To speed up the calculations the coordinates of the vertices are transformed to a coordinate system where $\mathbf{n}_\pi = (0, 0, 1)$ and the reference plane passes through the origin $O = (0, 0, 0)$. The projection of a v_i on the plane of the face f_j is then:

$$pp_{i,j}(x, y, z) = (x_{v_i}, y_{v_i}, -(A_{f_j}x_{v_i} + B_{f_j}y_{v_i} + D_{f_j})/C_{f_j}) \qquad (1)$$

where A_{f_j}, B_{f_j}, C_{f_j}, D_{f_j} are coefficients of the plane containing the face f_j.

The examination whether the projection point belongs to the triangle is done by the analysis of its barycentric coordinates $\beta_{1_{i,j}}$, $\beta_{2_{i,j}}$, $\beta_{3_{i,j}}$.

If $0 \leq \beta_{1_{i,j}}, \beta_{2_{i,j}}, \beta_{3_{i,j}} \leq 1$ and $z_{v_i} > z_{pp_{i,j}}$ self–occlusion is detected, all faces containing vertex v_i are moved to the set of occluded faces $\mathcal{F}_{occ}$.

To limit the search space, for each v_i only a subset of faces $\mathcal{F}_{v_i}$ is analyzed. The subset consists of faces for which the orthogonal projection of at least one vertex onto π belongs to the fixed neighborhood of the projection of v_i.

As the result, all faces are divided into the sets of visible $\mathcal{F}_{sup}$ and occluded $\mathcal{F}_{occ}$ faces, representing respectively the supporting surface and undercuts.

3.3 Estimation of Equator Curve

Locating the boundary can be done by tracing boundary edges - edges contained in only one face [6]. In most cases a boundary vertex (vertex on the edge) has two adjacent boundary vertices. A special vertex is the one with greater number of boundary neighborhood.

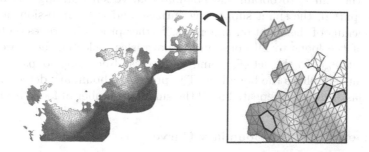

Fig. 3. Isles, holes, chains and special points of the boundary.

The boundary can be divided into loops surrounding the holes or isles and chains joining different special points (Fig. 3).

Orientation of the edge boundaries allows us for loops classification.

Denote $\mathcal{LV} = (v_1, v_2, \ldots, v_l)$ as the collection of ordered vertices on the boundary, and $\mathcal{LF} = (f_1, f_2, \ldots, f_l)$ as the collection adjacent faces. Let $\mathbf{v}_i = p_{v_i} - O(0,0,0)$ be position vector of boundary vertex and let $\mathbf{n}_{f_j}$ be the normal of adjacent face. Let the area vector of the loop be the sum of area vectors of oriented triangles constituted of the origin and two adjacent boundary vertices (Fig. 4a):

$$\mathbf{n}_{\mathcal{LV}} = \sum_{v_i \in \mathcal{LV}} d\mathbf{S}_i = \sum_{v_i \in \mathcal{LV}} \frac{\mathbf{v}_i \times \mathbf{v}_{i+1}}{2} \tag{2}$$

and the mean normal vectors of adjacent faces is

$$\mathbf{n}_{LF} = \sum_{f_i \in \mathcal{LF}} \frac{\mathbf{n}_{f_i}}{l} \tag{3}$$

The sign of the dot product $\mathbf{n}_{\mathcal{LF}} \cdot \mathbf{n}_{\mathcal{LV}}$ classifies the loop. Regarding $\mathbf{n}_{\mathcal{LF}}$ as the reference direction the isle is anticlockwise, the hole is clockwise (Fig. 4b, c).

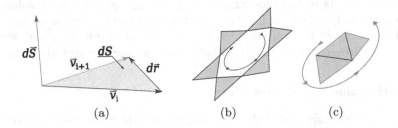

(a)   (b)   (c)

Fig. 4. Vector area and its application in loop classification.

While the aim is to obtain one boundary curve surrounding the maximal connected part of the splint supporting surface, and the impression procedure prevents locking of the splint on undercuts, further processing relies on the classification of the loops to fill holes and remove isles. Selected faces are moved from the set $\mathcal{F}_{occ}$ to the set $\mathcal{F}_{sup}$ and vice versa. Removing loops containing special points simplifies the boundary. The process of boundary detection, holes and isles classification is repeated until the smallest number of loops is obtained.

3.4   Smoothing of the Boundary Curve

At this stage, our boundary loop is still not smooth enough for practical use. We chose to smooth it by spline interpolation followed by a filtration.

Interpolation. For a given sequence of 3D points $\mathcal{LV}$ a parameter value t_i is assigned to each boundary vertex v_i such that $dt = \|p_i - p_{i-1}\|$ is a chord-length.

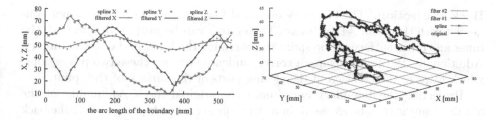

Fig. 5. Vertices of the boundary after the classification step, their spline interpolation and filtration with two filters.

Then the functions $X_s = x(t)$, $Y_s = y(t)$, $Z_s = z(t)$ can be computed yielding a 3D parametric curve. The cubic spline function takes the form [2]:

$$F_{S_i}(t) = a_{f_i}(t - t_i)^3 + b_{f_i}(t - t_i)^2 + c_{f_i}(t - t_i) + d_{f_i} \qquad (4)$$

where $t \in [t_i, t_{i+1}]$, F_{s_i} denotes functions X_{s_i}, Y_{s_i} or Z_{s_i} and a_{f_i} corresponding parameters a_{x_i}, a_{y_i}, a_{z_i} etc. The following assumptions are made: the function accepts data values in points $X_{s_i}(t_i) = x_i$, $Y_{s_i}(t_i) = y_i$, $Z_{s_i}(t_i) = z_i$ and $X_{s_{n-1}}(t_n) = x_n$, $Y_{s_{n-1}}(t_n) = y_n$, $Z_{s_{n-1}}(t_n) = z_n$;
the following conditions of continuity are fulfilled:
$$F_{s_i}(t_{i+1}) = F_{s_{i+1}}(t_{i+1}) \qquad F'_{s_i}(t_{i+1}) = F'_{s_{i+1}}(t_{i+1}) \qquad F''_{s_i}(t_{i+1}) = F''_{s_{i+1}}(t_{i+1})$$
and additionally in the case of natural cubic splines: $F''_{s_0}(t_0) = 0$, $F''_{s_{n-1}}(t_n) = 0$.

The spline function coefficients can be obtained as the solution of a system of linear equations [8]. A cubic spline preserves original data at the boundary vertices and performs interpolation in intervals between them yielding the functions which can be uniformly sampled for further processing. The samples sets $X_s(t)$, $Y_s(t)$, $Z_s(t)$ are obtained.

Filtration. A boundary smoothing effect can be achieved using low–pass filters. If the signal is uniformly sampled, it can be convolved with the filter window [10].

$$F_f(t_j) = \sum_{k=-w_f/2}^{k=w_f/2} h_f(k) F_s(t_j - k) \qquad (5)$$

where: $F_s(t_j)$ are samples of $X_s(t)$, $Y_s(t)$, $Z_s(t)$, and h_f accordingly h_x, h_y, h_z are window functions of the applied filters.

Different filter windows can be applied to each set of samples yielding different smoothing of the boundary in each dimension. While the boundary is localized on the lateral tooth surfaces, changes of $Z_f(t_j)$ are connected with a change of splint height while changes of $X_f(t_j)$ and $Y_f(t_j)$ make the boundary curve deviate from the mesh. The filtration should then be the strongest in Z dimension. In practice the Kaiser filter [7] with different sizes of the window was applied (Fig. 5).

There is also a possibility to apply additional constraints - for example user defined margin of the height of the splint $Z_f(t_j) = Z_f(t_j) + margin$.

Back Projection. The 3D curve obtained from the previous steps is not connected with the mesh $\mathcal{M}$ any more. Therefore it can be projected onto both the inner and outer surface of the splint to determine the inner and outer boundary. Additionally, the curve ensures a correspondence between these two projections, which helps in the creation of the closing parts of the surface of the splint.

Projecting the boundary curve onto the original mesh $\mathcal{M}$ quality of the obtained surface can be assessed. In order to preserve the topology of $\mathcal{M}$ the back projection is performed in such a way that for each $p_j(X_f(t_j), Y_f(t_j), Z_f(t_j))$ the closest $v_i \in \mathcal{V}$ is found. To close the loop, the shortest path in graph $\mathcal{M}$ between adjacent $v_i(p_j)$ and $v_m(p_{j+1})$ is found.

4 Results

The method was implemented in the Matlab R2014 enviroment. Detection of the self–occlusion, classification of boundary loops, and projection of a curve onto the mesh were implemented by the authors; cubic spline interpolation and filtration were done using supplied Matlab functions: csape.m, filter.m and kaiser.m.

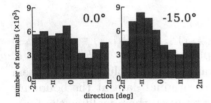 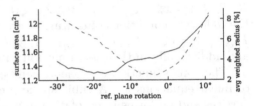

Fig. 6. Left: distributions of the directions of the normals projected onto the reference plane for inclination angles $\alpha = 0°$, $\alpha = -15°$ of the reference plane. Right: supporting surface area (blue) and imbalance vector length (dashed red) as a function of α.

In order to quantify the results quantitative parameters have to be proposed. The most straightforward seems to be the area of the supporting surface

$$S_{\mathcal{F}_{sup}} = \sum_{f_i \in \mathcal{F}_{sup}} S_{f_i} \tag{6}$$

As only the supporting surface can be the basis for building the splint it should be ensured that the splint is supported from all directions. In Fig. 6 the distribution of the projection of the normals to the faces $\mathbf{n}_{proj_{f_i}} = (n_{x_{f_i}}, n_{y_{f_i}}, 0)$ is illustrated for two different inclinations of the reference plane. The projections are represented with the angle of the vector $\gamma_i = atan2(\frac{n_{y_{f_i}}}{n_{x_{f_i}}})$. The distributions are not uniform and can be the basis of the balance evaluation:

$$\mathbf{b}_{\mathcal{F}_{sup}} = \frac{1}{S_{\mathcal{F}_{sup}}} \sum_{f_i \in \mathcal{F}_{sup}} \mathbf{n}_{proj_{f_i}} S_{f_i} \tag{7}$$

$b_{\mathcal{F}_{sup}}$ can be treated as the mean, surface weighted vector of the face normals projected onto the reference plane. It is also the horizontal component of the area vector of the supporting surface. The direction of $b_{\mathcal{F}_{sup}}$ is the the direction of the greatest imbalance, its length as a percentage of length of unitary vector $L_{b_{\mathcal{F}_{sup}}} = \|b_{\mathcal{F}_{sup}}\|$ can be treated as the deviation from the state of equilibrium. In the Fig. 6 the plots show the change of $S_{\mathcal{F}_{s}upp}$ and L_b as a function of the inclination angle α of the reference plane. The final criteria of the choice of the this angle should then be a compromise between the greatest area of the supporting surface and the smallest deviation from the state of equilibrium.

To evaluate further steps of processing, these parameters are measured after each step. Additionally the length of the boundary is measured.

$$l_{\mathcal{L}\mathcal{V}} = \sum_{v_i \in \mathcal{L}\mathcal{V}} \|p(v_{i+1}) - p(v_i)\| \tag{8}$$

Table 1. Selected parameters of the splint after subsequent processing stages depending on inclination of the reference plane (α).

α	Oclussion			Classification			Filter 1			Filter 2		
	S	l_b	$l_{\mathcal{L}\mathcal{V}}$	S	l_b	$l_{\mathcal{L}\mathcal{V}}$	S	l_b	$l_{\mathcal{L}\mathcal{V}}$	S	l_b	$l_{\mathcal{L}\mathcal{V}}$
0.0°	11.60	3.04	94.29	11.37	2.43	60.68	11.35	2.53	51.26	11.29	2.64	38.50
−5.0°	11.51	2.62	105.43	11.21	1.78	61.33	11.20	1.84	39.92	11.15	1.99	38.48
−7.5°	11.48	2.65	104.12	11.14	1.77	63.14	11.12	1.75	51.42	11.08	1.89	38.71
−10.0°	11.47	3.30	109.68	11.30	2.83	67.92	11.20	2.69	52.65	11.16	2.82	39.50
−15.0°	11.32	4.79	117.30	11.20	4.37	70.07	11.11	4.26	42.01	11.05	4.28	39.56

Table 1 gives a summary of the results for processing of splint surfaces for different inclination angles.

During the processing the area of the supporting surfaces slightly decreases, which is connected with smoothing of the curved parts of the boundary, which significantly reduces its length. The results shows some possibilities to quantify the quality of a splint boundary and inner surface of a splint, however, still not all factors (ex. splint height at a particular tooth) are included and still the operator's visual evaluation is of a great importance (Fig. 7).

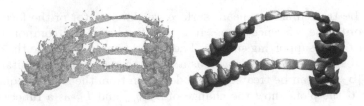

Fig. 7. Boundaries of the parts of the surface for different directions of insertions –
the results of self–occlusion detection function. Inclination of the model in a common
coordinate system, from top to bottom, corresponds to $0°$, $-5°$, $-10°$, $-15°$

5 Conclusions

An algorithm for automatic detection of tooth equators was presented. The first
estimation of tooth equator was done using a self–occlusion detection procedure.
The obtained boundary was jagged so it was cleaned by removing isles and filling
holes. After the cleaning, the cubic spline function was used as the first step of
filtration. Next a low–pass filter was applied. The resulting smooth path was
projected onto the surface of the splint. In this way the final boundary was
determined.

Some exemplary processing was done and illustrated. Parameters quantifying
the process were proposed and measured. The resulting curve can be projected
onto the inner and outer surface of the splint to create its closing surface and
also onto the initial surface to quantify the process.

Both methods of boundary estimation and methods of evaluation of its
parameters, presented here, are still in development phase and require further
work. But they can be the basis for a full automation of the process of splint
boundary estimation, including optimization for automatic selection of the direction of insertion.

References

1. Ash, M., Ramfjord, S., Schmidseder, J.: Terapia przy użyciu szyn okluzyjnych.
   Urban i Partner - Wydawnictwo Medyczne, Wrocław (1999)
2. de Boor, C.: A Practical Guide to Splines. No. 27 in Applied Mathematical Sciences, 1 edn. Springer-Verlag, New York (1978)
3. Botsch, M., Pauly, M., Rossl, C., Bischoff, S., Kobbelt, L.: Geometric modeling
   based on triangle meshes. In: SIGGRAPH 2006 (2006)
4. Chen, X., Li, X., Xu, L., Sun, Y., Politis, C., Egger, J.: Development of a computer-
   aided design software for dental splint in orthognathic surgery. Sci. Rep. **6**, 38867
   (2016)
5. Gateno, J., Xia, J., Teichgraeber, J.F., Rosen, A., Hultgren, B., Vadnais, T.: The
   precision of computer-generated surgical splints. JOMS **61**(7), 814–817 (2003)
6. Ju, T.: Robust repair of polygonal models. ACM Trans. Graph. **23**(3), 888–895
   (2004)

7. Kaiser, J.F.: Nonrecursive Digital Filter Design Using the I-Sinh Window Function. In: Proceedings of the 1974 IEEE IEEE International Symposium on Circuits and Systems, pp. 20–23 (1974)

8. Moon, B.S.: An explicit solution for the cubic spline interpolation for functions of a single variable. Appl. Math. Comput. **117**(2–3), 251–255 (2001)

9. Nasef, A.A., El-Beialy, A.R., Mostafa, Y.A.: Virtual techniques for designing and fabricating a retainer. AJODO **146**(3), 394–398 (2014)

10. Oppenheim, A.V., Schafer, R.: Digital Signal Processing. MIT video course, Prentice-Hall (1975)

11. Palaskar, J.N., Murali, R., Bansal, S.: Centric relation definition: a historical and contemporary prosthodontic persp. J. Ind. Prost. Soc. **13**(3), 149–154 (2013)

12. Pojda, D., Tomaka, A.A., Luchowski, L., Skabek, K., Tarnawski, M.: Applying computational geometry to designing an occlusal splint. In: CompIMAGE 2018, Kraków

13. de Rezende, A.B.: A new parallelometer. J. Prosthet. Dent. **21**(1), 79–85 (1969)

Identification of Factors that Affect Reproducibility of Mutation Calling Methods in Data Originating from the Next-Generation Sequencing

Roman Jaksik[1,2]([✉])[ID], Krzysztof Psiuk-Maksymowicz[1,2][ID], and Andrzej Swierniak[1,2]

[1] Institute of Automatic Control, Silesian University of Technology,
ul. Akademicka 16, 44-100 Gliwice, Poland
roman.jaksik@polsl.pl
[2] Biotechnology Centre, Silesian University of Technology,
ul. Krzywoustego 8, 44-100 Gliwice, Poland

Abstract. Identification of somatic mutations, based on data from next-generation sequencing of the DNA, has become one of the fundamental research strategies in oncology, with the goal to seek mechanisms underlying the process of carcinogenesis and resistance to commonly used therapies. Despite significant advances in the development of sequencing methods and data processing algorithms, the reproducibility of experiments is relatively low and depending significantly on the methods used to identify changes in the structure of the DNA. This is mainly due to the influence of three factors: (1) high heterogeneity of tumors due to which some mutations are characteristic for a small number of cells, (2) bias associated with the process of exome isolation and (3) specificity of data pre-processing strategies.

The aim of the work was to determine the impact of these factors on the identification of somatic mutations, allowing to determine the reasons for low reproducibility in such studies.

Keywords: Bioinformatic data analysis · Next-generation sequencing · Whole exome sequencing
Somatic mutations · Reproducibility of results

1 Introduction

Modern bioinformatics in large extent is concentrated on the analysis of data which originates from next-generation sequencing (NGS). Massive amounts of data produced by NGS presents a challenge for both data storage and analysis requiring advanced systems and tools for the successful application of this technology. There are already many systems for biomedical data management and analysis [1–3], some of which are in particular dedicated to NGS data analysis [4,5] or post-processing of such data by means of *e.g.* Gene Ontology tools [6].

© Springer Nature Switzerland AG 2018
T. Czachórski et al. (Eds.): ISCIS 2018, CCIS 935, pp. 264–271, 2018.
https://doi.org/10.1007/978-3-030-00840-6_29

Some of the massively parallel sequencing techniques are currently being introduced to the clinics. Both whole genome sequencing (WGS) and whole exome sequencing (WES) techniques have a huge potential in the application of so-called personalized medicine. One of the potential application of the WGS or targeted exome sequencing is to find intratumor genetic heterogeneity [7,8].

Unfortunately, none of those methods provides error-free results. The reproducibility of experiments is relatively low and depends significantly on the methods used to identify changes in the structure of the DNA. This is mainly due to the influence of three factors: the process of data filtration [9], high heterogeneity of tumors through which some subclasses are characteristic for too few cells [10], and bias introduced by the process of exome isolation [11].

In general, mutations can be subdivided into germline and somatic. Unlike the germline mutations, somatic mutations are accumulated during the life and are not transmitted to descendants. Identification of single nucleotide variants (SNV) based on NGS data have been successfully adapted to detect somatic variants using multiple tissue samples of a single patient. These variants correspond to mutations that have occurred *de novo* within groups of somatic cells. This is possible by high-throughput sequencing technologies that parallelize the sequencing process producing up to billions of short reads (fragments of sequenced DNA molecules) per one sample. To determine DNA sequence of an individual the reads need to be aligned in a specific order, which is possible only if the coverage, *i.e.* the number of mapped reads per position in the reference sequence, is high enough.

2   Materials and Methods

2.1   Materials

In this study, we used WES data collected from six primary breast cancer samples for which two technical replicates were performed at the level of sequencing and additional samples from matched peripheral blood leukocytes. These data come from the study by a Weiwei Shi et al. [8] and are publicly available in the Sequence Read Archive (SRA) database under accession ID SRP070662.

2.2   Methods

Detection of Somatic Point Mutations. Quality control was conducted using FastQC and FastQ Screen. Sequencing reads were aligned to the GRCh37 reference genome, using BWA mem algorithm [12]. Aligned reads were processed using MarkDuplicates algorithm from the Picard tool set and BaseRecalibrator from the Genome Analysis Toolkit (GATK). Somatic mutations were identified using MuTect2 [13] based on tumor sample, for which we had two technical replicates, and a control sample derived from healthy cells. All variants were annotated using Variant Effect Predictor [15].

3   Results

3.1   Reproducibility of Exome Sequencing

For each of the six patients, we identified two sets of somatic mutations based on exome sequencing of a tumor sample in two technical replicates, both of which were compared to a common control sample extracted from healthy cells. Figure 1 shows Venn diagrams with intersection and relative complements between technical replicates for all six samples. The reproducibility is very low considering that the only expected variability in the experiment is of technical origin. The average Jaccard index is 0.16 meaning that only 16% all identified variants are common between both replicates.

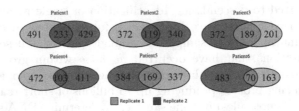

Fig. 1. Venn diagrams showing intersection and relative complements of technical replicates sets from six patients.

The most possible reasons for such low reproducibility can be associated with:

(a) Variations in the sensitivity level - in a case of subclonal mutations which are observed only in a small fraction of the tumor cells the results might differ due to a random sampling of the sequencing reads that support the finding;

(b) Availability of sites for mutation calling - differences in the coverage level between both replicates at specific genomic positions;

(c) Specificity of mutation calling algorithm - variability in mutation calling criteria which result from the fact that both replicates are analyzed independently.

Additionally, differences in the data quality between both samples can also have a profound effect on the reproducibility level, however, in such a case, we would observe high differences in the number of variants detected using one of the replicates which are not the case here, except for one of the patients (patient 6). The quality is reasonably uniform across replicates, showing only significant differences comparing to the control samples (e.g. much lower Phread quality scores for reads from patient 2), this, however, affects both replicates equally.

3.2 Variations in the Sensitivity Level

The most intuitive reason for the lack of reproducibility might be related to high heterogeneity of cancer resulting in some of the mutations being present only in a small proportion of cancer cells. In such a case the lower is the fraction of cells with a particular mutation the probability of obtaining a significant number of reads necessary to make a finding also drops. Due to sampling effect, a particular mutation might be detected in one sample but not in the other one reducing the overall concordance level. To test this hypothesis we divide mutations into two groups, concordant and discordant between the replicates. If indeed the discordant variants are associated with differences in the sensitivity level, they should predominantly contain variants which low variant allele frequency (VAF).

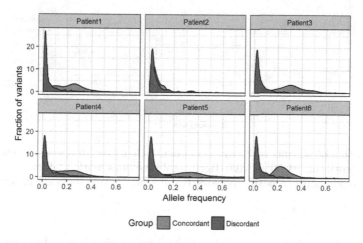

Fig. 2. Smoothed distribution of variant allele frequencies between concordant and discordant variants. All distributions are normalized to the area under the curve equal to one.

Figure 2 shows the normalized, smoothed distribution of VAF for both variant groups. In all cases, the differences in VAF between both groups are significant showing that indeed the variants specific to a single replicate have a low VAF. The only exception is Patient 2 for which the distributions are similar.

3.3 Availability of Sites for Mutation Calling

Exome sequencing relies on the ability to extract only specific portions of the DNA using sequence-specific probes, similar to those used in oligonucleotide microarray experiments. However due to various probe-specific effects [16] the exome extraction process is biased towards regions of specific nucleotide composition, which might differ among samples in a single experiment. Additionally, various technical aspects of the experiment might lead to differences in the total number of reads obtained for a specific replicate. For those reasons, some positions might have sufficient coverage to call variants in one sample but not in the other one.

To test this hypothesis we analyzed the coverage levels of all variants detected in at least one replicate and calculated the fraction of such positions which are characterized by a specific minimal coverage level.

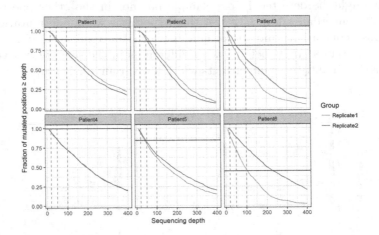

Fig. 3. Fraction of variants with sequencing depth that exceeds specific levels. Vertical lines mark depths of: 20, 50 and 100. Horizontal blue lines mark differences in the total number of reads between both replicates (total reads in one replicate divided by the other).

Figure 2 shows that in a case of patient 3 and 6 significant differences in the coverage level can be observed which are associated with high differences in the total number of reads obtained for a particular replicate (20% and 50% less for one replicate in a case of patient 3 and 6 respectively). In both of those cases, we can expect low concordance between replicates however as for the remaining ones the only differences are observable between the fraction of positions with coverage above 100x.

3.4   Specificity of Mutation Calling Algorithm

Most of the algorithms used to detect mutations rely not only on the detection of differences in the sequencing reads compared to the reference genome, using all reads available for a specific position, but also on various post processing steps which the main goal is to separate real variants from the sequencing artifacts. The outcome of the filtering step relies heavily on the coverage and number of reads that support the variant in the control sample as compared to tumor, length of the read and position of the variant inside it, Phread quality of the positions that show changes (confidence of the sequencing scanner) and the number of other variants which were detected in the surrounding region. MuTect2 uses multiple filters which remove on average 95% of all positions that show any differences compared to the reference genome in the tumor sample. However, since there is a possibility of committing type II error (filtering out actual mutations) we hypothesize that some of the discrepancies between replicates might be a result of committing the type II error in only one of the samples.

To verify this hypothesis we identified all MuTect2 filters which removed a particular position in only one of the replicates (see Fig. 4). They turned up to be predominantly: LOD_T fstar, clustered events, homologous mapping event and multiple events in alternative allele.

LOD_T *fstar* filter rejects a variant with a tumor LOD (log odds) score (Eq. 1) below a given threshold value ($\approx$6.3), suggesting insufficient evidence of its presence in the tumor sample.

$$LOD_T = log_{10} \left(\frac{P(\text{observed data in tumor} - \text{site is mutated})}{P(\text{observed data in tumor} - \text{site is reference})} \right) \quad (1)$$

Clustered events filter rejects FPs caused by misalignments evidenced by the alternate alleles being clustered at a consistent distance from the start or end of the read alignment. *Homologous mapping event* and *multiple events alt allele* filters remove sites at which multiple events (various mutations or indels) were observed in tumor or in tumor and normal cells respectively. Multiple various variants at the same position are very unlikely due to low mutation rate and usually indicate sequencing errors.

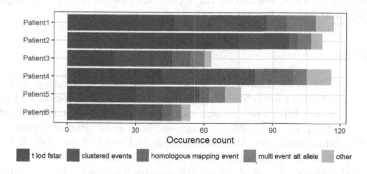

Fig. 4. MuTect2 filters (LOD_T fstar, clustered events, homologous mapping event and multiple events alt allele filters) which treat differentially individual variants between both technical replicates.

Figure 4 shows that the main differences result from filters which are affected by the coverage at specific mutated positions, however, there is no correlation between them and the statistics shown in Fig. 3 suggesting the influence of random sampling and differences at the level of exome capture process.

4   Discussion and Concluding Remarks

This study shows that the of reproducibility of experiments which aim to detect somatic mutations, based on whole exome sequencing experiments can be low, resulting predominantly from the variant filtration procedure and differences in the number of supporting reads at a particular position, which is only affected to a small degree by the total number of reads obtained for a particular sample. This however, does not concern only sub-clonal variants which are found in a small number of cells used for sequencing.

Despite significant reproducibility issues exome sequencing is an invaluable tool for the study of various genetic diseases. It might not provide answers with absolute confidence, however it significantly limits the search space allowing to validate the outcomes with more precise single site-specific methods. Improvements in the detection of neurological diseases [17], study of mechanism associated with Mendelian disorders [18] and identification of cancer associated genes [7,8] are just few examples in which DNA sequencing provided invaluable knowledge, that would be inaccessible without the existence of this technology.

Acknowledgements. This work was partially supported by the National Centre for Research and Development grant No. Strategmed2/267398/4/NCBR/2015 (KPM), the National Science Centre grant No. 2016/23/D/ST7/03665 (RJ), and by internal grant of Institute of Automatic Control BK-204/RAu1/2017 (AS).

Calculations were carried out by means of the infrastructure of the Ziemowit computer cluster (www.ziemowit.hpc.polsl.pl) in the Laboratory of Bioinformatics and Computational Biology, The Biotechnology, Bioengineering and Bioinformatics Centre Silesian BIO-FARMA, created in the POIG.02.01.00-00-166/08 and expanded in the POIG.02.03.01-00-040/13 projects.

References

1. Luo, J., Wu, M., Gopukumar, D., Zhao, Y.: Big data application in biomedical research and health care: a literature review. Biomed. Inf. Insights **8**, 1–10 (2016)
2. Bensz, W., et al.: Integrated System supporting research on environment related cancers. In: Król, D., Madeyski, L., Nguyen, N.T. (eds.) Recent Developments in Intelligent Information and Database Systems. SCI, vol. 642, pp. 399–409. Springer, Cham (2016). https://doi.org/10.1007/978-3-319-31277-4_35
3. Psiuk-Maksymowicz, K., et al.: A holistic approach to testing biomedical hypotheses and analysis of biomedical data. In: Kozielski, S., Mrozek, D., Kasprowski, P., Małysiak-Mrozek, B., Kostrzewa, D. (eds.) BDAS 2015-2016. CCIS, vol. 613, pp. 449–462. Springer, Cham (2016). https://doi.org/10.1007/978-3-319-34099-9_34
4. Afgan, E., Baker, D., van den Beek, M., Blankenberg, D., Bouvier, D., Cech, M., Chilton, J.: The Galaxy platform for accessible, reproducible and collaborative biomedical analyses: 2016 update. Nucleic Acids Res. **44**(W1), W3–W10 (2016)
5. Psiuk-Maksymowicz, K., Mrozek, D., Jaksik, R., Borys, D., Fujarewicz, K., Swierniak, A.: Scalability of a genomic data analysis in the biotest platform. In: Nguyen, N.T., Tojo, S., Nguyen, L.M., Trawiński, B. (eds.) ACIIDS 2017. LNCS (LNAI), vol. 10192, pp. 741–752. Springer, Cham (2017). https://doi.org/10.1007/978-3-319-54430-4_71

6. Gruca, A., Jaksik, R., Psiuk-Maksymowicz, K.: Functional interpretation of gene sets: semantic-based clustering of gene ontology terms on the biotest platform. In: Gruca, A., Czachórski, T., Harezlak, K., Kozielski, S., Piotrowska, A. (eds.) ICMMI 2017. AISC, vol. 659, pp. 125–136. Springer, Cham (2018). https://doi.org/10.1007/978-3-319-67792-7_13

7. Gerlinger, M., Rowan, A.J., Horswell, S., Larkin, J., Endesfelder, D., Gronroos, E., Martinez, P., Matthews, N.: Intratumor heterogeneity and branched evolution revealed by multiregion sequencing. N. Engl. J. Med. **366**, 883–892 (2012)

8. Shi, W., Ng, C.K.Y., Lim, R.S., Jiang, T., Kumar, S., Li, X., Wali, V.B., Piscuoglio, S., Gerstein, M.B., Chagpar, A.B., Weigelt, B., Pusztai, L., Reis-Filho, J.S., Hatzis, C.: Reliability of whole-exome sequencing for assessing intratumor genetic heterogeneity. bioRxiv (2018)

9. Derryberry, D.Z., Cowperthwaite, M.C., Wilke, C.O.: Reproducibility of SNV-calling in multiple sequencing runs from single tumors. PeerJ **4**, e1508 (2016)

10. Qi, Y., Liu, X., Liu, C., Wang, B., Hess, K.R., Symmans, W.F., Shi, W., Pusztai, L.: Reproducibility of variant calls in replicate next generation sequencing experiments. PLoS One **7**, e0119230 (2015)

11. Meynert, A.M., Ansari, M., FitzPatrick, D.R., Taylor, M.S.: Variant detection sensitivity and biases in whole genome and exome sequencing. BMC Bioinform. **15**, 247 (2014)

12. Li, H.: Aligning sequence reads, clone sequences and assembly contigs with BWA-MEM. arXiv.org p. arXiv:1303.3997 (2013)

13. Cibulskis, C., Lawrence, M.S., Carter, S.L., Sivachenko, A., Jaffe, D., Sougnez, C., Gabriel, S., Meyerson, M., Lander, E.S., Getz, G.: Sensitive detection of somatic point mutations in impure and heterogeneous cancer samples. Nat. Biotechnol. **31**, 213–219 (2013)

14. Metzker, M.L.: Sequencing technologies – the next generation. Nat. Rev. Genet. **11**(1), 31–46 (2010)

15. McLaren, W., Gil, L., Hunt, S.E., Riat, H.S., Ritchie, G.R., Thormann, A., Flicek, P., Cunningham, F.: The ensembl variant effect predictor. Genome Biol **17**(1), 122 (2016)

16. Jaksik, R., Marczyk, M., Polanska, J., Rzeszowska-Wolny, J.: Sources of high variance between probe signals in affymetrix short oligonucleotide microarrays. Sensors **14**, 532–548 (2014)

17. Vissers, L., van Nimwegen, K., Schieving, J., Kamsteeg, E., Kleefstra, T., Yntema, H., Pfundt, R., van der Wilt, G.J., Krabbenborg, L., Brunner, H., van der Burg, S., Grutters, J., Veltman, J., Willemsen, M.: A clinical utility study of exome sequencing versus conventional genetic testing in pediatric neurology. Genet. Med. **19**, 1055–1063 (2017)

18. Bamshad, M.J., Ng, S.B., Bigham, A.W., Tabor, H.K., Emond, M.J., Nickerson, D.A., Shendure, J.: Exome sequencing as a tool for Mendelian disease gene discovery. Nat. Rev. Genet. **12**, 745–755 (2011)

Author Index

Printed in the United States
by Bookmasters

Printed in the United States
By Bookmasters